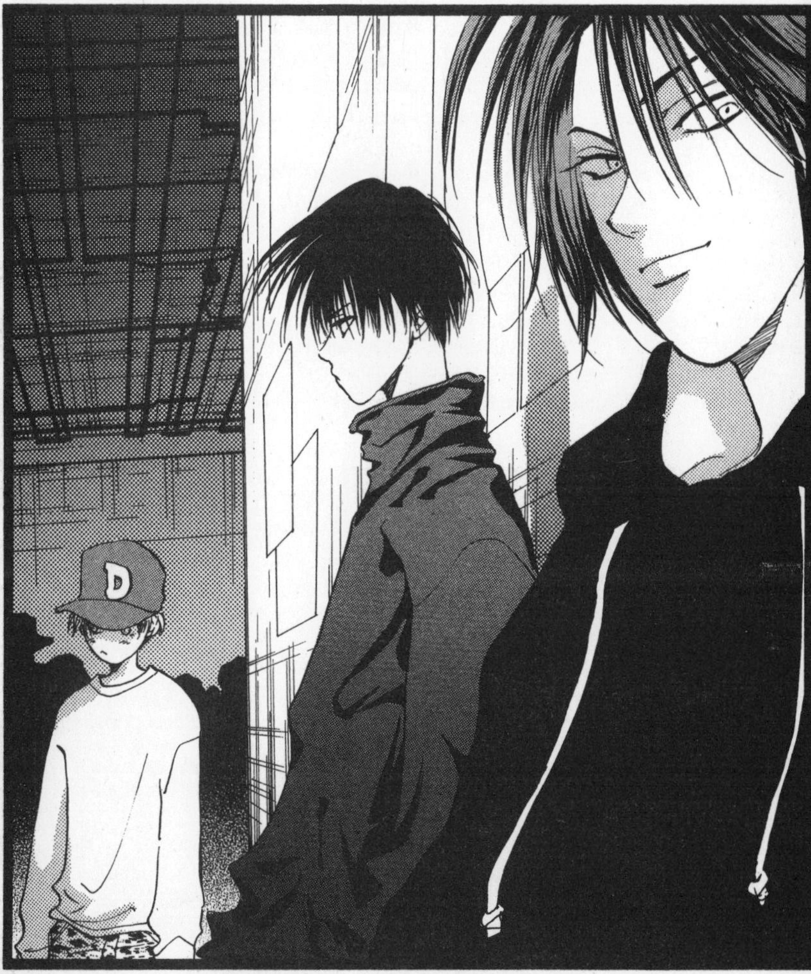

Hands Off! Vol. 1
Created by Kasane Katsumoto

Translation - Asuka Yoshizu
English Adaptation - Lianne Sentar
Copy Editors - Suzanne Waldman and Chrissy Schilling
Retouch and Lettering - Haruko Furukawa
Production Artists - John Lo and James Dashiell
Cover Design - Patrick Hook

Editor - Nicole Monastirsky
Digital Imaging Manager - Chris Buford
Pre-Press Manager - Antonio DePietro
Production Managers - Jennifer Miller and Mutsumi Miyazaki
Art Director - Matt Alford
Managing Editor - Jill Freshney
VP of Production - Ron Klamert
President and C.O.O. - John Parker
Publisher and C.E.O. - Stuart Levy

A  Manga

TOKYOPOP Inc.
5900 Wilshire Blvd. Suite 2000
Los Angeles, CA 90036

E-mail: info@TOKYOPOP.com
Come visit us online at www.TOKYOPOP.com

ISBN: 1-59532-153-5

First TOKYOPOP printing: October 2004
10 9 8 7 6 5 4 3 2 1
Printed in the USA

Volume 1

by

Kasane Katsumoto

HAMBURG // LONDON // LOS ANGELES // TOKYO

CONTENTS

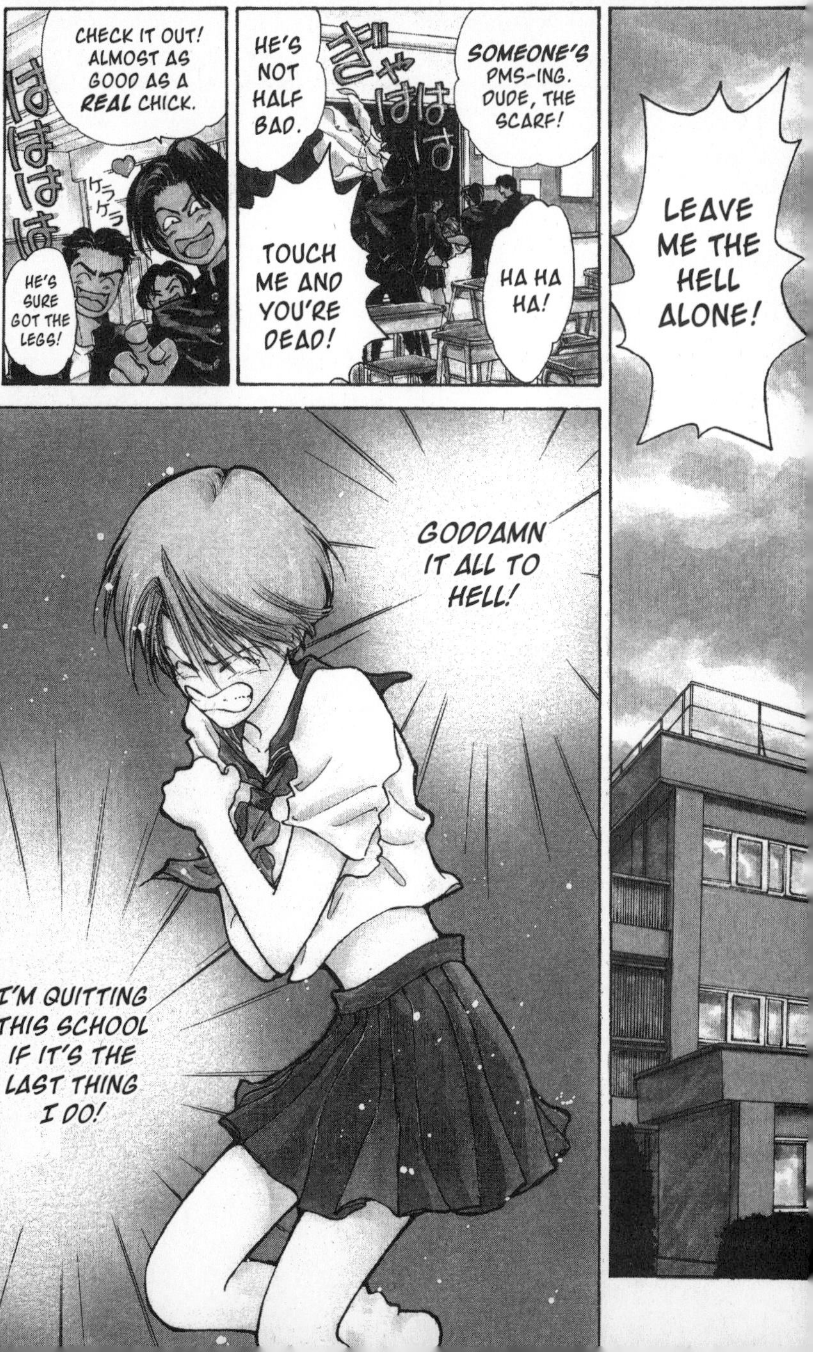
LEAVE ME THE HELL ALONE!
SOMEONE'S PMS-ING. DUDE, THE SCARF!
ぎゃははは
HE'S NOT HALF BAD.
HA HA HA!
TOUCH ME AND YOU'RE DEAD!
CHECK IT OUT! ALMOST AS GOOD AS A REAL CHICK.
ケラケラ
はははは
HE'S SURE GOT THE LEGS!
GODDAMN IT ALL TO HELL!
I'M QUITTING THIS SCHOOL IF IT'S THE LAST THING I DO!

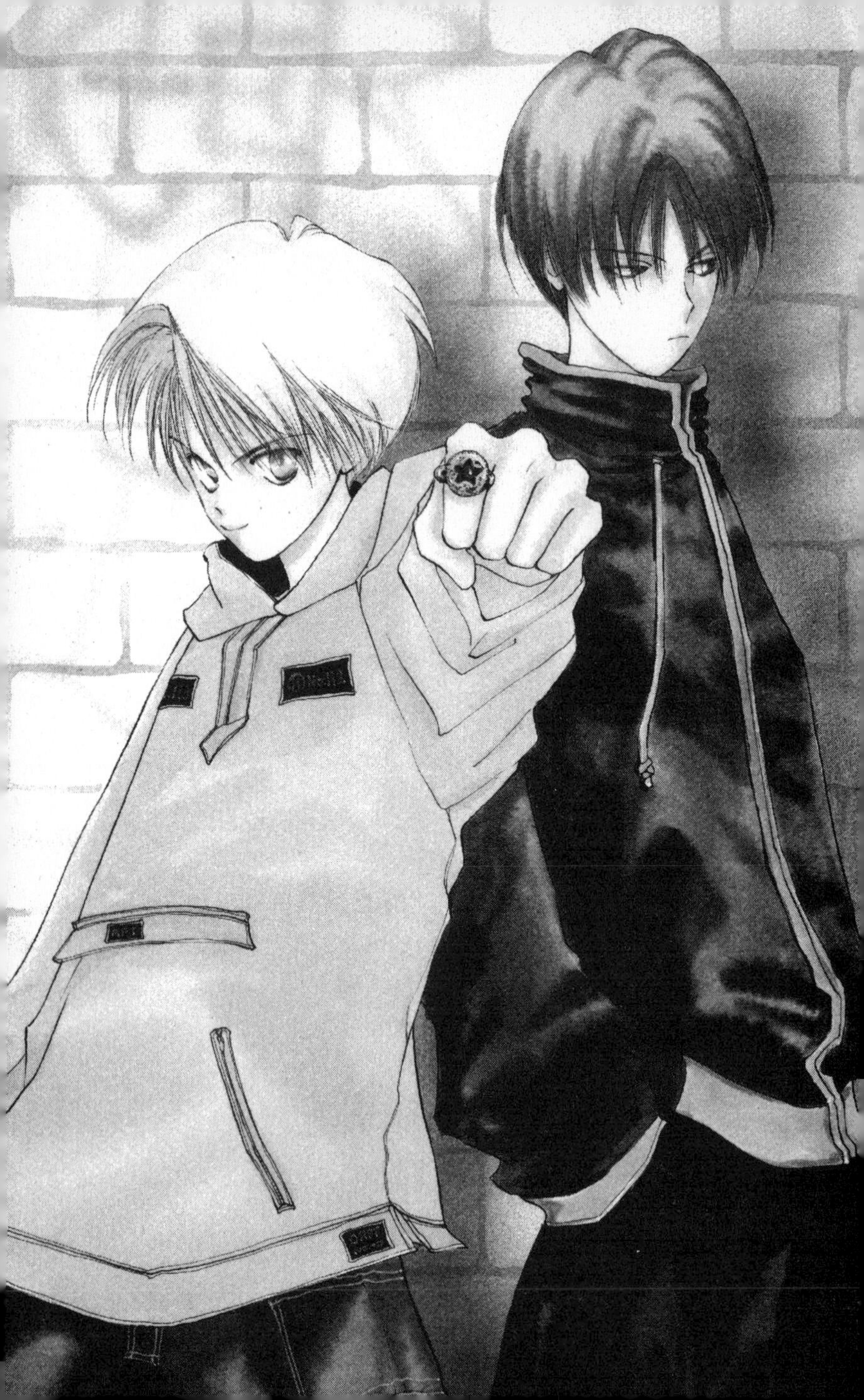

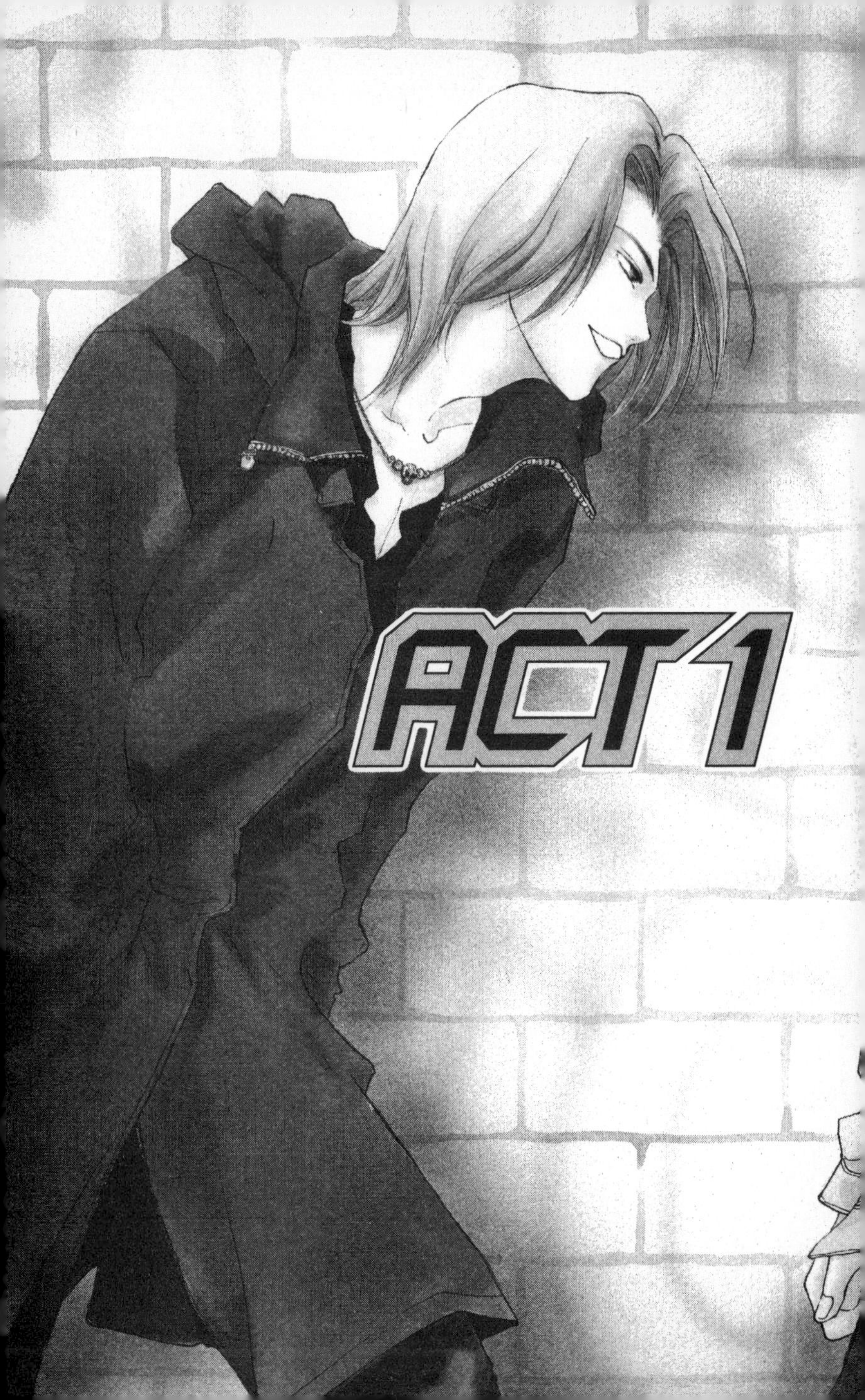
ACT 1

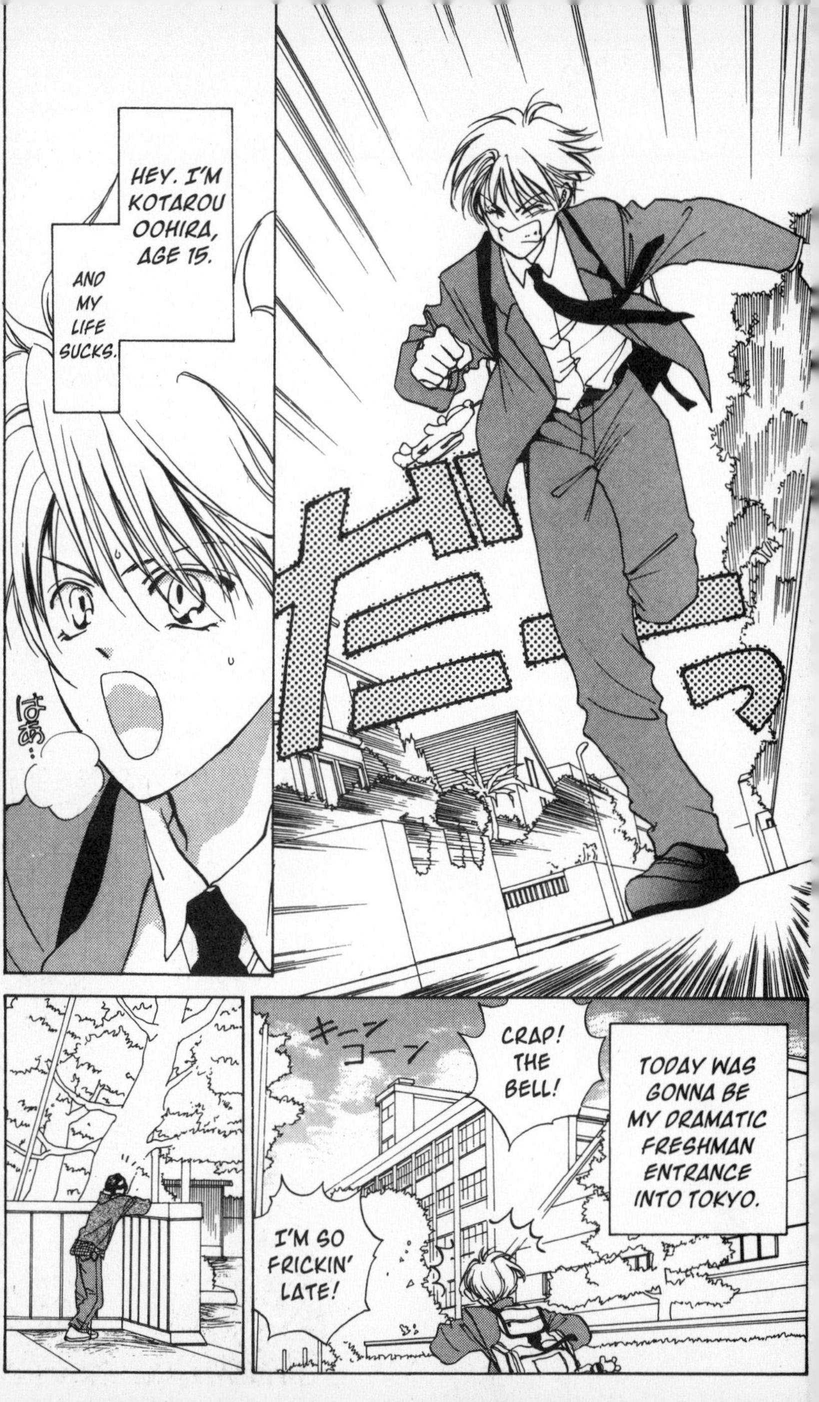
HEY. I'M KOTAROU OOHIRA, AGE 15.
AND MY LIFE SUCKS.
はぁ…
TODAY WAS GONNA BE MY DRAMATIC FRESHMAN ENTRANCE INTO TOKYO.
CRAP! THE BELL!
キーンコーン
I'M SO FRICKIN' LATE!

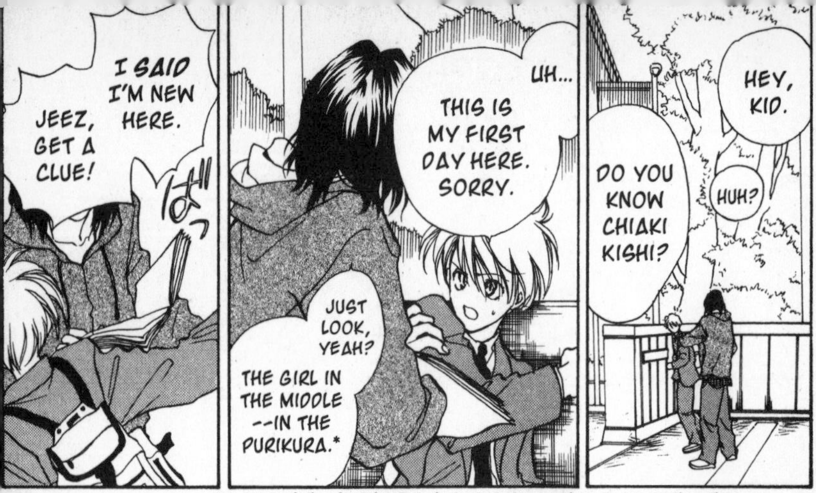
HEY, KID.
HUH?
DO YOU KNOW CHIAKI KISHI?
UH...
THIS IS MY FIRST DAY HERE. SORRY.
JUST LOOK, YEAH?
THE GIRL IN THE MIDDLE --IN THE PURIKURA.*
I SAID I'M NEW HERE.
JEEZ, GET A CLUE!
ばっ

*An abbreviation for Print Club--instant photo machines that make tiny stickers.

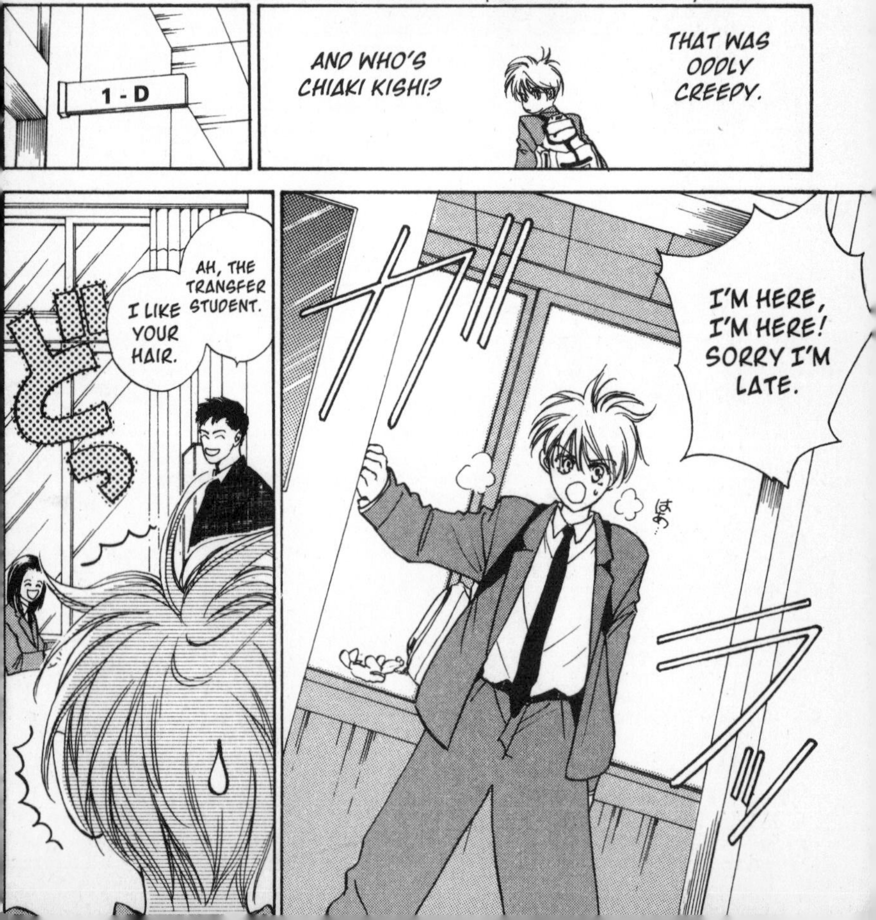
THAT WAS ODDLY CREEPY.
AND WHO'S CHIAKI KISHI?
1 - D
I'M HERE, I'M HERE! SORRY I'M LATE.
AH, THE TRANSFER STUDENT.
I LIKE YOUR HAIR.

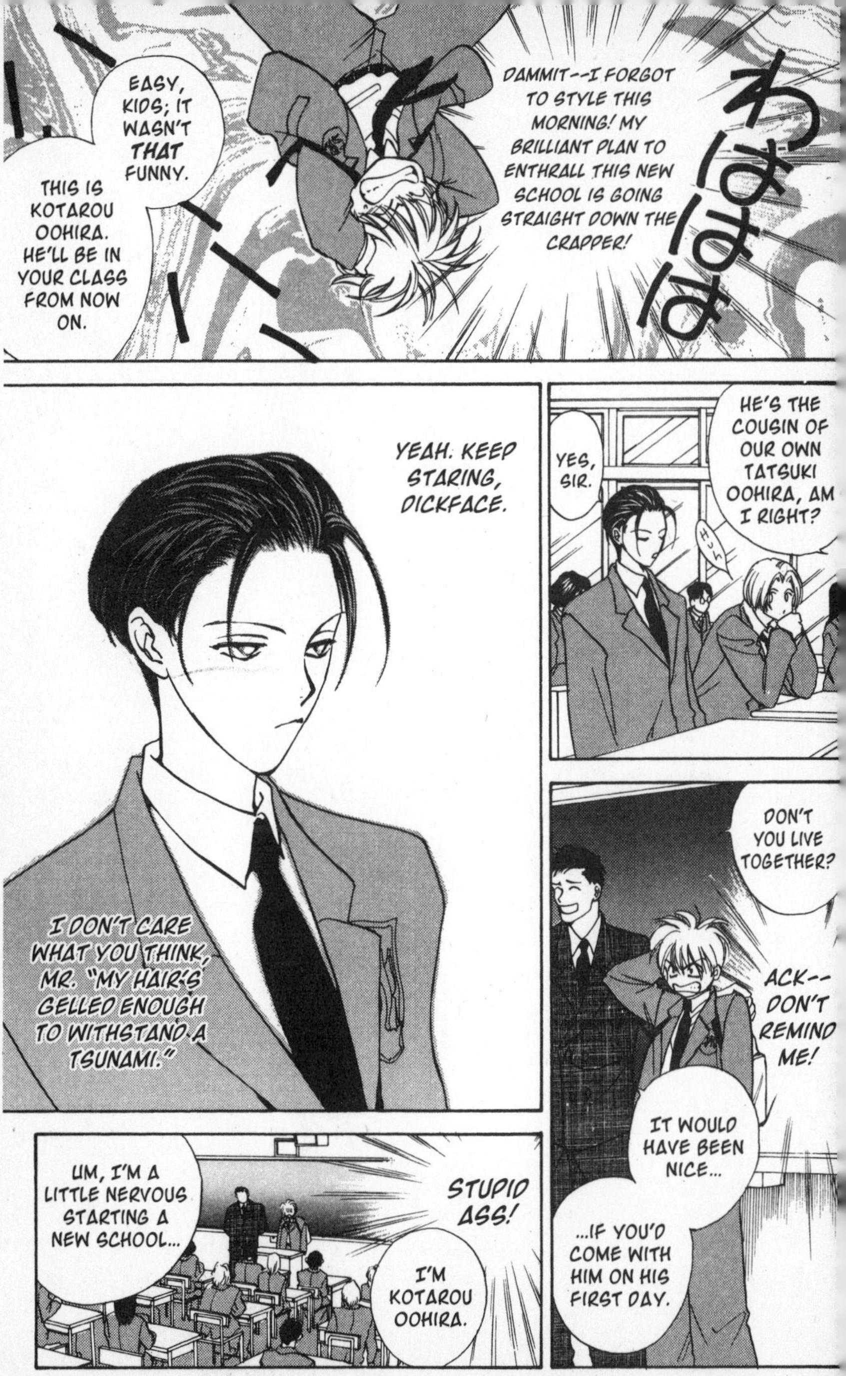

わははは
DAMMIT--I FORGOT TO STYLE THIS MORNING! MY BRILLIANT PLAN TO ENTHRALL THIS NEW SCHOOL IS GOING STRAIGHT DOWN THE CRAPPER!
EASY, KIDS; IT WASN'T **THAT** FUNNY.
THIS IS KOTAROU OOHIRA. HE'LL BE IN YOUR CLASS FROM NOW ON.
HE'S THE COUSIN OF OUR OWN TATSUKI OOHIRA, AM I RIGHT?
Huh
YES, SIR.
YEAH. KEEP STARING, DICKFACE.
I DON'T CARE WHAT YOU THINK, MR. "MY HAIR'S GELLED ENOUGH TO WITHSTAND A TSUNAMI."
DON'T YOU LIVE TOGETHER?
ACK--DON'T REMIND ME!
IT WOULD HAVE BEEN NICE...
...IF YOU'D COME WITH HIM ON HIS FIRST DAY.
UM, I'M A LITTLE NERVOUS STARTING A NEW SCHOOL...
STUPID ASS!
I'M KOTAROU OOHIRA.

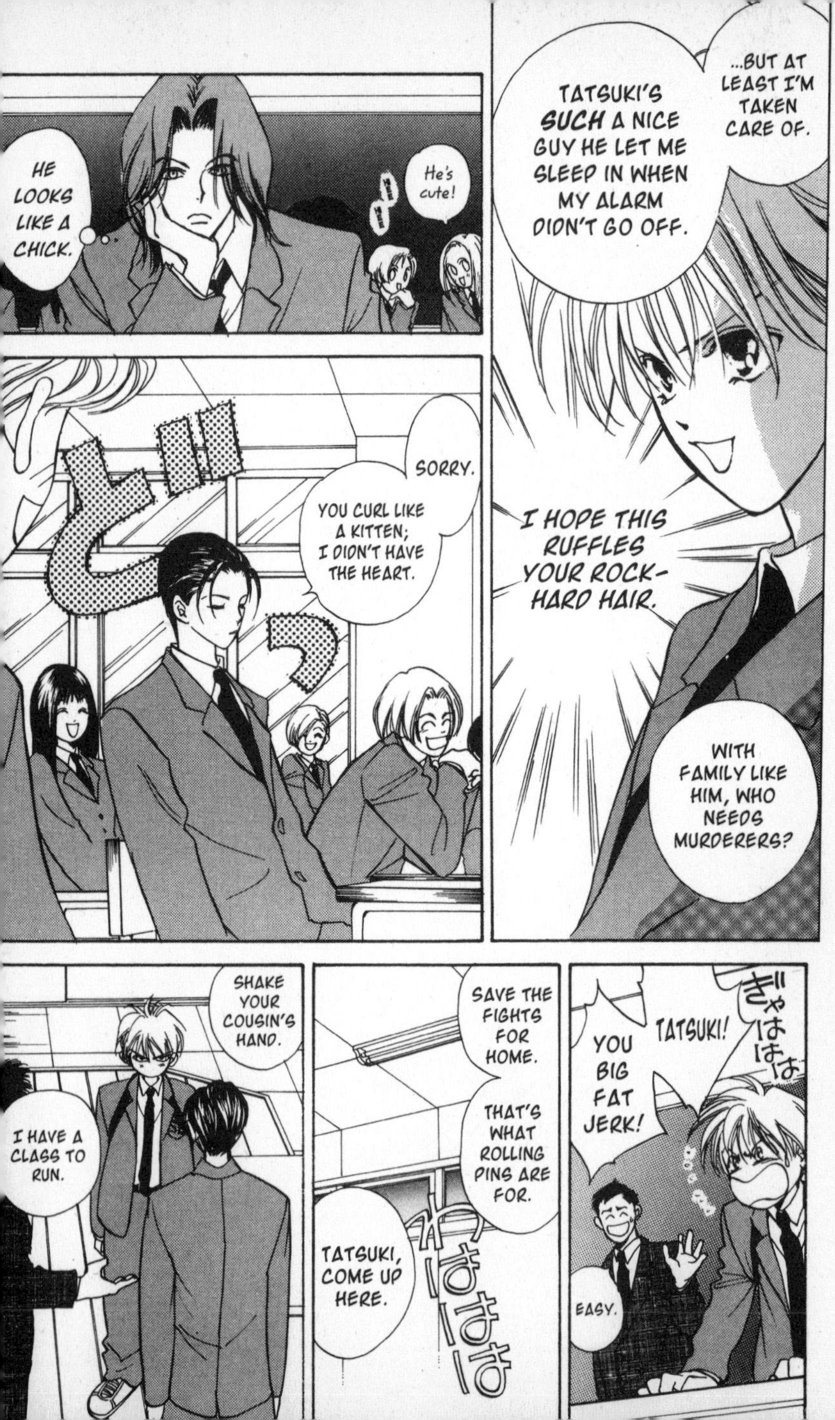
...BUT AT LEAST I'M TAKEN CARE OF.
TATSUKI'S SUCH A NICE GUY HE LET ME SLEEP IN WHEN MY ALARM DIDN'T GO OFF.
I HOPE THIS RUFFLES YOUR ROCK-HARD HAIR.
WITH FAMILY LIKE HIM, WHO NEEDS MURDERERS?
He's cute!
HEE HEE
HE LOOKS LIKE A CHICK.
SORRY.
YOU CURL LIKE A KITTEN; I DIDN'T HAVE THE HEART.
どっ
ぎゃははは
TATSUKI!
YOU BIG FAT JERK!
EASY.
SAVE THE FIGHTS FOR HOME.
THAT'S WHAT ROLLING PINS ARE FOR.
わははは
TATSUKI, COME UP HERE.
SHAKE YOUR COUSIN'S HAND.
I HAVE A CLASS TO RUN.

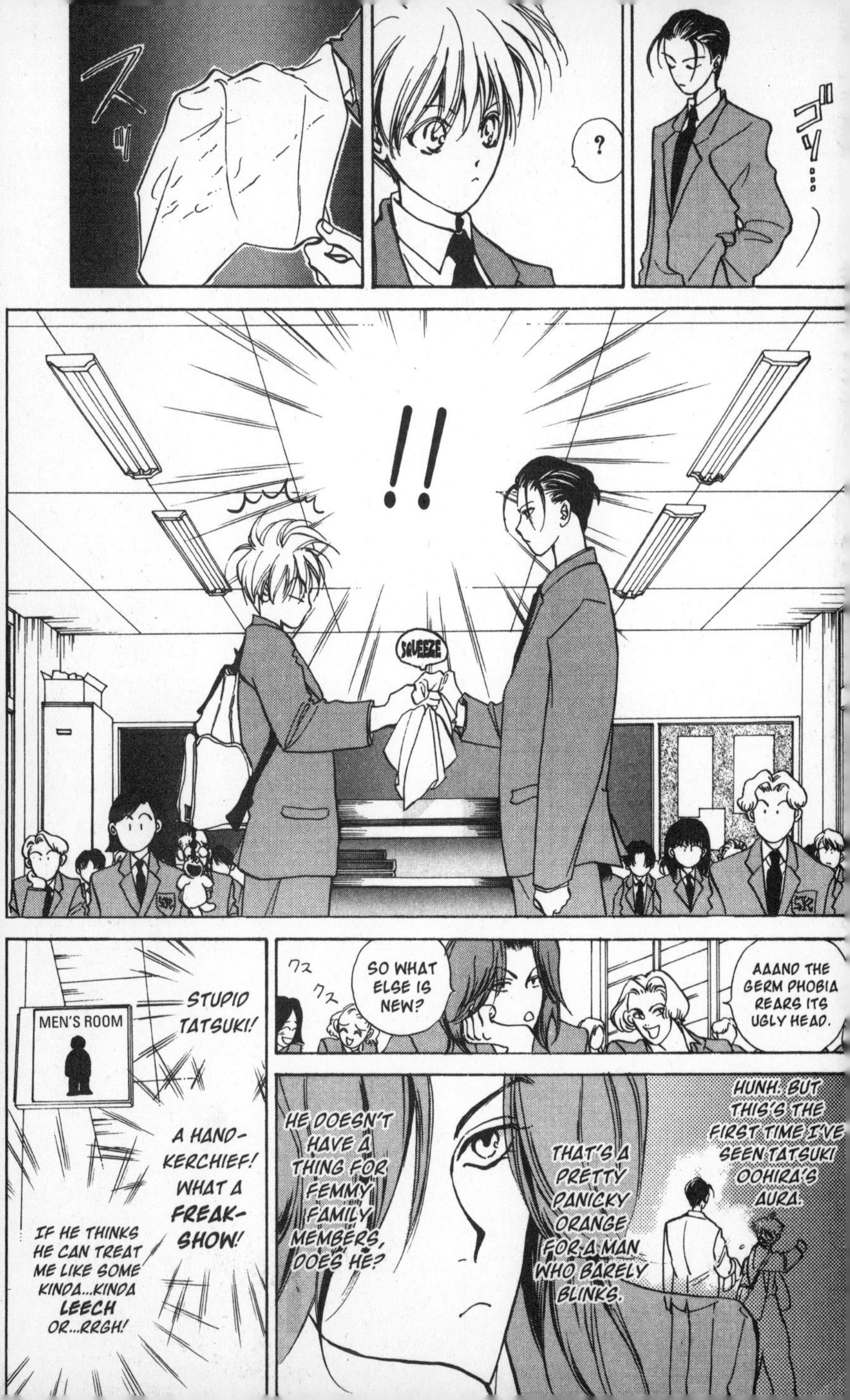

ゴソ...
?
スッ
!!
SQUEEZE
AAAND THE GERM PHOBIA REARS ITS UGLY HEAD.
SO WHAT ELSE IS NEW?
クス クス
STUPID TATSUKI!
MEN'S ROOM
A HAND-KERCHIEF! WHAT A FREAK-SHOW!
IF HE THINKS HE CAN TREAT ME LIKE SOME KINDA...KINDA LEECH OR...RRGH!
HUNH. BUT THIS'S THE FIRST TIME I'VE SEEN TATSUKI OOHIRA'S AURA.
THAT'S A PRETTY PANICKY ORANGE FOR A MAN WHO BARELY BLINKS.
HE DOESN'T HAVE A THING FOR FEMMY FAMILY MEMBERS, DOES HE?

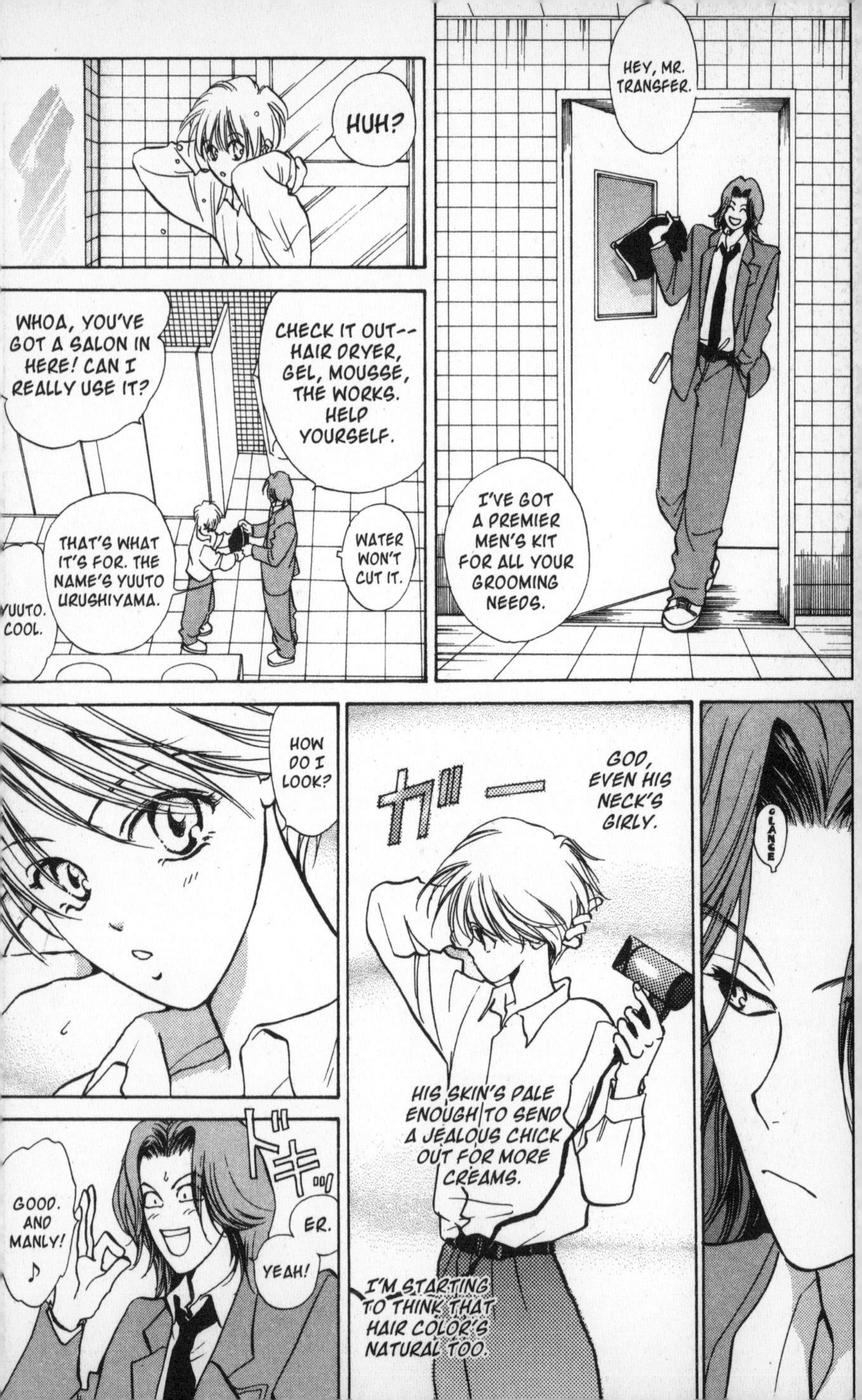
HEY, MR. TRANSFER.
I'VE GOT A PREMIER MEN'S KIT FOR ALL YOUR GROOMING NEEDS.
HUH?
CHECK IT OUT-- HAIR DRYER, GEL, MOUSSE, THE WORKS. HELP YOURSELF.
WHOA, YOU'VE GOT A SALON IN HERE! CAN I REALLY USE IT?
WATER WON'T CUT IT.
THAT'S WHAT IT'S FOR. THE NAME'S YUUTO URUSHIYAMA.
YUUTO. COOL.
GLANCE
ガー
GOD, EVEN HIS NECK'S GIRLY.
HIS SKIN'S PALE ENOUGH TO SEND A JEALOUS CHICK OUT FOR MORE CREAMS.
I'M STARTING TO THINK THAT HAIR COLOR'S NATURAL TOO.
HOW DO I LOOK?
ドキ
ER.
YEAH!
GOOD. AND MANLY! ♪

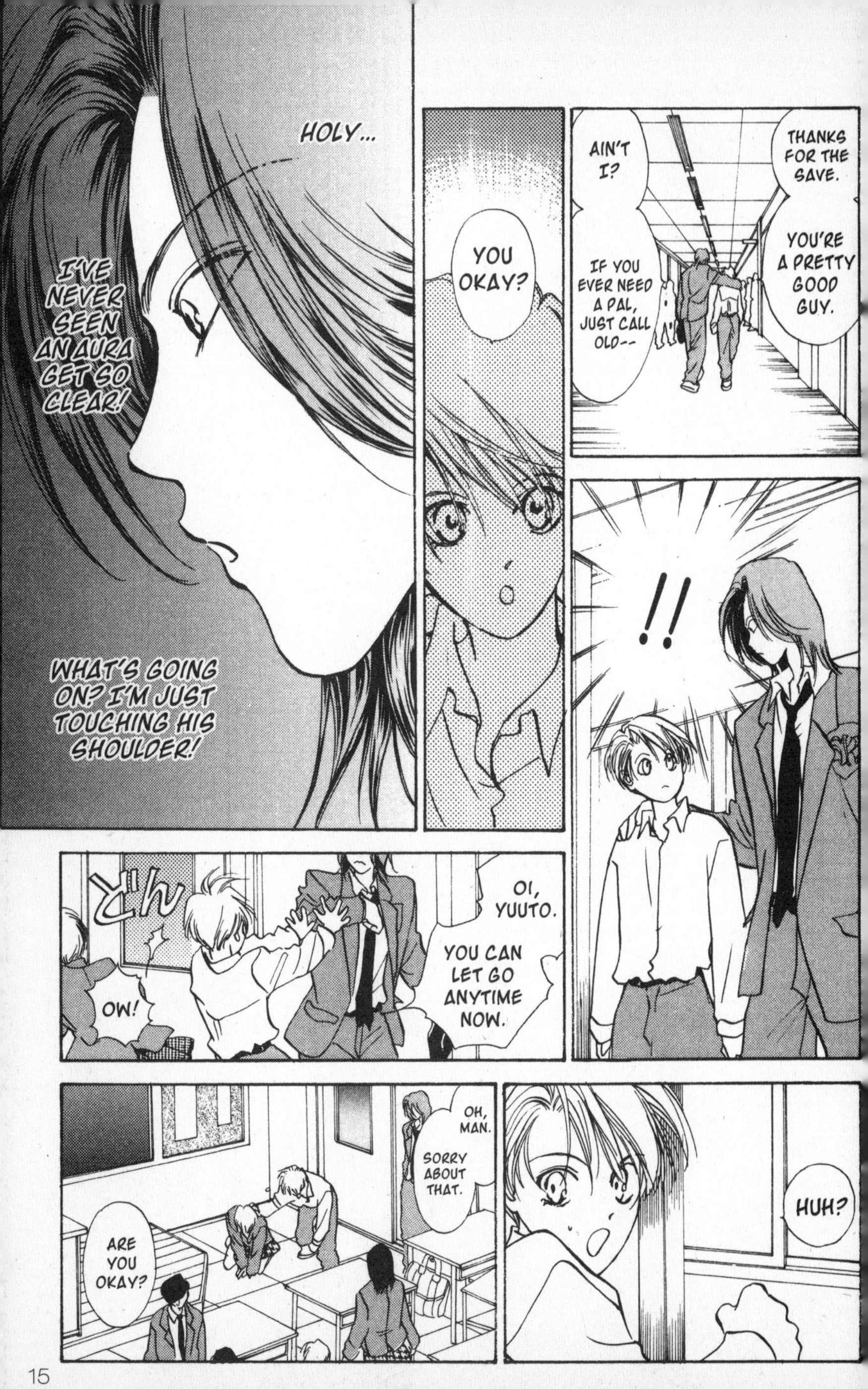
THANKS FOR THE SAVE.
YOU'RE A PRETTY GOOD GUY.
AIN'T I?
IF YOU EVER NEED A PAL, JUST CALL OLD--
!!
YOU OKAY?
HOLY...
I'VE NEVER SEEN AN AURA GET SO CLEAR!
WHAT'S GOING ON? I'M JUST TOUCHING HIS SHOULDER!
OI, YUUTO.
YOU CAN LET GO ANYTIME NOW.
OW!
HUH?
OH, MAN.
SORRY ABOUT THAT.
ARE YOU OKAY?

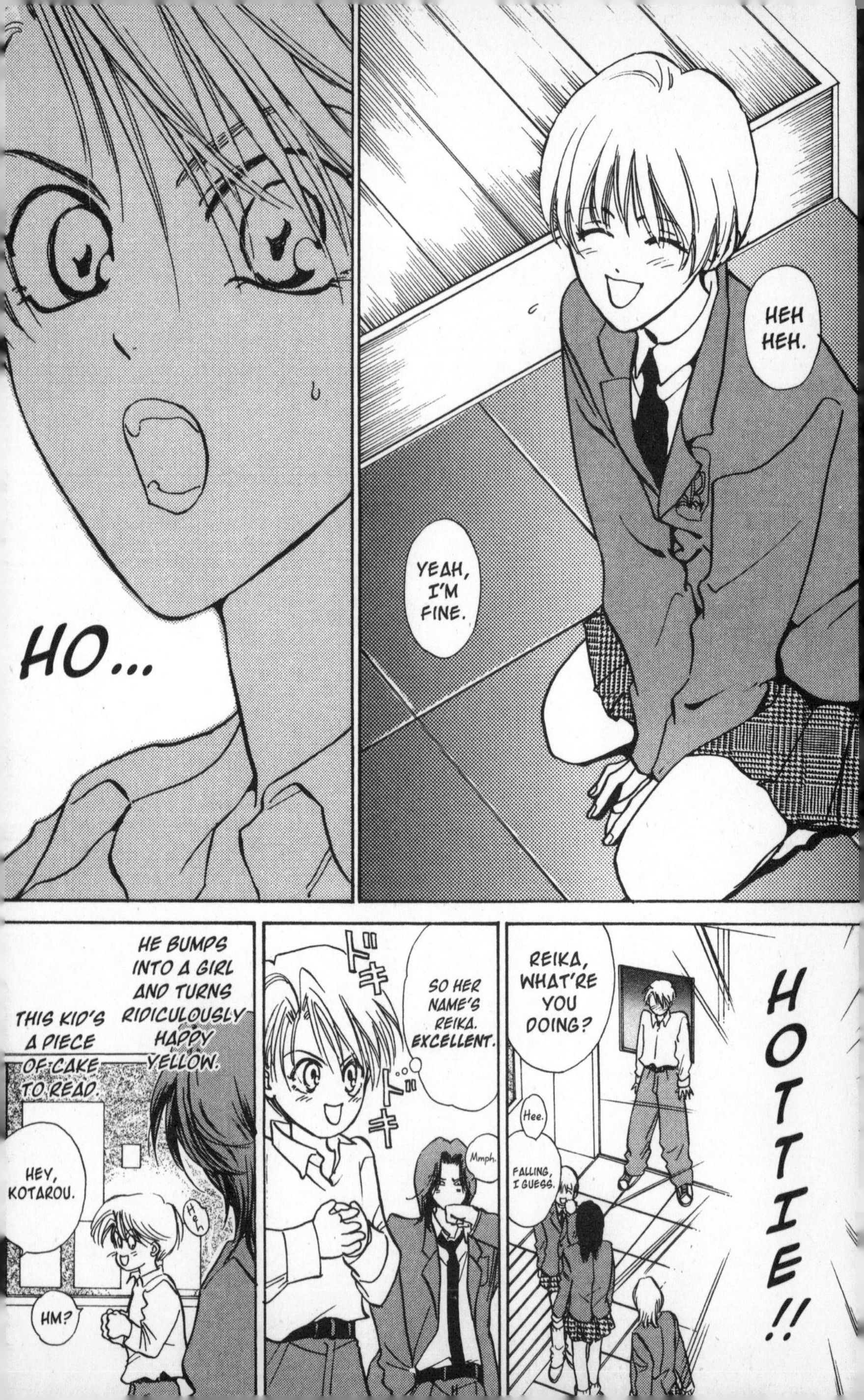
HEH HEH.
YEAH, I'M FINE.
HO...
REIKA, WHAT'RE YOU DOING?
Hee.
FALLING, I GUESS.
HOTTIE!!
ドキ
ドキ
SO HER NAME'S REIKA. EXCELLENT.
Mmph.
HE BUMPS INTO A GIRL AND TURNS RIDICULOUSLY HAPPY YELLOW.
THIS KID'S A PIECE OF CAKE TO READ.
HEY, KOTAROU.
Heh
HM?

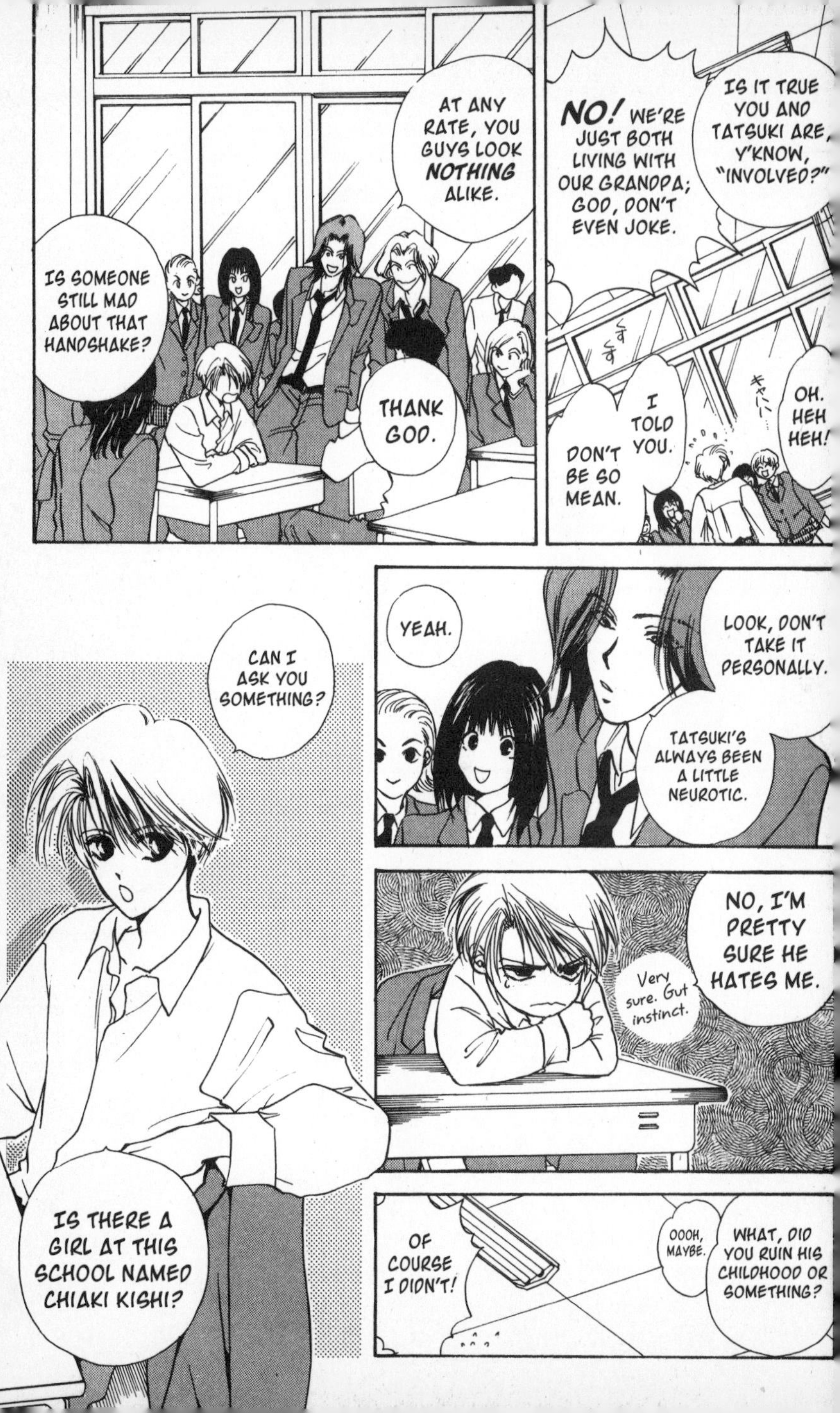
IS IT TRUE YOU AND TATSUKI ARE, Y'KNOW, "INVOLVED?"
NO! WE'RE JUST BOTH LIVING WITH OUR GRANDPA; GOD, DON'T EVEN JOKE.
OH. HEH HEH!
キャハハ…
くすくす
I TOLD YOU.
DON'T BE SO MEAN.
AT ANY RATE, YOU GUYS LOOK NOTHING ALIKE.
THANK GOD.
IS SOMEONE STILL MAD ABOUT THAT HANDSHAKE?
LOOK, DON'T TAKE IT PERSONALLY.
YEAH.
TATSUKI'S ALWAYS BEEN A LITTLE NEUROTIC.
NO, I'M PRETTY SURE HE HATES ME.
Very sure. Gut instinct.
WHAT, DID YOU RUIN HIS CHILDHOOD OR SOMETHING?
OOOH, MAYBE.
OF COURSE I DIDN'T!
CAN I ASK YOU SOMETHING?
IS THERE A GIRL AT THIS SCHOOL NAMED CHIAKI KISHI?

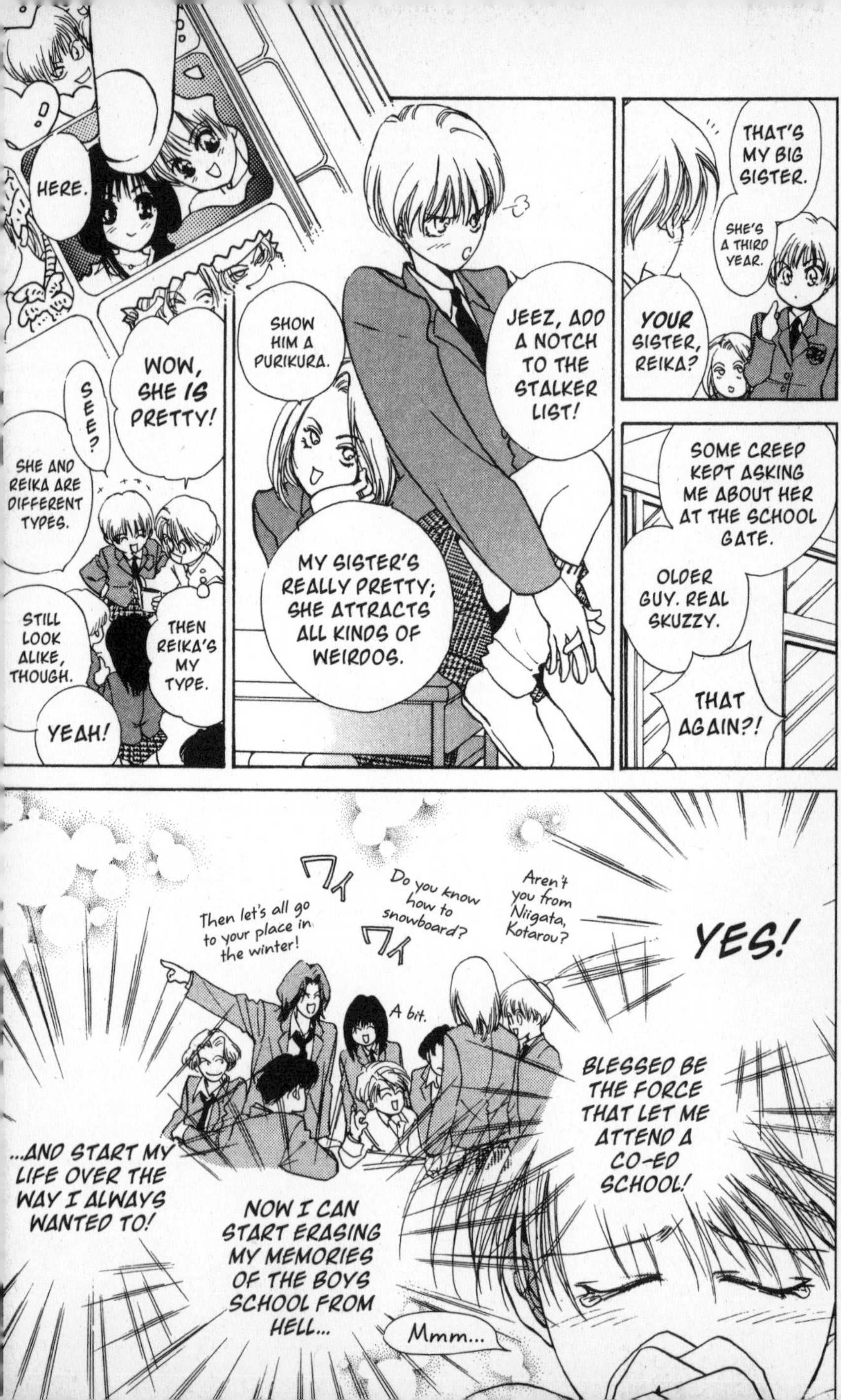
THAT'S MY BIG SISTER.
SHE'S A THIRD YEAR.
YOUR SISTER, REIKA?
SOME CREEP KEPT ASKING ME ABOUT HER AT THE SCHOOL GATE.
OLDER GUY. REAL SKUZZY.
THAT AGAIN?!
JEEZ, ADD A NOTCH TO THE STALKER LIST!
SHOW HIM A PURIKURA.
MY SISTER'S REALLY PRETTY; SHE ATTRACTS ALL KINDS OF WEIRDOS.
HERE.
WOW, SHE IS PRETTY!
SEE?
SHE AND REIKA ARE DIFFERENT TYPES.
THEN REIKA'S MY TYPE.
STILL LOOK ALIKE, THOUGH.
YEAH!
YES!
BLESSED BE THE FORCE THAT LET ME ATTEND A CO-ED SCHOOL!
Aren't you from Niigata, Kotarou?
Do you know how to snowboard?
ワイ
ワイ
Then let's all go to your place in the winter!
A bit.
NOW I CAN START ERASING MY MEMORIES OF THE BOYS SCHOOL FROM HELL...
...AND START MY LIFE OVER THE WAY I ALWAYS WANTED TO!
Mmm...

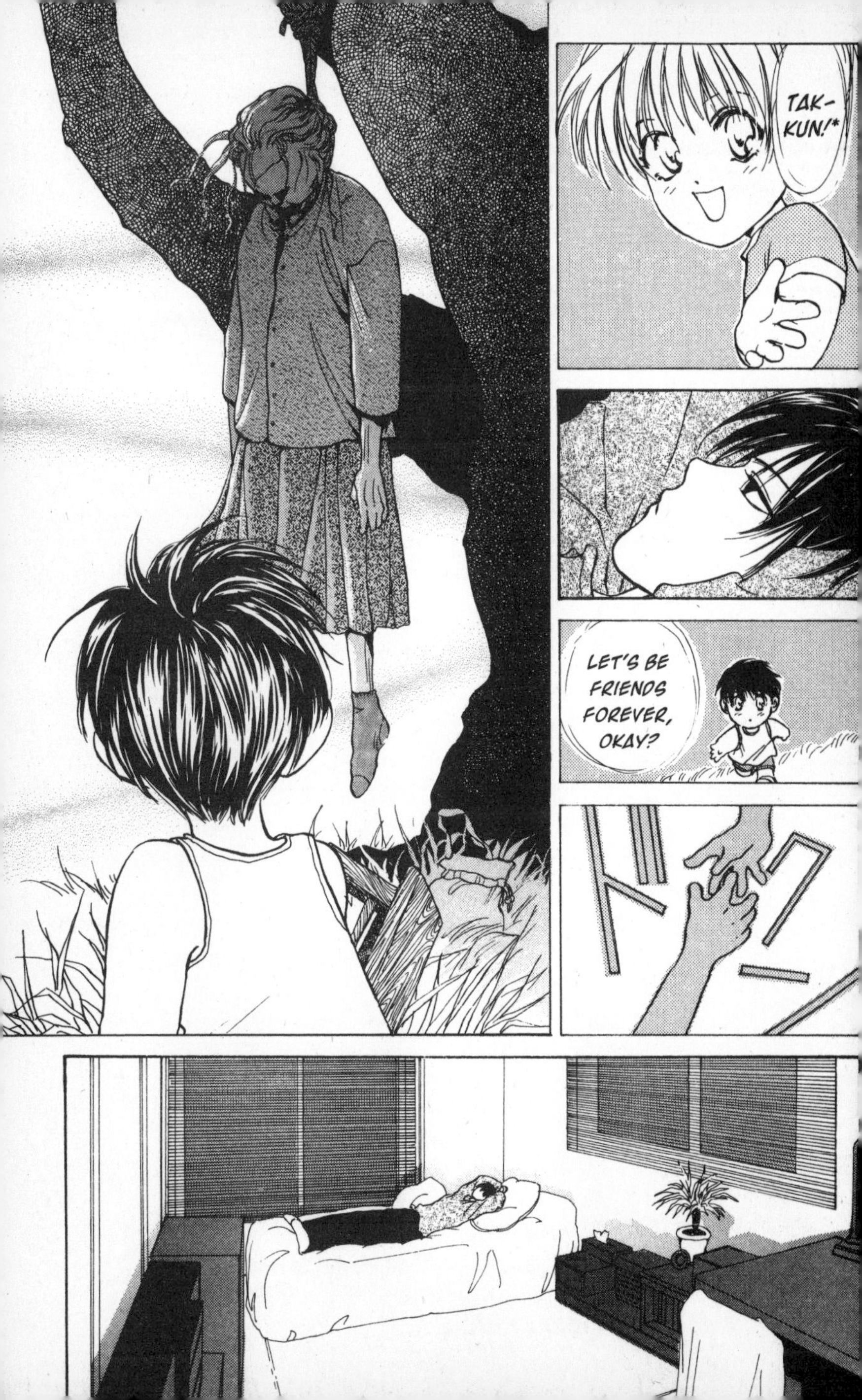
TAK-KUN!*
LET'S BE FRIENDS FOREVER, OKAY?

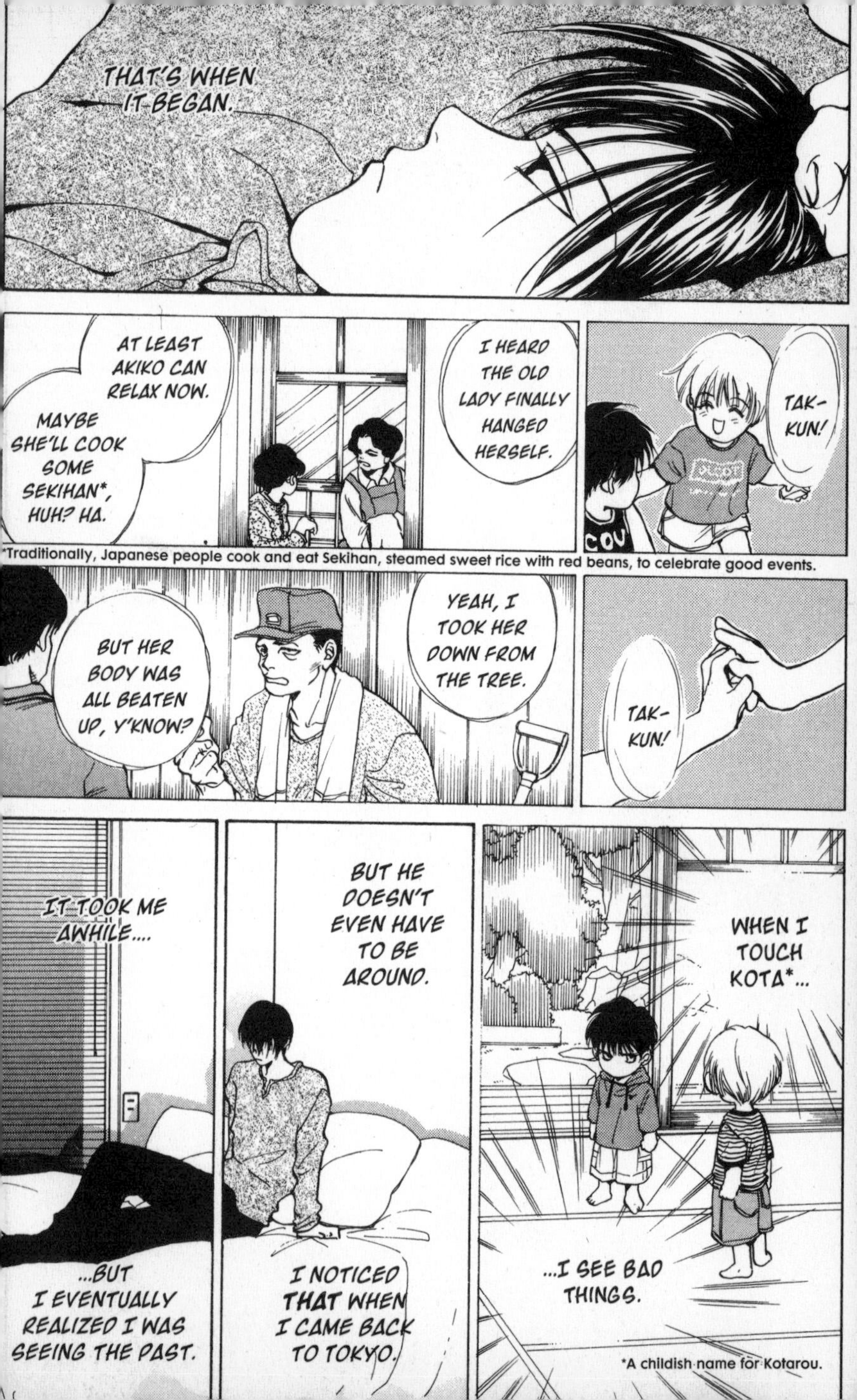
THAT'S WHEN IT BEGAN.
TAK-KUN!
I HEARD THE OLD LADY FINALLY HANGED HERSELF.
AT LEAST AKIKO CAN RELAX NOW.
MAYBE SHE'LL COOK SOME SEKIHAN*, HUH? HA.
TAK-KUN!
YEAH, I TOOK HER DOWN FROM THE TREE.
BUT HER BODY WAS ALL BEATEN UP, Y'KNOW?
WHEN I TOUCH KOTA*...
...I SEE BAD THINGS.
BUT HE DOESN'T EVEN HAVE TO BE AROUND.
I NOTICED THAT WHEN I CAME BACK TO TOKYO.
IT TOOK ME AWHILE....
...BUT I EVENTUALLY REALIZED I WAS SEEING THE PAST.

*Traditionally, Japanese people cook and eat Sekihan, steamed sweet rice with red beans, to celebrate good events.

*A childish name for Kotarou.

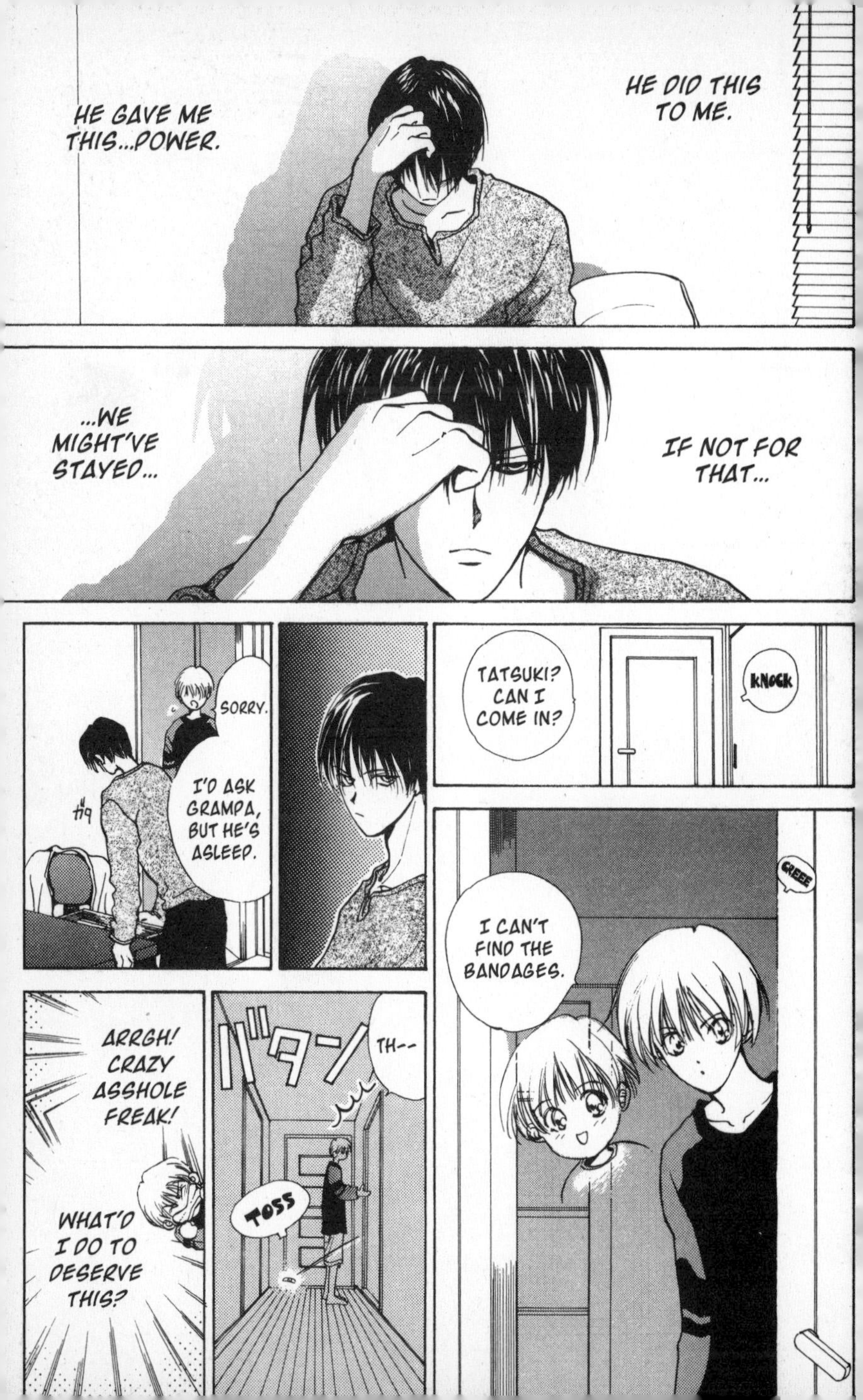
HE DID THIS TO ME.
HE GAVE ME THIS...POWER.
IF NOT FOR THAT...
...WE MIGHT'VE STAYED...
KNOCK
TATSUKI? CAN I COME IN?
CREEE
I CAN'T FIND THE BANDAGES.
SORRY.
I'D ASK GRAMPA, BUT HE'S ASLEEP.
TH--
バタン
TOSS
ARRGH! CRAZY ASSHOLE FREAK!
WHAT'D I DO TO DESERVE THIS?

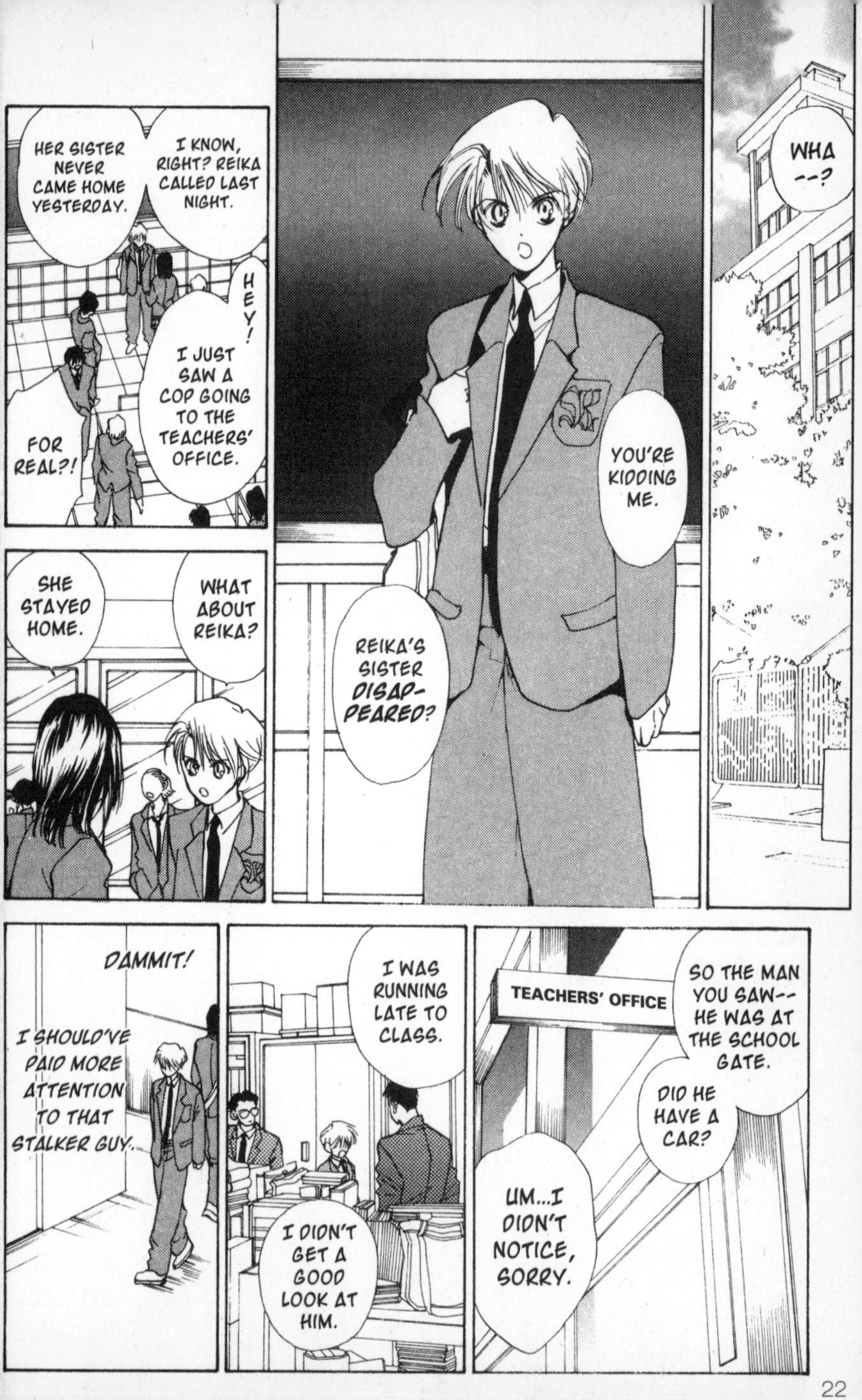
WHA--?
YOU'RE KIDDING ME.
REIKA'S SISTER DISAPPEARED?
I KNOW, RIGHT? REIKA CALLED LAST NIGHT.
HER SISTER NEVER CAME HOME YESTERDAY.
HEY!
I JUST SAW A COP GOING TO THE TEACHERS' OFFICE.
FOR REAL?!
WHAT ABOUT REIKA?
SHE STAYED HOME.
TEACHERS' OFFICE
SO THE MAN YOU SAW--HE WAS AT THE SCHOOL GATE.
DID HE HAVE A CAR?
UM...I DIDN'T NOTICE, SORRY.
I WAS RUNNING LATE TO CLASS.
I DIDN'T GET A GOOD LOOK AT HIM.
DAMMIT!
I SHOULD'VE PAID MORE ATTENTION TO THAT STALKER GUY.

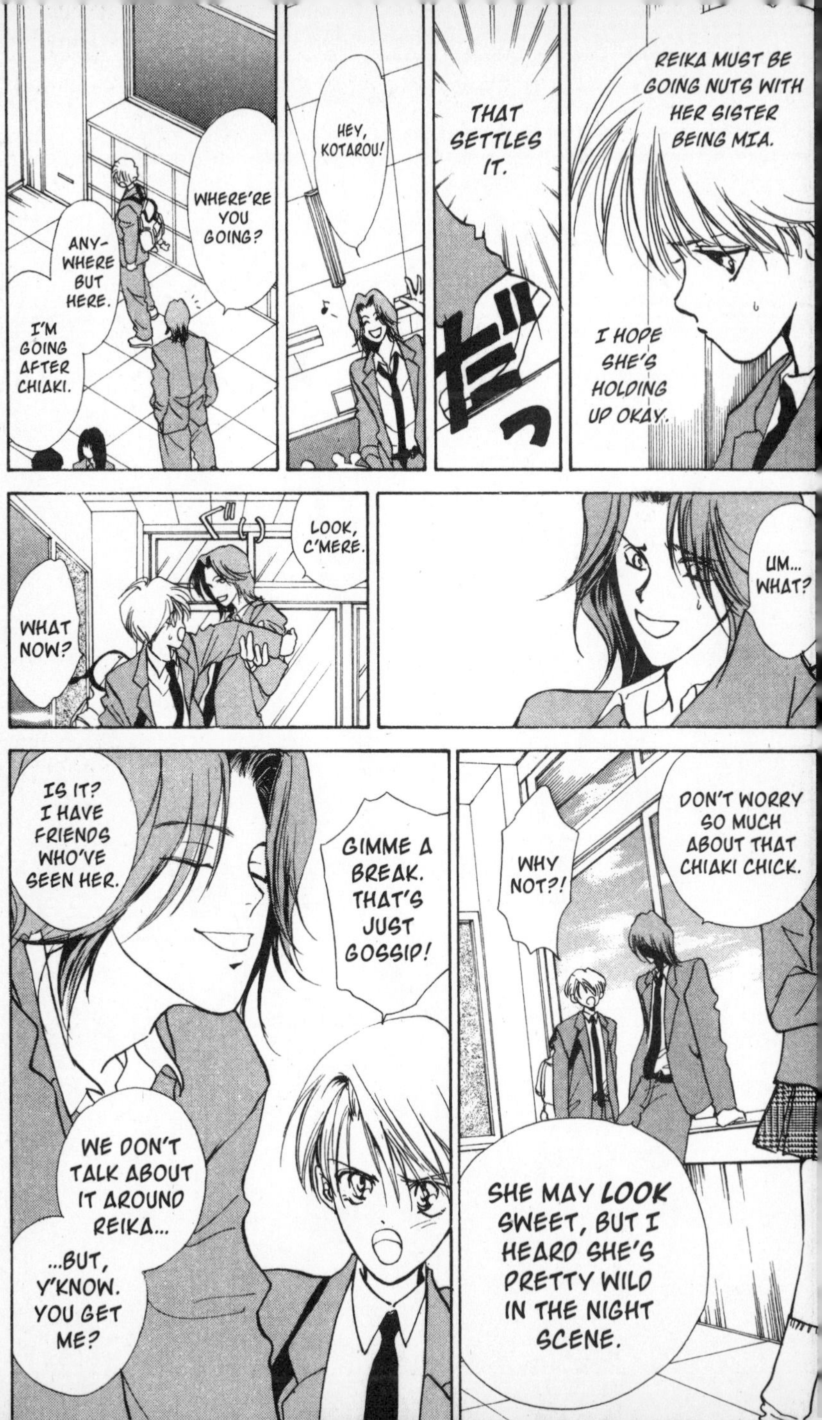
REIKA MUST BE GOING NUTS WITH HER SISTER BEING MIA.
I HOPE SHE'S HOLDING UP OKAY.
THAT SETTLES IT.
HEY, KOTAROU!
WHERE'RE YOU GOING?
ANY-WHERE BUT HERE.
I'M GOING AFTER CHIAKI.
UM... WHAT?
LOOK, C'MERE.
WHAT NOW?
DON'T WORRY SO MUCH ABOUT THAT CHIAKI CHICK.
WHY NOT?!
SHE MAY LOOK SWEET, BUT I HEARD SHE'S PRETTY WILD IN THE NIGHT SCENE.
GIMME A BREAK. THAT'S JUST GOSSIP!
IS IT? I HAVE FRIENDS WHO'VE SEEN HER.
WE DON'T TALK ABOUT IT AROUND REIKA...
...BUT, Y'KNOW. YOU GET ME?

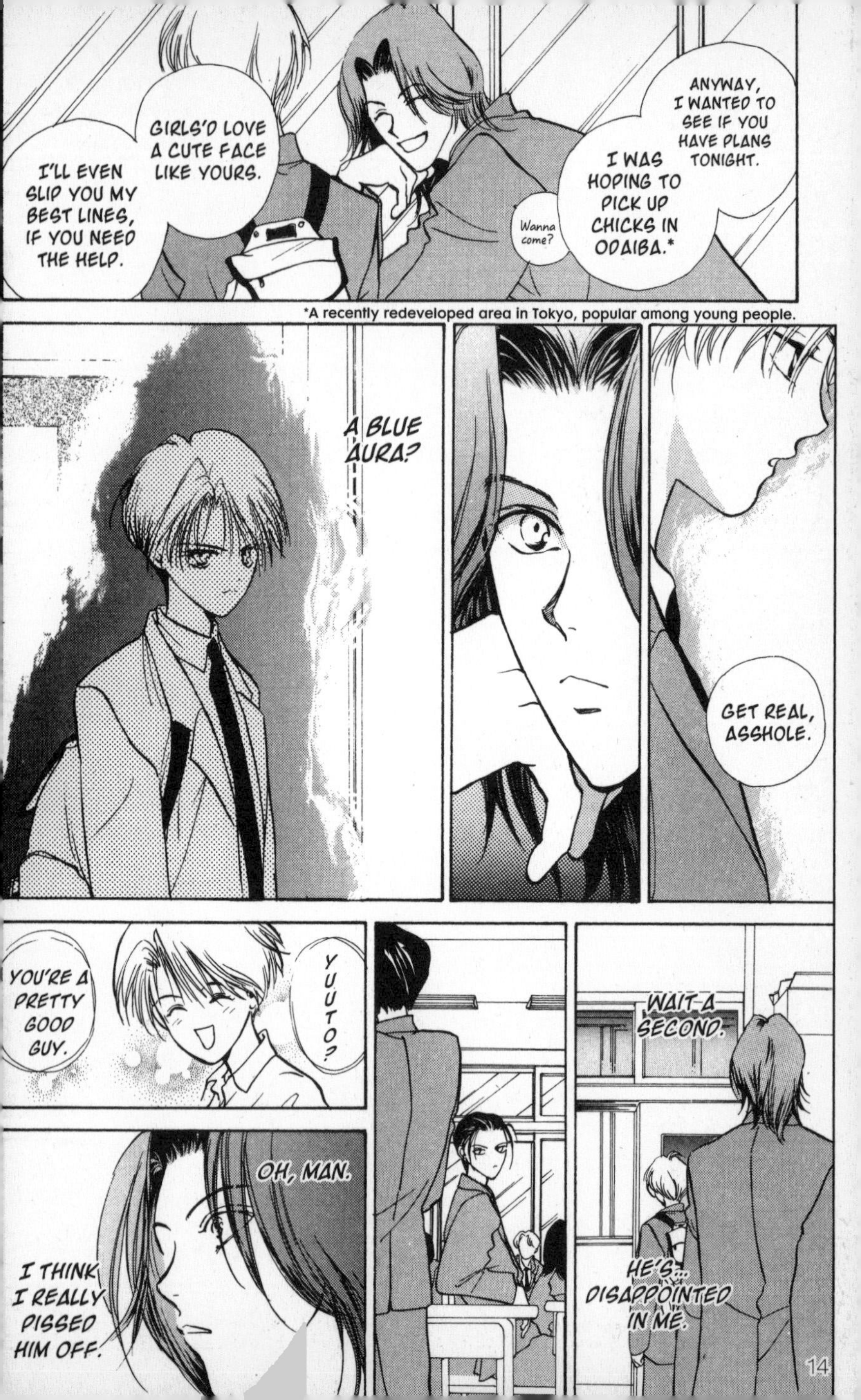
ANYWAY, I WANTED TO SEE IF YOU HAVE PLANS TONIGHT.
I WAS HOPING TO PICK UP CHICKS IN ODAIBA.*
Wanna come?
GIRLS'D LOVE A CUTE FACE LIKE YOURS.
I'LL EVEN SLIP YOU MY BEST LINES, IF YOU NEED THE HELP.
GET REAL, ASSHOLE.
A BLUE AURA?
WAIT A SECOND.
HE'S... DISAPPOINTED IN ME.
YUUTO?
YOU'RE A PRETTY GOOD GUY.
OH, MAN.
I THINK I REALLY PISSED HIM OFF.

*A recently redeveloped area in Tokyo, popular among young people.

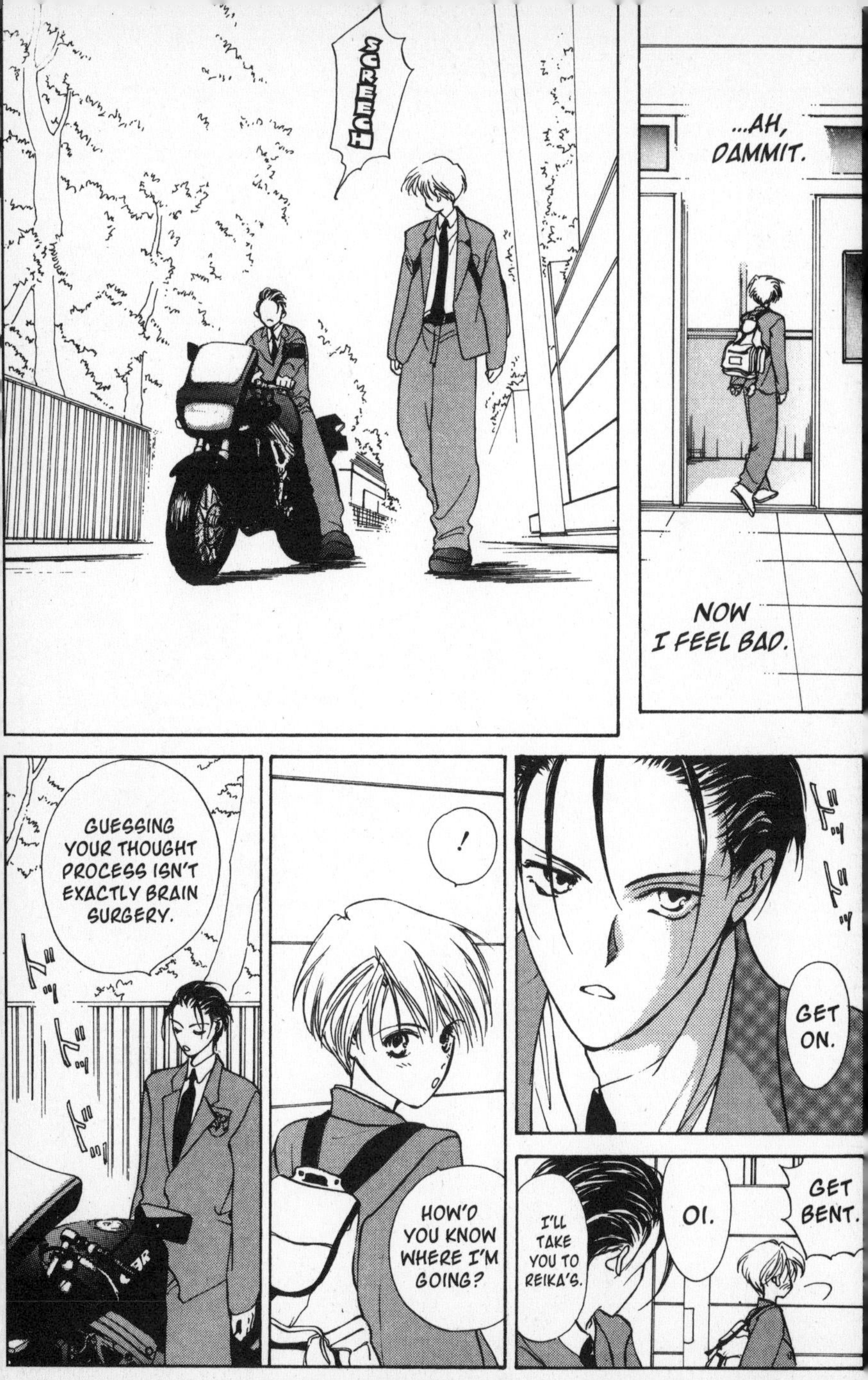
...AH, DAMMIT.
NOW I FEEL BAD.
SCREECH
GET ON.
GET BENT.
OI.
I'LL TAKE YOU TO REIKA'S.
!
HOW'D YOU KNOW WHERE I'M GOING?
GUESSING YOUR THOUGHT PROCESS ISN'T EXACTLY BRAIN SURGERY.

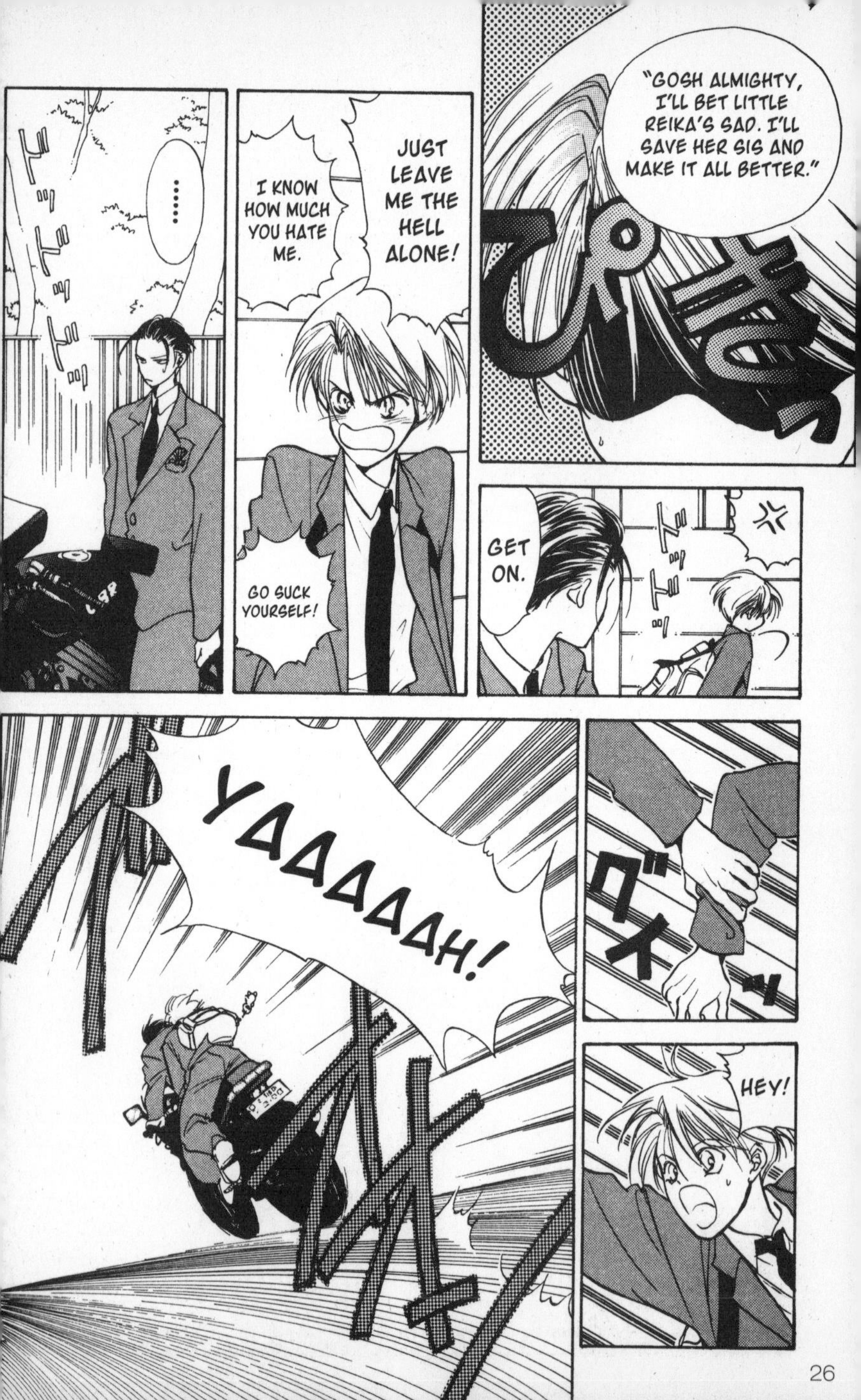

"GOSH ALMIGHTY, I'LL BET LITTLE REIKA'S SAD. I'LL SAVE HER SIS AND MAKE IT ALL BETTER."
ぴきっ
GET ON.
JUST LEAVE ME THE HELL ALONE!
I KNOW HOW MUCH YOU HATE ME.
GO SUCK YOURSELF!
......
グイッ
HEY!
YAAAAAH!

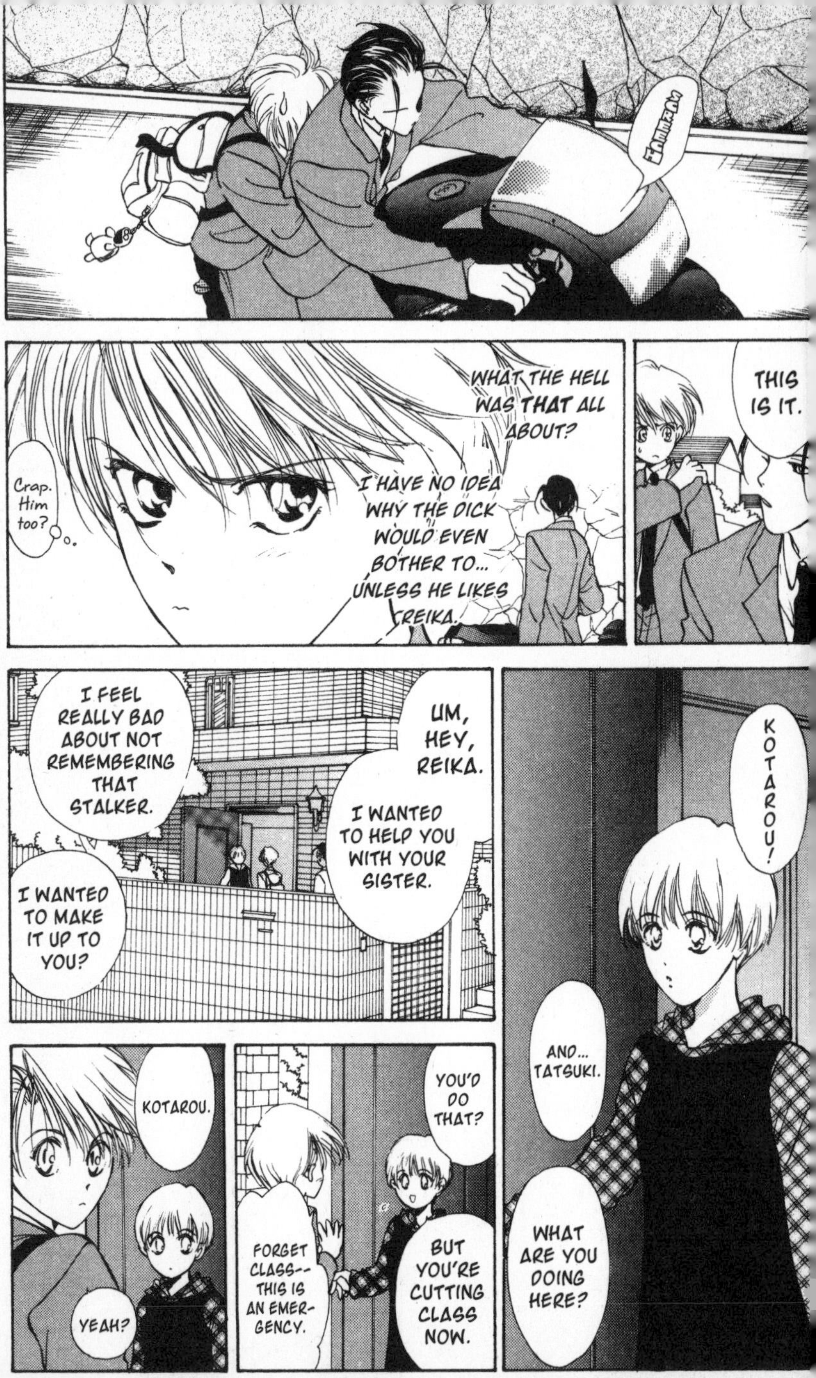
SCREECH
THIS IS IT.
WHAT THE HELL WAS **THAT** ALL ABOUT?
I HAVE NO IDEA WHY THE DICK WOULD EVEN BOTHER TO... UNLESS HE LIKES REIKA.
Crap. Him too?
KOTAROU!
AND... TATSUKI.
WHAT ARE YOU DOING HERE?
UM, HEY, REIKA.
I WANTED TO HELP YOU WITH YOUR SISTER.
I FEEL REALLY BAD ABOUT NOT REMEMBERING THAT STALKER.
I WANTED TO MAKE IT UP TO YOU?
YOU'D DO THAT?
BUT YOU'RE CUTTING CLASS NOW.
FORGET CLASS--THIS IS AN EMERGENCY.
KOTAROU.
YEAH?

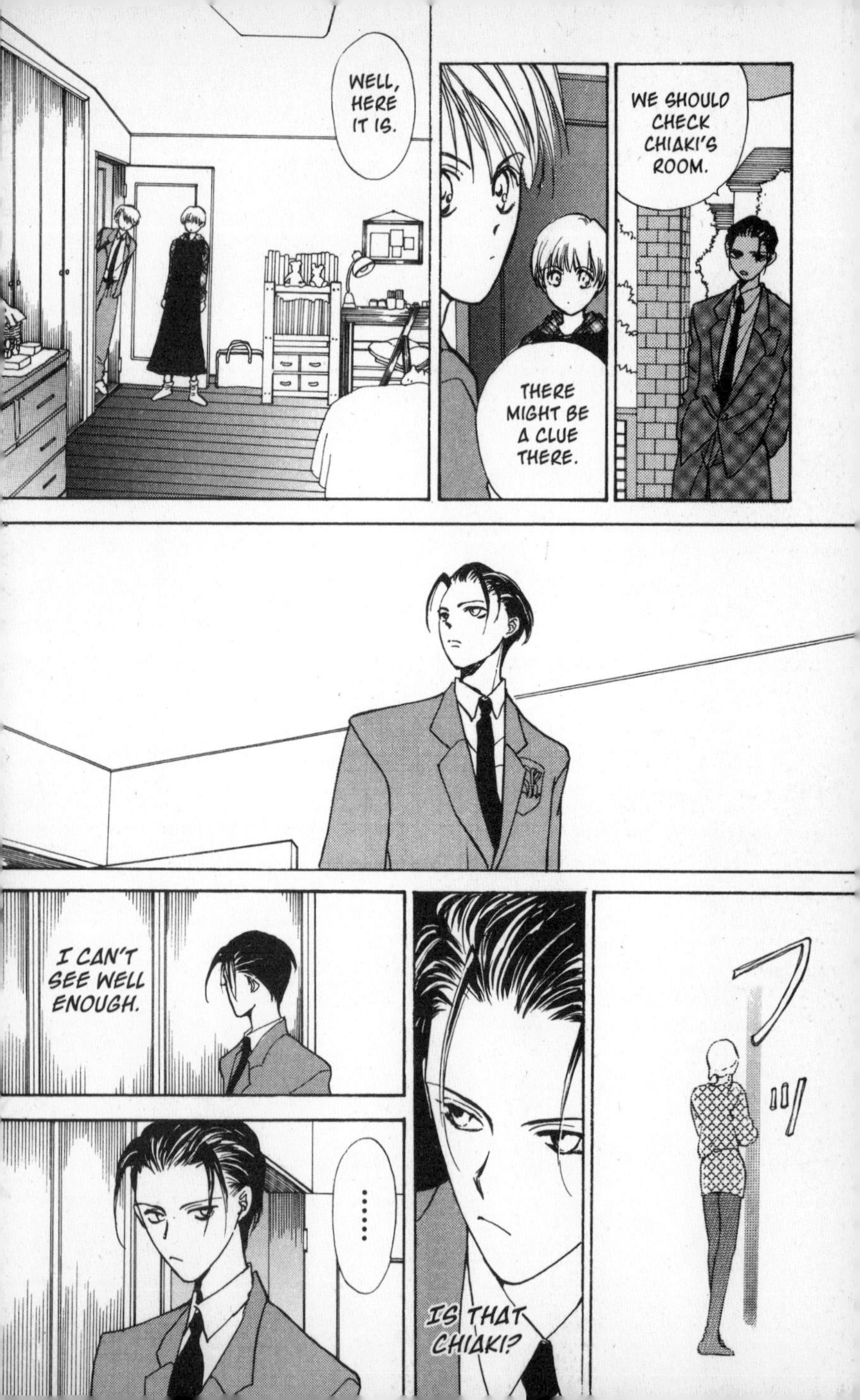
WE SHOULD CHECK CHIAKI'S ROOM.
THERE MIGHT BE A CLUE THERE.
WELL, HERE IT IS.
IS THAT CHIAKI?
I CAN'T SEE WELL ENOUGH.
......

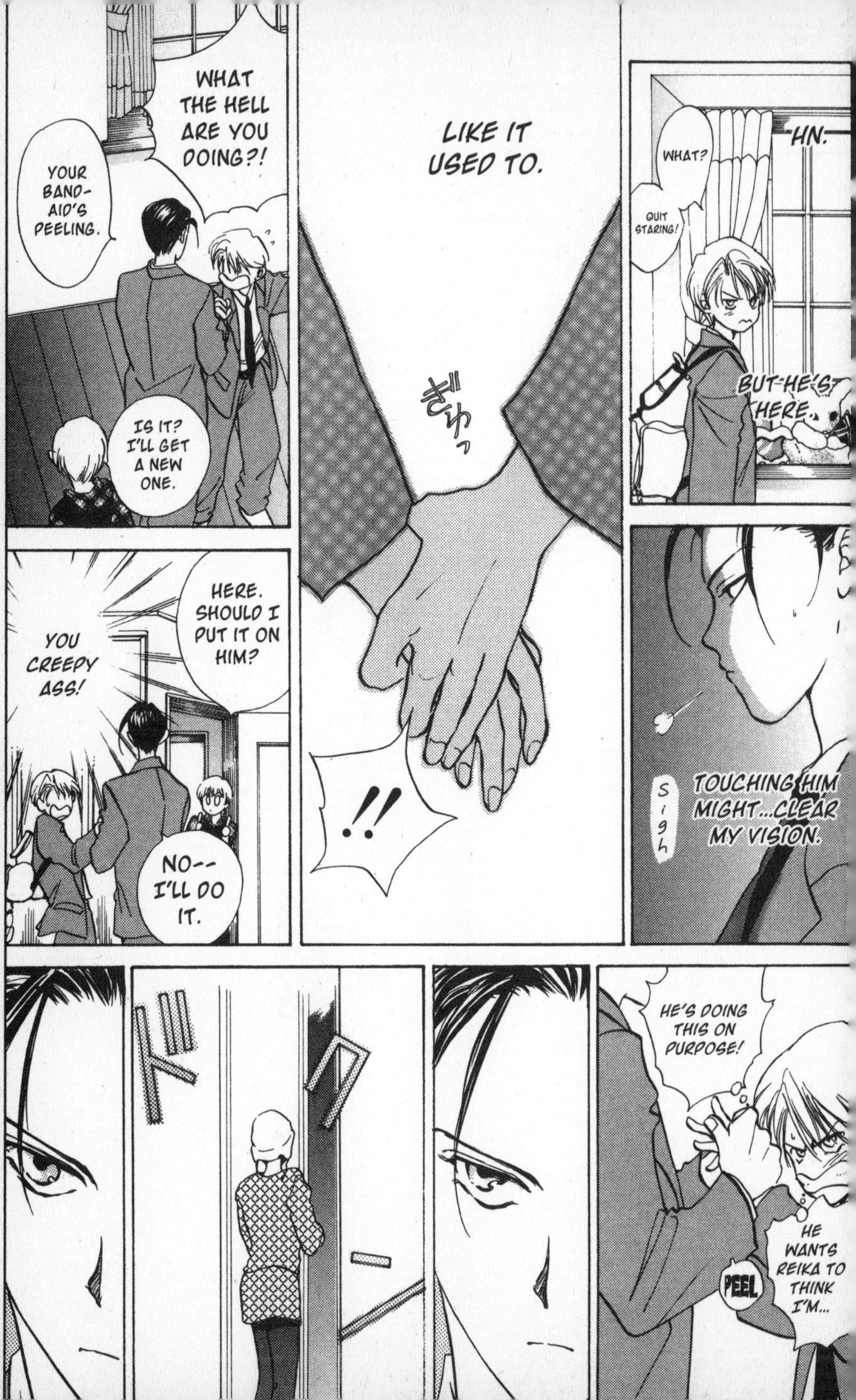

WHAT?
QUIT STARING!
HN.
BUT HE'S HERE.
Sigh
TOUCHING HIM MIGHT...CLEAR MY VISION.
LIKE IT USED TO.
ぎゅっ
!!
WHAT THE HELL ARE YOU DOING?!
YOUR BAND-AID'S PEELING.
IS IT? I'LL GET A NEW ONE.
HERE. SHOULD I PUT IT ON HIM?
YOU CREEPY ASS!
NO-- I'LL DO IT.
HE'S DOING THIS ON PURPOSE!
HE WANTS REIKA TO THINK I'M...
PEEL

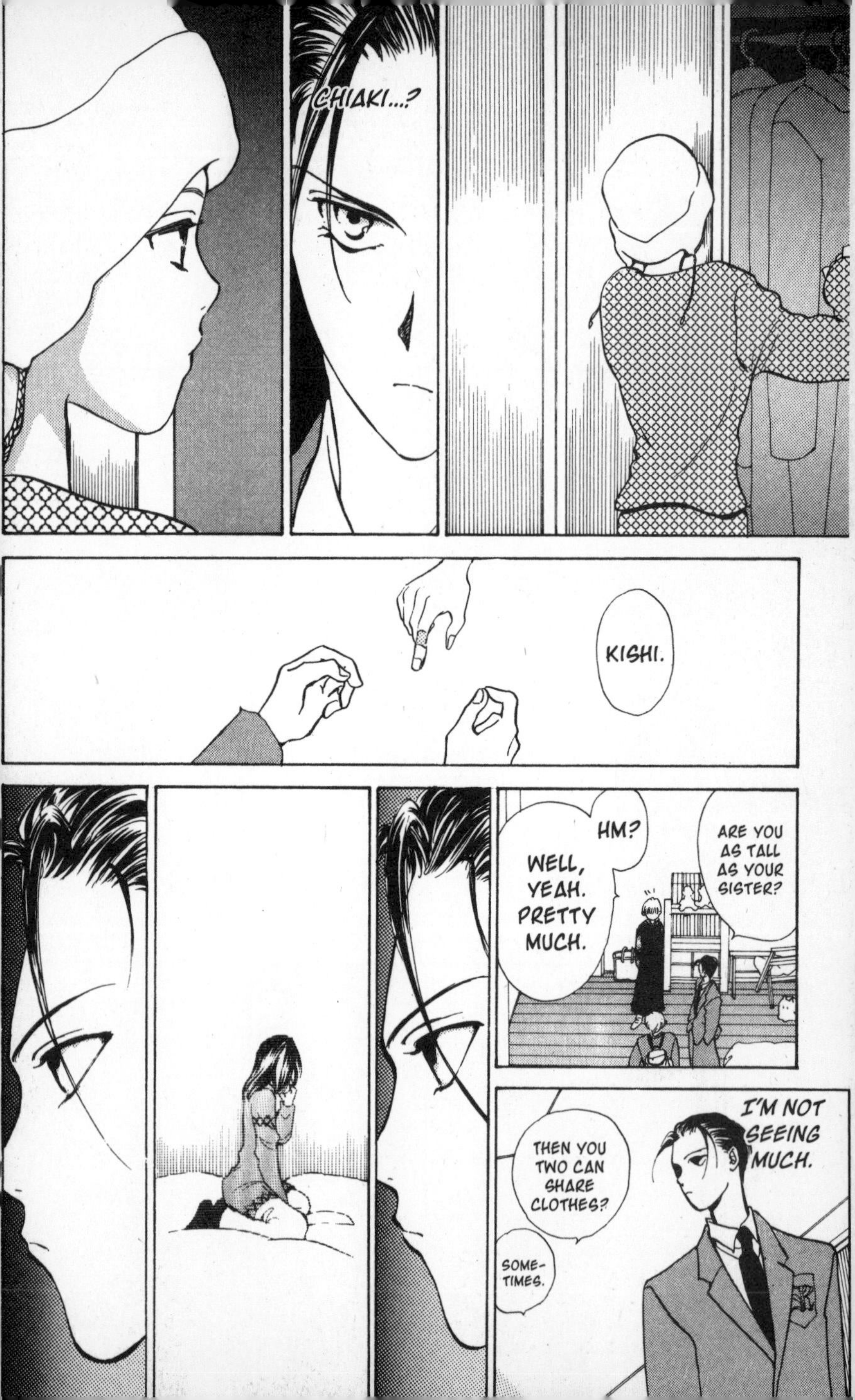
CHIAKI...?
KISHI.
ARE YOU AS TALL AS YOUR SISTER?
HM? WELL, YEAH. PRETTY MUCH.
I'M NOT SEEING MUCH.
THEN YOU TWO CAN SHARE CLOTHES?
SOME-TIMES.

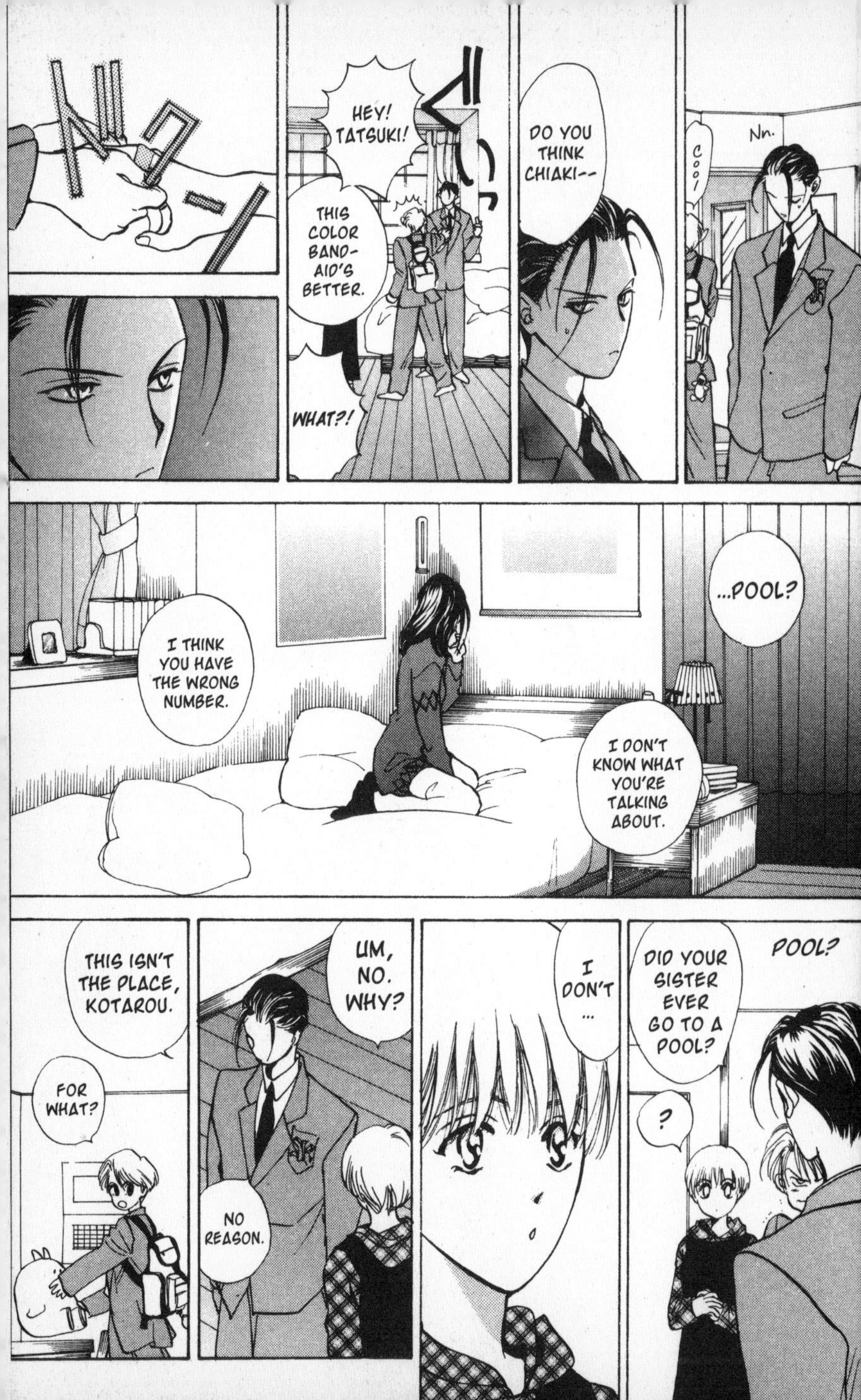
Nn.
Cool
DO YOU THINK CHIAKI--
HEY! TATSUKI!
THIS COLOR BAND-AID'S BETTER.
WHAT?!
...POOL?
I DON'T KNOW WHAT YOU'RE TALKING ABOUT.
I THINK YOU HAVE THE WRONG NUMBER.
POOL?
DID YOUR SISTER EVER GO TO A POOL?
?
I DON'T ...
UM, NO. WHY?
NO REASON.
THIS ISN'T THE PLACE, KOTAROU.
FOR WHAT?

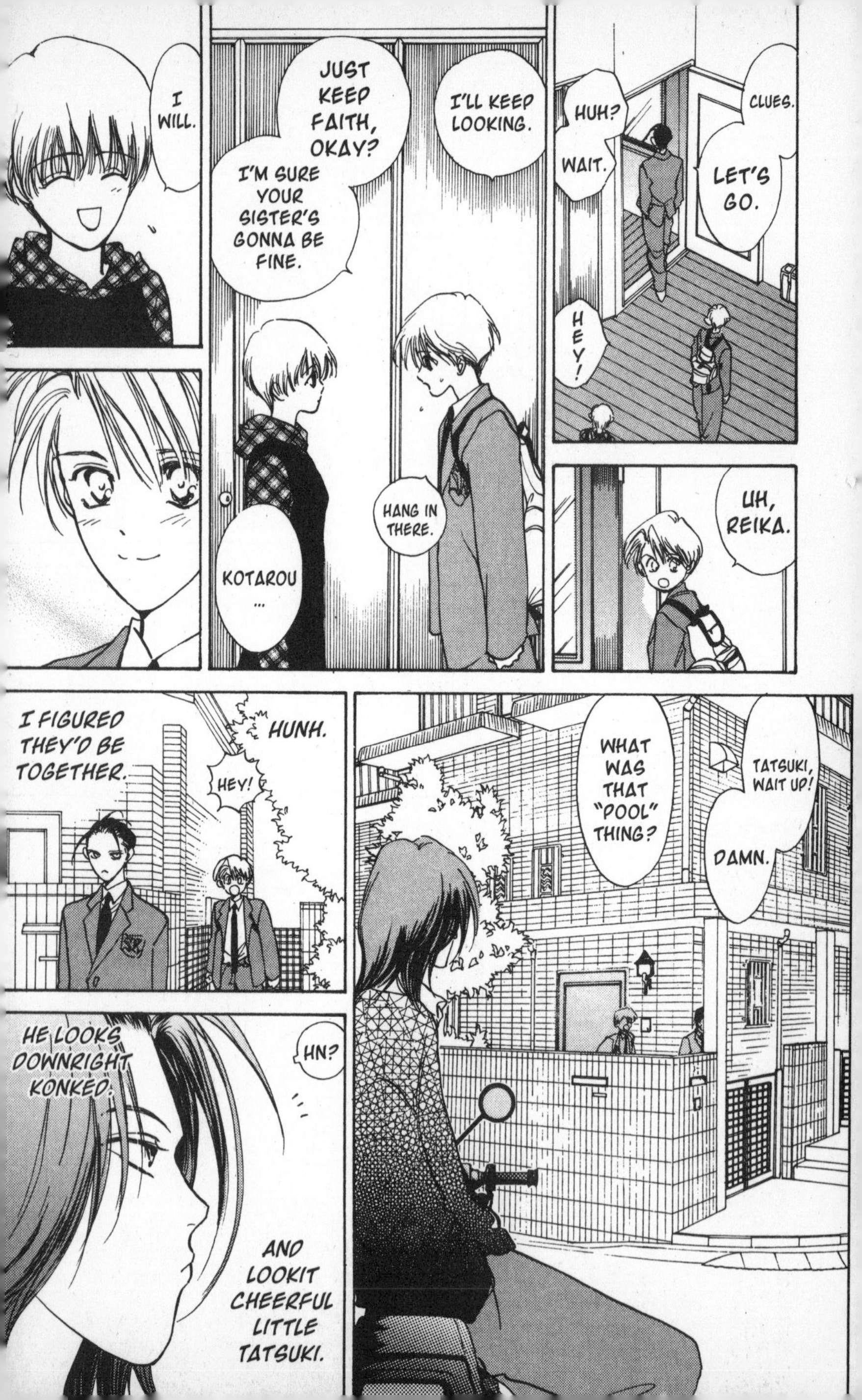
CLUES.
LET'S GO.
HUH?
WAIT.
HEY!
UH, REIKA.
I'LL KEEP LOOKING.
JUST KEEP FAITH, OKAY?
I'M SURE YOUR SISTER'S GONNA BE FINE.
HANG IN THERE.
KOTAROU ...
I WILL.
TATSUKI, WAIT UP!
WHAT WAS THAT "POOL" THING?
DAMN.
HUNH.
I FIGURED THEY'D BE TOGETHER.
HEY!
HN?
HE LOOKS DOWNRIGHT KONKED.
AND LOOKIT CHEERFUL LITTLE TATSUKI.

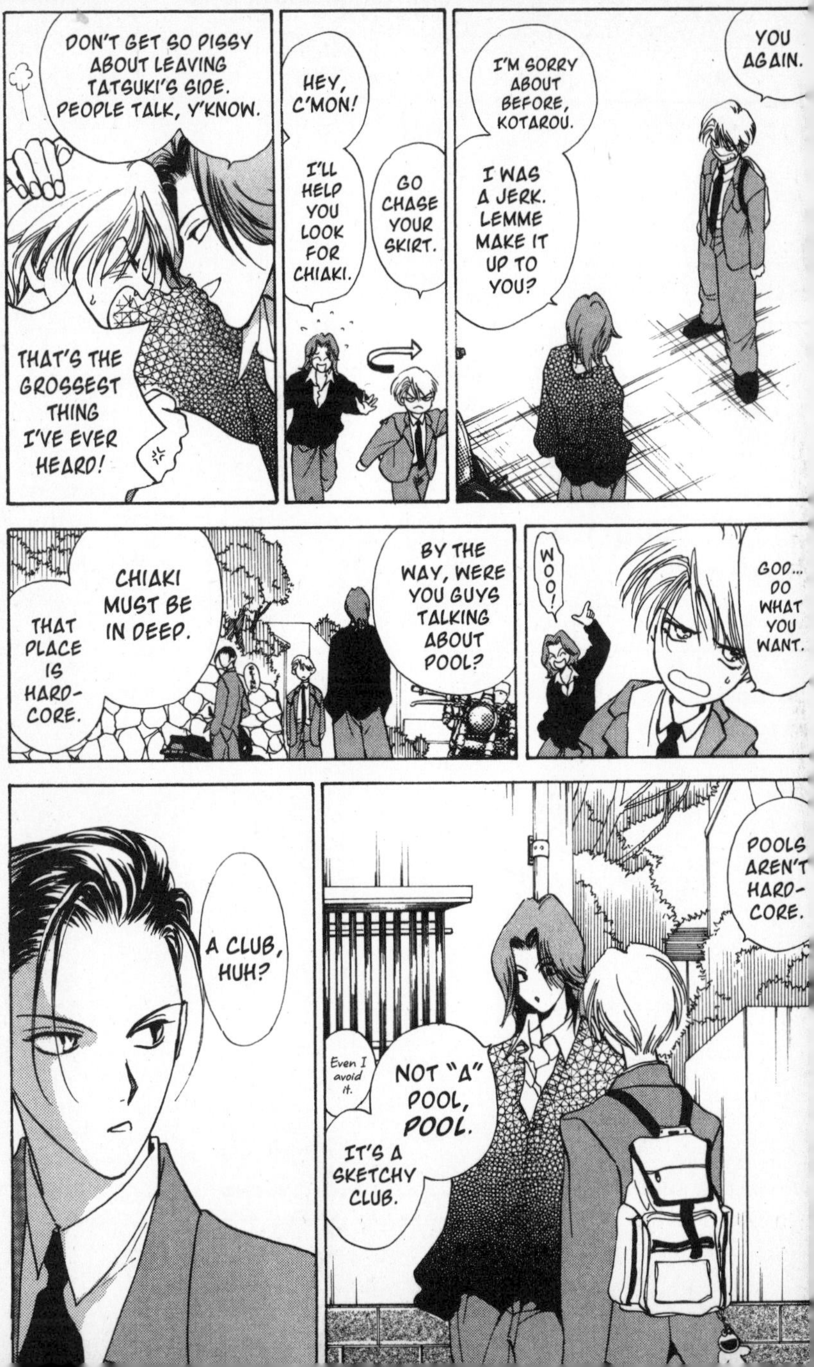
YOU AGAIN.
I'M SORRY ABOUT BEFORE, KOTAROU.
I WAS A JERK. LEMME MAKE IT UP TO YOU?
GO CHASE YOUR SKIRT.
HEY, C'MON!
I'LL HELP YOU LOOK FOR CHIAKI.
DON'T GET SO PISSY ABOUT LEAVING TATSUKI'S SIDE. PEOPLE TALK, Y'KNOW.
THAT'S THE GROSSEST THING I'VE EVER HEARD!
GOD... DO WHAT YOU WANT.
WOO!
BY THE WAY, WERE YOU GUYS TALKING ABOUT POOL?
CHIAKI MUST BE IN DEEP.
THAT PLACE IS HARD-CORE.
POOLS AREN'T HARD-CORE.
NOT "A" POOL, POOL.
IT'S A SKETCHY CLUB.
Even I avoid it.
A CLUB, HUH?

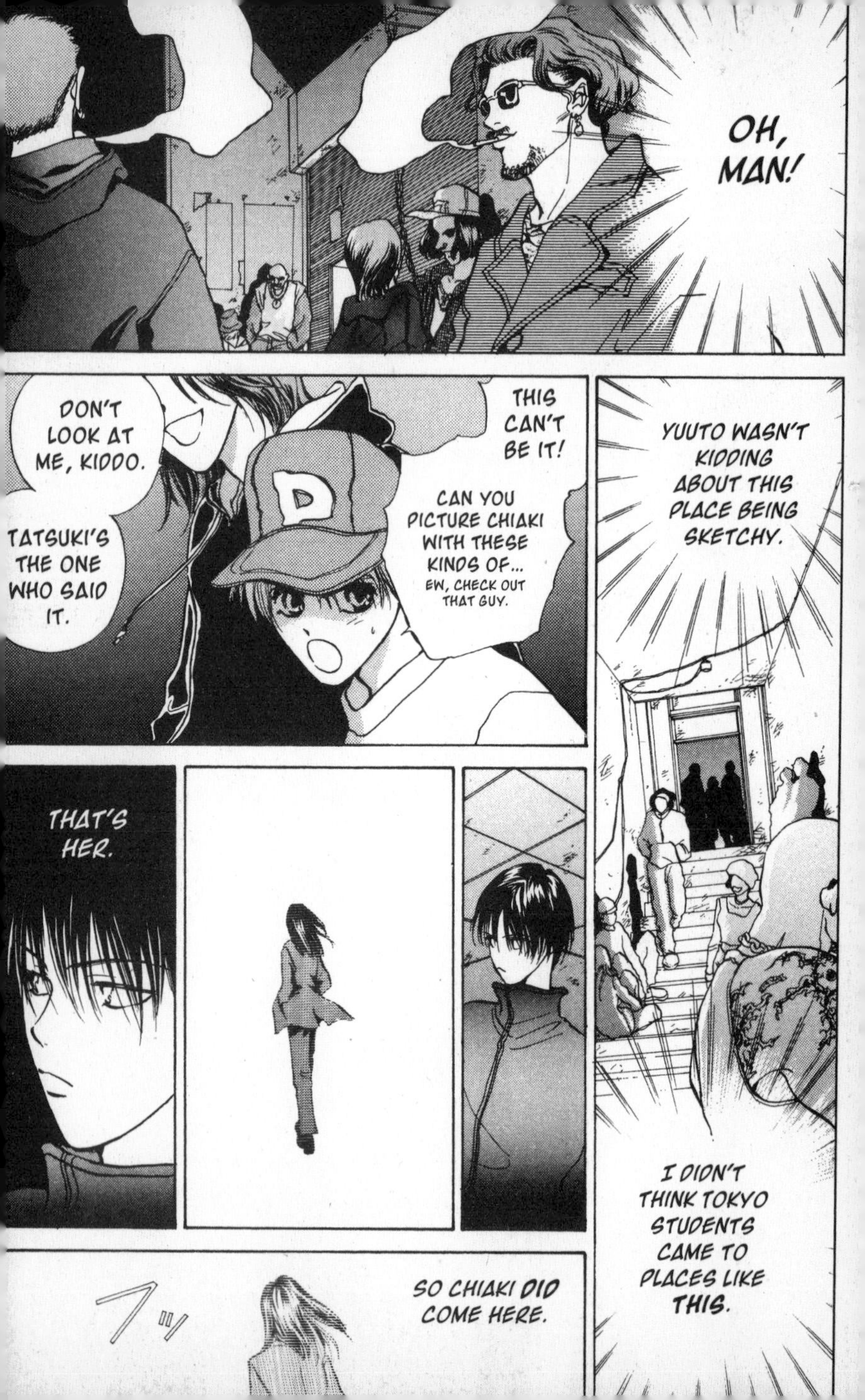
OH, MAN!
YUUTO WASN'T KIDDING ABOUT THIS PLACE BEING SKETCHY.
I DIDN'T THINK TOKYO STUDENTS CAME TO PLACES LIKE THIS.
THIS CAN'T BE IT!
CAN YOU PICTURE CHIAKI WITH THESE KINDS OF...
EW, CHECK OUT THAT GUY.
DON'T LOOK AT ME, KIDDO.
TATSUKI'S THE ONE WHO SAID IT.
THAT'S HER.
SO CHIAKI DID COME HERE.
フッ

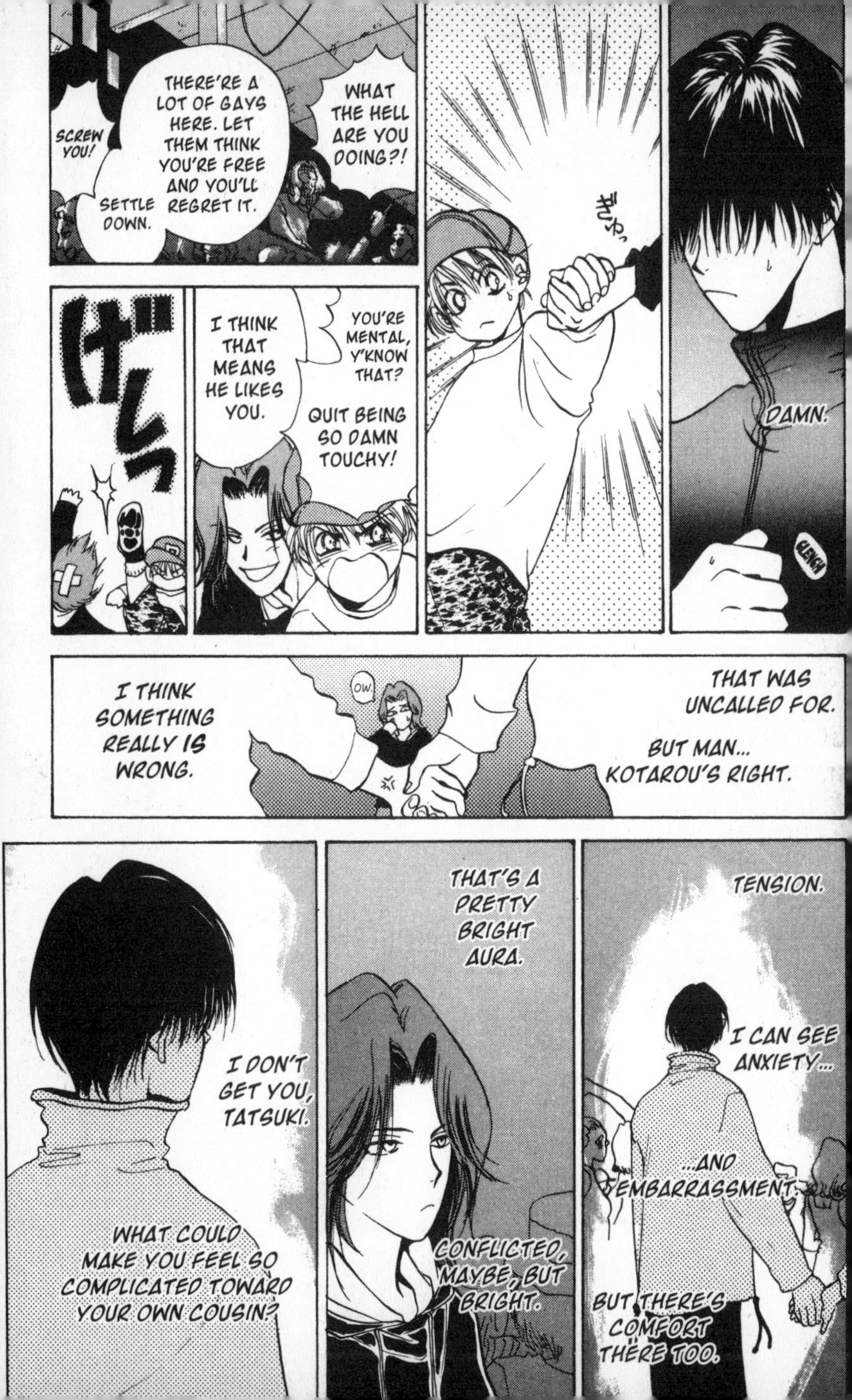
DAMN.
CLENCH
WHAT THE HELL ARE YOU DOING?!
THERE'RE A LOT OF GAYS HERE. LET THEM THINK YOU'RE FREE AND YOU'LL REGRET IT.
SCREW YOU!
SETTLE DOWN.
YOU'RE MENTAL, Y'KNOW THAT?
QUIT BEING SO DAMN TOUCHY!
I THINK THAT MEANS HE LIKES YOU.
げしっ
THAT WAS UNCALLED FOR.
BUT MAN... KOTAROU'S RIGHT.
OW!
I THINK SOMETHING REALLY IS WRONG.
TENSION.
I CAN SEE ANXIETY...
...AND EMBARRASSMENT.
BUT THERE'S COMFORT THERE TOO.
THAT'S A PRETTY BRIGHT AURA.
CONFLICTED, MAYBE, BUT BRIGHT.
I DON'T GET YOU, TATSUKI.
WHAT COULD MAKE YOU FEEL SO COMPLICATED TOWARD YOUR OWN COUSIN?

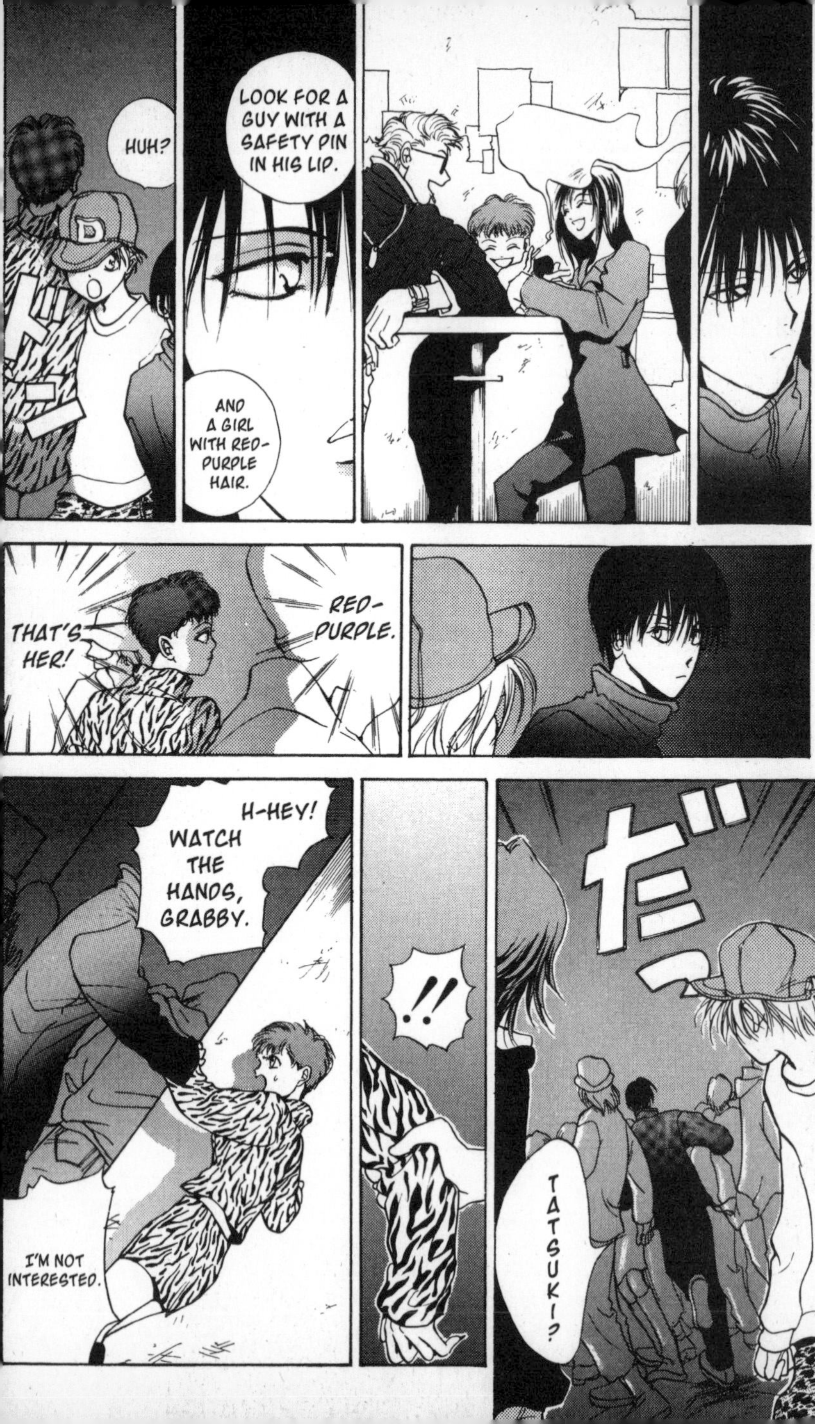
LOOK FOR A GUY WITH A SAFETY PIN IN HIS LIP.
AND A GIRL WITH RED-PURPLE HAIR.
HUH?
RED-PURPLE.
THAT'S HER!
ダッ
TATSUKI?
!!
H-HEY!
WATCH THE HANDS, GRABBY.
I'M NOT INTERESTED.

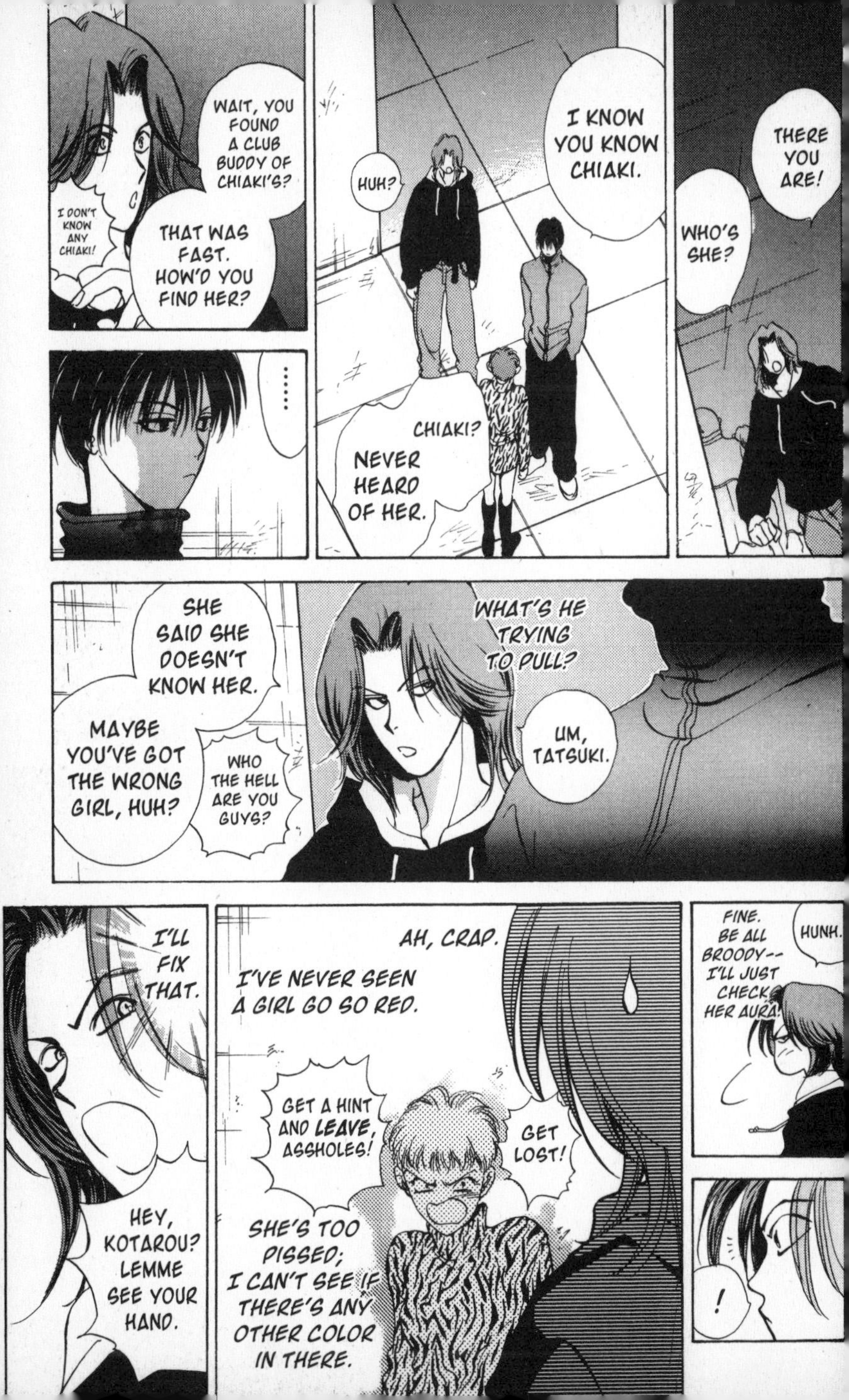
THERE YOU ARE!
WHO'S SHE?
I KNOW YOU KNOW CHIAKI.
HUH?
CHIAKI? NEVER HEARD OF HER.
WAIT, YOU FOUND A CLUB BUDDY OF CHIAKI'S?
I DON'T KNOW ANY CHIAKI!
THAT WAS FAST. HOW'D YOU FIND HER?
......
WHAT'S HE TRYING TO PULL?
UM, TATSUKI.
SHE SAID SHE DOESN'T KNOW HER.
WHO THE HELL ARE YOU GUYS?
MAYBE YOU'VE GOT THE WRONG GIRL, HUH?
HUNH.
FINE. BE ALL BROODY-- I'LL JUST CHECK HER AURA.
!
AH, CRAP.
I'VE NEVER SEEN A GIRL GO SO RED.
GET LOST!
GET A HINT AND LEAVE, ASSHOLES!
SHE'S TOO PISSED; I CAN'T SEE IF THERE'S ANY OTHER COLOR IN THERE.
I'LL FIX THAT.
HEY, KOTAROU? LEMME SEE YOUR HAND.

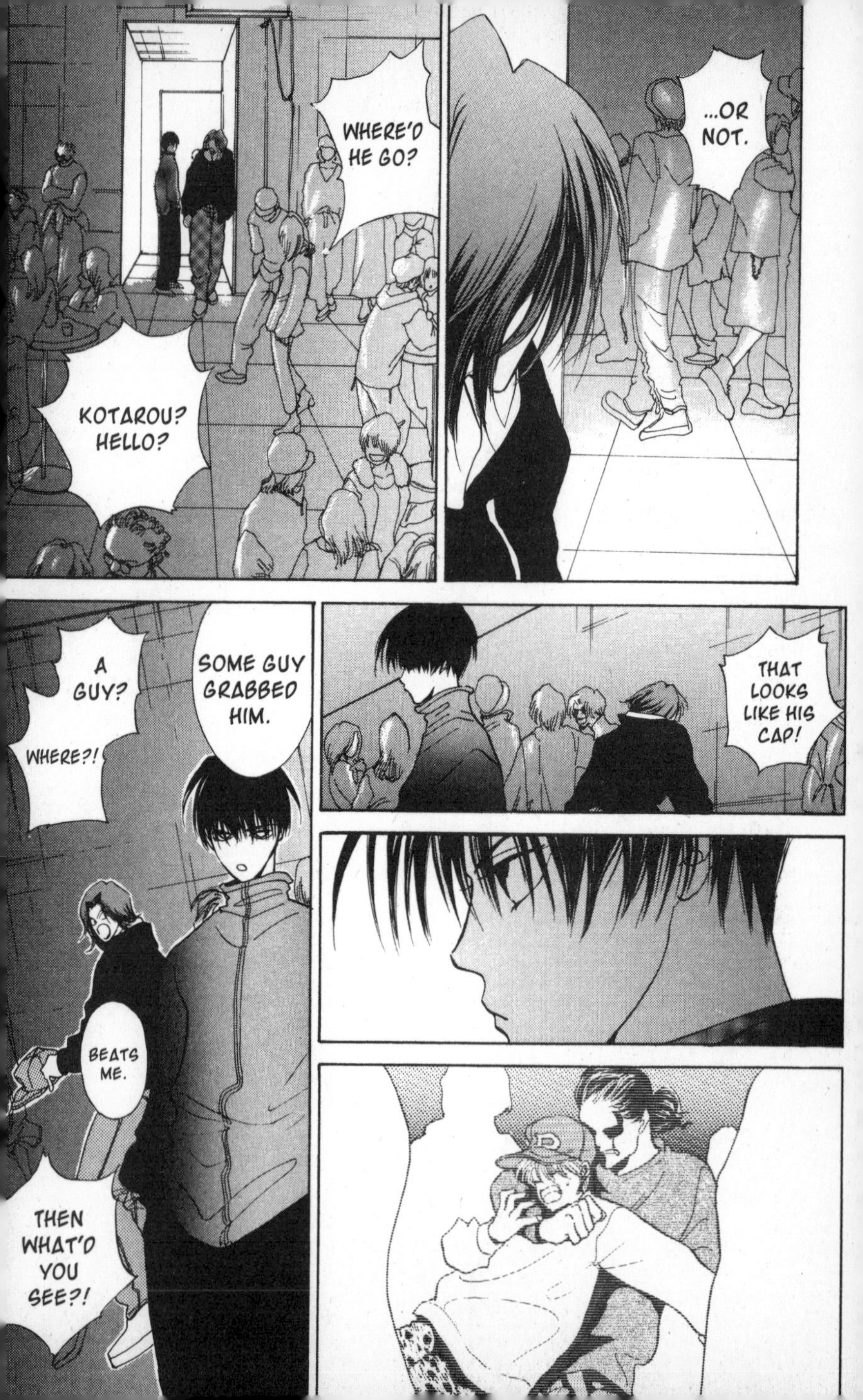
...OR NOT.
WHERE'D HE GO?
KOTAROU? HELLO?
THAT LOOKS LIKE HIS CAP!
SOME GUY GRABBED HIM.
A GUY?
WHERE?!
BEATS ME.
THEN WHAT'D YOU SEE?!

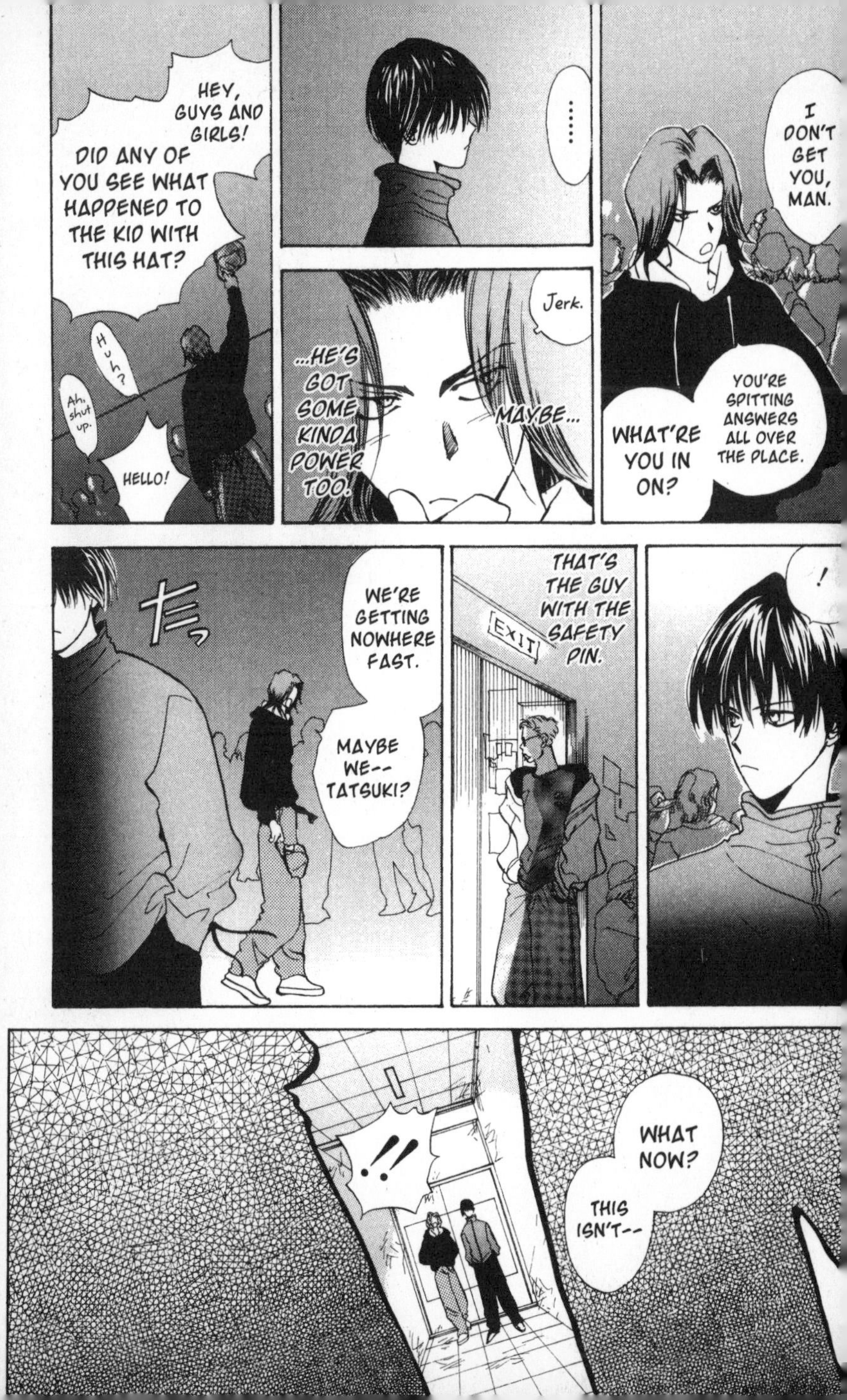
I DON'T GET YOU, MAN.
YOU'RE SPITTING ANSWERS ALL OVER THE PLACE.
WHAT'RE YOU IN ON?
......
Jerk.
MAYBE...
...HE'S GOT SOME KINDA POWER TOO!
HEY, GUYS AND GIRLS!
DID ANY OF YOU SEE WHAT HAPPENED TO THE KID WITH THIS HAT?
Huh?
Ah, shut up.
HELLO!
!
THAT'S THE GUY WITH THE SAFETY PIN.
EXIT
WE'RE GETTING NOWHERE FAST.
MAYBE WE-- TATSUKI!?
WHAT NOW?
THIS ISN'T--
!!

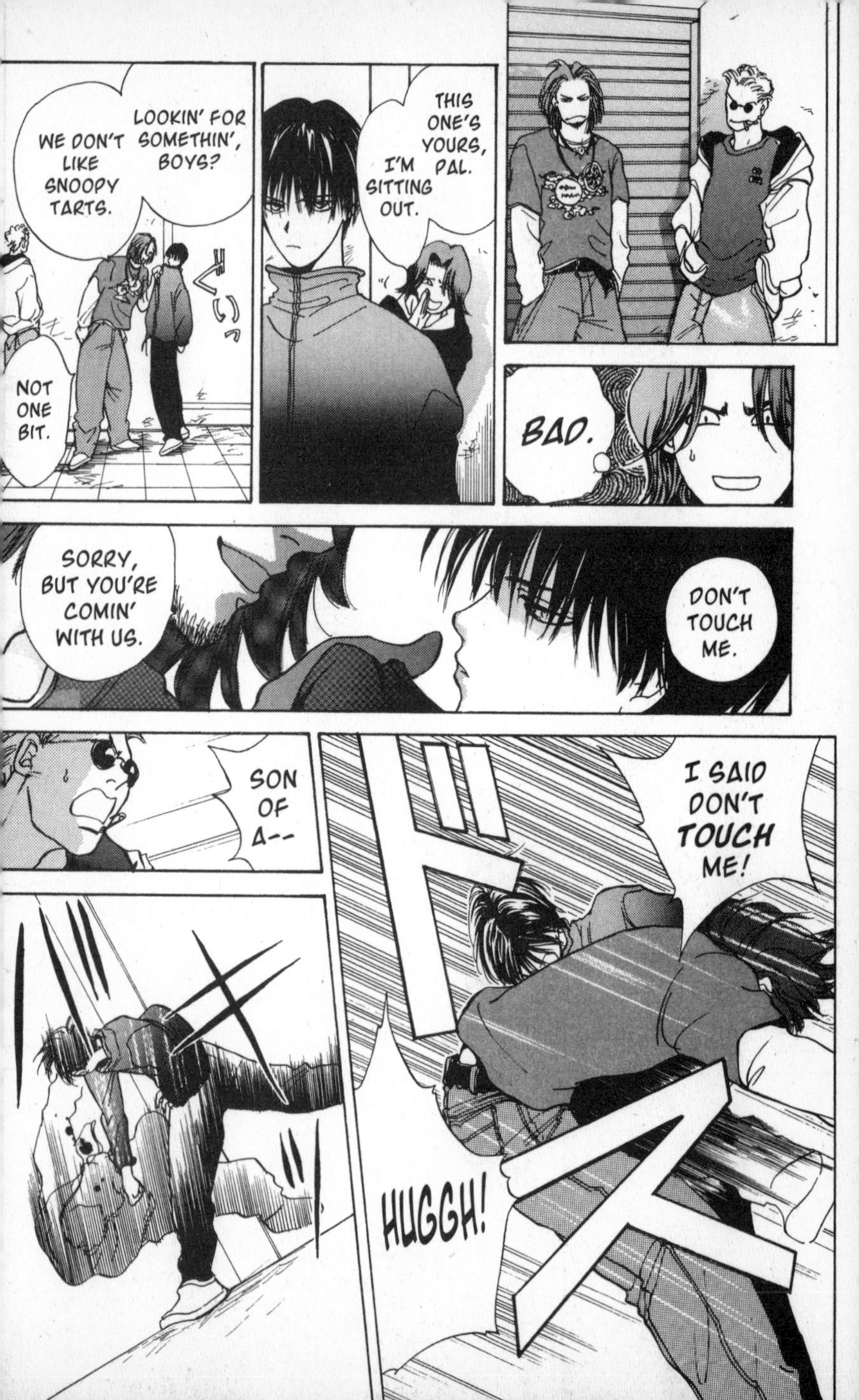
BAD.
THIS ONE'S YOURS, PAL.
I'M SITTING OUT.
LOOKIN' FOR SOMETHIN', BOYS?
WE DON'T LIKE SNOOPY TARTS.
NOT ONE BIT.
SORRY, BUT YOU'RE COMIN' WITH US.
DON'T TOUCH ME.
I SAID DON'T TOUCH ME!
HUGGH!
SON OF A--

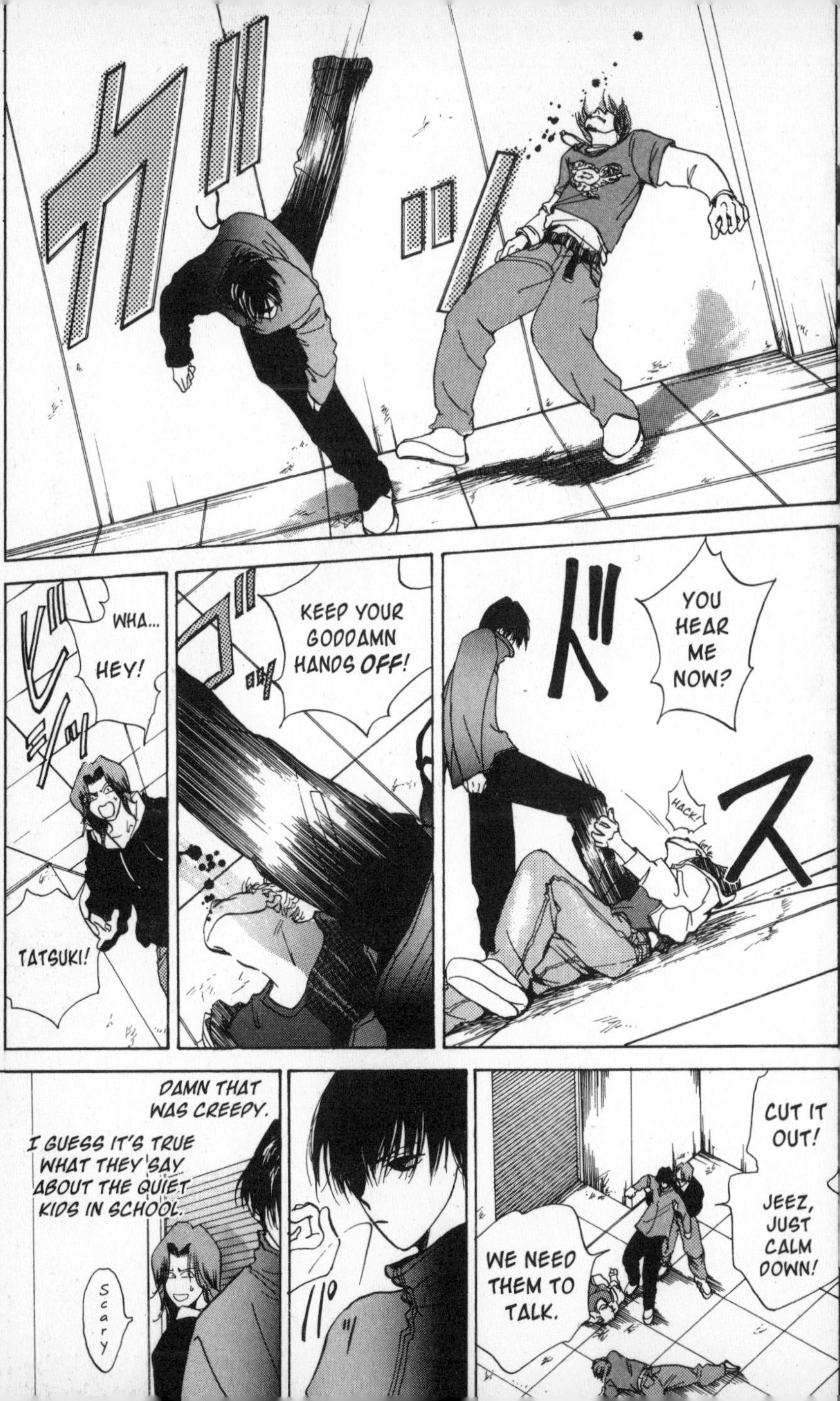
YOU HEAR ME NOW?
HACK!
KEEP YOUR GODDAMN HANDS OFF!
WHA...
HEY!
TATSUKI!
CUT IT OUT!
JEEZ, JUST CALM DOWN!
WE NEED THEM TO TALK.
DAMN THAT WAS CREEPY.
I GUESS IT'S TRUE WHAT THEY SAY ABOUT THE QUIET KIDS IN SCHOOL.
Scary

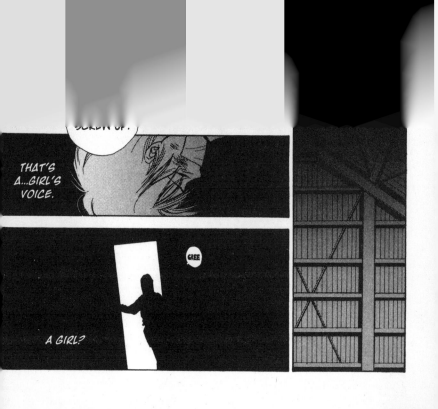

SCREW UP!

THAT'S A...GIRL'S VOICE.

GREE

A GIRL?

WAIT A SECOND. SOMEBODY HIT ME...

...AND PUSHED ME IN A CAR!

OW.

MY FACE HURTS.

WHERE AM I?

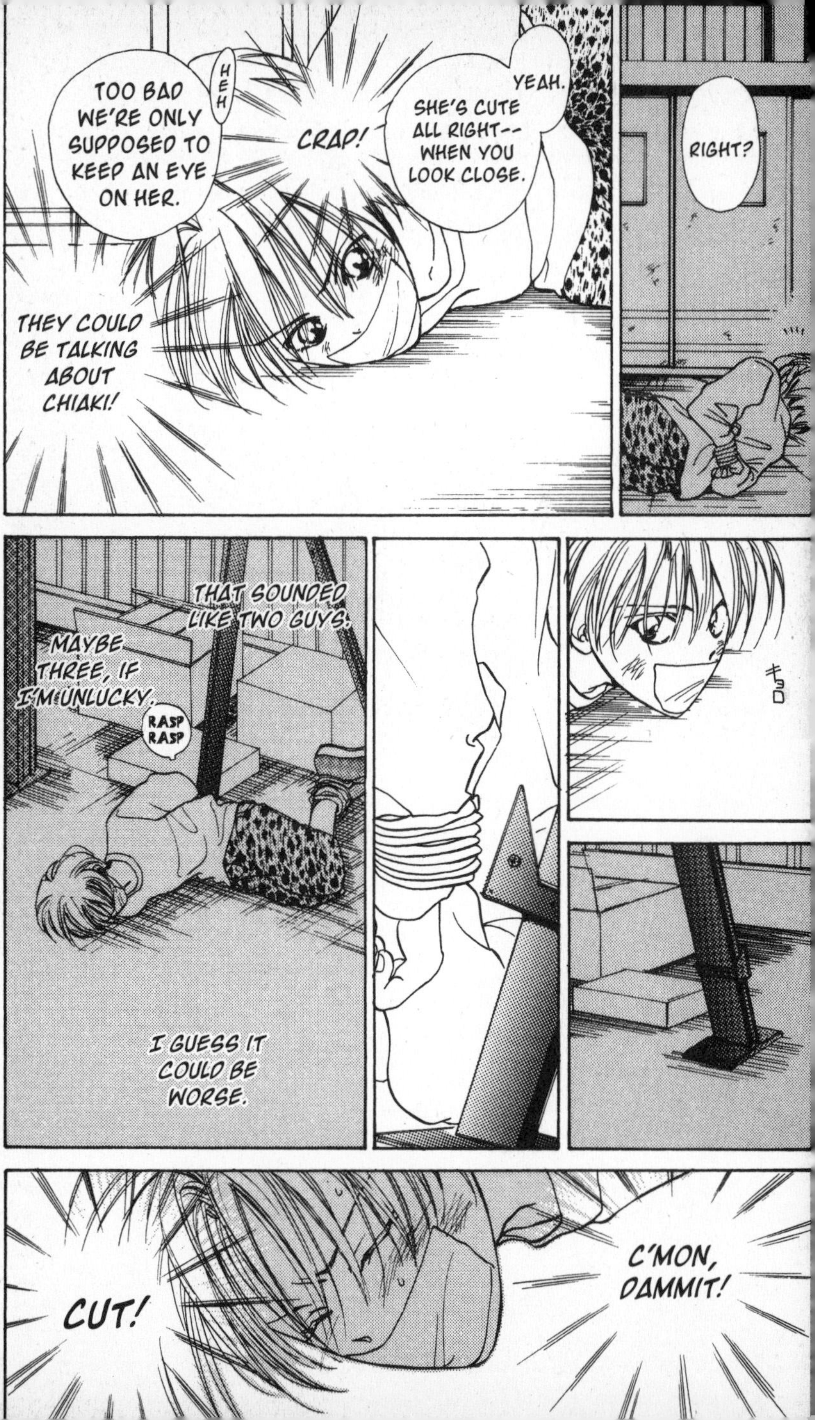
RIGHT?
YEAH. SHE'S CUTE ALL RIGHT-- WHEN YOU LOOK CLOSE.
CRAP!
HEH
TOO BAD WE'RE ONLY SUPPOSED TO KEEP AN EYE ON HER.
THEY COULD BE TALKING ABOUT CHIAKI!
キョロ
THAT SOUNDED LIKE TWO GUYS.
MAYBE THREE, IF I'M UNLUCKY.
RASP RASP
I GUESS IT COULD BE WORSE.
C'MON, DAMMIT!
CUT!

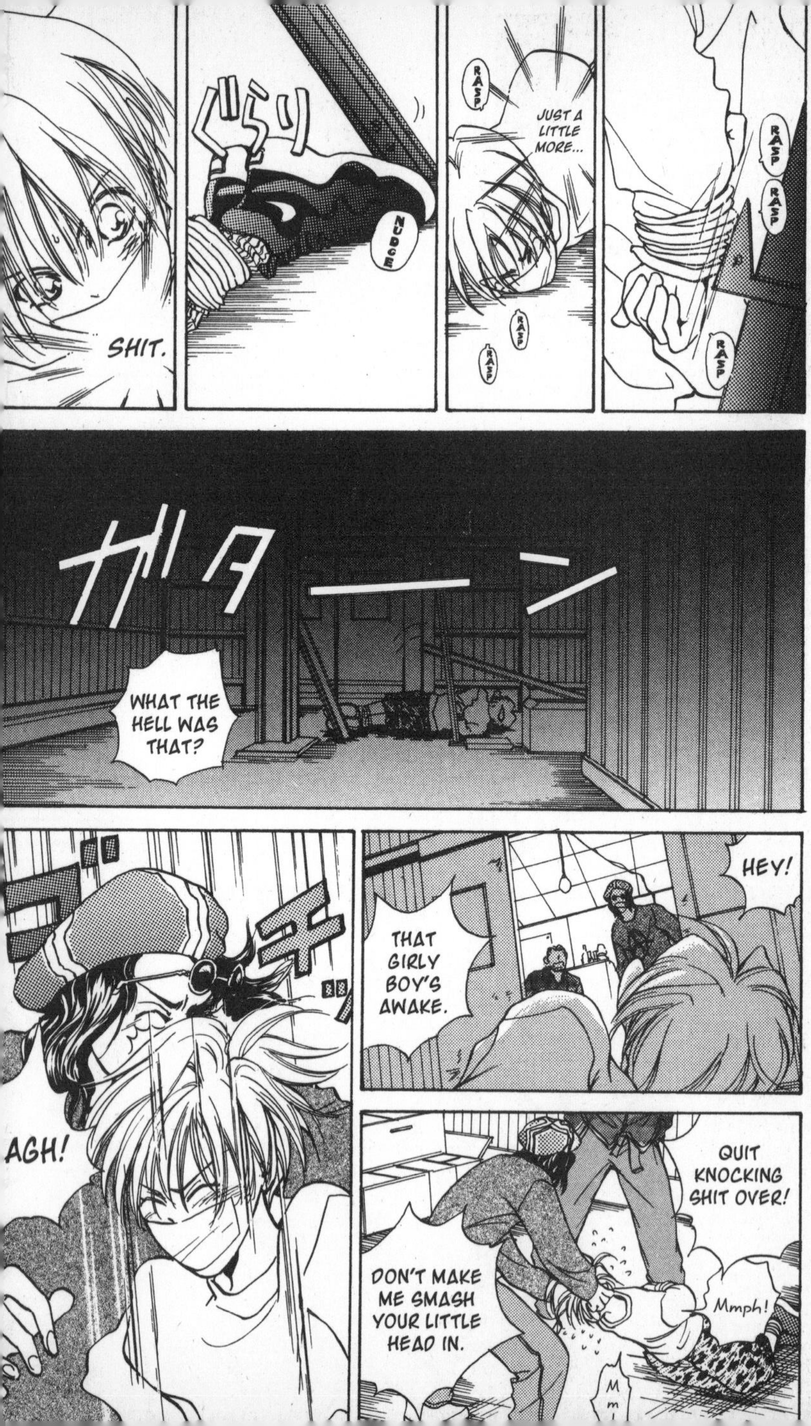
RASP
RASP
RASP
RASP
JUST A LITTLE MORE...
RASP
RASP
ぐらり
NUDGE
SHIT.
ガターーン
WHAT THE HELL WAS THAT?
HEY!
THAT GIRLY BOY'S AWAKE.
QUIT KNOCKING SHIT OVER!
DON'T MAKE ME SMASH YOUR LITTLE HEAD IN.
Mmph!
Mm
AGH!

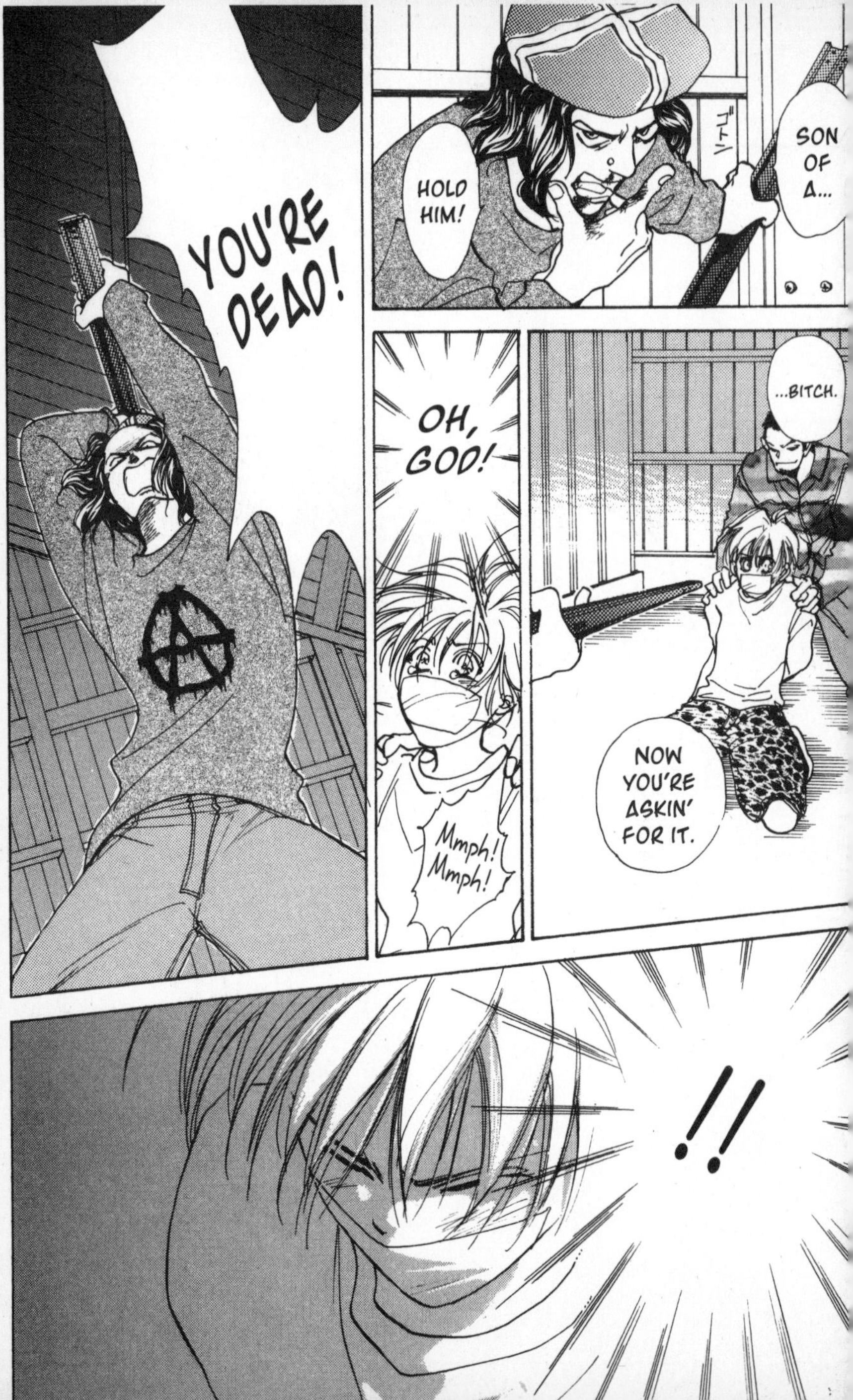

SON OF A...
ゴトン
HOLD HIM!
...BITCH.
NOW YOU'RE ASKIN' FOR IT.
OH, GOD!
Mmph! Mmph!
YOU'RE DEAD!
!!

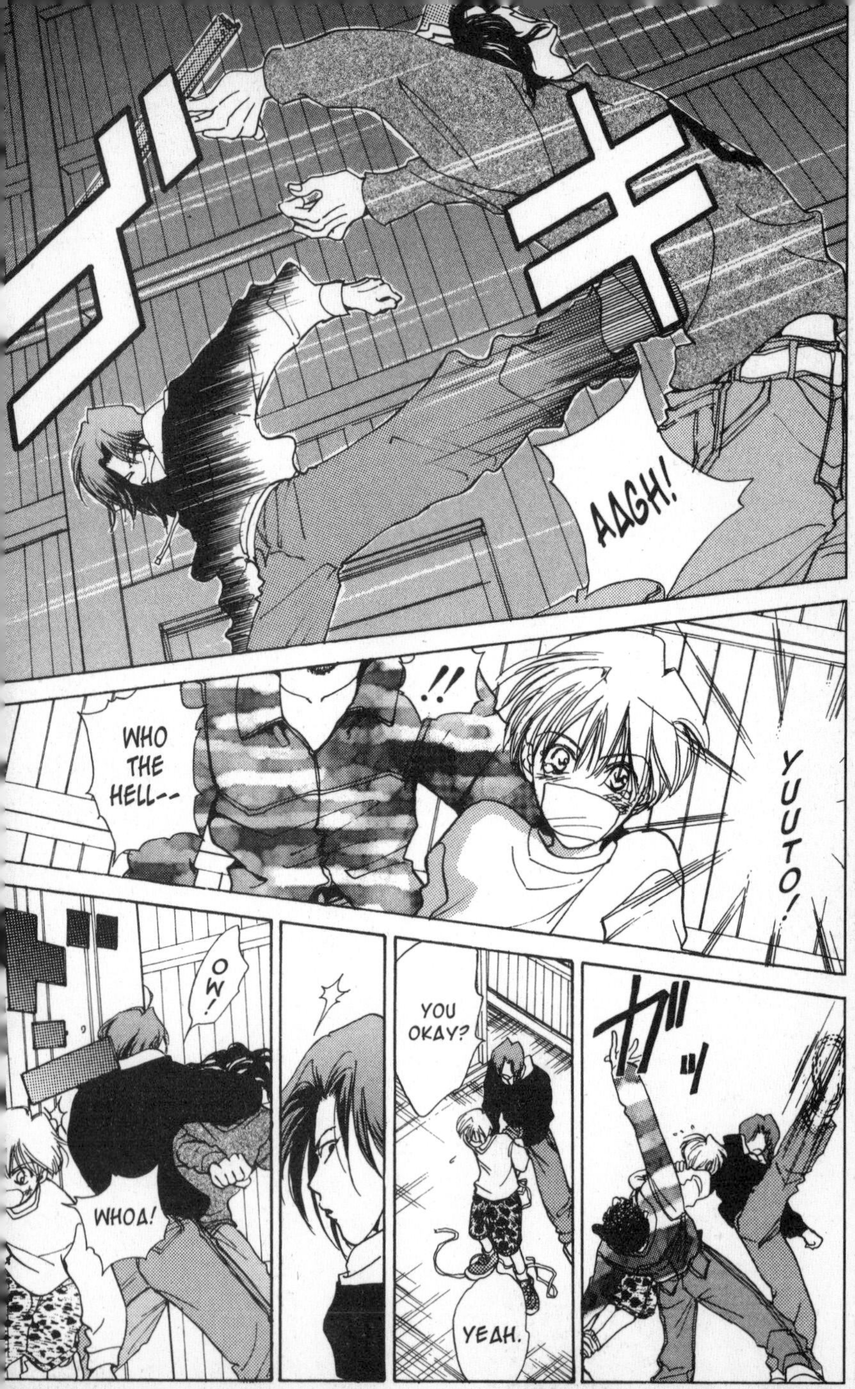
AAGH!
YUUTO!!
!!
WHO THE HELL--
YOU OKAY?
YEAH.
OW!
WHOA!

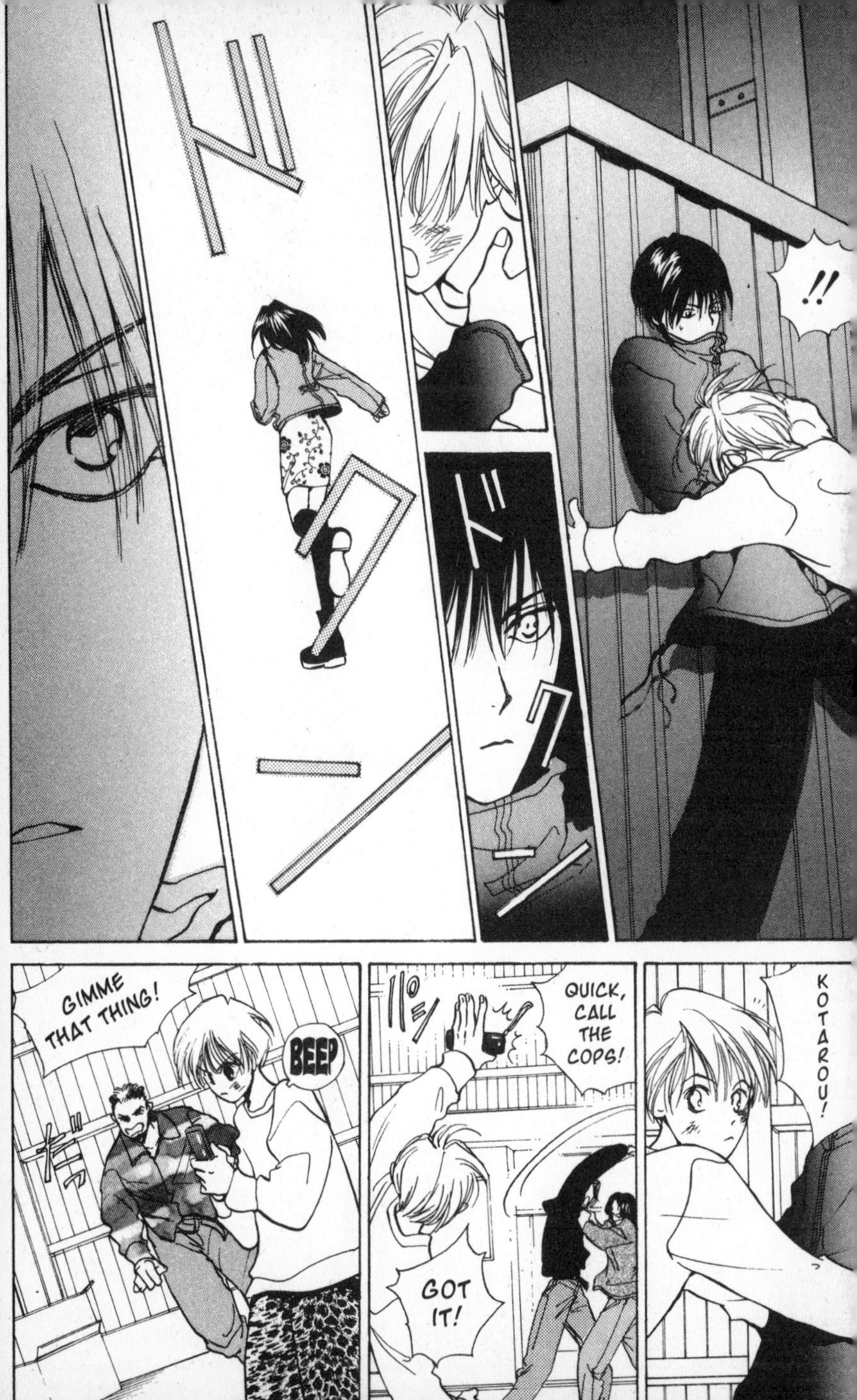
!!
KOTAROU!
QUICK, CALL THE COPS!
GOT IT!
GIMME THAT THING!
BEEP

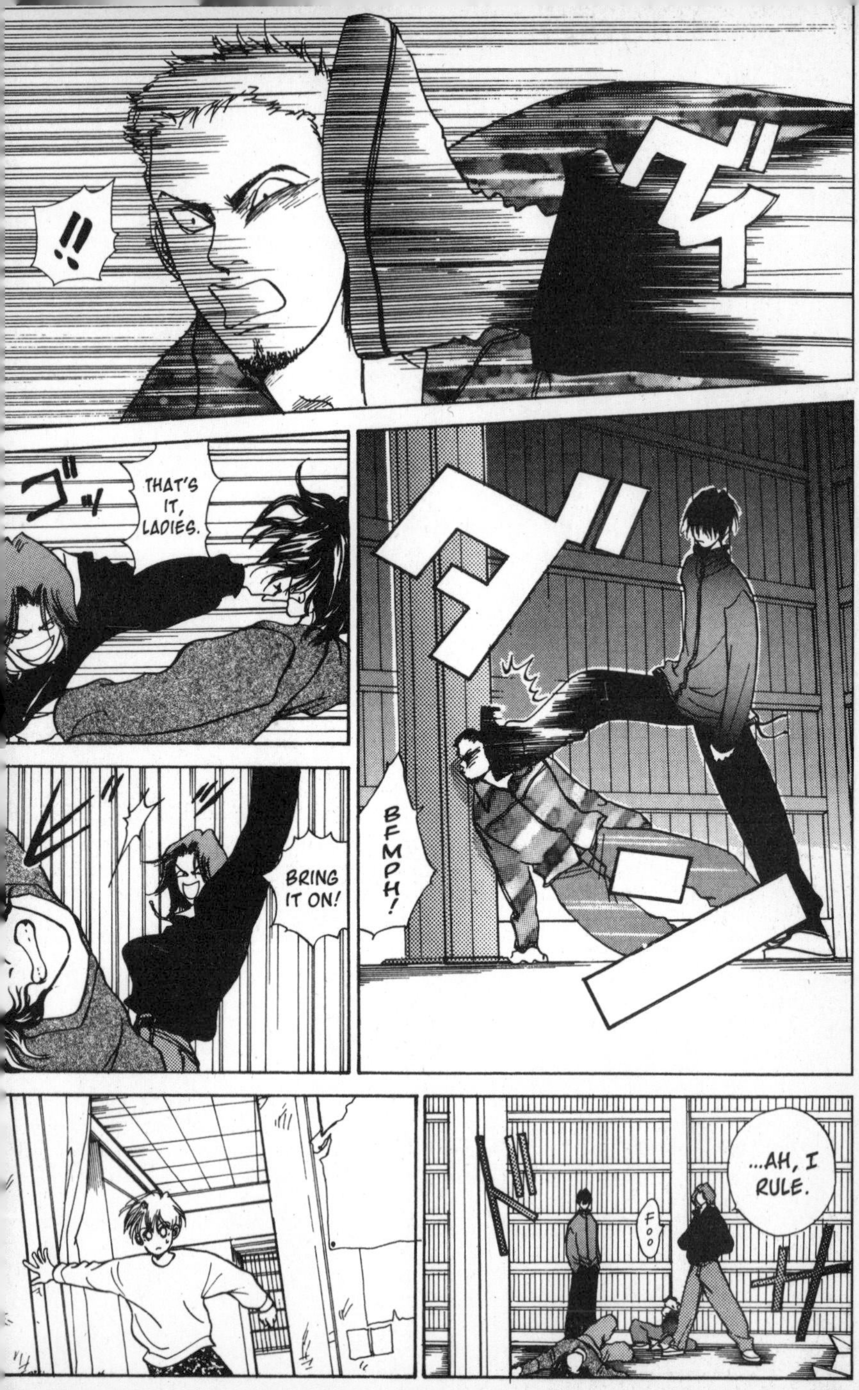
!!
BFMPH!
THAT'S IT, LADIES.
BRING IT ON!
...AH, I RULE.
Foo

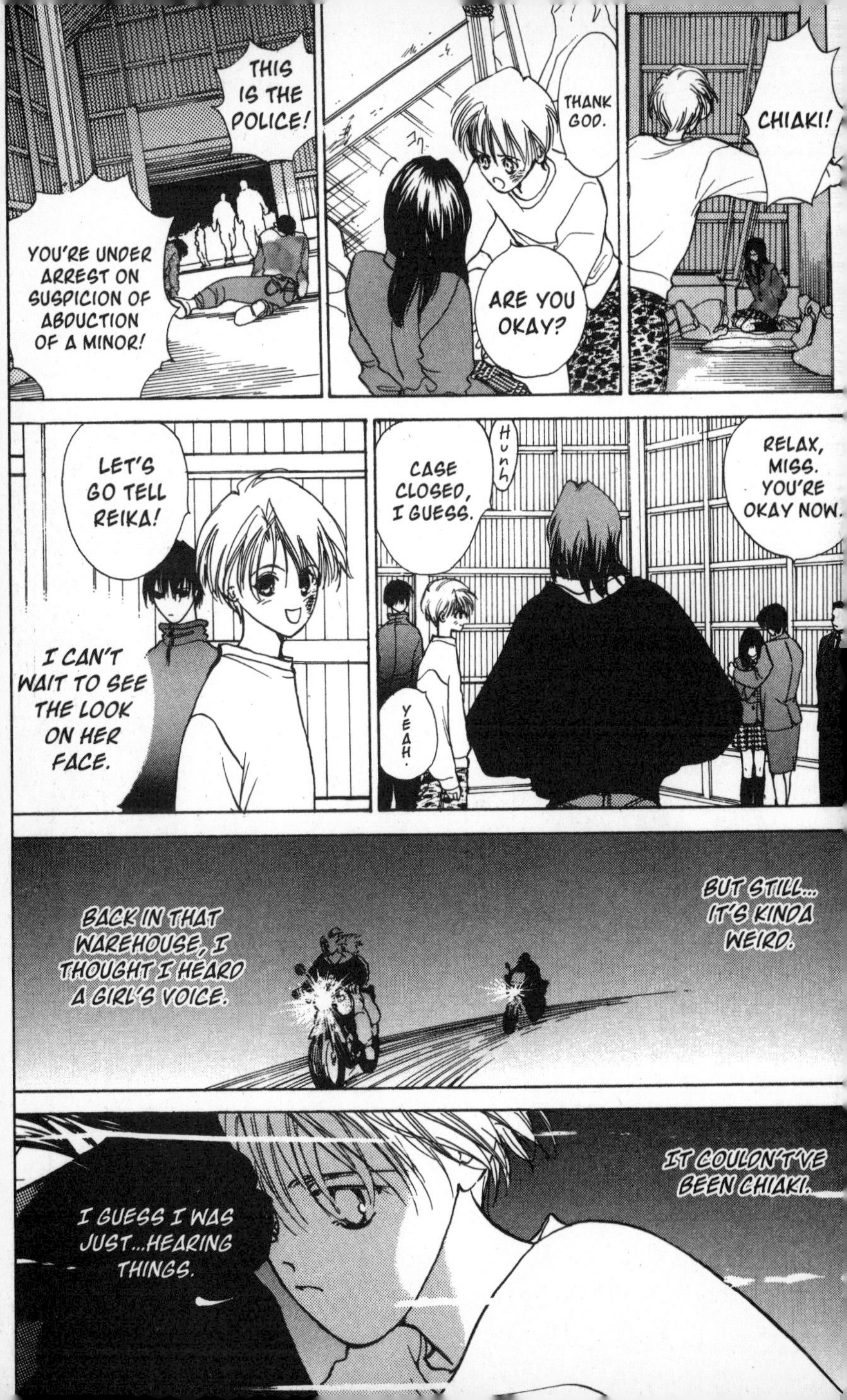
CHIAKI!
THANK GOD.
ARE YOU OKAY?
THIS IS THE POLICE!
YOU'RE UNDER ARREST ON SUSPICION OF ABDUCTION OF A MINOR!
RELAX, MISS. YOU'RE OKAY NOW.
Hunh
CASE CLOSED, I GUESS.
YEAH.
LET'S GO TELL REIKA!
I CAN'T WAIT TO SEE THE LOOK ON HER FACE.
BUT STILL... IT'S KINDA WEIRD.
BACK IN THAT WAREHOUSE, I THOUGHT I HEARD A GIRL'S VOICE.
IT COULDN'T'VE BEEN CHIAKI.
I GUESS I WAS JUST...HEARING THINGS.

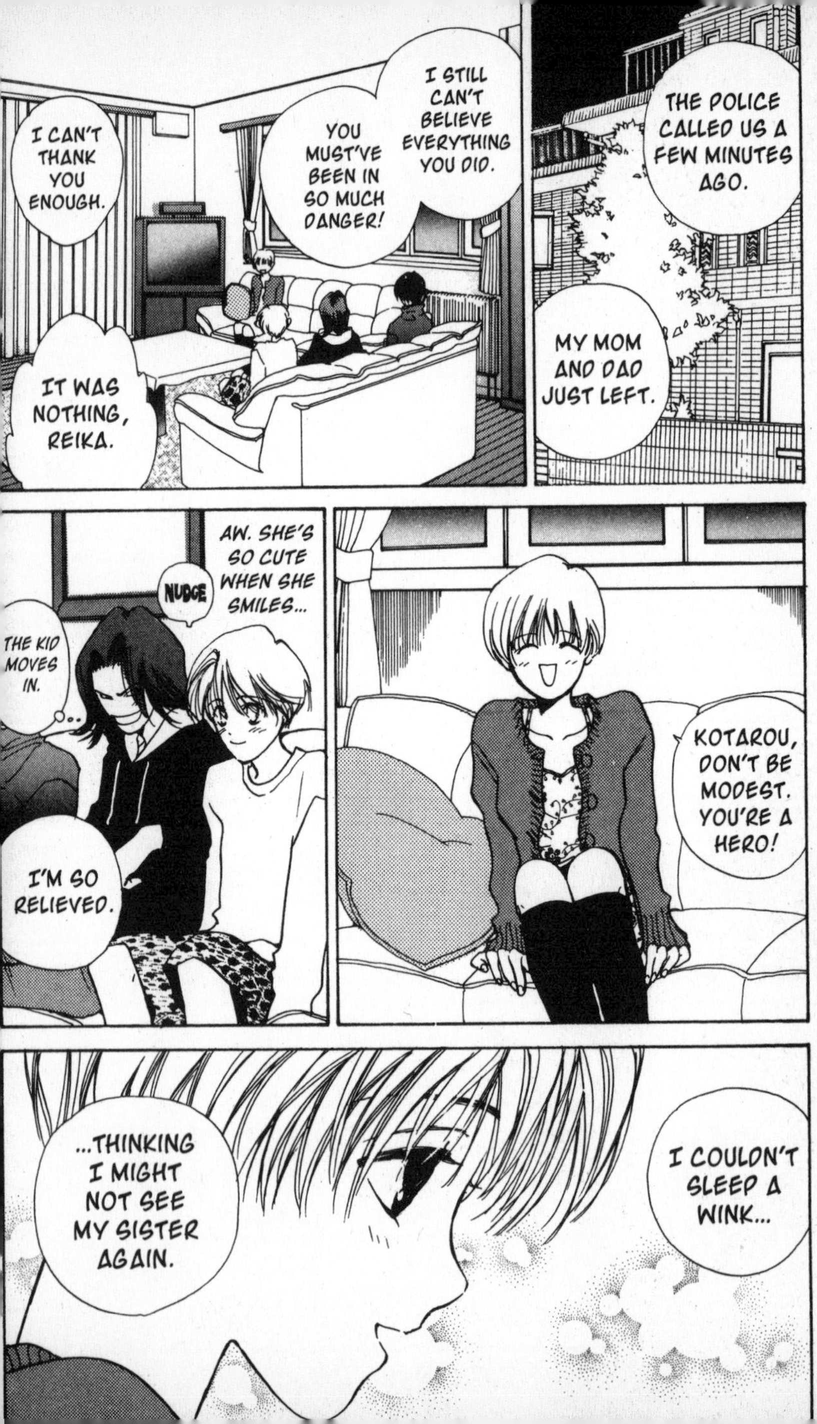
THE POLICE CALLED US A FEW MINUTES AGO.
MY MOM AND DAD JUST LEFT.
I STILL CAN'T BELIEVE EVERYTHING YOU DID.
YOU MUST'VE BEEN IN SO MUCH DANGER!
I CAN'T THANK YOU ENOUGH.
IT WAS NOTHING, REIKA.
KOTAROU, DON'T BE MODEST. YOU'RE A HERO!
AW. SHE'S SO CUTE WHEN SHE SMILES...
NUDGE
THE KID MOVES IN.
I'M SO RELIEVED.
I COULDN'T SLEEP A WINK...
...THINKING I MIGHT NOT SEE MY SISTER AGAIN.

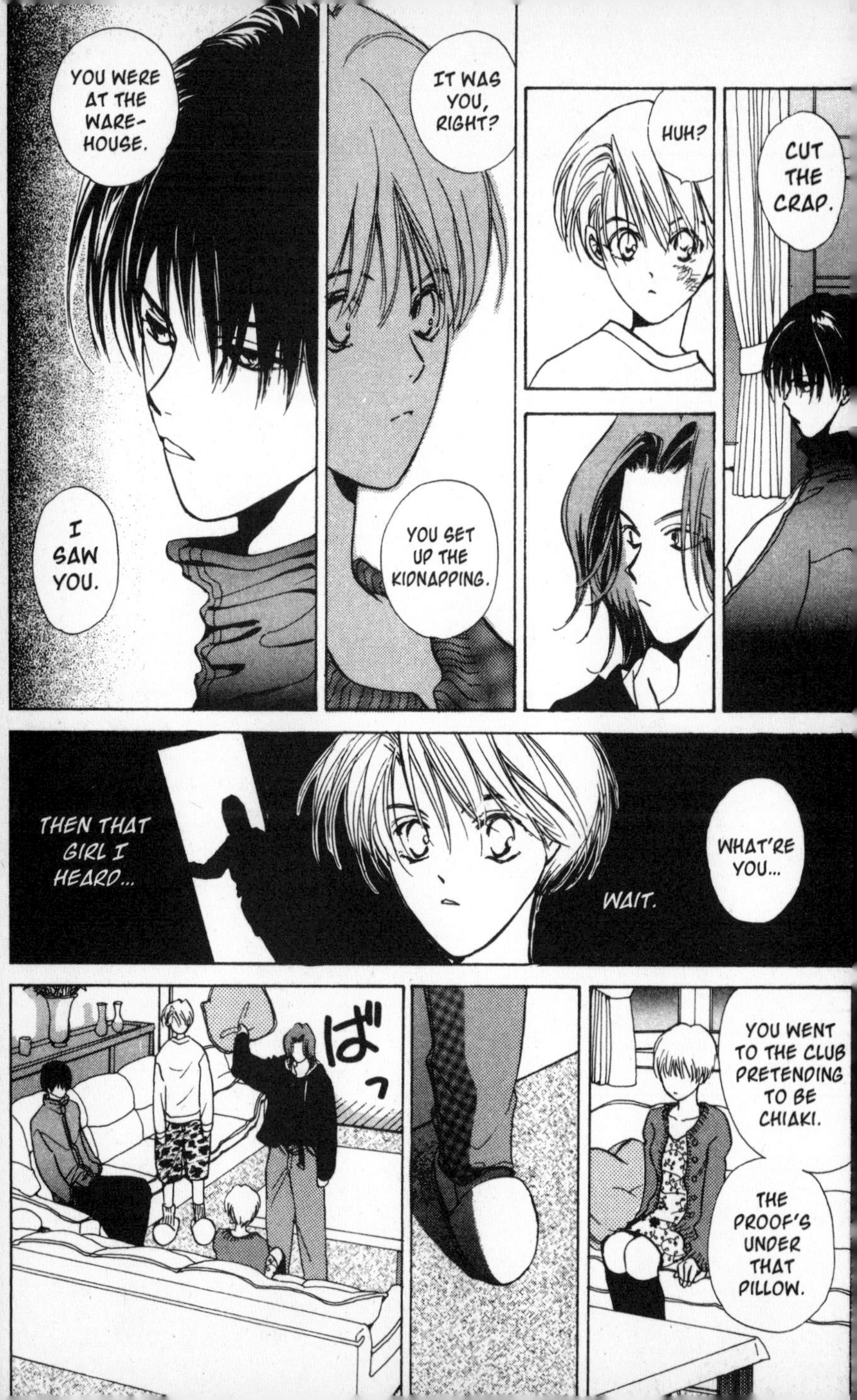
CUT THE CRAP.
HUH?
IT WAS YOU, RIGHT?
YOU SET UP THE KIDNAPPING.
YOU WERE AT THE WARE-HOUSE.
I SAW YOU.
WHAT'RE YOU...
WAIT.
THEN THAT GIRL I HEARD...
YOU WENT TO THE CLUB PRETENDING TO BE CHIAKI.
THE PROOF'S UNDER THAT PILLOW.
ばっ

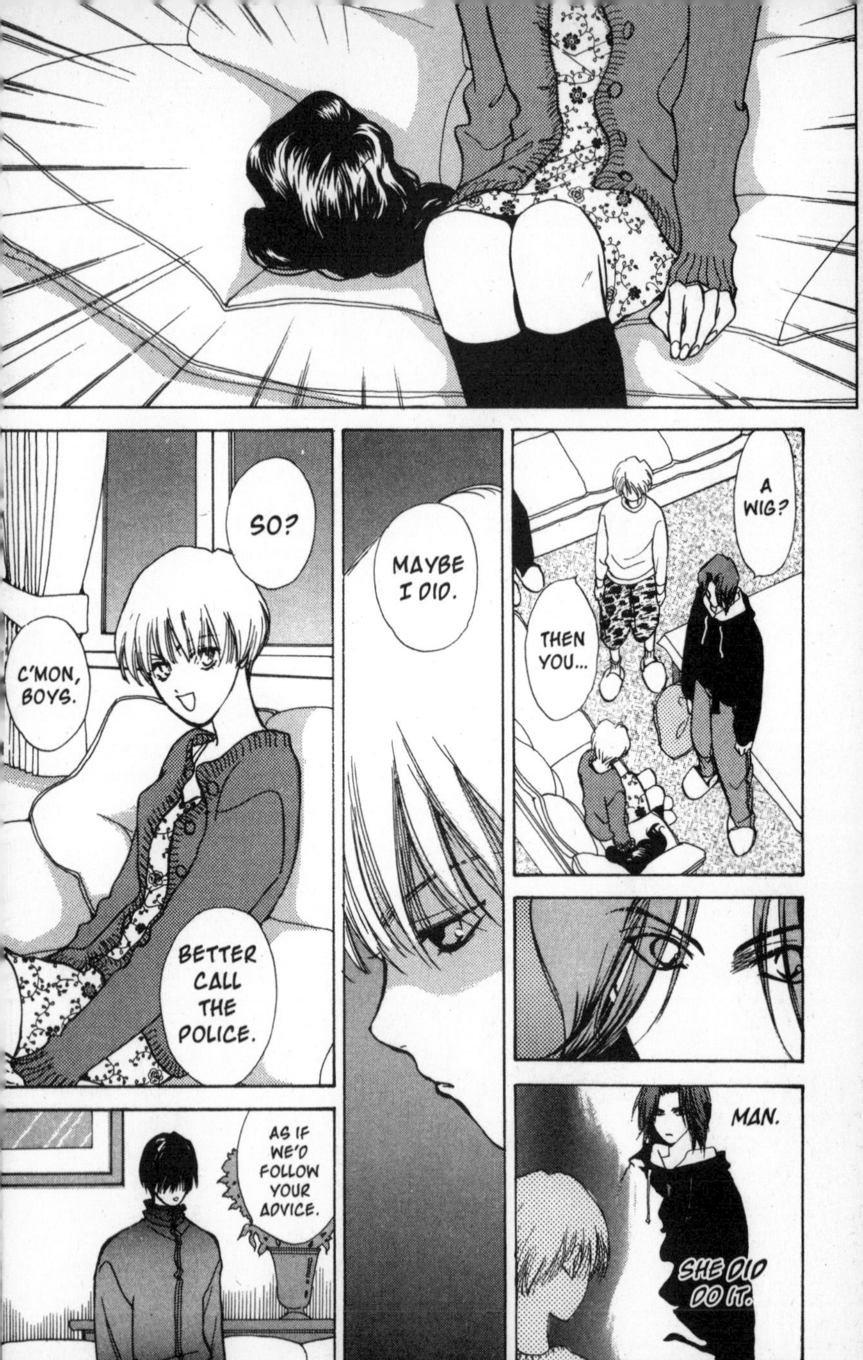
A WIG?
THEN YOU...
MAN.
SHE DID DO IT.
MAYBE I DID.
SO?
C'MON, BOYS.
BETTER CALL THE POLICE.
AS IF WE'D FOLLOW YOUR ADVICE.

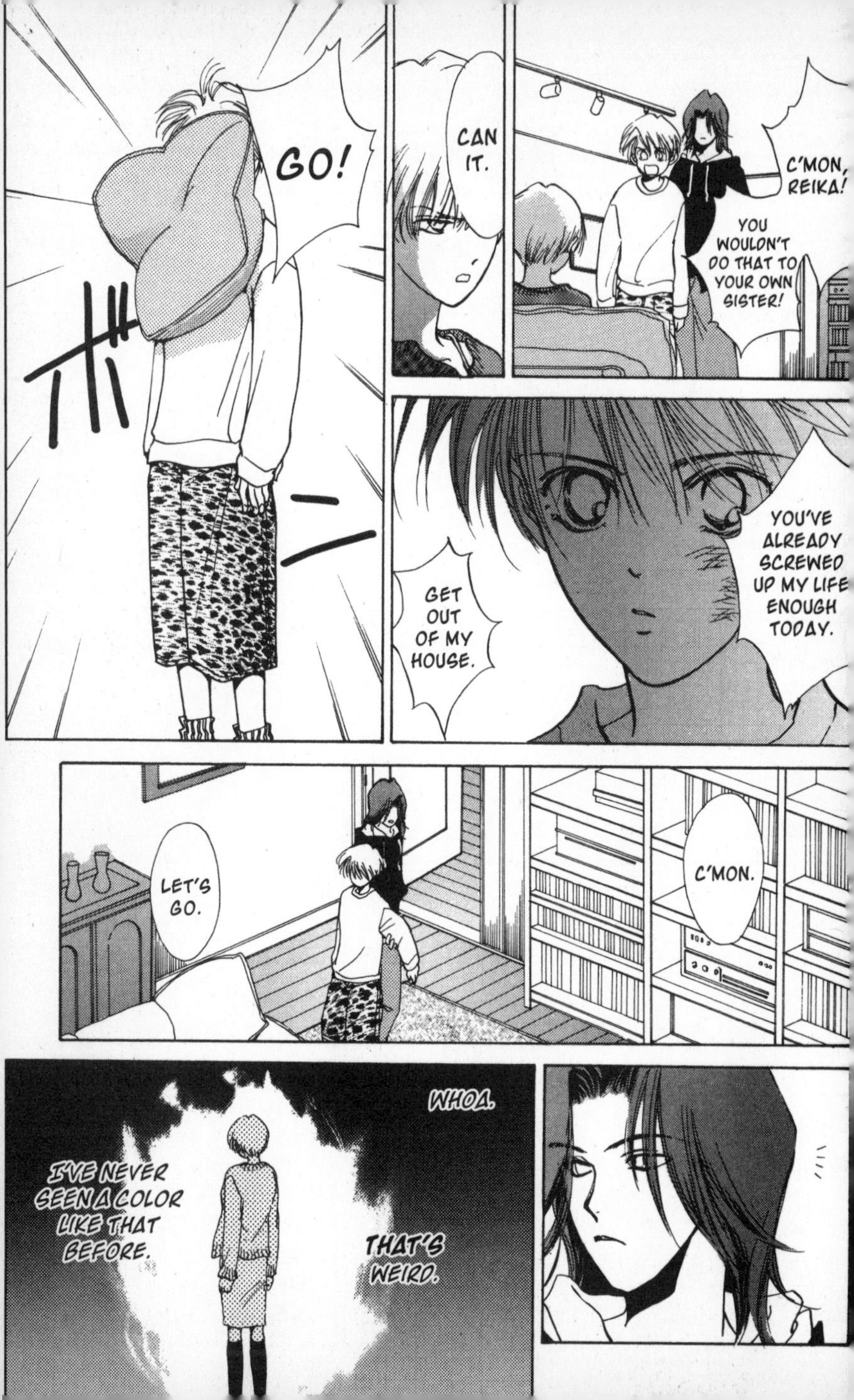
C'MON, REIKA!
YOU WOULDN'T DO THAT TO YOUR OWN SISTER!
CAN IT.
YOU'VE ALREADY SCREWED UP MY LIFE ENOUGH TODAY.
GET OUT OF MY HOUSE.
GO!
C'MON.
LET'S GO.
WHOA.
I'VE NEVER SEEN A COLOR LIKE THAT BEFORE.
THAT'S WEIRD.

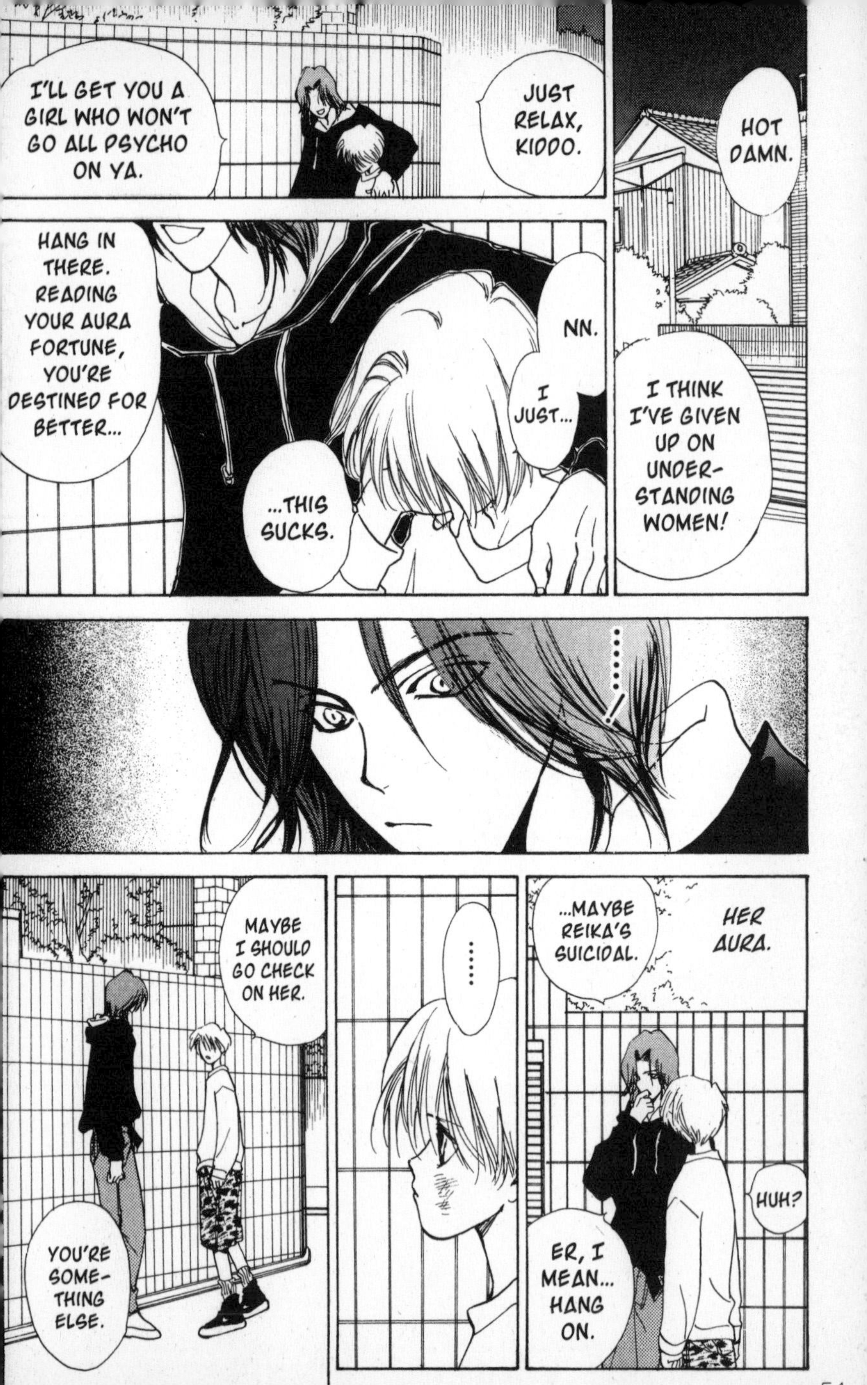
HOT DAMN.
I THINK I'VE GIVEN UP ON UNDER-STANDING WOMEN!
JUST RELAX, KIDDO.
I'LL GET YOU A GIRL WHO WON'T GO ALL PSYCHO ON YA.
NN.
I JUST...
...THIS SUCKS.
HANG IN THERE. READING YOUR AURA FORTUNE, YOU'RE DESTINED FOR BETTER...
......!
HER AURA.
...MAYBE REIKA'S SUICIDAL.
HUH?
ER, I MEAN... HANG ON.
......
MAYBE I SHOULD GO CHECK ON HER.
YOU'RE SOME-THING ELSE.

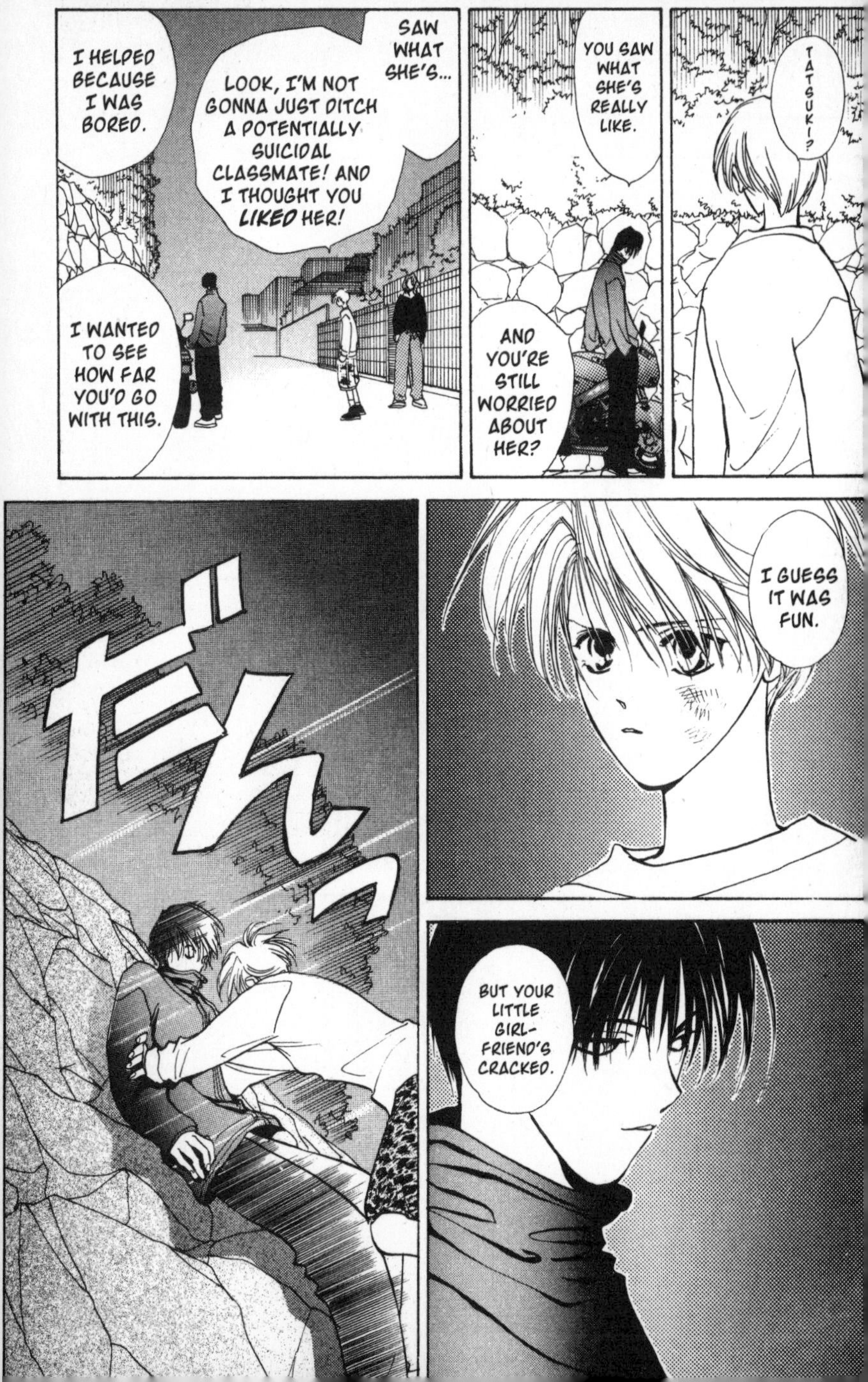
TATSUKI?
YOU SAW WHAT SHE'S REALLY LIKE.
AND YOU'RE STILL WORRIED ABOUT HER?
SAW WHAT SHE'S...
LOOK, I'M NOT GONNA JUST DITCH A POTENTIALLY SUICIDAL CLASSMATE! AND I THOUGHT YOU LIKED HER!
I HELPED BECAUSE I WAS BORED.
I WANTED TO SEE HOW FAR YOU'D GO WITH THIS.
I GUESS IT WAS FUN.
BUT YOUR LITTLE GIRL-FRIEND'S CRACKED.
だんっ

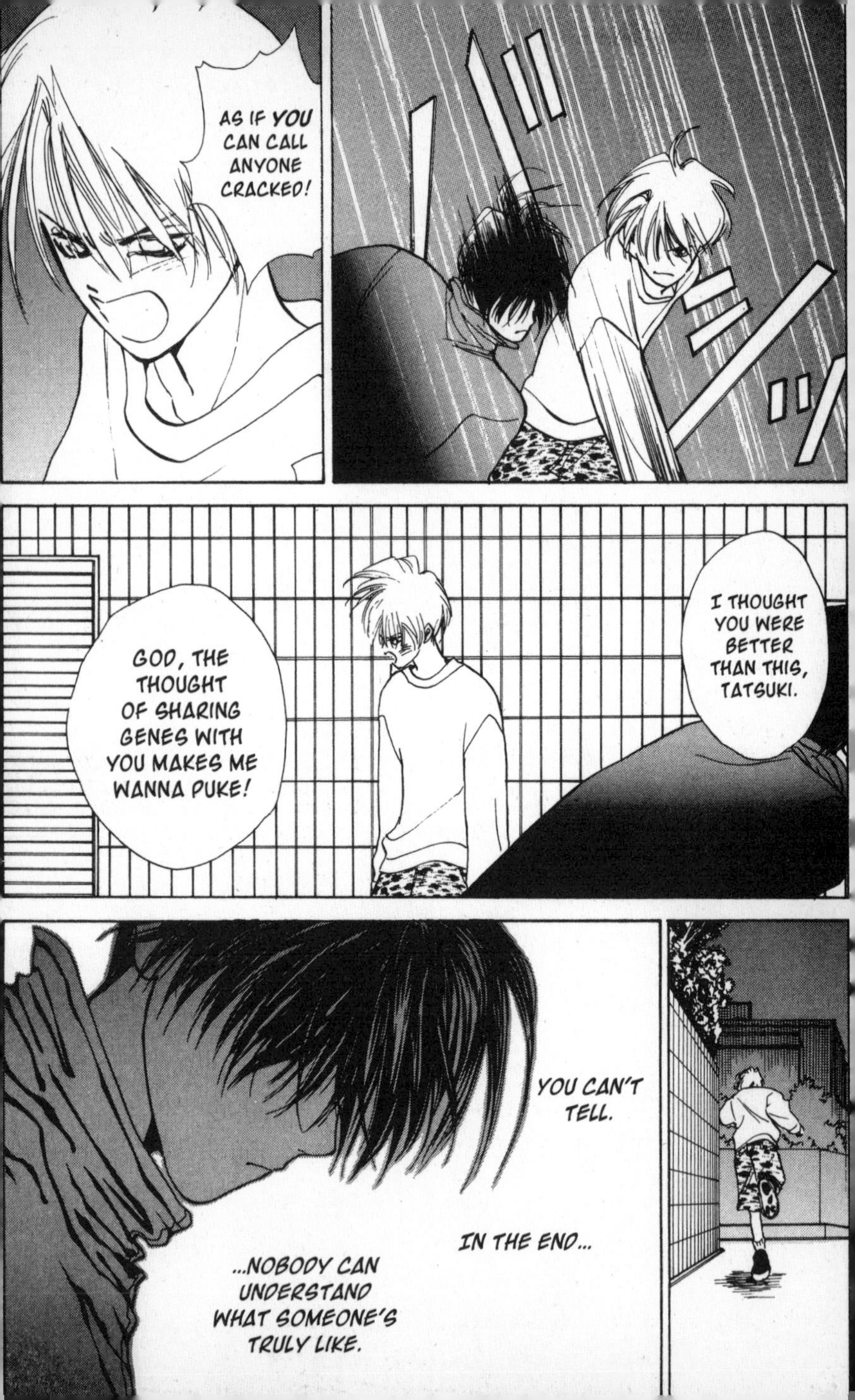
AS IF YOU CAN CALL ANYONE CRACKED!
I THOUGHT YOU WERE BETTER THAN THIS, TATSUKI.
GOD, THE THOUGHT OF SHARING GENES WITH YOU MAKES ME WANNA PUKE!
YOU CAN'T TELL.
IN THE END...
...NOBODY CAN UNDERSTAND WHAT SOMEONE'S TRULY LIKE.

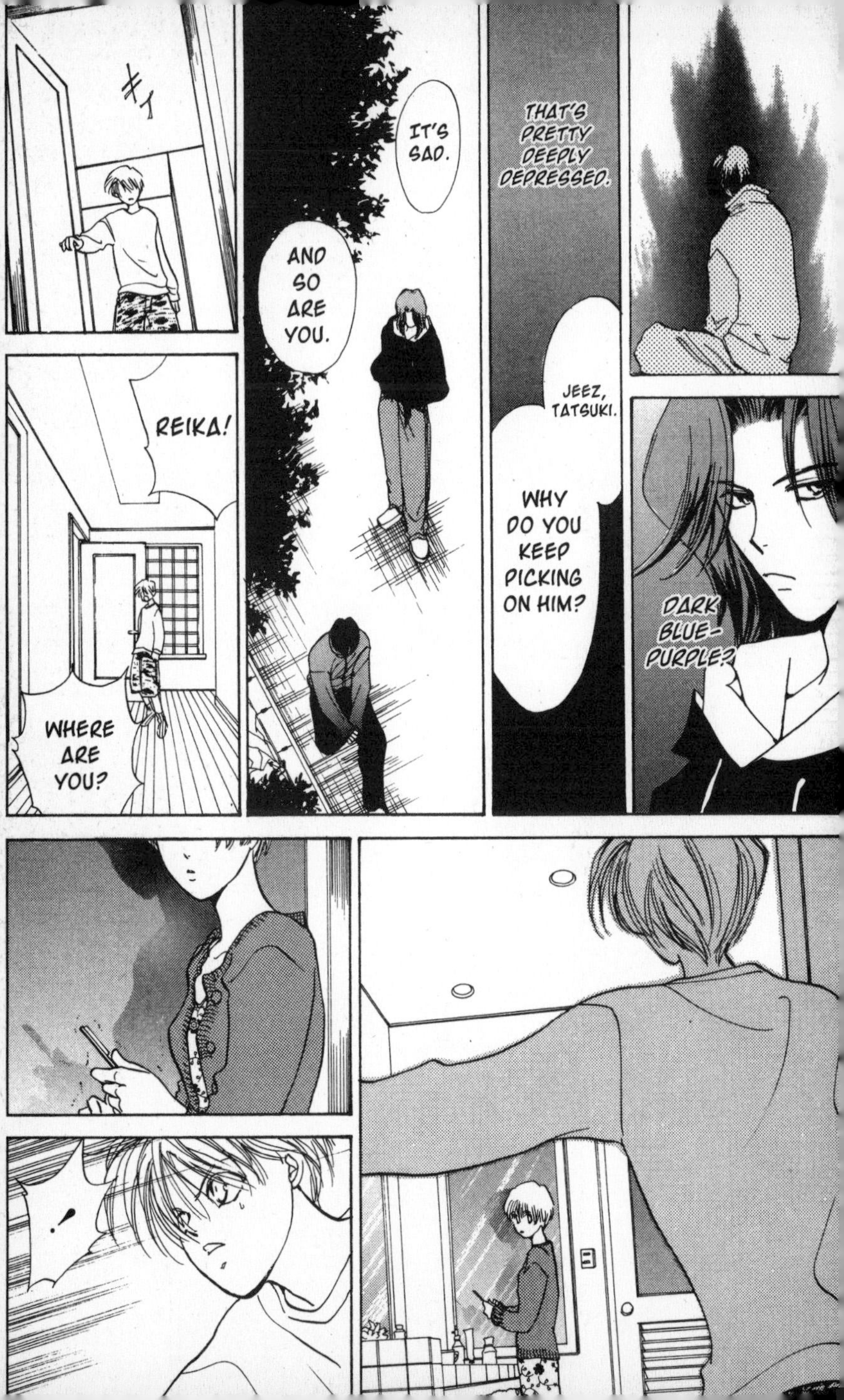
DARK BLUE-PURPLE?
THAT'S PRETTY DEEPLY DEPRESSED.
JEEZ, TATSUKI.
WHY DO YOU KEEP PICKING ON HIM?
IT'S SAD.
AND SO ARE YOU.
キィ
REIKA!
WHERE ARE YOU?
!

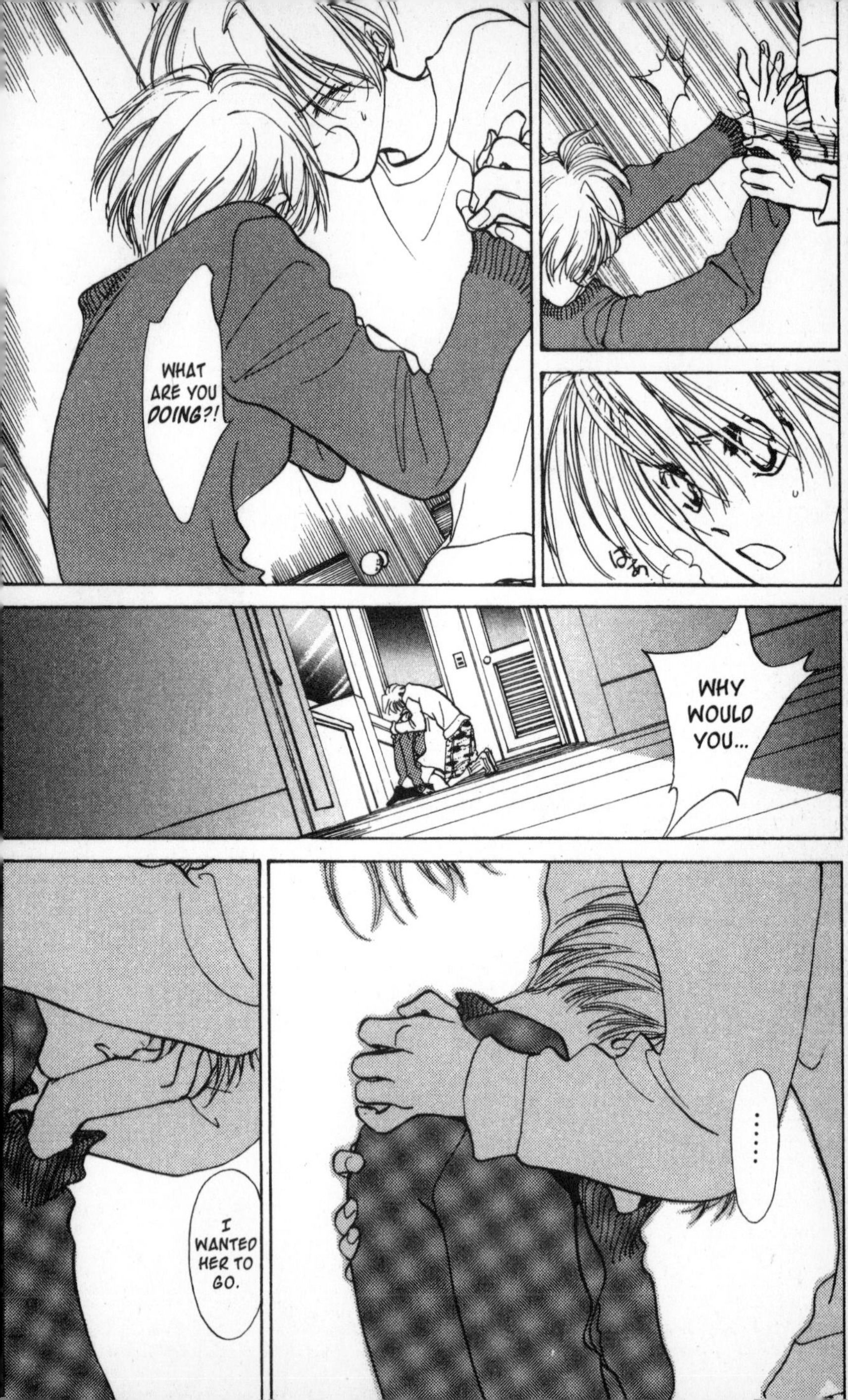
WHAT ARE YOU DOING?!
WHY WOULD YOU...
......
I WANTED HER TO GO.

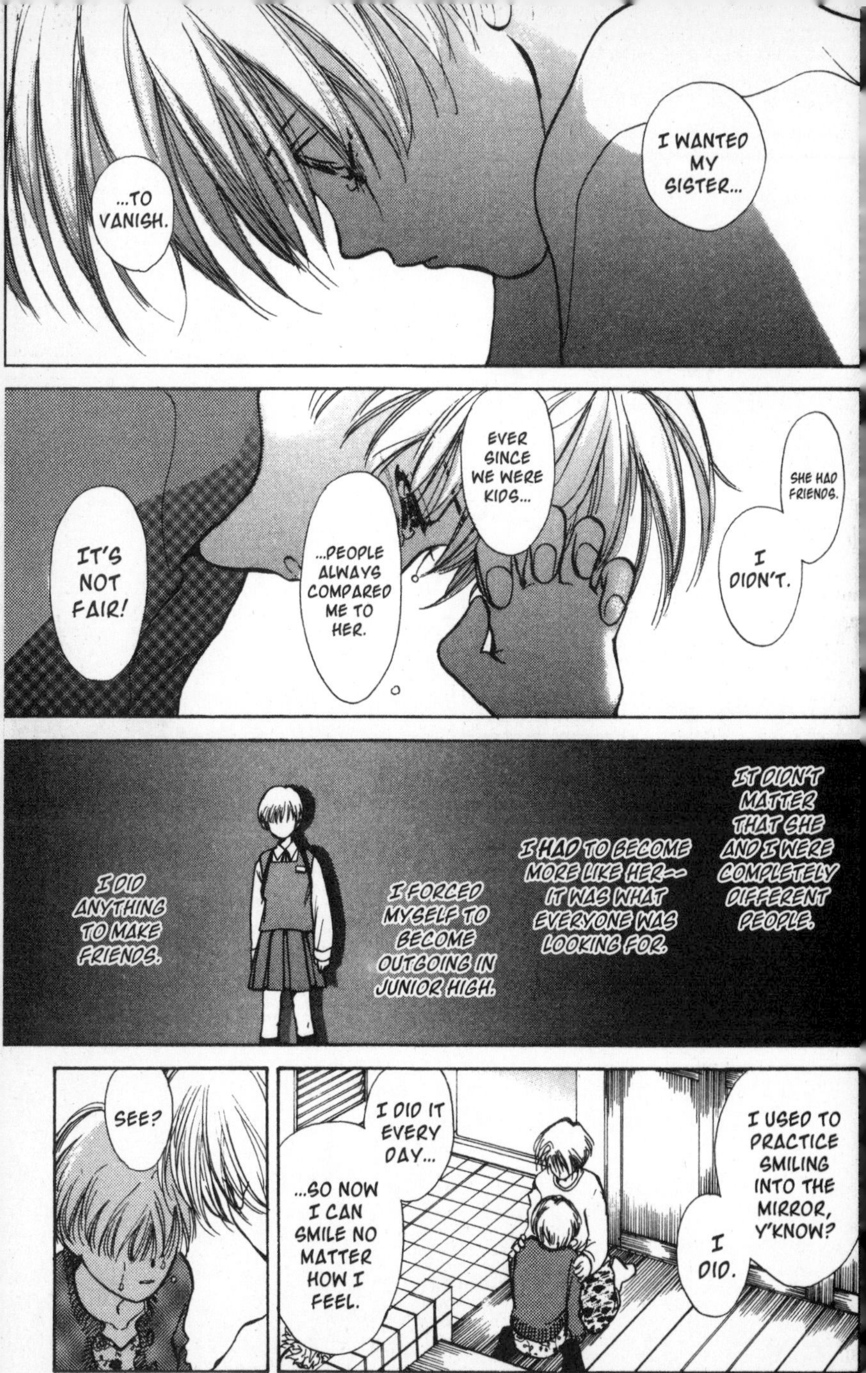
I WANTED MY SISTER...
...TO VANISH.
SHE HAD FRIENDS.
I DIDN'T.
EVER SINCE WE WERE KIDS...
...PEOPLE ALWAYS COMPARED ME TO HER.
IT'S NOT FAIR!
IT DIDN'T MATTER THAT SHE AND I WERE COMPLETELY DIFFERENT PEOPLE.
I HAD TO BECOME MORE LIKE HER-- IT WAS WHAT EVERYONE WAS LOOKING FOR.
I FORCED MYSELF TO BECOME OUTGOING IN JUNIOR HIGH.
I DID ANYTHING TO MAKE FRIENDS.
I USED TO PRACTICE SMILING INTO THE MIRROR, Y'KNOW?
I DID.
I DID IT EVERY DAY...
...SO NOW I CAN SMILE NO MATTER HOW I FEEL.
SEE?

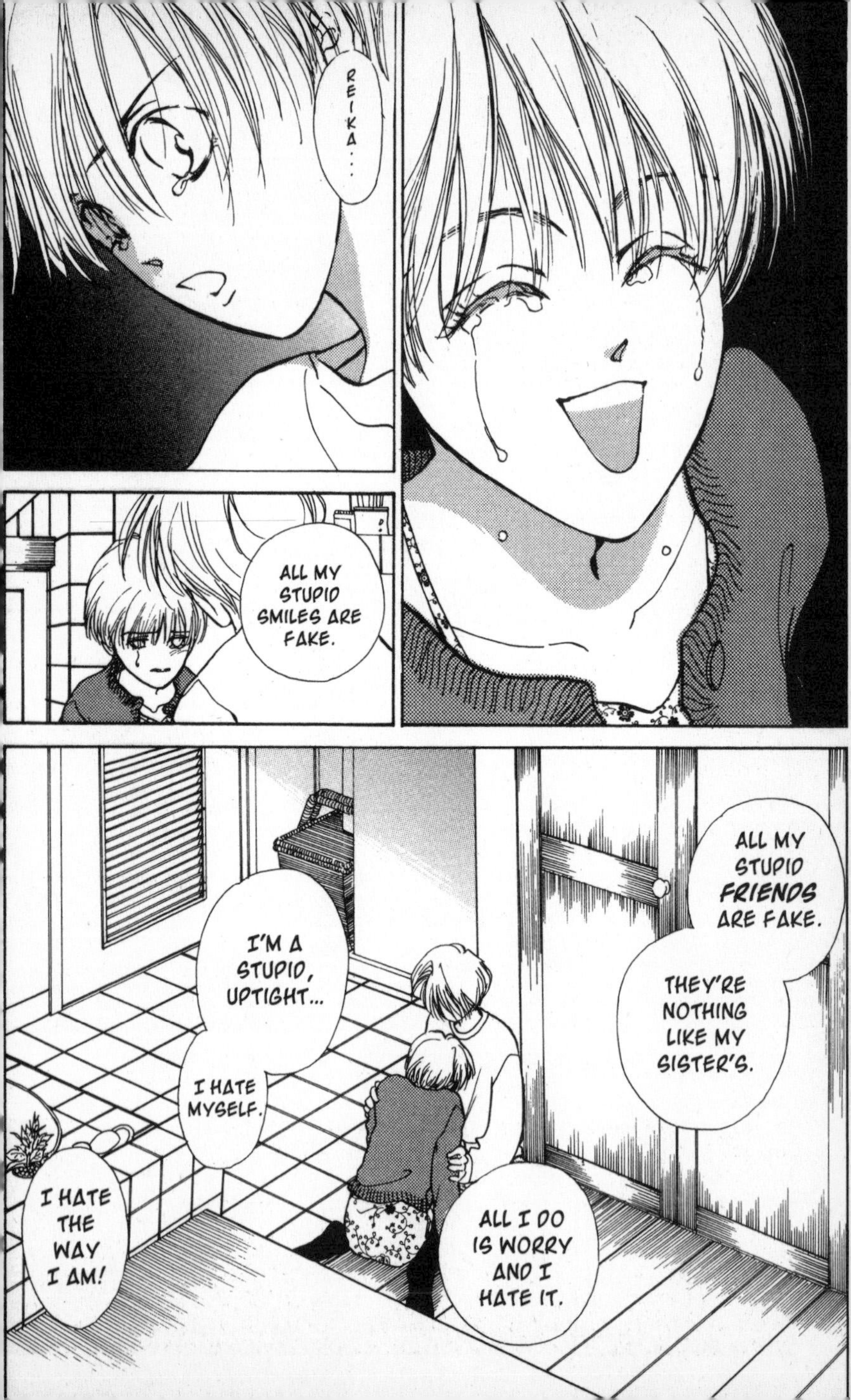
REIKA...
ALL MY STUPID SMILES ARE FAKE.
ALL MY STUPID FRIENDS ARE FAKE.
THEY'RE NOTHING LIKE MY SISTER'S.
I'M A STUPID, UPTIGHT...
I HATE MYSELF.
ALL I DO IS WORRY AND I HATE IT.
I HATE THE WAY I AM!

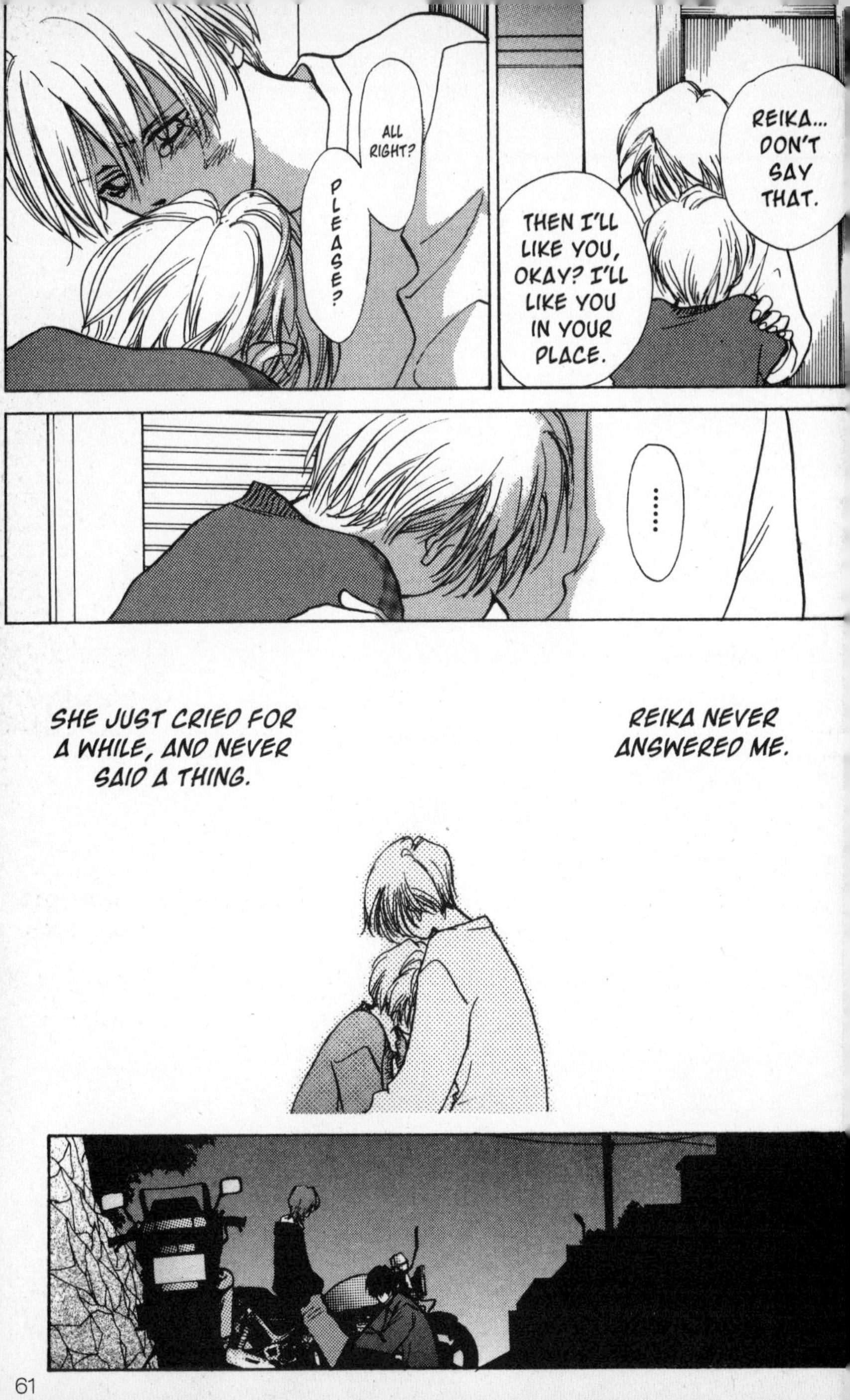
REIKA... DON'T SAY THAT.
THEN I'LL LIKE YOU, OKAY? I'LL LIKE YOU IN YOUR PLACE.
ALL RIGHT?
PLEASE?
……
REIKA NEVER ANSWERED ME.
SHE JUST CRIED FOR A WHILE, AND NEVER SAID A THING.

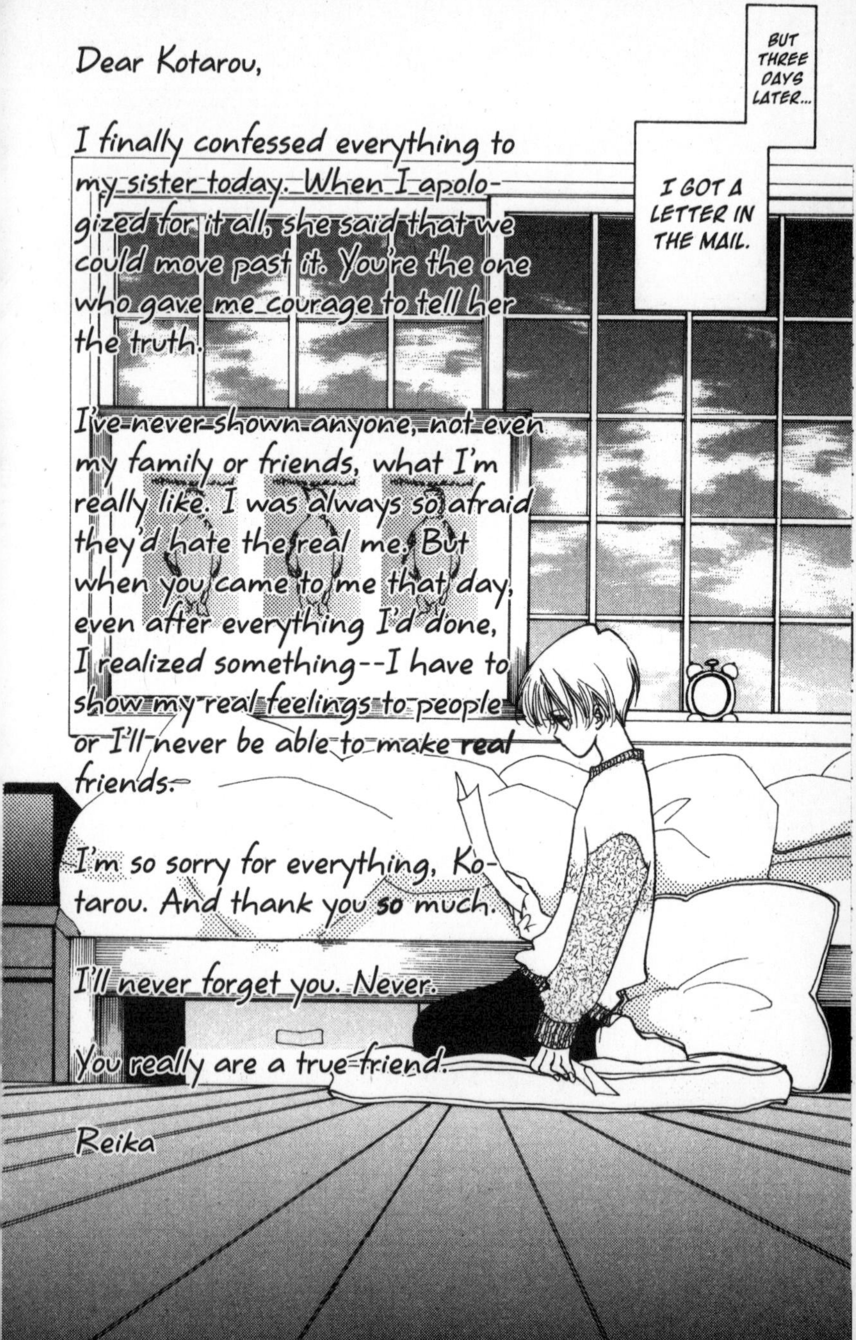
BUT THREE DAYS LATER...
I GOT A LETTER IN THE MAIL.
Dear Kotarou,
I finally confessed everything to my sister today. When I apologized for it all, she said that we could move past it. You're the one who gave me courage to tell her the truth.
I've never shown anyone, not even my family or friends, what I'm really like. I was always so afraid they'd hate the real me. But when you came to me that day, even after everything I'd done, I realized something--I have to show my real feelings to people or I'll never be able to make real friends.
I'm so sorry for everything, Kotarou. And thank you so much.
I'll never forget you. Never.
You really are a true friend.
Reika

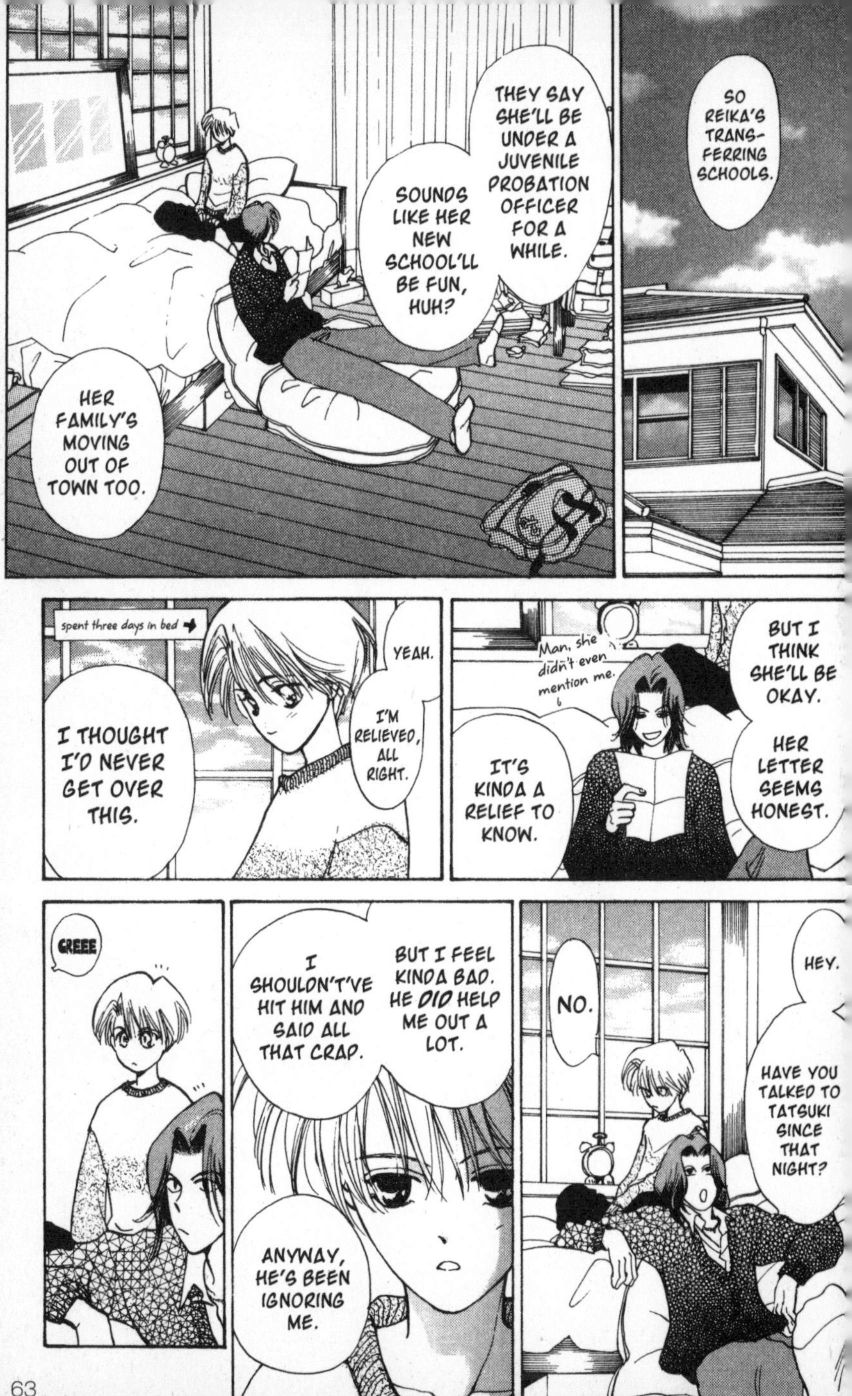
SO REIKA'S TRANS-FERRING SCHOOLS.
THEY SAY SHE'LL BE UNDER A JUVENILE PROBATION OFFICER FOR A WHILE.
SOUNDS LIKE HER NEW SCHOOL'LL BE FUN, HUH?
HER FAMILY'S MOVING OUT OF TOWN TOO.
BUT I THINK SHE'LL BE OKAY.
HER LETTER SEEMS HONEST.
Man, she didn't even mention me.
IT'S KINDA A RELIEF TO KNOW.
YEAH.
I'M RELIEVED, ALL RIGHT.
spent three days in bed
I THOUGHT I'D NEVER GET OVER THIS.
HEY.
HAVE YOU TALKED TO TATSUKI SINCE THAT NIGHT?
NO.
BUT I FEEL KINDA BAD. HE *DID* HELP ME OUT A LOT.
I SHOULDN'T'VE HIT HIM AND SAID ALL THAT CRAP.
ANYWAY, HE'S BEEN IGNORING ME.
GREEE

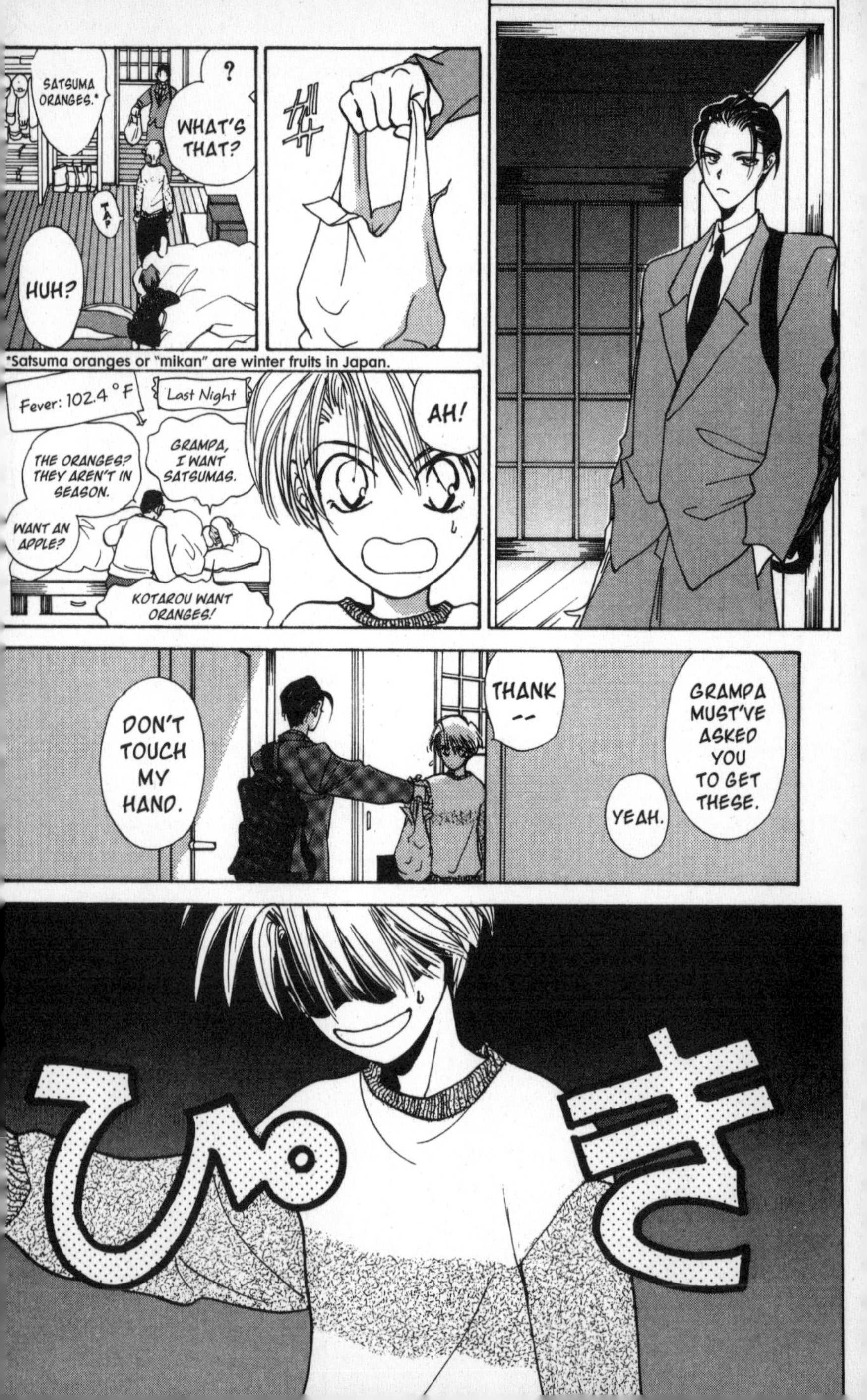
ガサ
?
WHAT'S THAT?
SATSUMA ORANGES.*
TAP
HUH?
AH!
Last Night
Fever: 102.4 °F
GRAMPA, I WANT SATSUMAS.
THE ORANGES? THEY AREN'T IN SEASON.
WANT AN APPLE?
KOTAROU WANT ORANGES!
GRAMPA MUST'VE ASKED YOU TO GET THESE.
YEAH.
THANK --
DON'T TOUCH MY HAND.
ぴき
*Satsuma oranges or "mikan" are winter fruits in Japan.

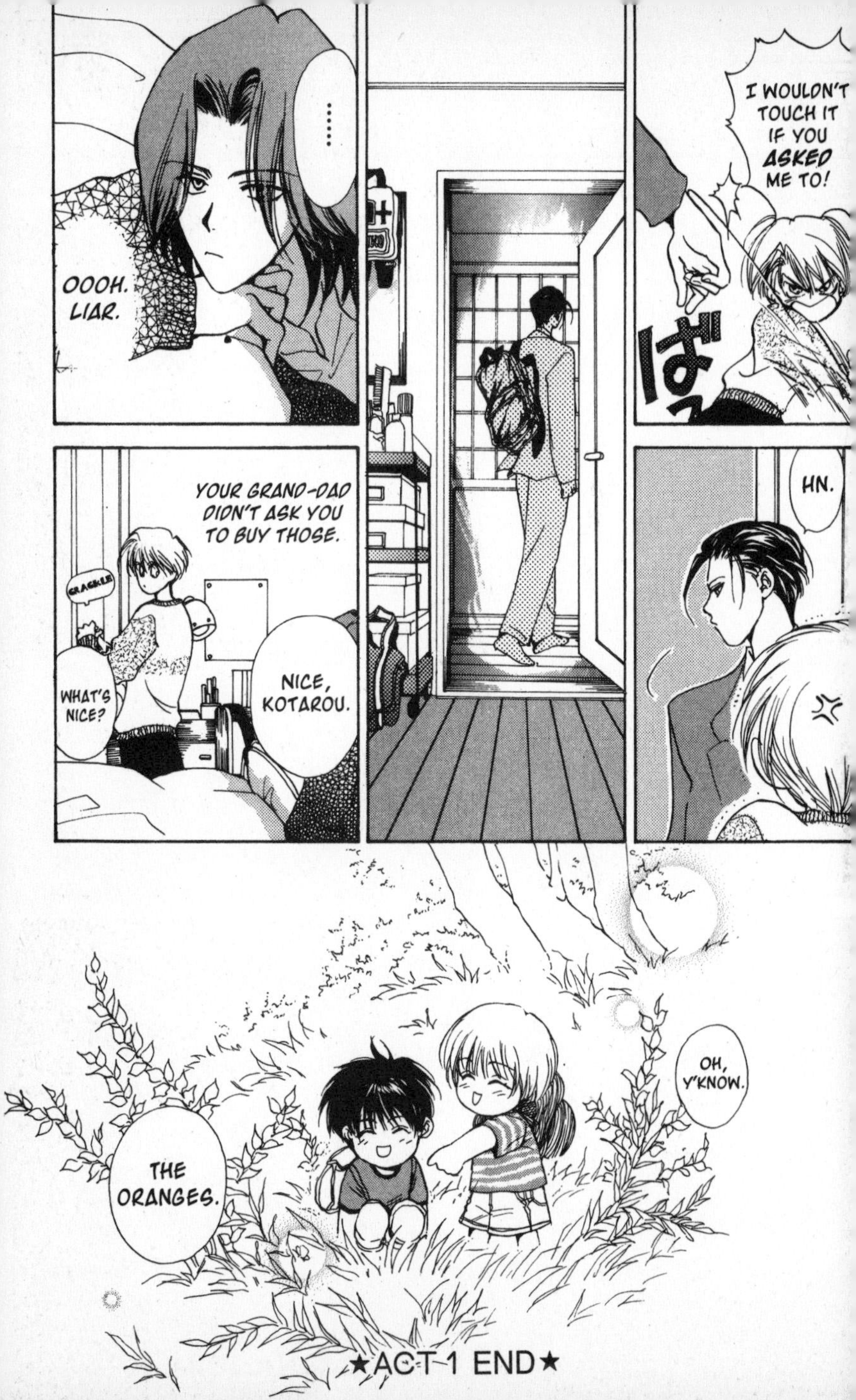
I WOULDN'T TOUCH IT IF YOU ASKED ME TO!
ば
HN.
......
OOOH. LIAR.
YOUR GRAND-DAD DIDN'T ASK YOU TO BUY THOSE.
NICE, KOTAROU.
CRACKLE
WHAT'S NICE?
OH, Y'KNOW.
THE ORANGES.

★ACT 1 END★

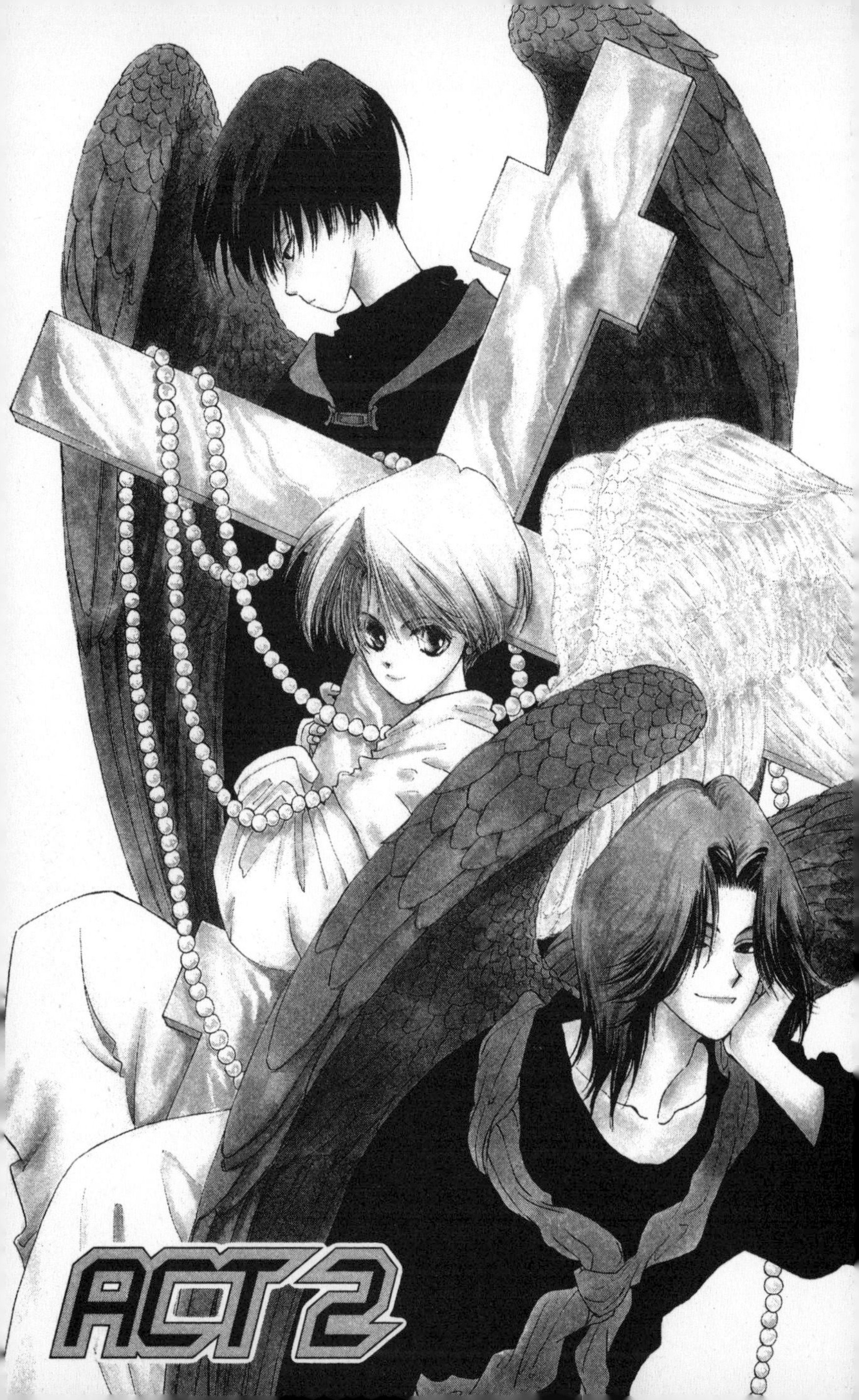
ACT 2

ACT 2

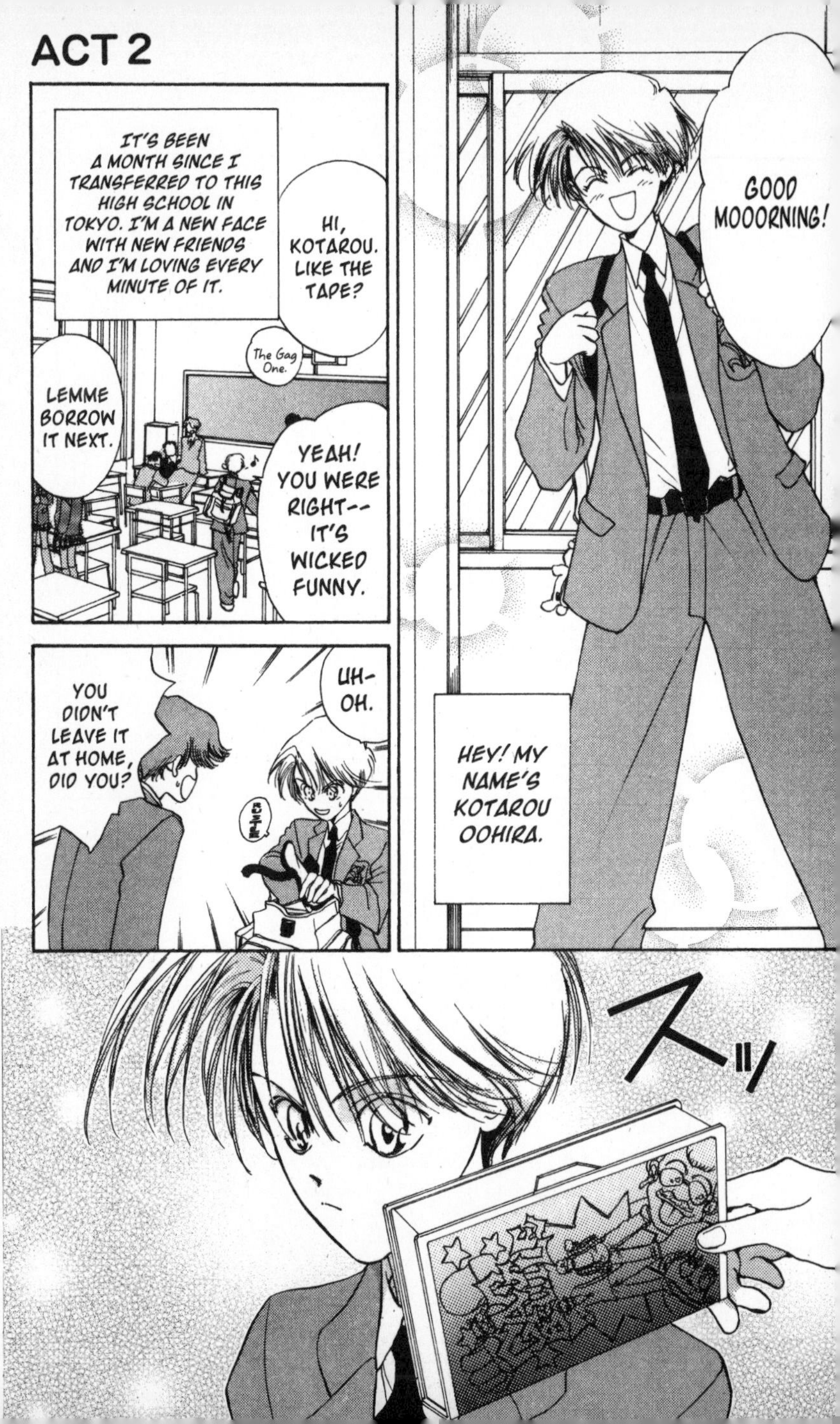
GOOD MOOORNING!
HEY! MY NAME'S KOTAROU OOHIRA.
IT'S BEEN A MONTH SINCE I TRANSFERRED TO THIS HIGH SCHOOL IN TOKYO. I'M A NEW FACE WITH NEW FRIENDS AND I'M LOVING EVERY MINUTE OF IT.
HI, KOTAROU. LIKE THE TAPE?
The Gag One.
YEAH! YOU WERE RIGHT-- IT'S WICKED FUNNY.
LEMME BORROW IT NEXT.
UH-OH.
RUSTLE
YOU DIDN'T LEAVE IT AT HOME, DID YOU?
スッ

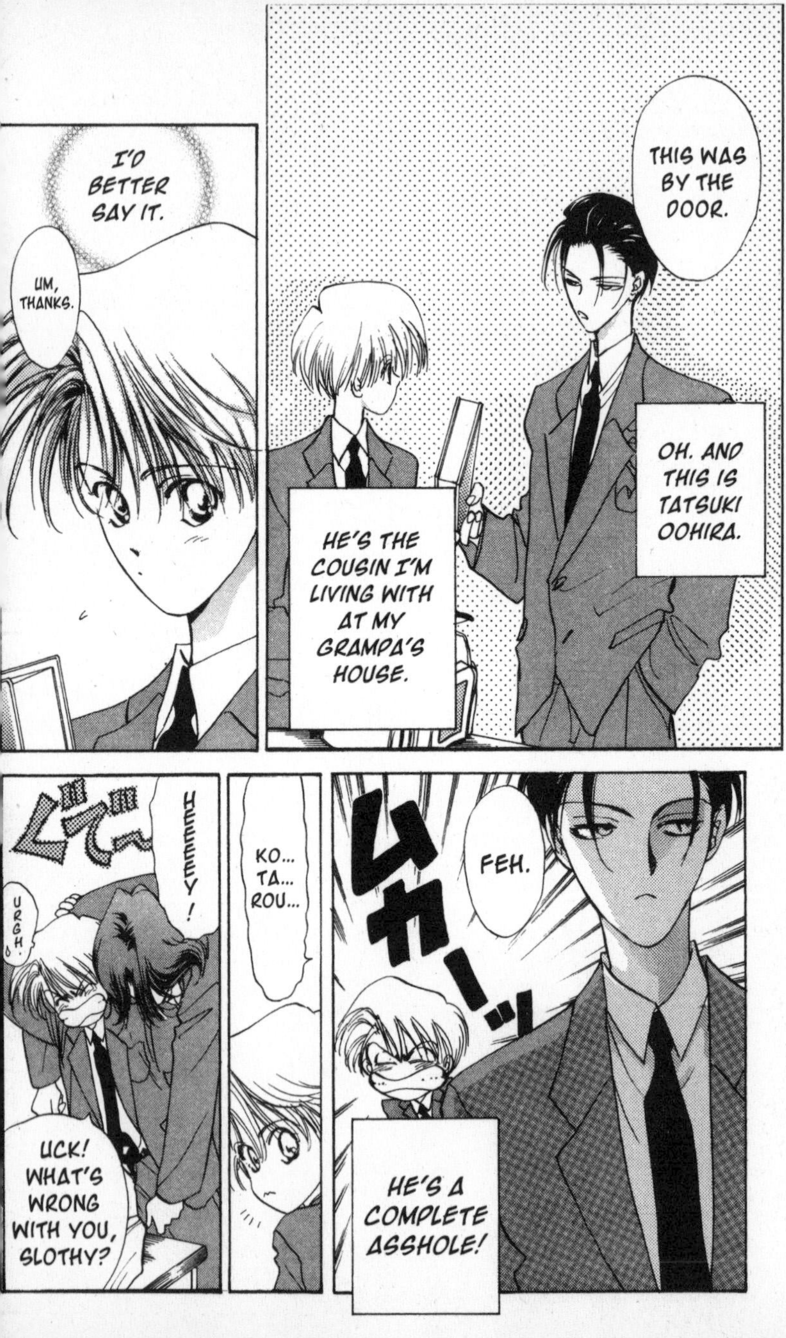
THIS WAS BY THE DOOR.
OH. AND THIS IS TATSUKI OOHIRA.
HE'S THE COUSIN I'M LIVING WITH AT MY GRAMPA'S HOUSE.
I'D BETTER SAY IT.
UM, THANKS.
ムカーッ
FEH.
HE'S A COMPLETE ASSHOLE!
KO... TA... ROU...
ぐでー
HEEEEY!
URGH.
UCK! WHAT'S WRONG WITH YOU, SLOTHY?

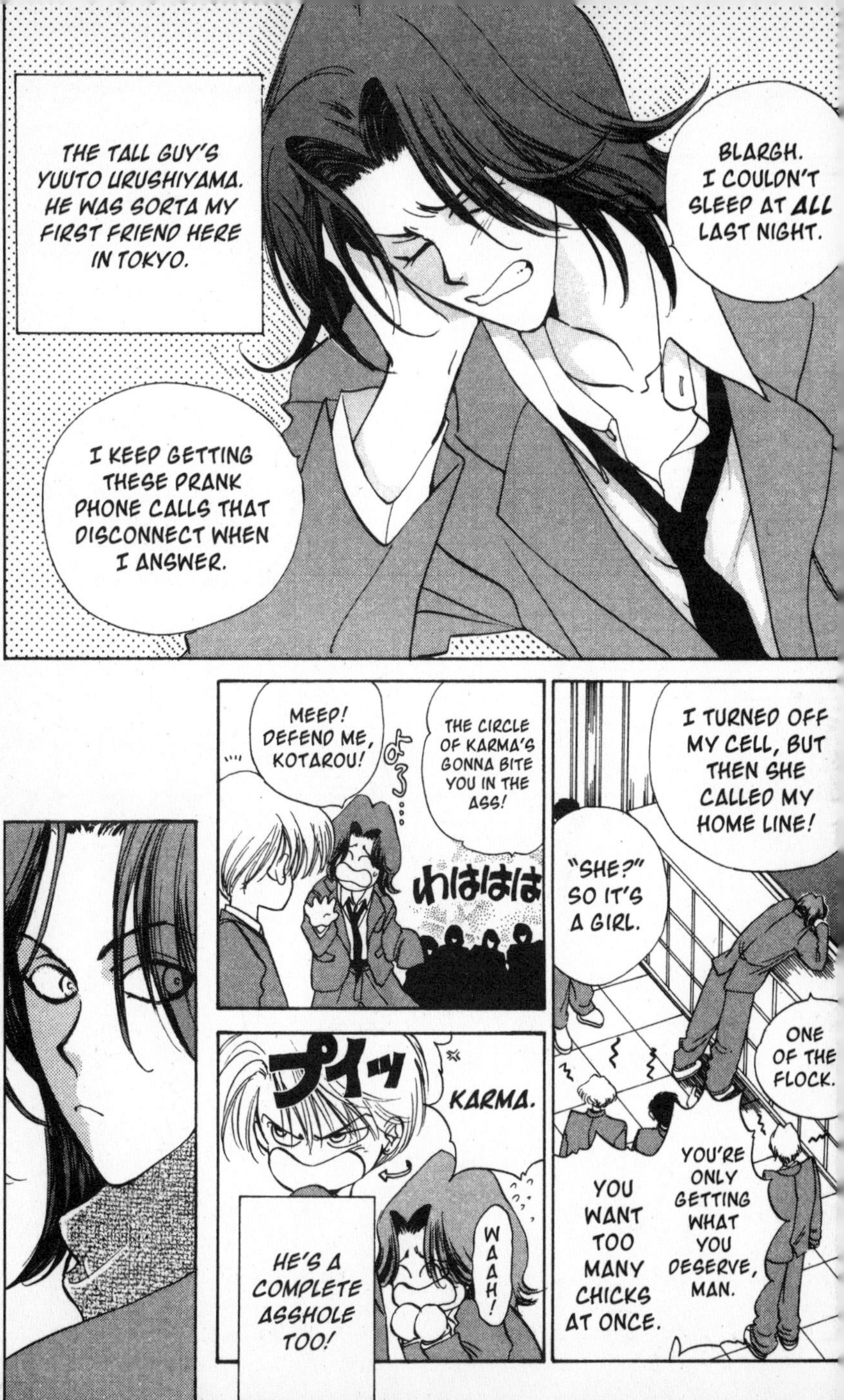
BLARGH. I COULDN'T SLEEP AT **ALL** LAST NIGHT.
THE TALL GUY'S YUUTO URUSHIYAMA. HE WAS SORTA MY FIRST FRIEND HERE IN TOKYO.
I KEEP GETTING THESE PRANK PHONE CALLS THAT DISCONNECT WHEN I ANSWER.
I TURNED OFF MY CELL, BUT THEN SHE CALLED MY HOME LINE!
"SHE?" SO IT'S A GIRL.
ONE OF THE FLOCK.
YOU'RE ONLY GETTING WHAT YOU DESERVE, MAN.
YOU WANT TOO MANY CHICKS AT ONCE.
THE CIRCLE OF KARMA'S GONNA BITE YOU IN THE ASS!
MEEP! DEFEND ME, KOTAROU!
わははは
プイッ
KARMA.
WAAAH!
HE'S A COMPLETE ASSHOLE TOO!

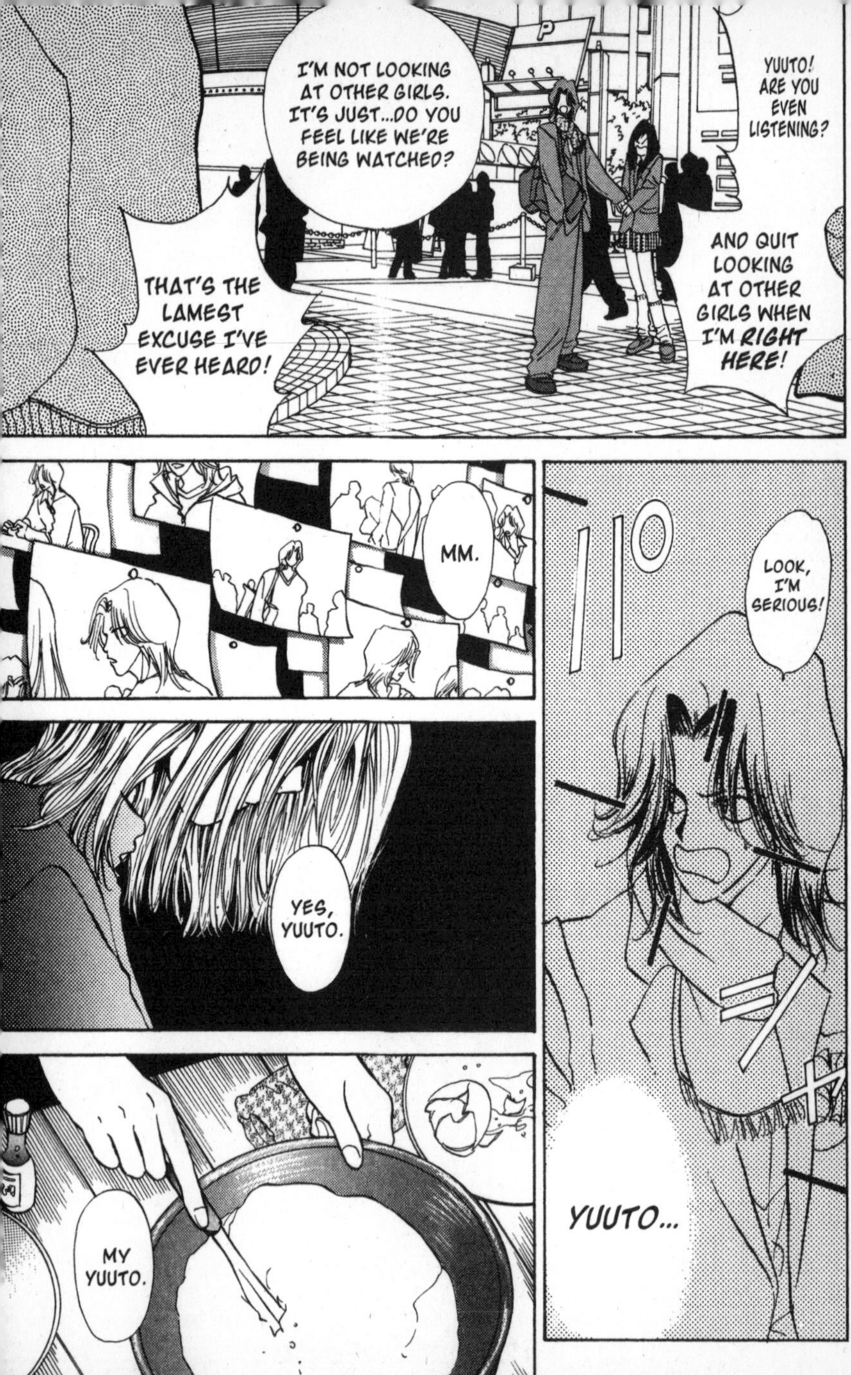
YUUTO! ARE YOU EVEN LISTENING?
AND QUIT LOOKING AT OTHER GIRLS WHEN I'M *RIGHT HERE*!
I'M NOT LOOKING AT OTHER GIRLS. IT'S JUST...DO YOU FEEL LIKE WE'RE BEING WATCHED?
THAT'S THE LAMEST EXCUSE I'VE EVER HEARD!
LOOK, I'M SERIOUS!
YUUTO...
MM.
YES, YUUTO.
MY YUUTO.

ACT 2

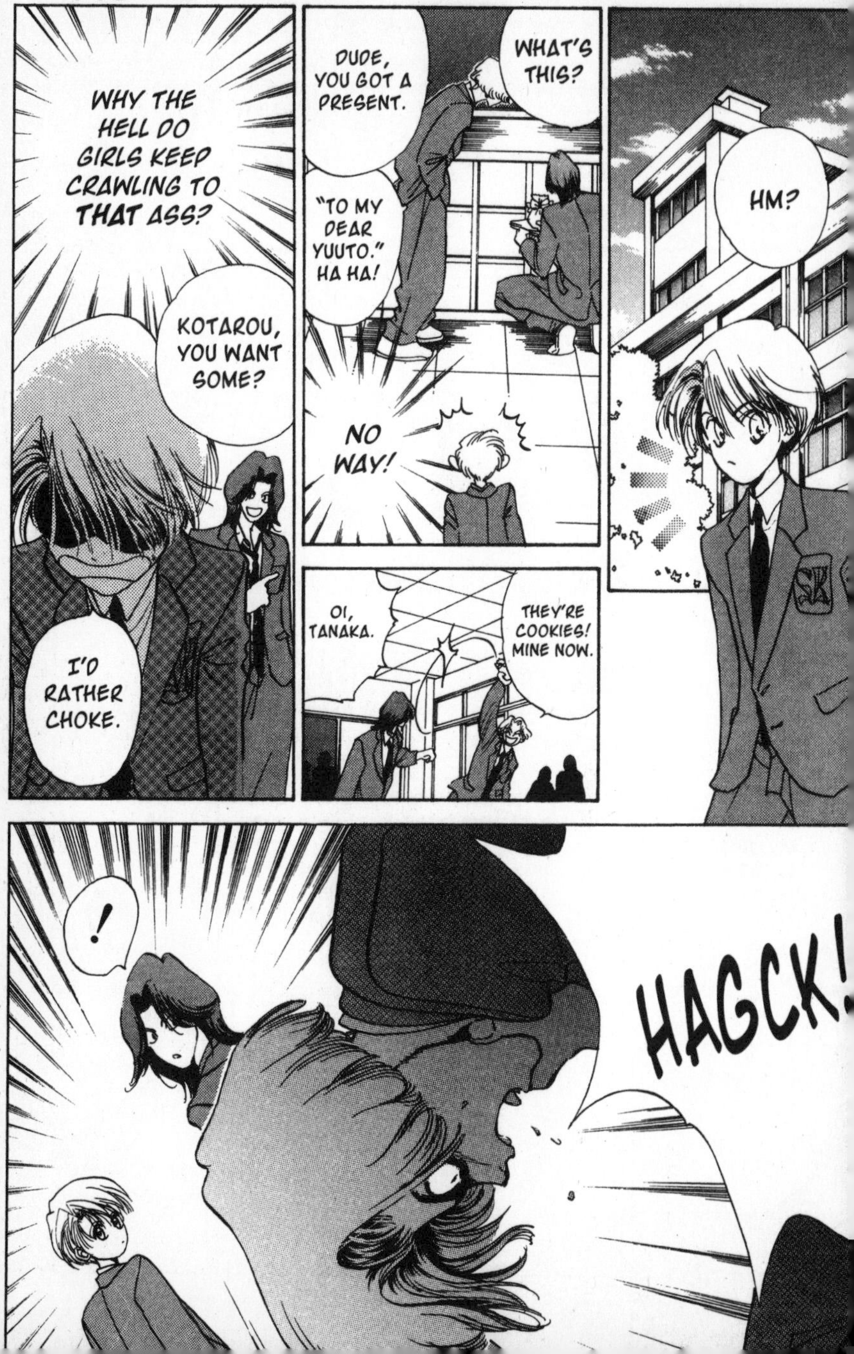
HM?
WHAT'S THIS?
DUDE, YOU GOT A PRESENT.
"TO MY DEAR YUUTO." HA HA!
NO WAY!
THEY'RE COOKIES! MINE NOW.
OI, TANAKA.
WHY THE HELL DO GIRLS KEEP CRAWLING TO THAT ASS?
KOTAROU, YOU WANT SOME?
I'D RATHER CHOKE.
HAGCK!
!

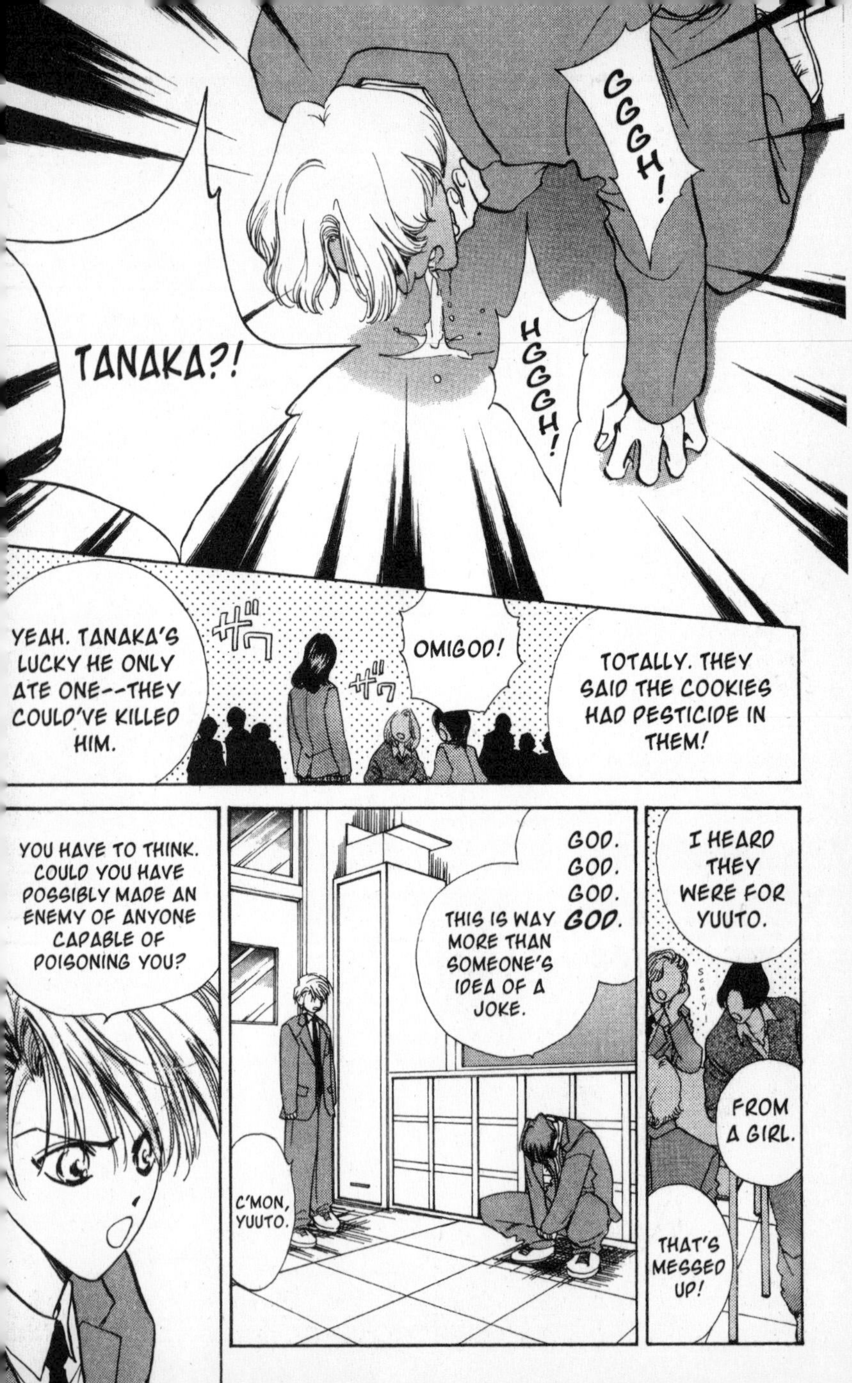
GGGH!
HGGGH!
TANAKA?!
TOTALLY. THEY SAID THE COOKIES HAD PESTICIDE IN THEM!
OMIGOD!
ザワ
ザワ
YEAH. TANAKA'S LUCKY HE ONLY ATE ONE--THEY COULD'VE KILLED HIM.
I HEARD THEY WERE FOR YUUTO.
Scary!
FROM A GIRL.
THAT'S MESSED UP!
GOD. GOD. GOD. GOD.
THIS IS WAY MORE THAN SOMEONE'S IDEA OF A JOKE.
C'MON, YUUTO.
YOU HAVE TO THINK. COULD YOU HAVE POSSIBLY MADE AN ENEMY OF ANYONE CAPABLE OF POISONING YOU?

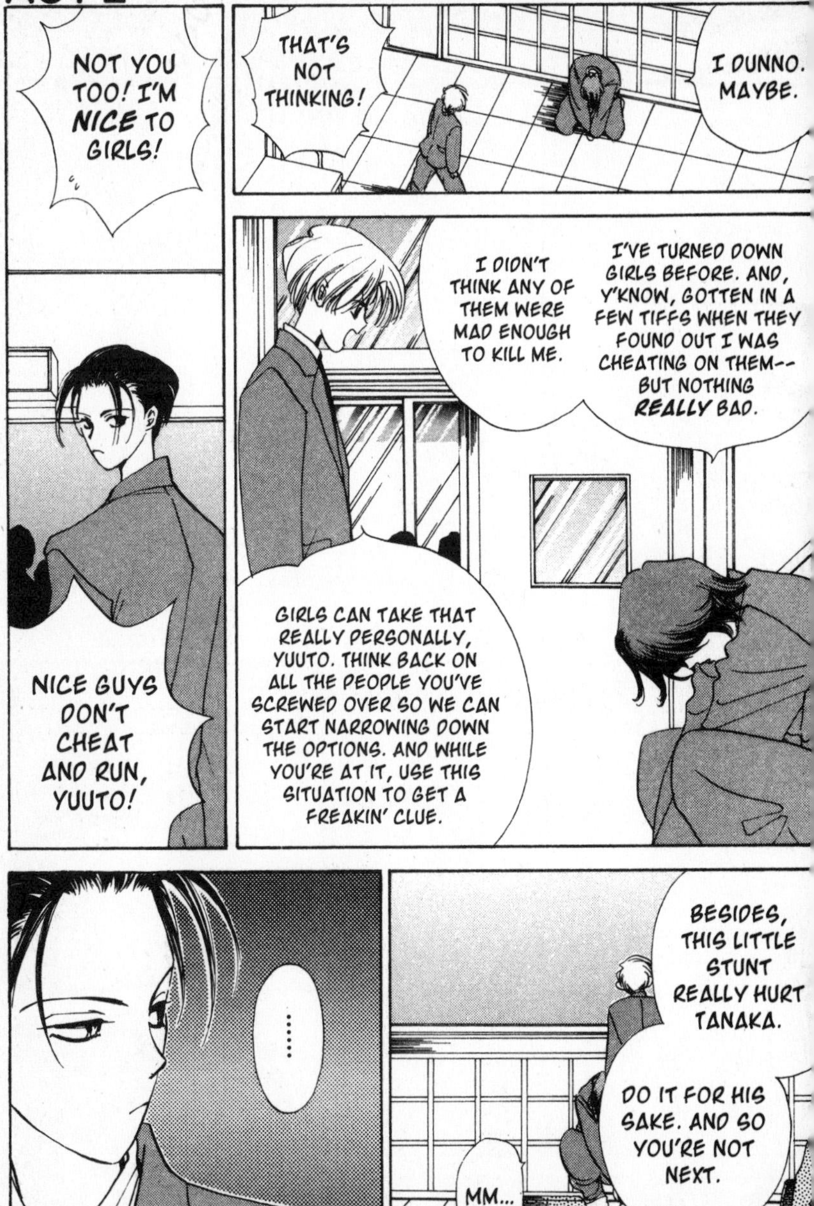
I DUNNO. MAYBE.
THAT'S NOT THINKING!
NOT YOU TOO! I'M *NICE* TO GIRLS!
I'VE TURNED DOWN GIRLS BEFORE. AND, Y'KNOW, GOTTEN IN A FEW TIFFS WHEN THEY FOUND OUT I WAS CHEATING ON THEM-- BUT NOTHING *REALLY* BAD.
I DIDN'T THINK ANY OF THEM WERE MAD ENOUGH TO KILL ME.
GIRLS CAN TAKE THAT REALLY PERSONALLY, YUUTO. THINK BACK ON ALL THE PEOPLE YOU'VE SCREWED OVER SO WE CAN START NARROWING DOWN THE OPTIONS. AND WHILE YOU'RE AT IT, USE THIS SITUATION TO GET A FREAKIN' CLUE.
NICE GUYS DON'T CHEAT AND RUN, YUUTO!
BESIDES, THIS LITTLE STUNT REALLY HURT TANAKA.
DO IT FOR HIS SAKE. AND SO YOU'RE NOT NEXT.
MM...
......

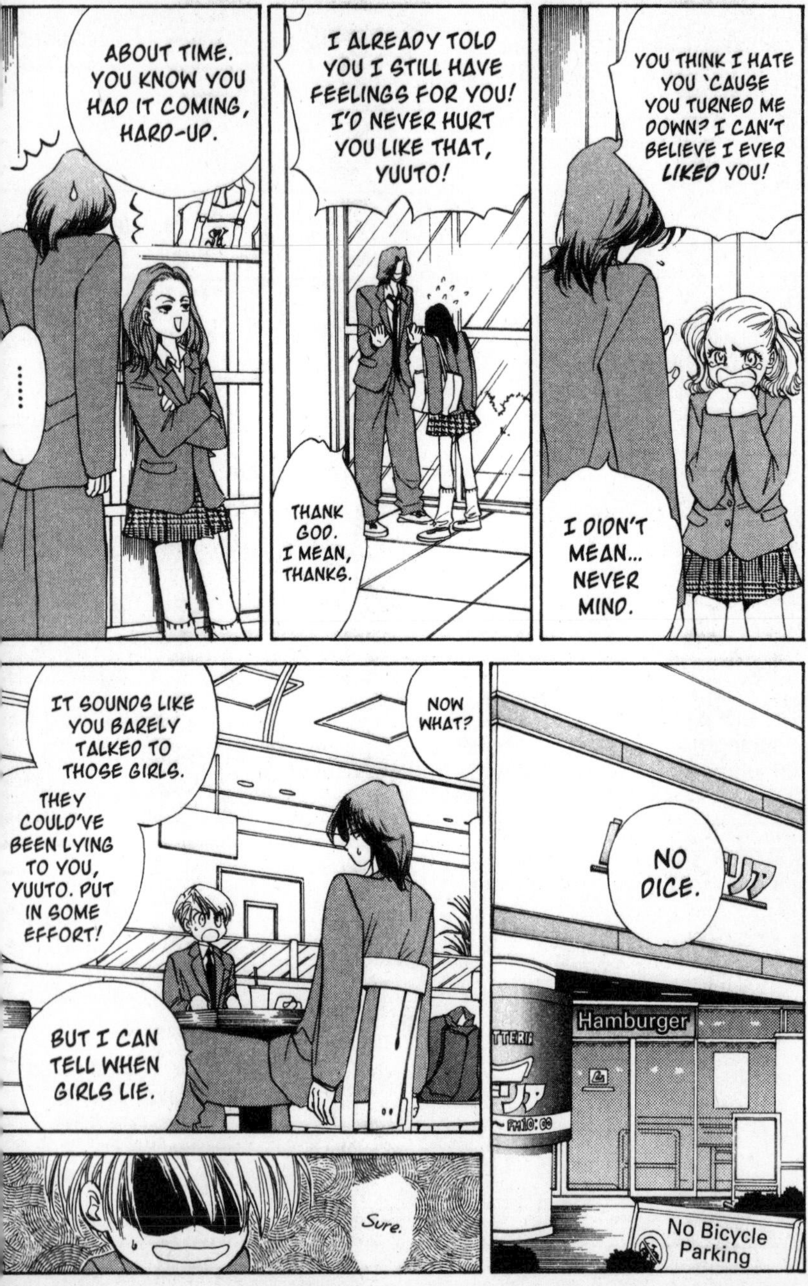
YOU THINK I HATE YOU 'CAUSE YOU TURNED ME DOWN? I CAN'T BELIEVE I EVER *LIKED* YOU!
I DIDN'T MEAN... NEVER MIND.
I ALREADY TOLD YOU I STILL HAVE FEELINGS FOR YOU! I'D NEVER HURT YOU LIKE THAT, YUUTO!
THANK GOD. I MEAN, THANKS.
ABOUT TIME. YOU KNOW YOU HAD IT COMING, HARD-UP.
......
NO DICE.
Hamburger
No Bicycle Parking
NOW WHAT?
IT SOUNDS LIKE YOU BARELY TALKED TO THOSE GIRLS.
THEY COULD'VE BEEN LYING TO YOU, YUUTO. PUT IN SOME EFFORT!
BUT I CAN TELL WHEN GIRLS LIE.
Sure.

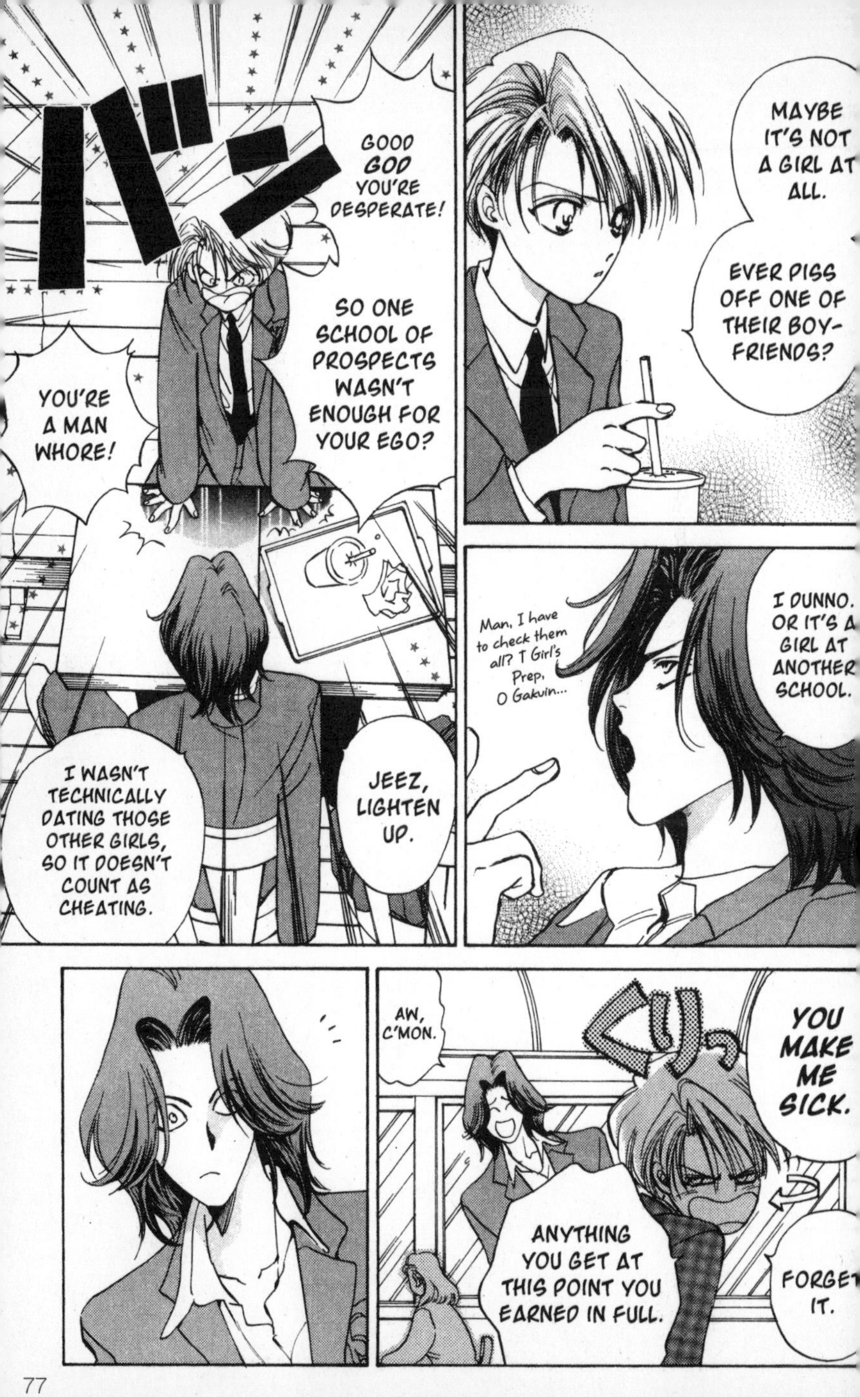
MAYBE IT'S NOT A GIRL AT ALL.
EVER PISS OFF ONE OF THEIR BOY-FRIENDS?
I DUNNO. OR IT'S A GIRL AT ANOTHER SCHOOL.
Man, I have to check them all? T Girl's Prep, O Gakuin...
GOOD GOD YOU'RE DESPERATE!
SO ONE SCHOOL OF PROSPECTS WASN'T ENOUGH FOR YOUR EGO?
YOU'RE A MAN WHORE!
JEEZ, LIGHTEN UP.
I WASN'T TECHNICALLY DATING THOSE OTHER GIRLS, SO IT DOESN'T COUNT AS CHEATING.
YOU MAKE ME SICK.
AW, C'MON.
FORGET IT.
ANYTHING YOU GET AT THIS POINT YOU EARNED IN FULL.

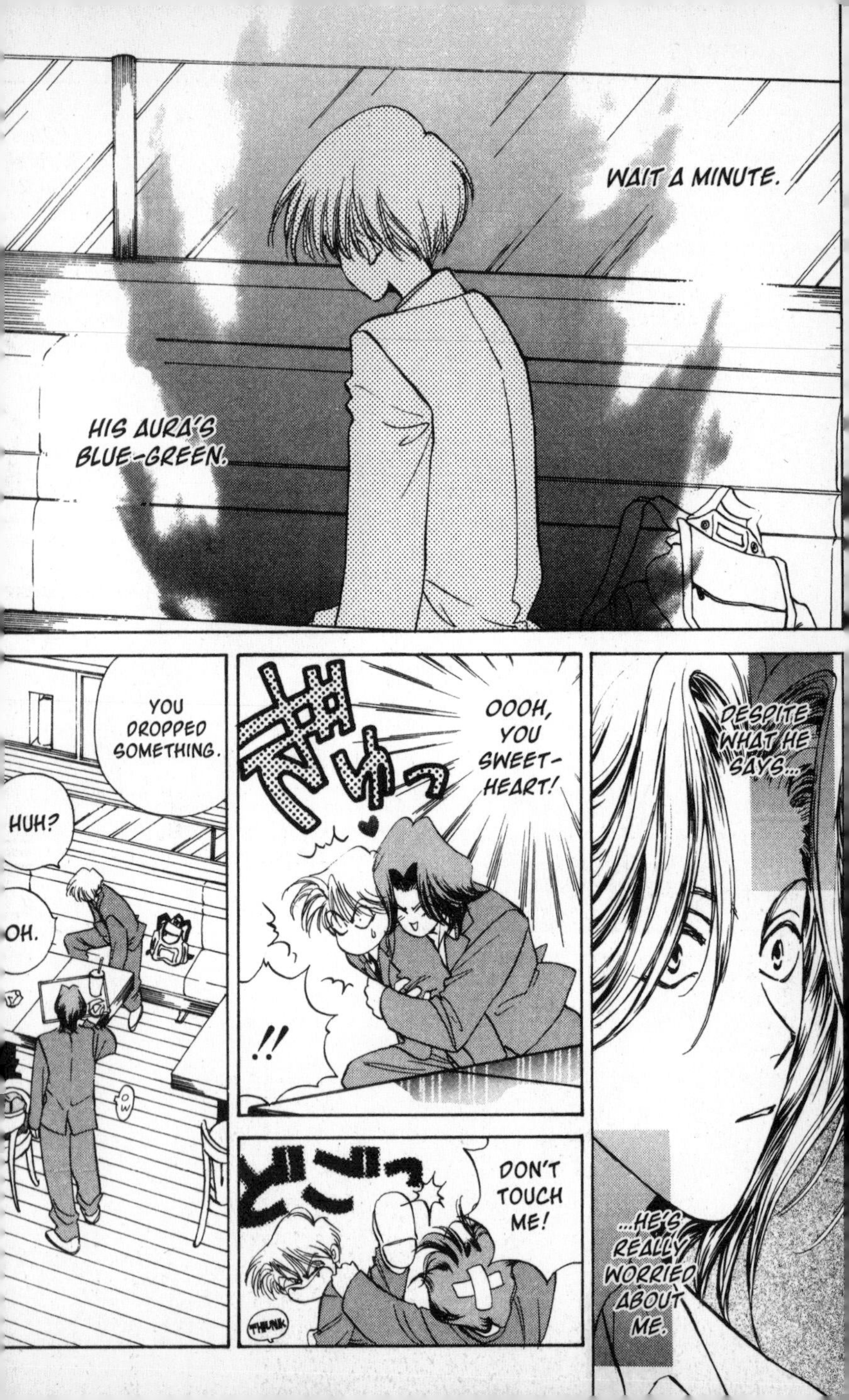
WAIT A MINUTE.
HIS AURA'S BLUE-GREEN.
DESPITE WHAT HE SAYS...
...HE'S REALLY WORRIED ABOUT ME.
OOOH, YOU SWEET-HEART!
!!
DON'T TOUCH ME!
THUNK
YOU DROPPED SOMETHING.
HUH?
OH.
OW

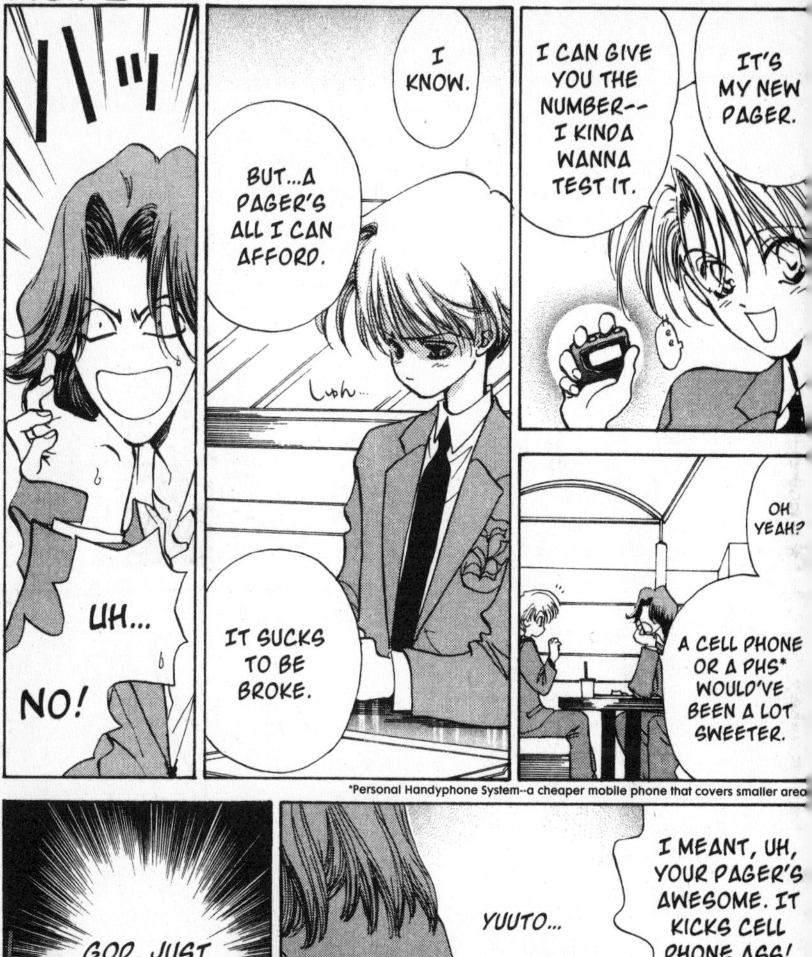
IT'S MY NEW PAGER.
I CAN GIVE YOU THE NUMBER-- I KINDA WANNA TEST IT.
OH YEAH?
A CELL PHONE OR A PHS* WOULD'VE BEEN A LOT SWEETER.
I KNOW.
BUT...A PAGER'S ALL I CAN AFFORD.
しゅん...
IT SUCKS TO BE BROKE.
ハッ
UH...
NO!

*Personal Handyphone System--a cheaper mobile phone that covers smaller area

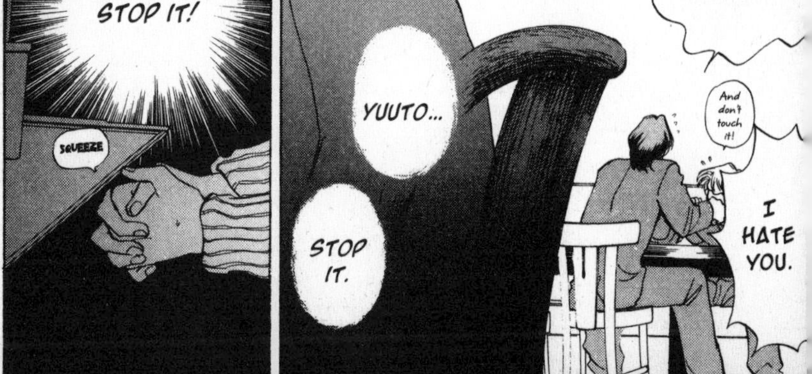
I MEANT, UH, YOUR PAGER'S AWESOME. IT KICKS CELL PHONE ASS!
YUUTO...
And don't touch it!
YUUTO...
I HATE YOU.
STOP IT.
GOD, JUST STOP IT!
SQUEEZE

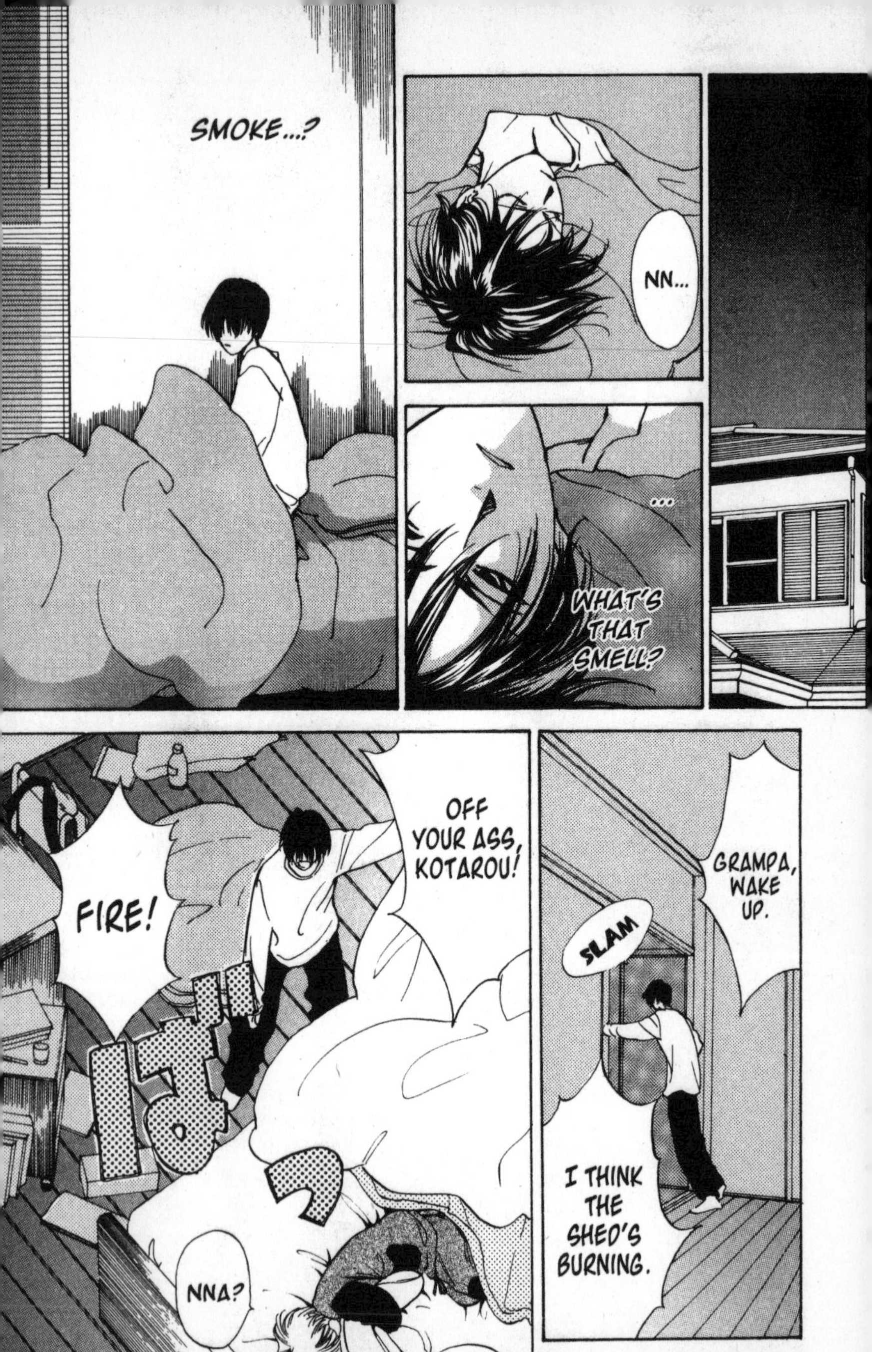
NN...
...
WHAT'S THAT SMELL?
SMOKE...?
GRAMPA, WAKE UP.
SLAM
I THINK THE SHED'S BURNING.
OFF YOUR ASS, KOTAROU!
FIRE!
NNA?

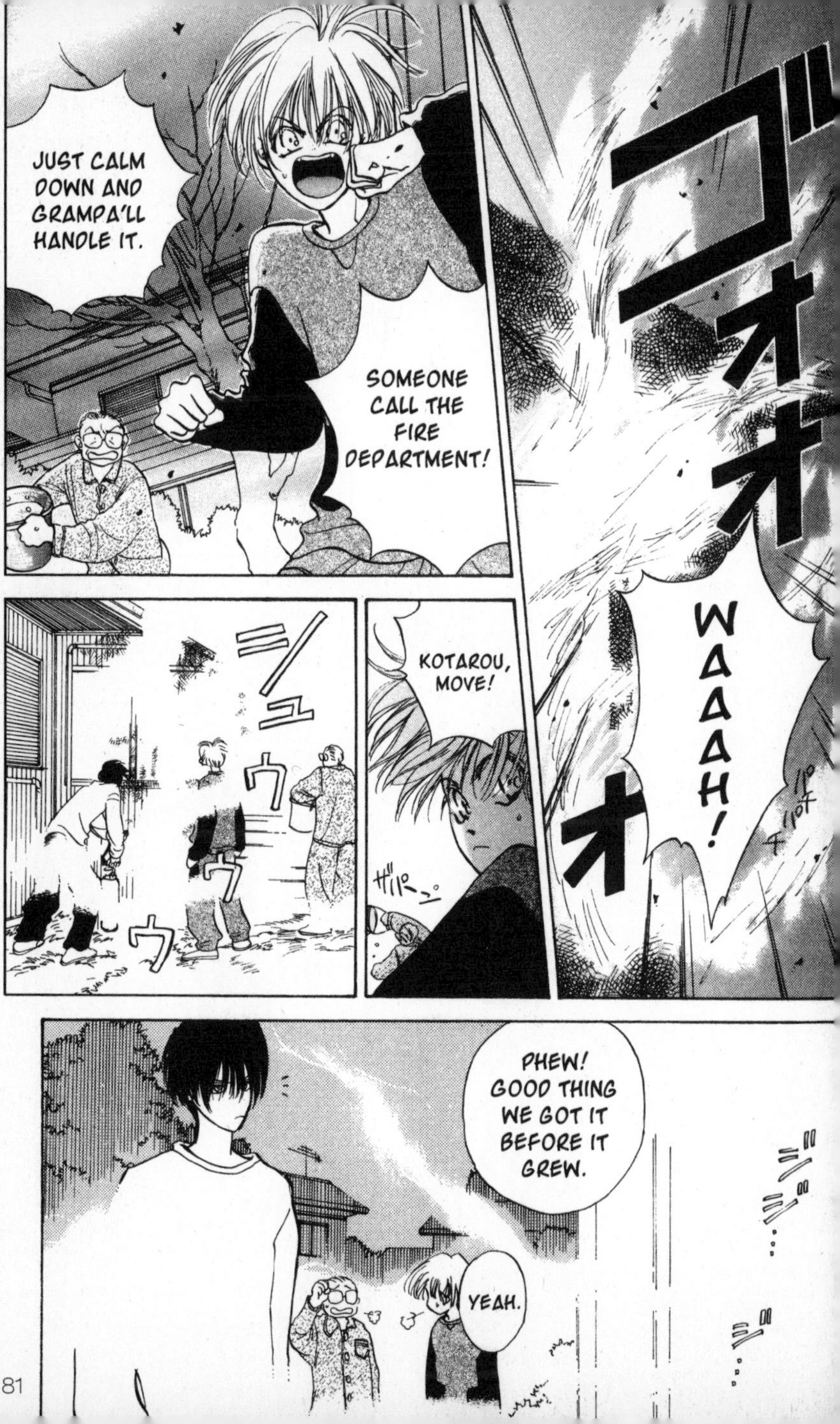

ゴオオオ
WAAAAH!
JUST CALM DOWN AND GRAMPA'LL HANDLE IT.
SOMEONE CALL THE FIRE DEPARTMENT!
KOTAROU, MOVE!
シュウウウ
PHEW! GOOD THING WE GOT IT BEFORE IT GREW.
YEAH.

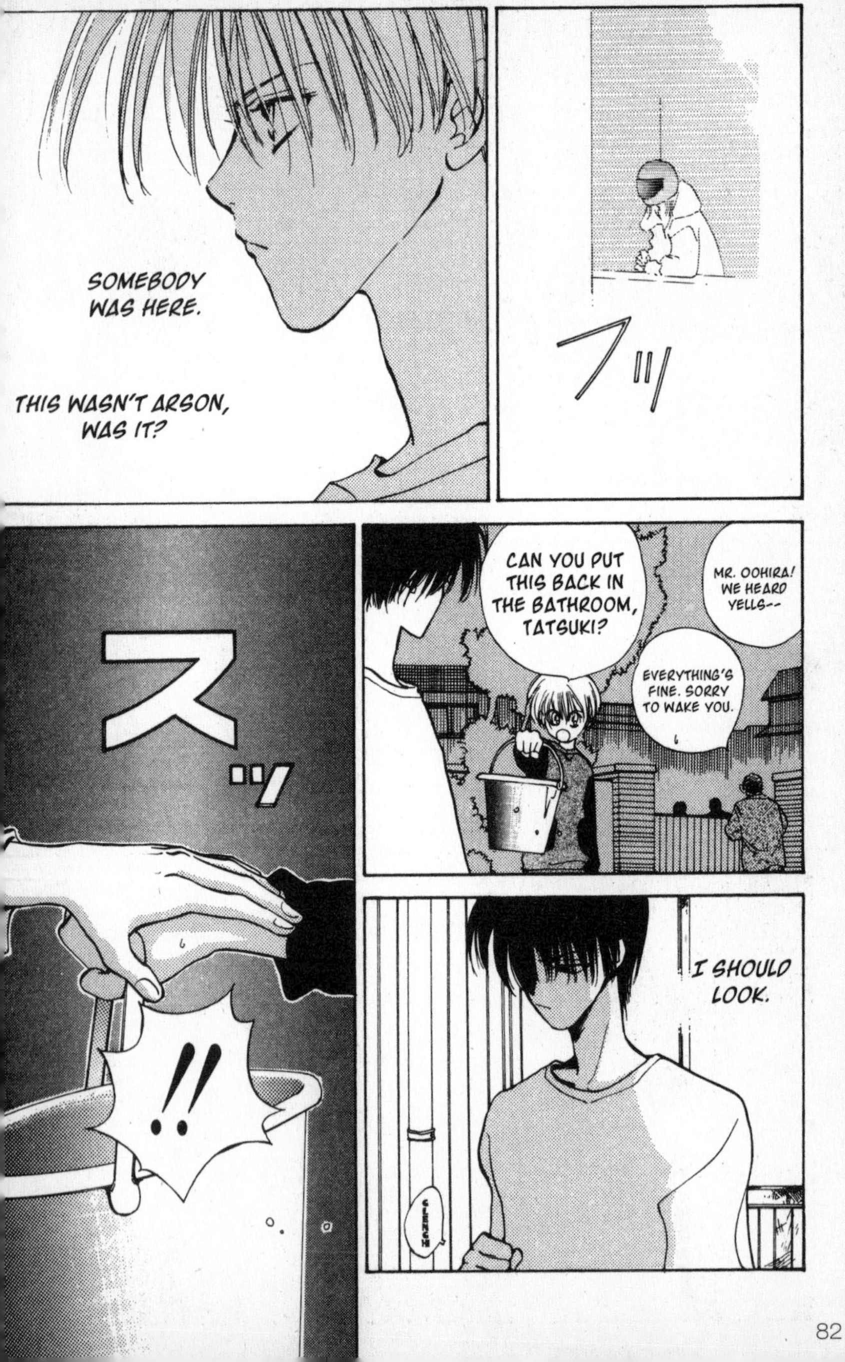
フッ
SOMEBODY WAS HERE.
THIS WASN'T ARSON, WAS IT?
MR. OOHIRA! WE HEARD YELLS--
EVERYTHING'S FINE. SORRY TO WAKE YOU.
CAN YOU PUT THIS BACK IN THE BATHROOM, TATSUKI?
I SHOULD LOOK.
CLENCH
スッ
!!

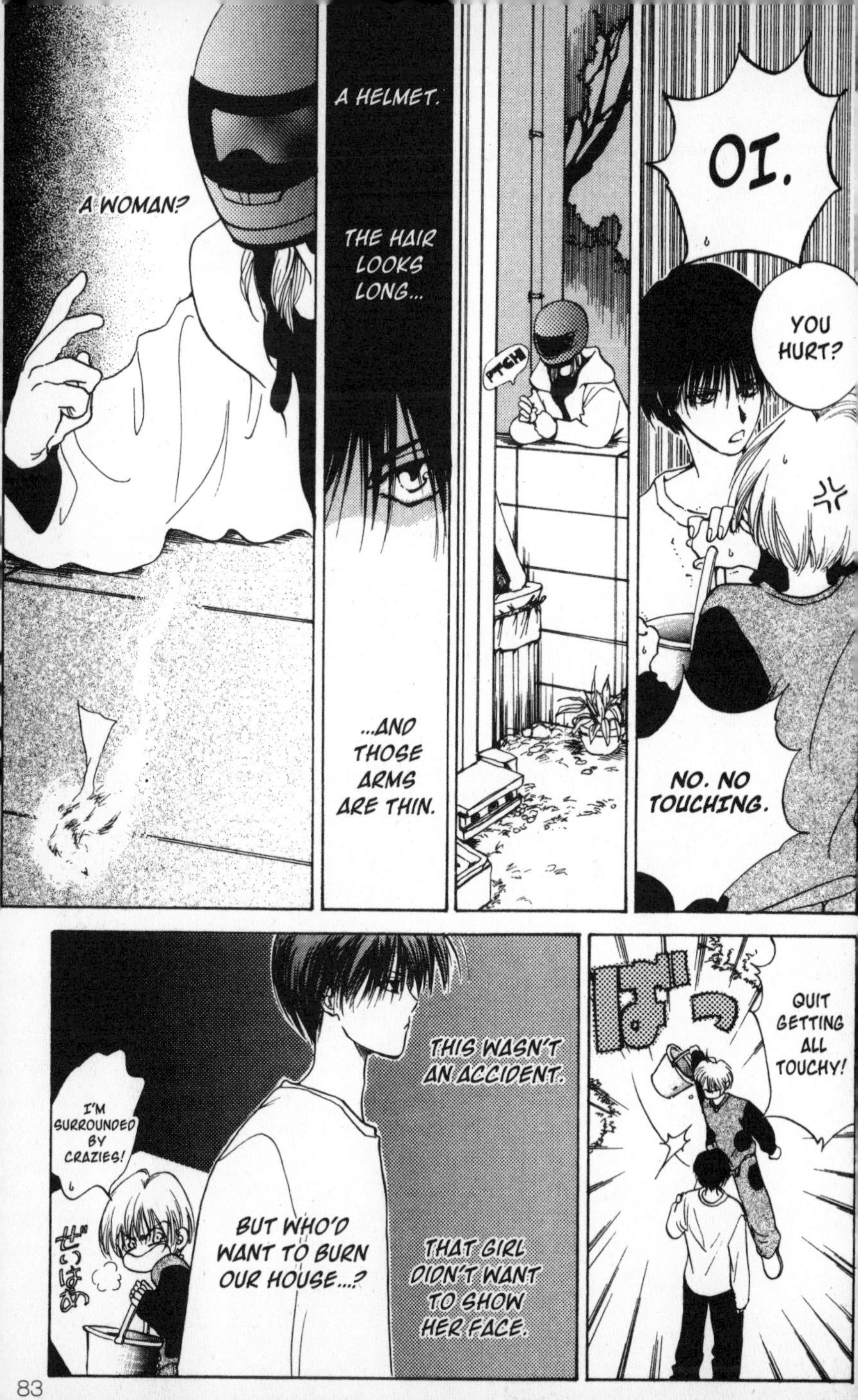
OI.
YOU HURT?
NO. NO TOUCHING.
PTCH
A HELMET.
THE HAIR LOOKS LONG...
...AND THOSE ARMS ARE THIN.
A WOMAN?
ばっ
QUIT GETTING ALL TOUCHY!
THIS WASN'T AN ACCIDENT.
THAT GIRL DIDN'T WANT TO SHOW HER FACE.
BUT WHO'D WANT TO BURN OUR HOUSE...?
I'M SURROUNDED BY CRAZIES!
ぜいはあ

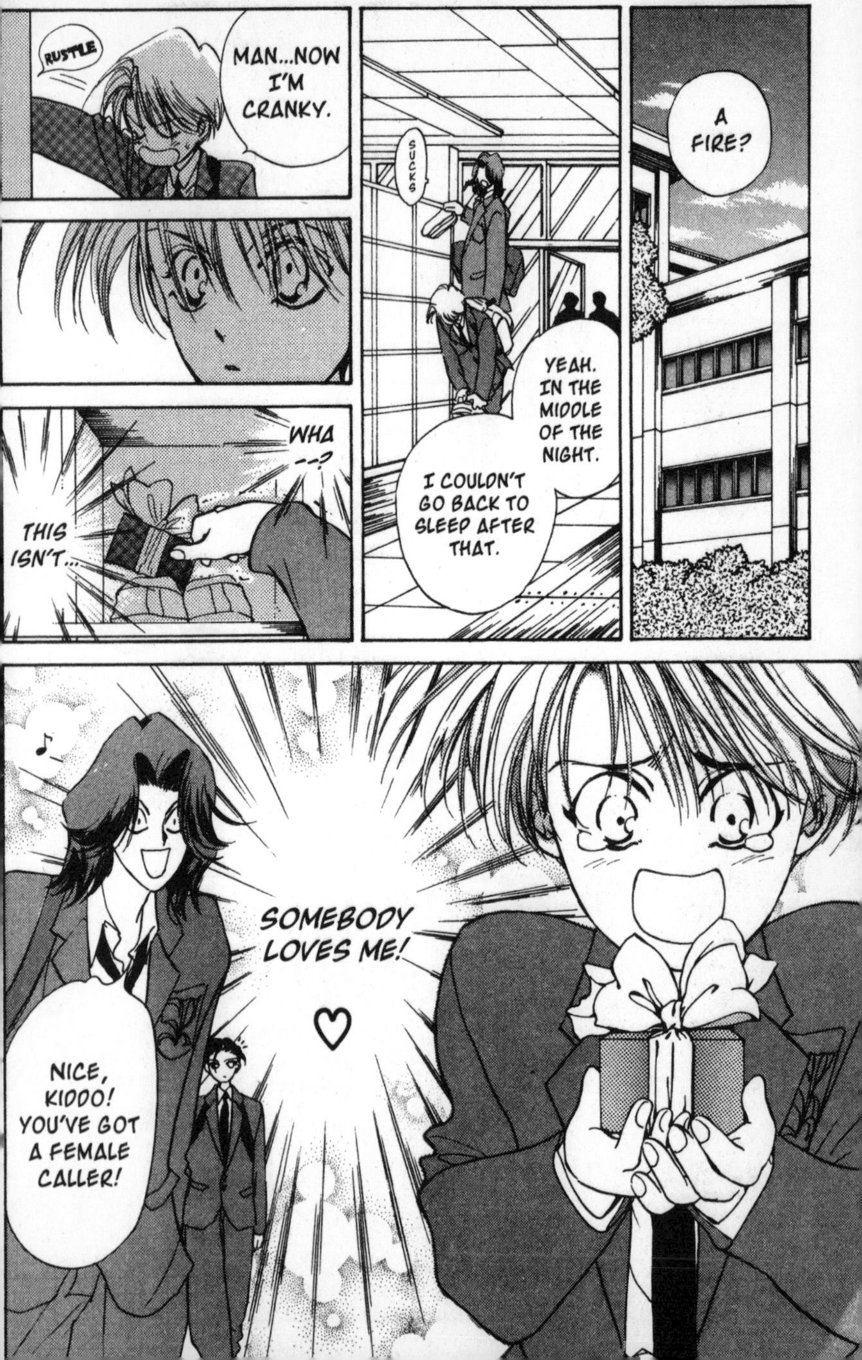
A FIRE?
SUCKS
YEAH. IN THE MIDDLE OF THE NIGHT.
I COULDN'T GO BACK TO SLEEP AFTER THAT.
RUSTLE
MAN...NOW I'M CRANKY.
WHA--?
THIS ISN'T...
SOMEBODY LOVES ME! ♥
♪
NICE, KIDDO! YOU'VE GOT A FEMALE CALLER!

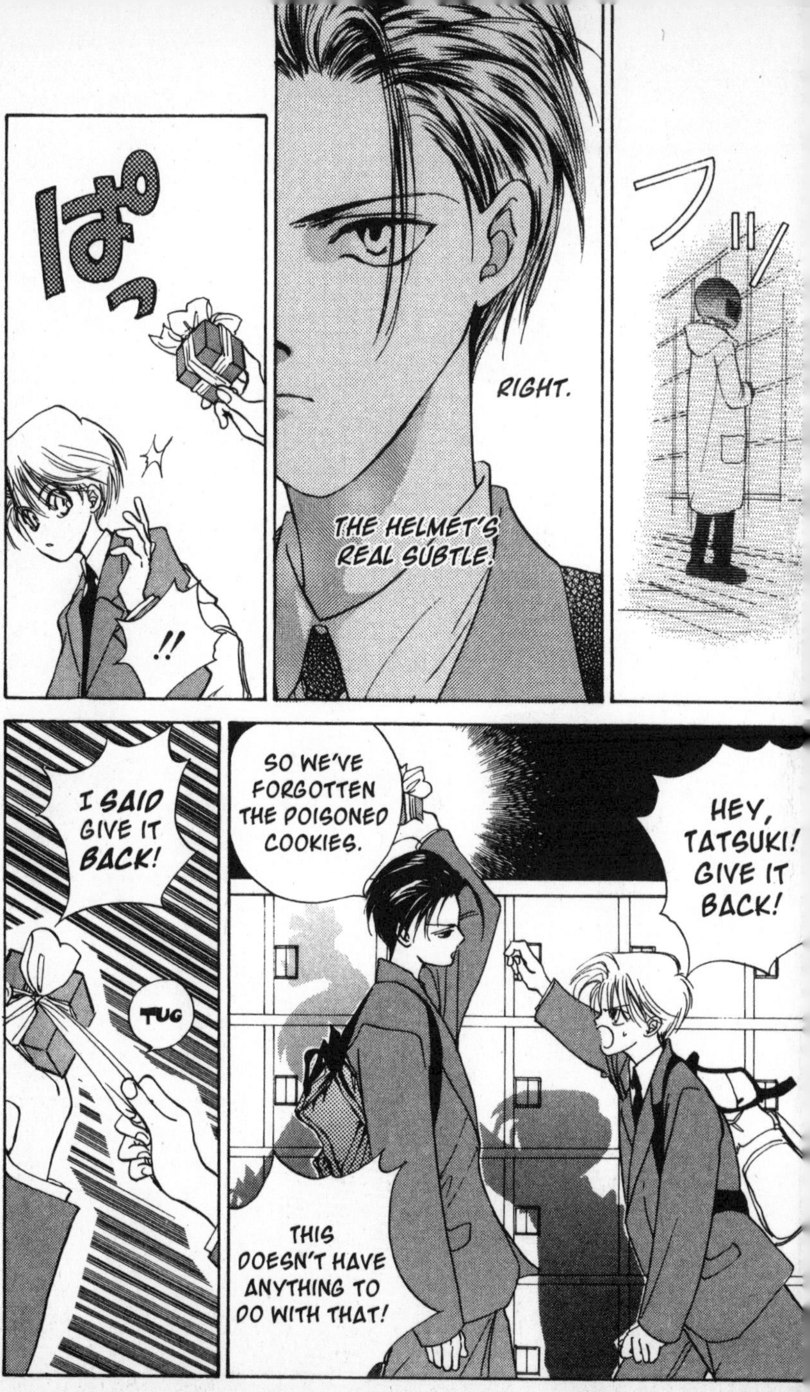
フッ
RIGHT.
THE HELMET'S REAL SUBTLE.
ぱっ
!!
HEY, TATSUKI! GIVE IT BACK!
SO WE'VE FORGOTTEN THE POISONED COOKIES.
THIS DOESN'T HAVE ANYTHING TO DO WITH THAT!
I SAID GIVE IT BACK!
TUG

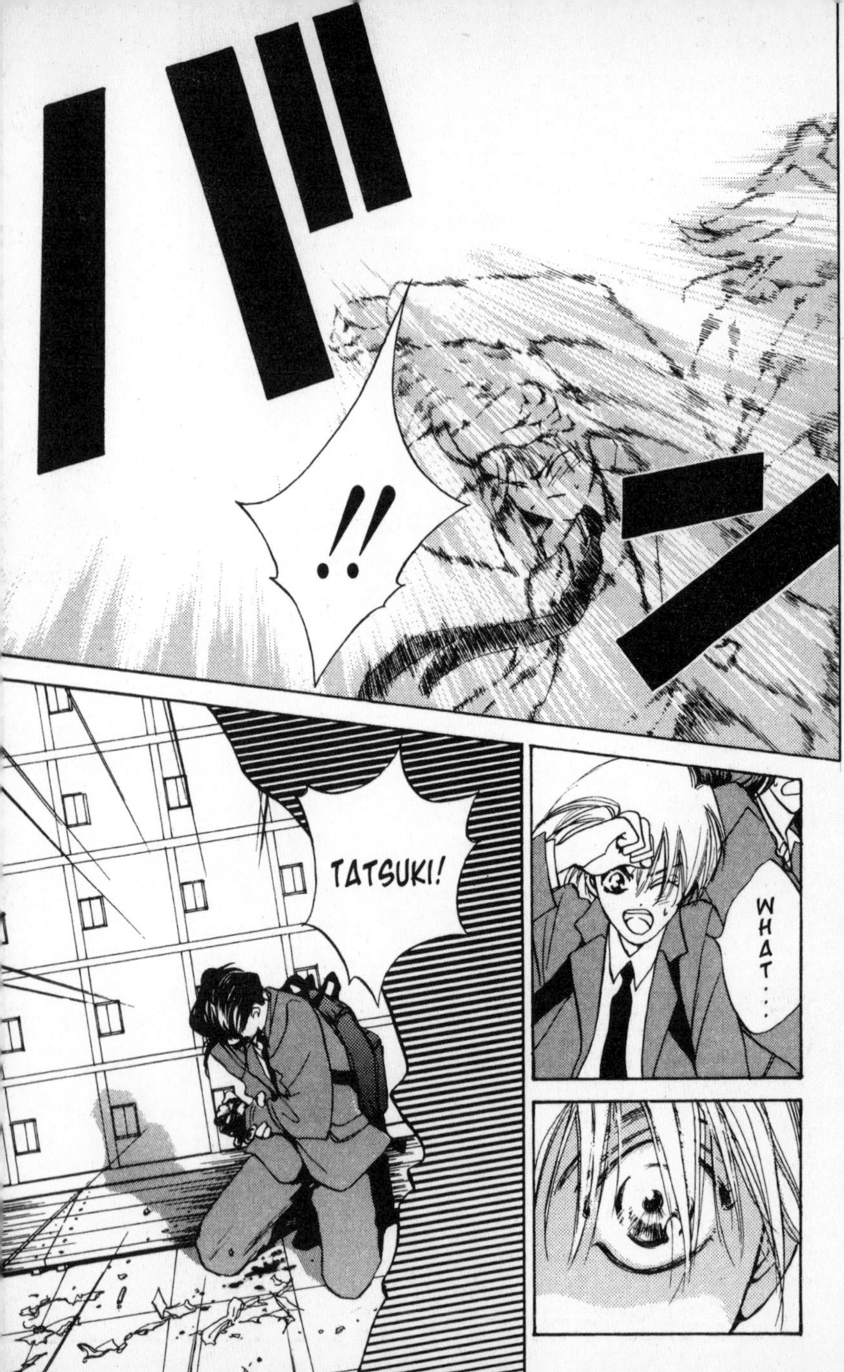
!!
WHAT...
TATSUKI!

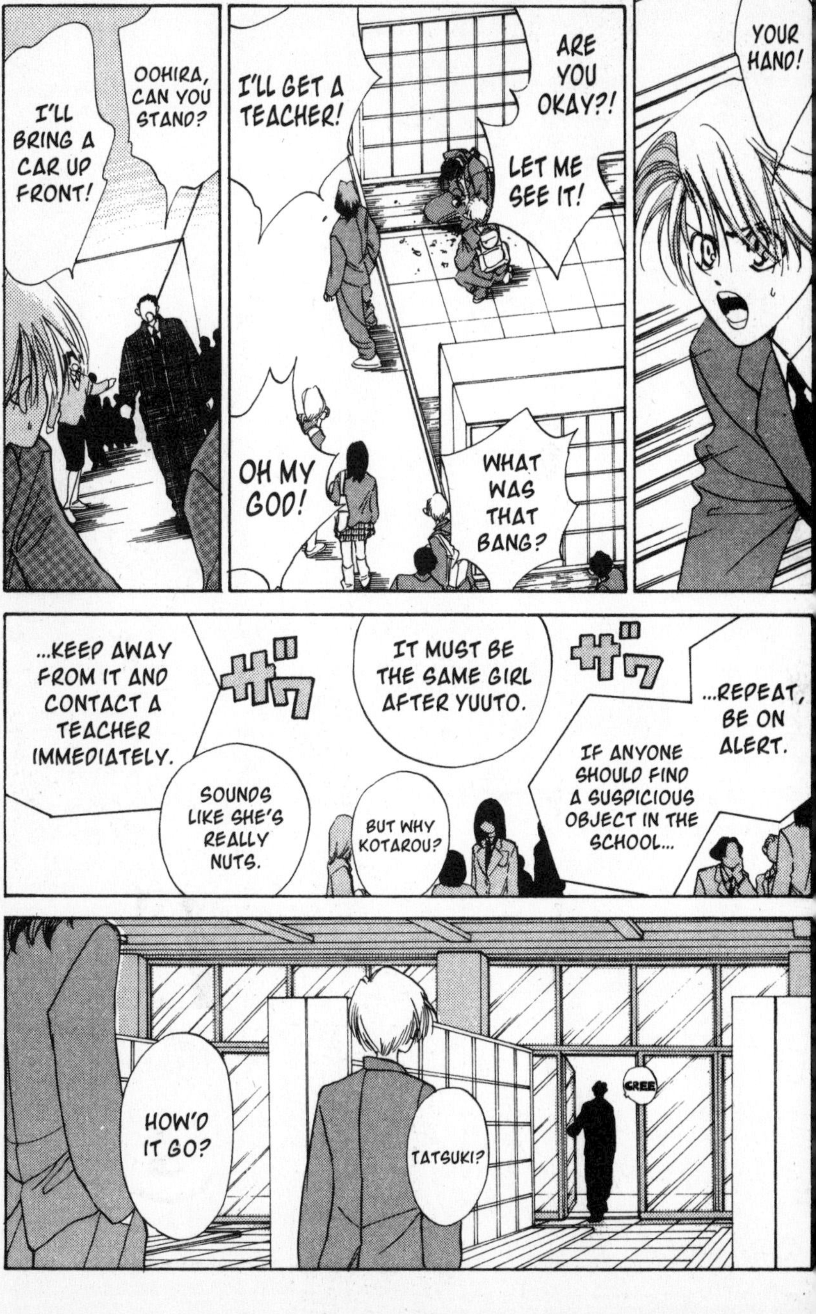
YOUR HAND!
ARE YOU OKAY?!
LET ME SEE IT!
I'LL GET A TEACHER!
WHAT WAS THAT BANG?
OH MY GOD!
OOHIRA, CAN YOU STAND?
I'LL BRING A CAR UP FRONT!
...REPEAT, BE ON ALERT.
IF ANYONE SHOULD FIND A SUSPICIOUS OBJECT IN THE SCHOOL...
ザワ
IT MUST BE THE SAME GIRL AFTER YUUTO.
BUT WHY KOTAROU?
ザワ
SOUNDS LIKE SHE'S REALLY NUTS.
...KEEP AWAY FROM IT AND CONTACT A TEACHER IMMEDIATELY.
GREE
TATSUKI?
HOW'D IT GO?

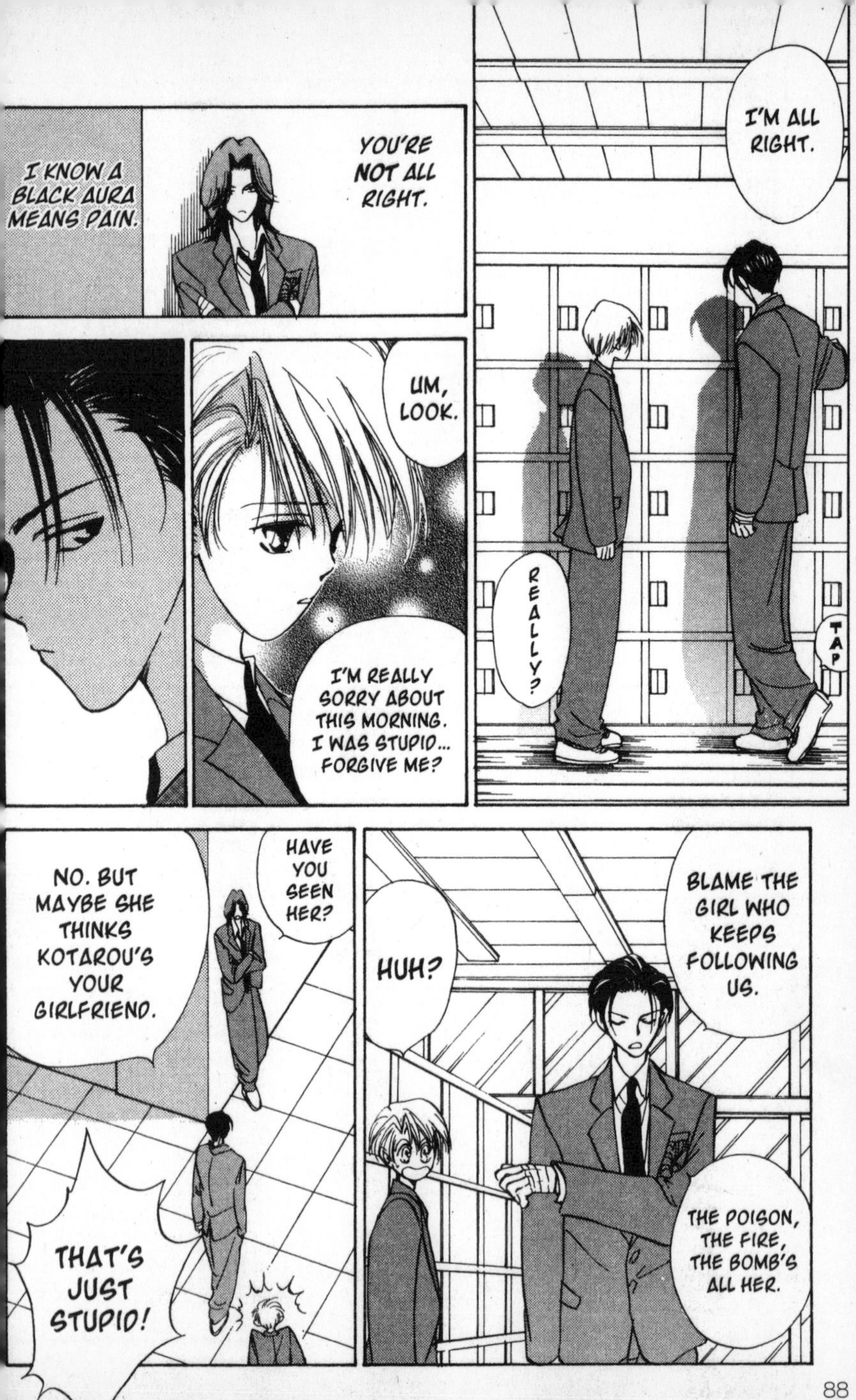
I'M ALL RIGHT.
REALLY?
TAP
YOU'RE NOT ALL RIGHT.
I KNOW A BLACK AURA MEANS PAIN.
UM, LOOK.
I'M REALLY SORRY ABOUT THIS MORNING. I WAS STUPID... FORGIVE ME?
BLAME THE GIRL WHO KEEPS FOLLOWING US.
HUH?
THE POISON, THE FIRE, THE BOMB'S ALL HER.
HAVE YOU SEEN HER?
NO. BUT MAYBE SHE THINKS KOTAROU'S YOUR GIRLFRIEND.
THAT'S JUST STUPID!

ACT 2

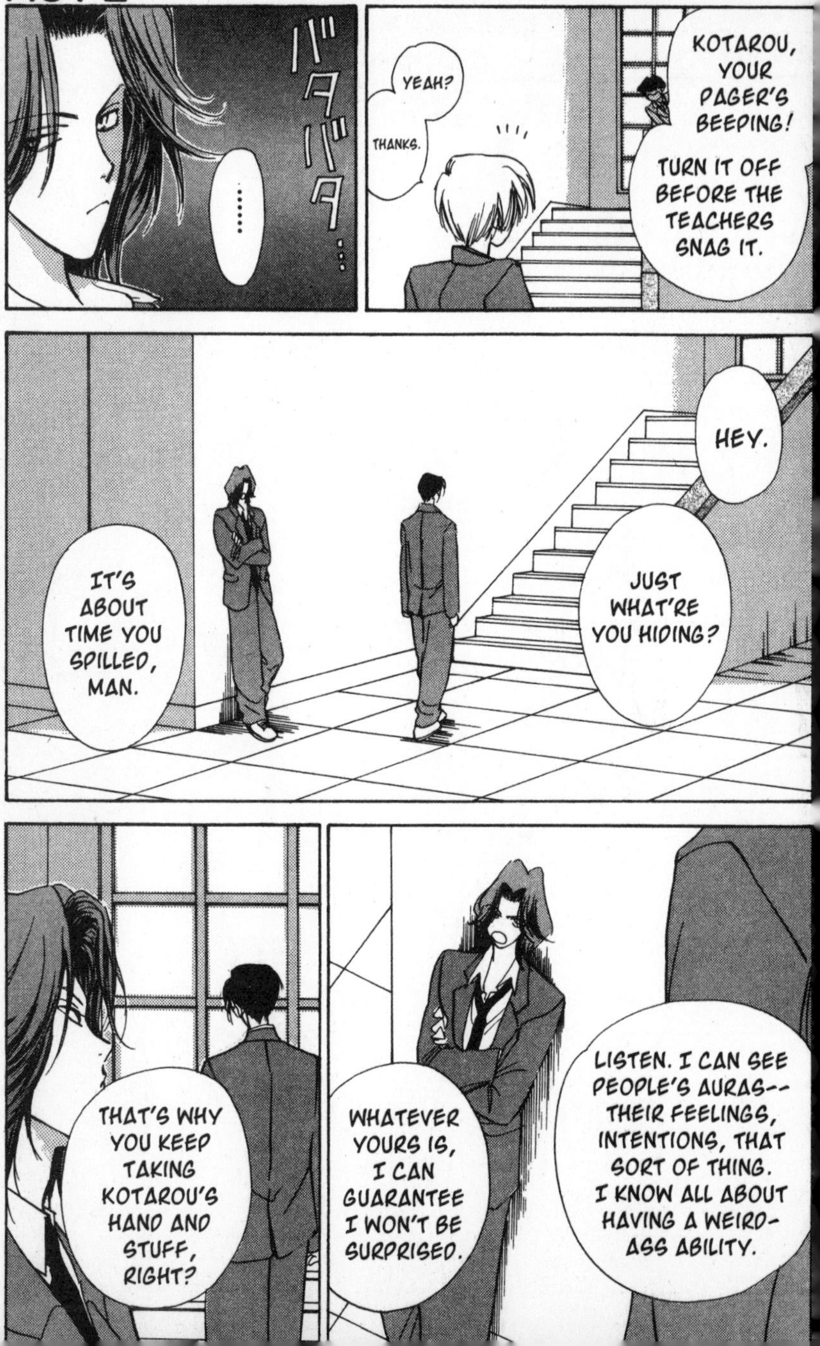
KOTAROU, YOUR PAGER'S BEEPING!
TURN IT OFF BEFORE THE TEACHERS SNAG IT.
YEAH?
THANKS.
バタバタ...
......
HEY.
JUST WHAT'RE YOU HIDING?
IT'S ABOUT TIME YOU SPILLED, MAN.
LISTEN. I CAN SEE PEOPLE'S AURAS--THEIR FEELINGS, INTENTIONS, THAT SORT OF THING. I KNOW ALL ABOUT HAVING A WEIRD-ASS ABILITY.
WHATEVER YOURS IS, I CAN GUARANTEE I WON'T BE SURPRISED.
THAT'S WHY YOU KEEP TAKING KOTAROU'S HAND AND STUFF, RIGHT?

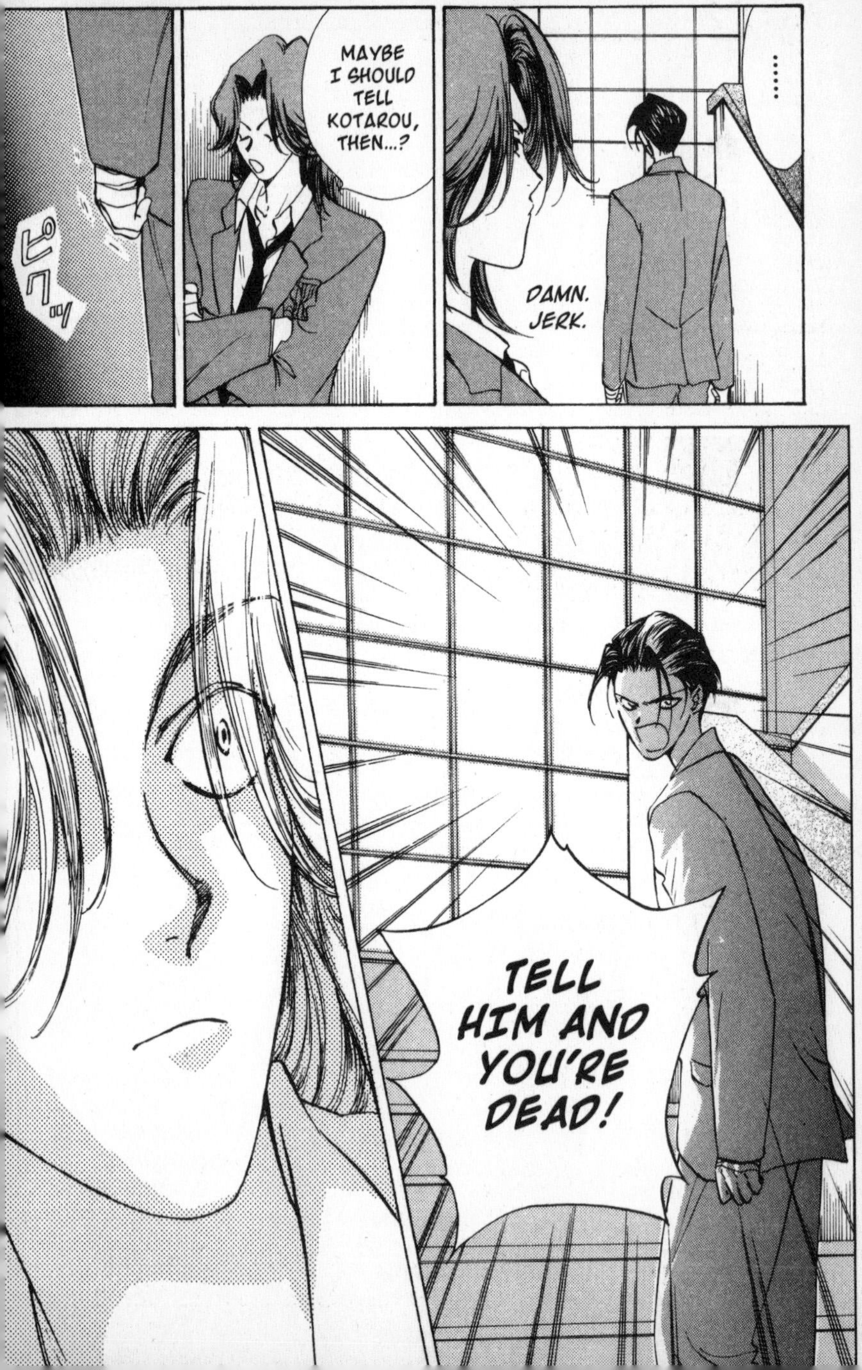
......
DAMN. JERK.
MAYBE I SHOULD TELL KOTAROU, THEN...?
ピクッ
TELL HIM AND YOU'RE DEAD!

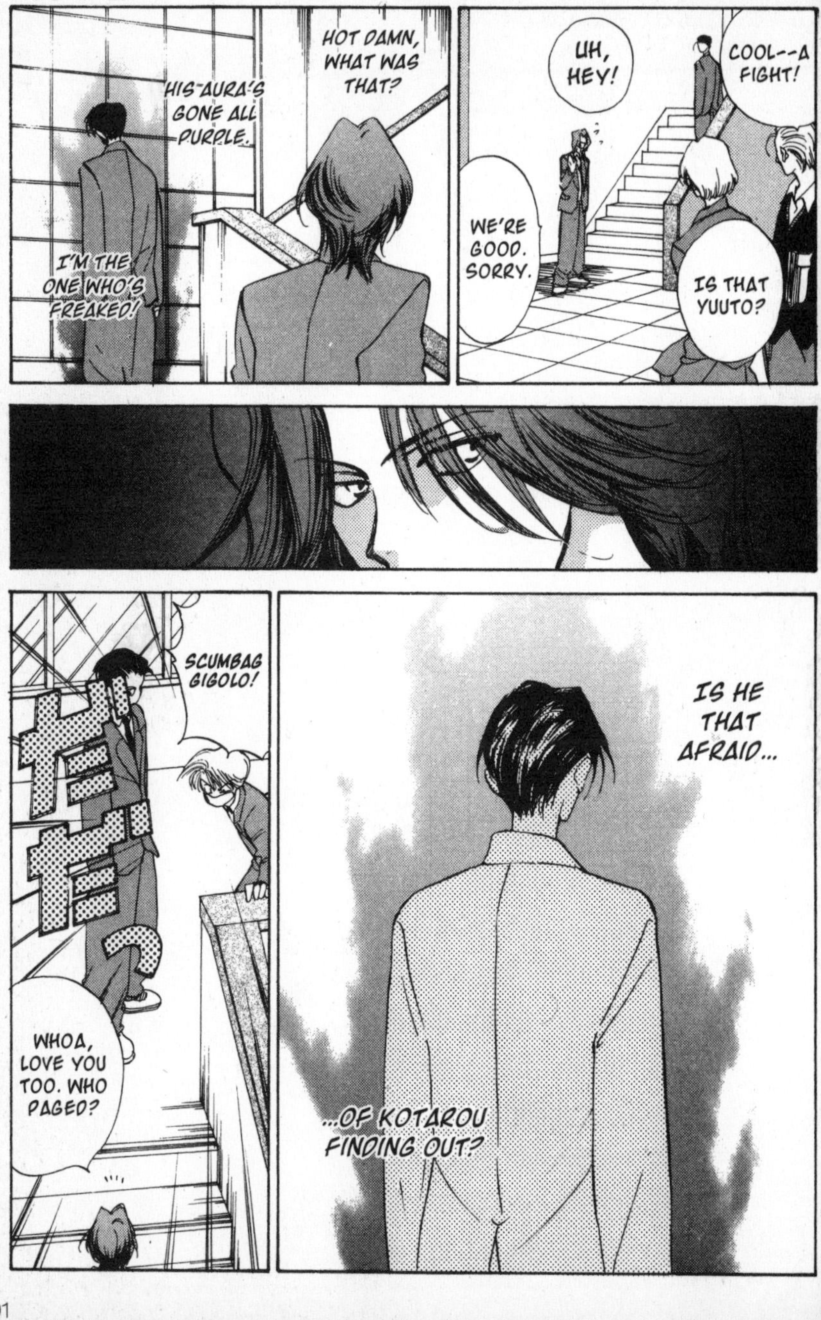
COOL--A FIGHT!
UH, HEY!
IS THAT YUUTO?
WE'RE GOOD. SORRY.
HOT DAMN, WHAT WAS THAT?
HIS AURA'S GONE ALL PURPLE.
I'M THE ONE WHO'S FREAKED!
IS HE THAT AFRAID...
...OF KOTAROU FINDING OUT?
SCUMBAG GIGOLO!
WHOA, LOVE YOU TOO. WHO PAGED?

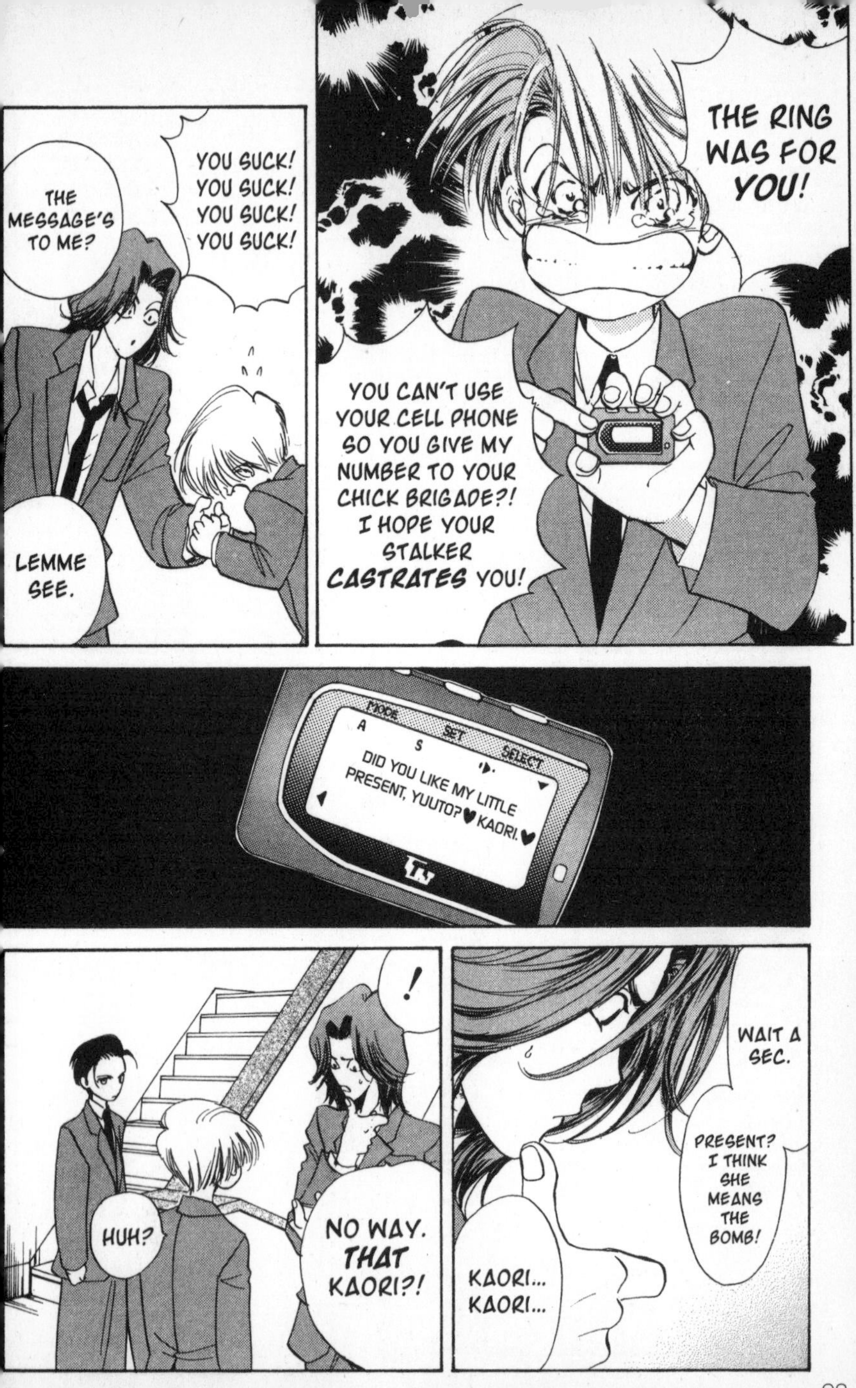
THE RING WAS FOR YOU!
YOU CAN'T USE YOUR CELL PHONE SO YOU GIVE MY NUMBER TO YOUR CHICK BRIGADE?! I HOPE YOUR STALKER CASTRATES YOU!
YOU SUCK! YOU SUCK! YOU SUCK! YOU SUCK!
THE MESSAGE'S TO ME?
LEMME SEE.
MODE
A
SET
S
SELECT
DID YOU LIKE MY LITTLE PRESENT, YUUTO?♥ KAORI.♥
WAIT A SEC.
PRESENT? I THINK SHE MEANS THE BOMB!
KAORI... KAORI...
!
NO WAY. THAT KAORI?!
HUH?

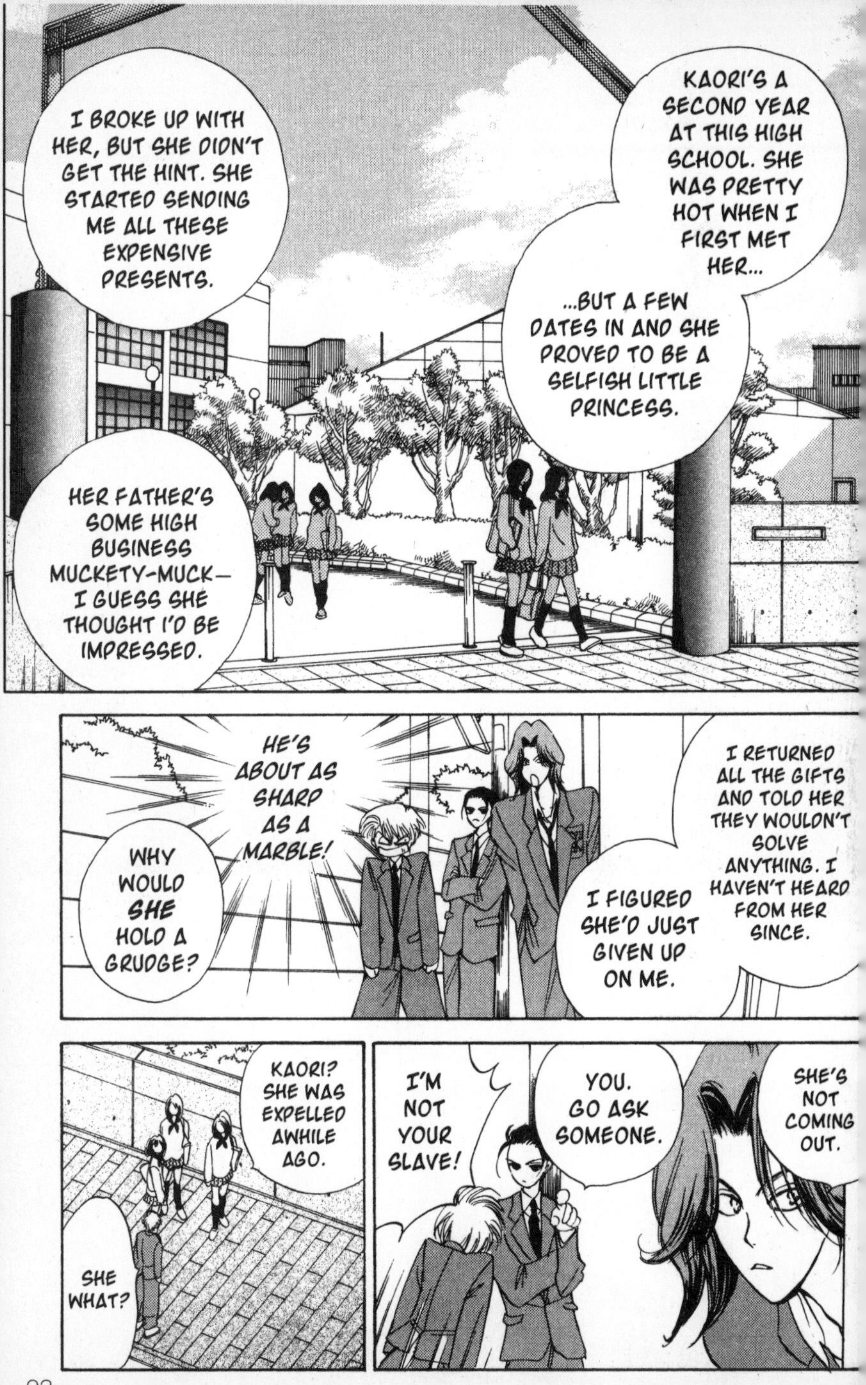
KAORI'S A SECOND YEAR AT THIS HIGH SCHOOL. SHE WAS PRETTY HOT WHEN I FIRST MET HER...
...BUT A FEW DATES IN AND SHE PROVED TO BE A SELFISH LITTLE PRINCESS.
I BROKE UP WITH HER, BUT SHE DIDN'T GET THE HINT. SHE STARTED SENDING ME ALL THESE EXPENSIVE PRESENTS.
HER FATHER'S SOME HIGH BUSINESS MUCKETY-MUCK—I GUESS SHE THOUGHT I'D BE IMPRESSED.
I RETURNED ALL THE GIFTS AND TOLD HER THEY WOULDN'T SOLVE ANYTHING. I HAVEN'T HEARD FROM HER SINCE.
I FIGURED SHE'D JUST GIVEN UP ON ME.
HE'S ABOUT AS SHARP AS A MARBLE!
WHY WOULD **SHE** HOLD A GRUDGE?
SHE'S NOT COMING OUT.
YOU. GO ASK SOMEONE.
I'M NOT YOUR SLAVE!
KAORI? SHE WAS EXPELLED AWHILE AGO.
SHE WHAT?

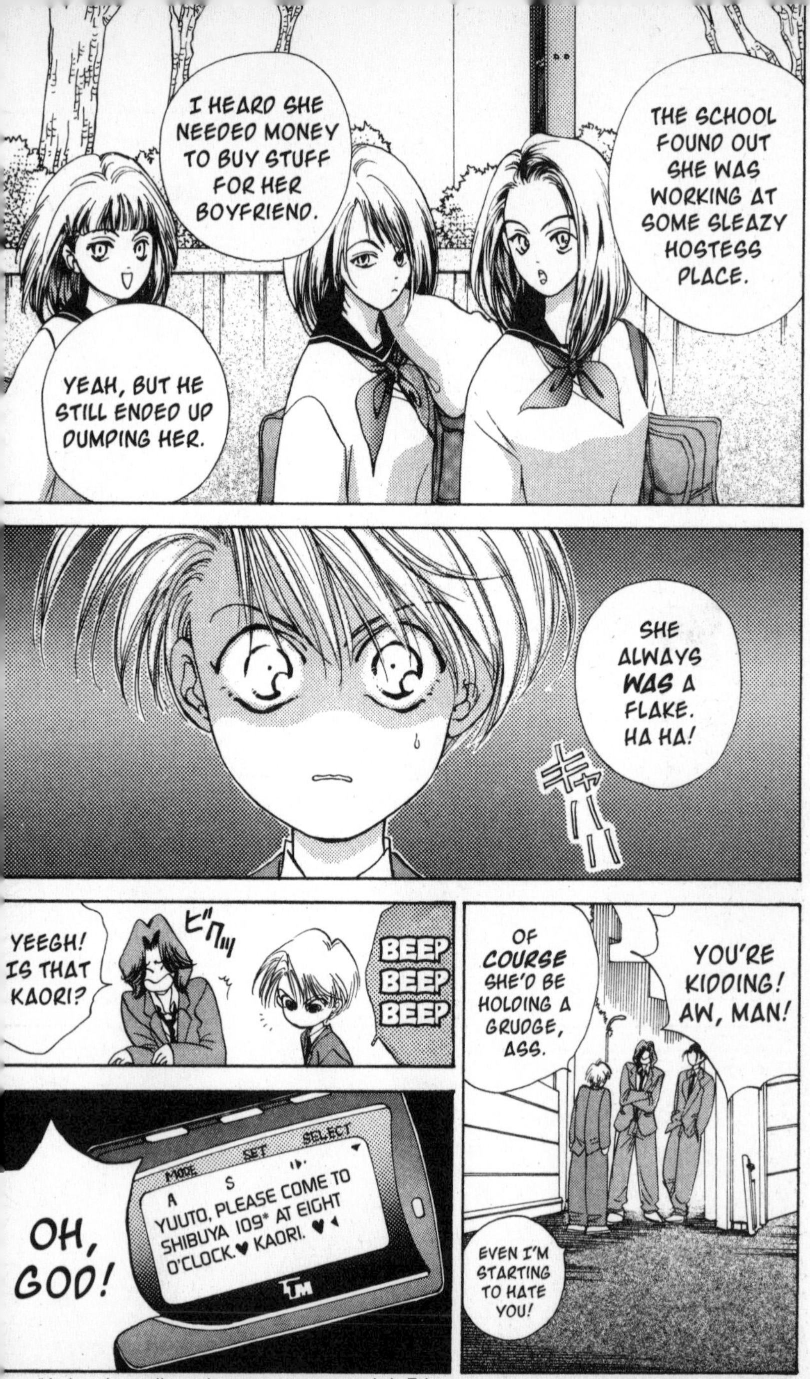
THE SCHOOL FOUND OUT SHE WAS WORKING AT SOME SLEAZY HOSTESS PLACE.
I HEARD SHE NEEDED MONEY TO BUY STUFF FOR HER BOYFRIEND.
YEAH, BUT HE STILL ENDED UP DUMPING HER.
SHE ALWAYS WAS A FLAKE. HA HA!
キャハハ
YOU'RE KIDDING! AW, MAN!
OF COURSE SHE'D BE HOLDING A GRUDGE, ASS.
EVEN I'M STARTING TO HATE YOU!
BEEP BEEP BEEP
ビクッ
YEEGH! IS THAT KAORI?
MODE SET SELECT
YUUTO, PLEASE COME TO SHIBUYA 109* AT EIGHT O'CLOCK.♥ KAORI. ♥
OH, GOD!

*A shopping mall popular among young people in Tokyo.

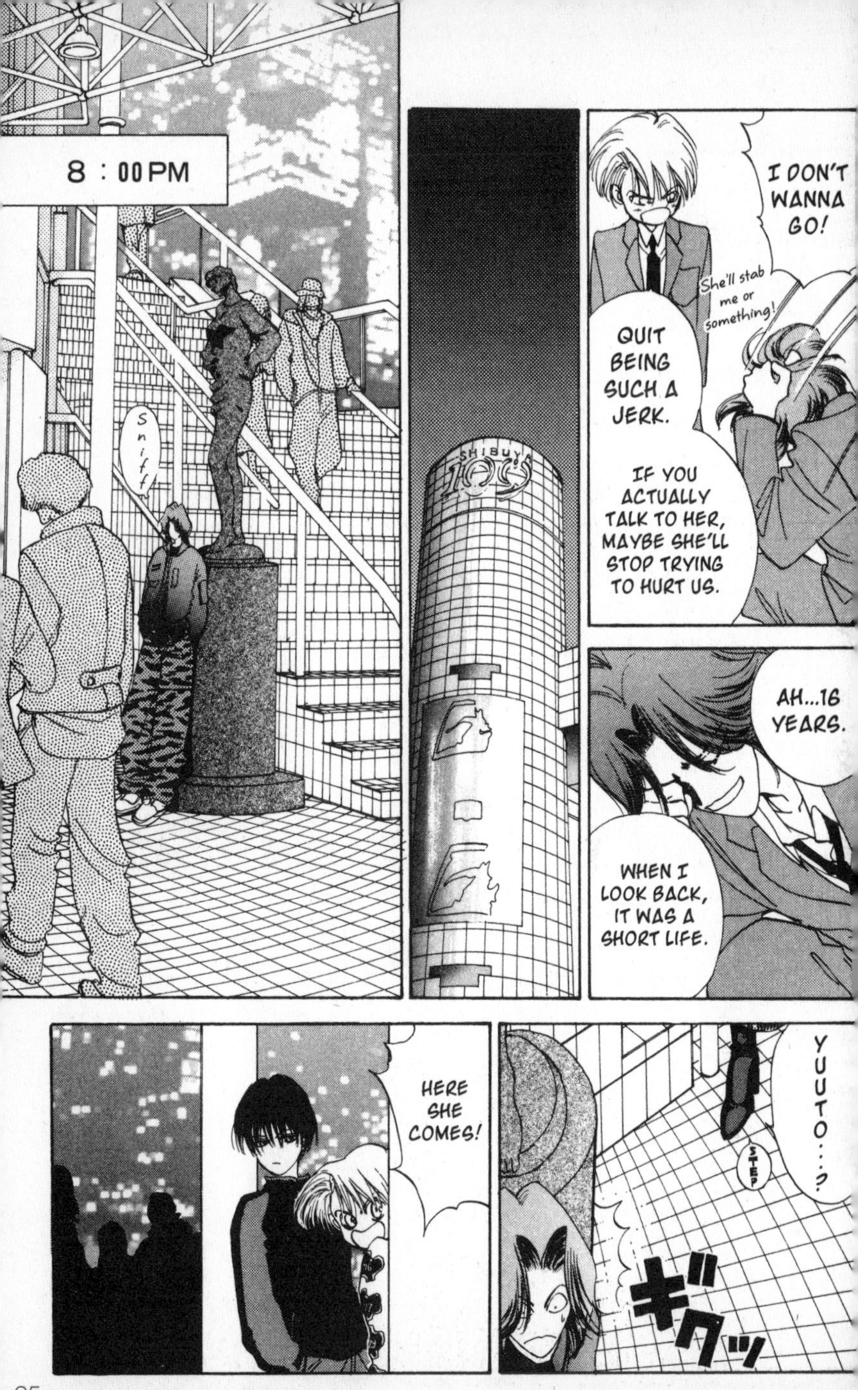
I DON'T WANNA GO!
She'll stab me or something!
QUIT BEING SUCH A JERK.
IF YOU ACTUALLY TALK TO HER, MAYBE SHE'LL STOP TRYING TO HURT US.
AH...16 YEARS.
WHEN I LOOK BACK, IT WAS A SHORT LIFE.
SHIBUYA 109
8 : 00 PM
Sniff
YUUTO...?
STEP
ギクッ
HERE SHE COMES!

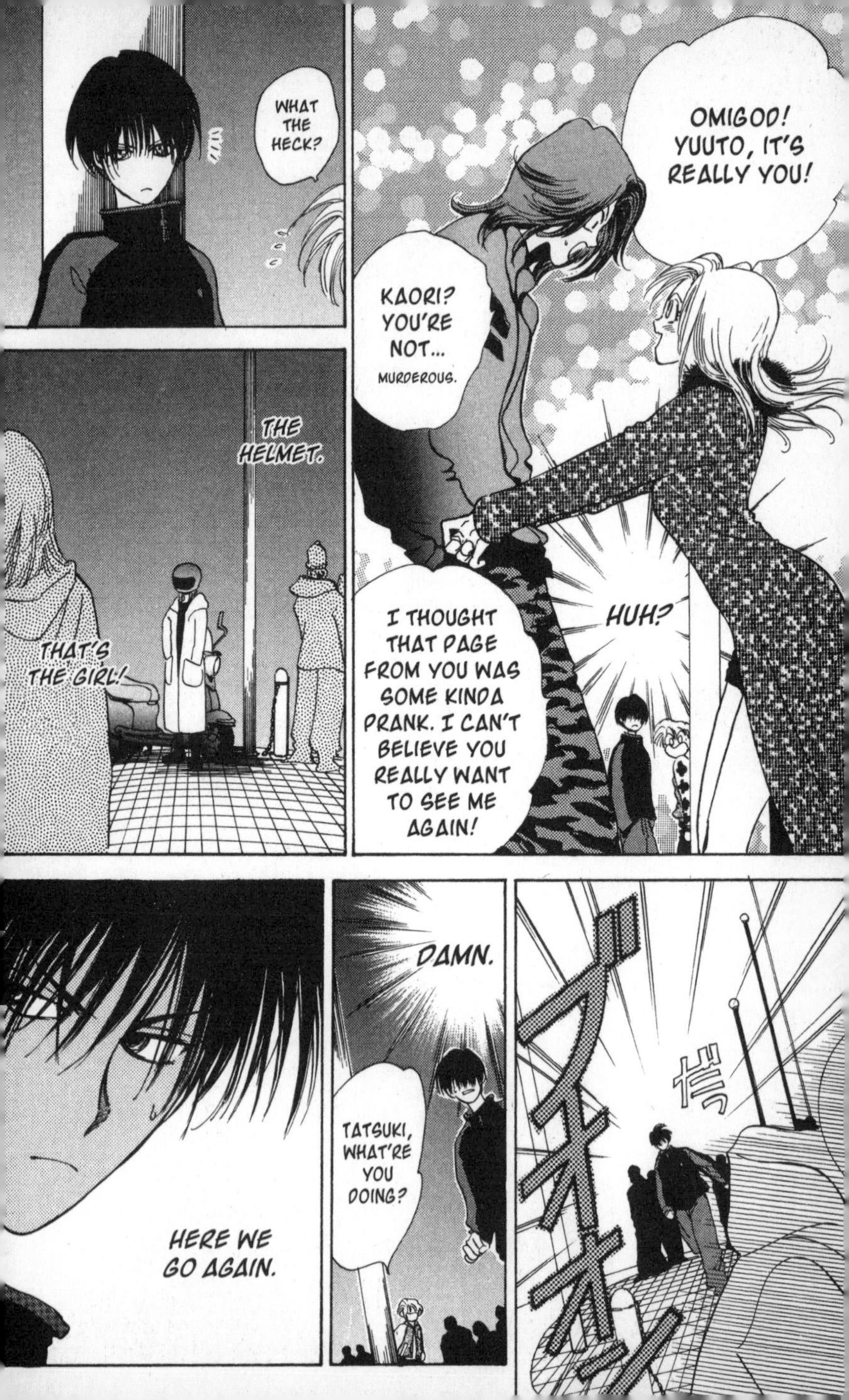
OMIGOD! YUUTO, IT'S REALLY YOU!
KAORI? YOU'RE NOT... MURDEROUS.
HUH?
I THOUGHT THAT PAGE FROM YOU WAS SOME KINDA PRANK. I CAN'T BELIEVE YOU REALLY WANT TO SEE ME AGAIN!
WHAT THE HECK?
THE HELMET.
THAT'S THE GIRL!
DAMN.
TATSUKI, WHAT'RE YOU DOING?
HERE WE GO AGAIN.

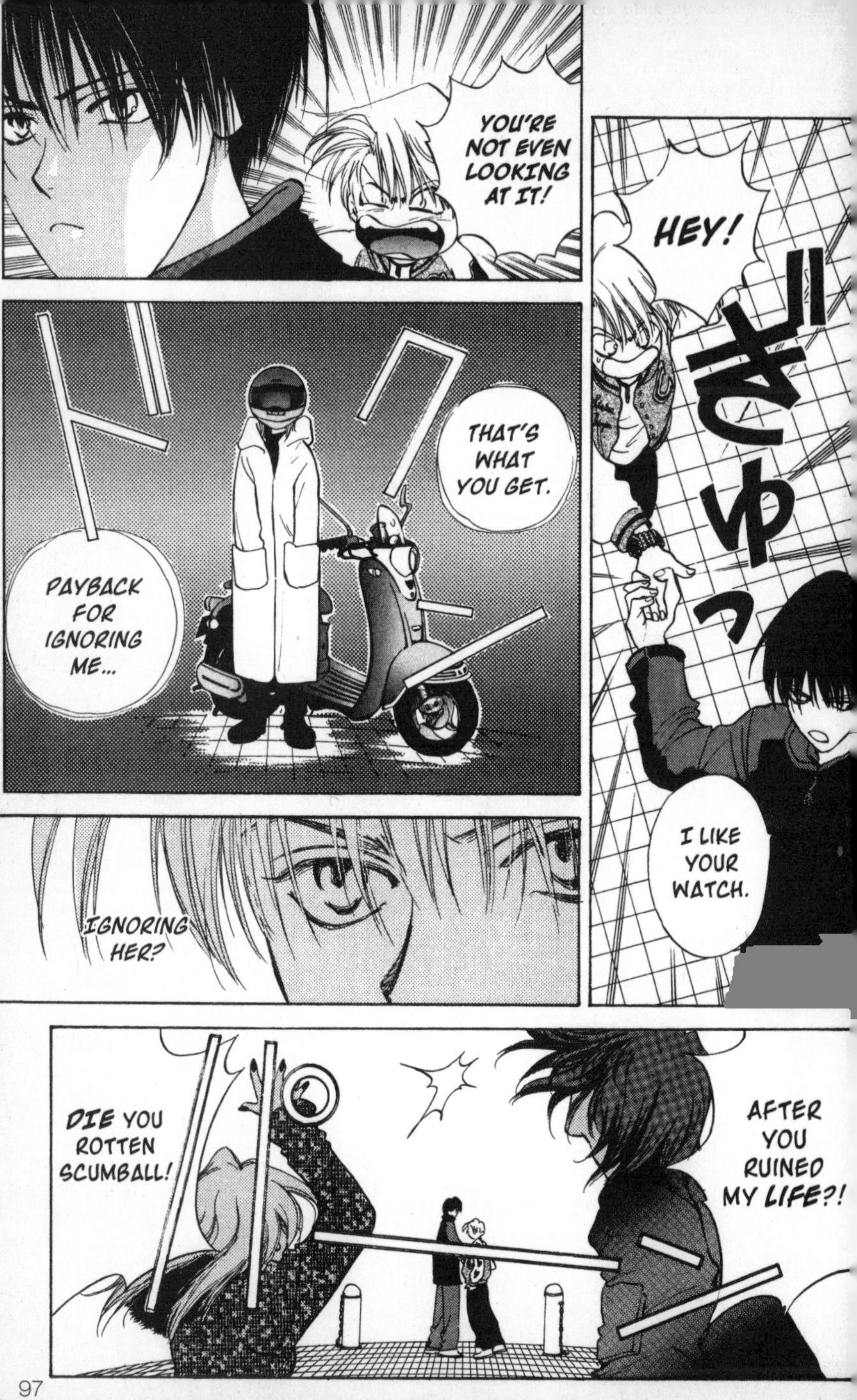
HEY!
ぎゅっ
I LIKE YOUR WATCH.
YOU'RE NOT EVEN LOOKING AT IT!
THAT'S WHAT YOU GET.
PAYBACK FOR IGNORING ME...
IGNORING HER?
AFTER YOU RUINED MY *LIFE*?!
DIE YOU ROTTEN SCUMBALL!

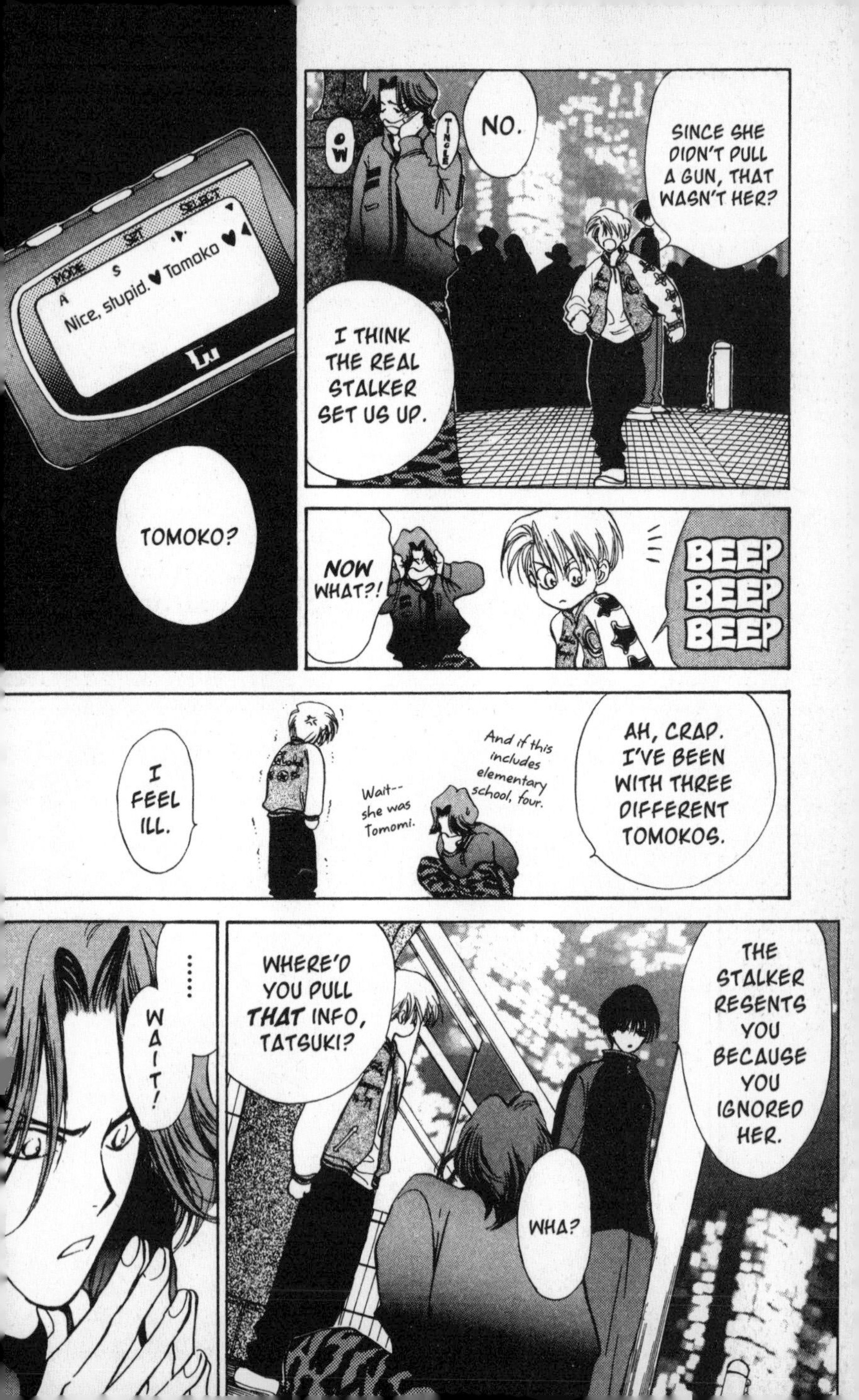
SINCE SHE DIDN'T PULL A GUN, THAT WASN'T HER?
NO.
TINGLE
OW
I THINK THE REAL STALKER SET US UP.
BEEP BEEP BEEP
NOW WHAT?!
MODE SET SELECT
Nice, stupid. ♥ Tomoko ♥
TOMOKO?
AH, CRAP. I'VE BEEN WITH THREE DIFFERENT TOMOKOS.
And if this includes elementary school, four.
Wait-- she was Tomomi.
I FEEL ILL.
THE STALKER RESENTS YOU BECAUSE YOU IGNORED HER.
WHA?
WHERE'D YOU PULL THAT INFO, TATSUKI?
......
WAIT!

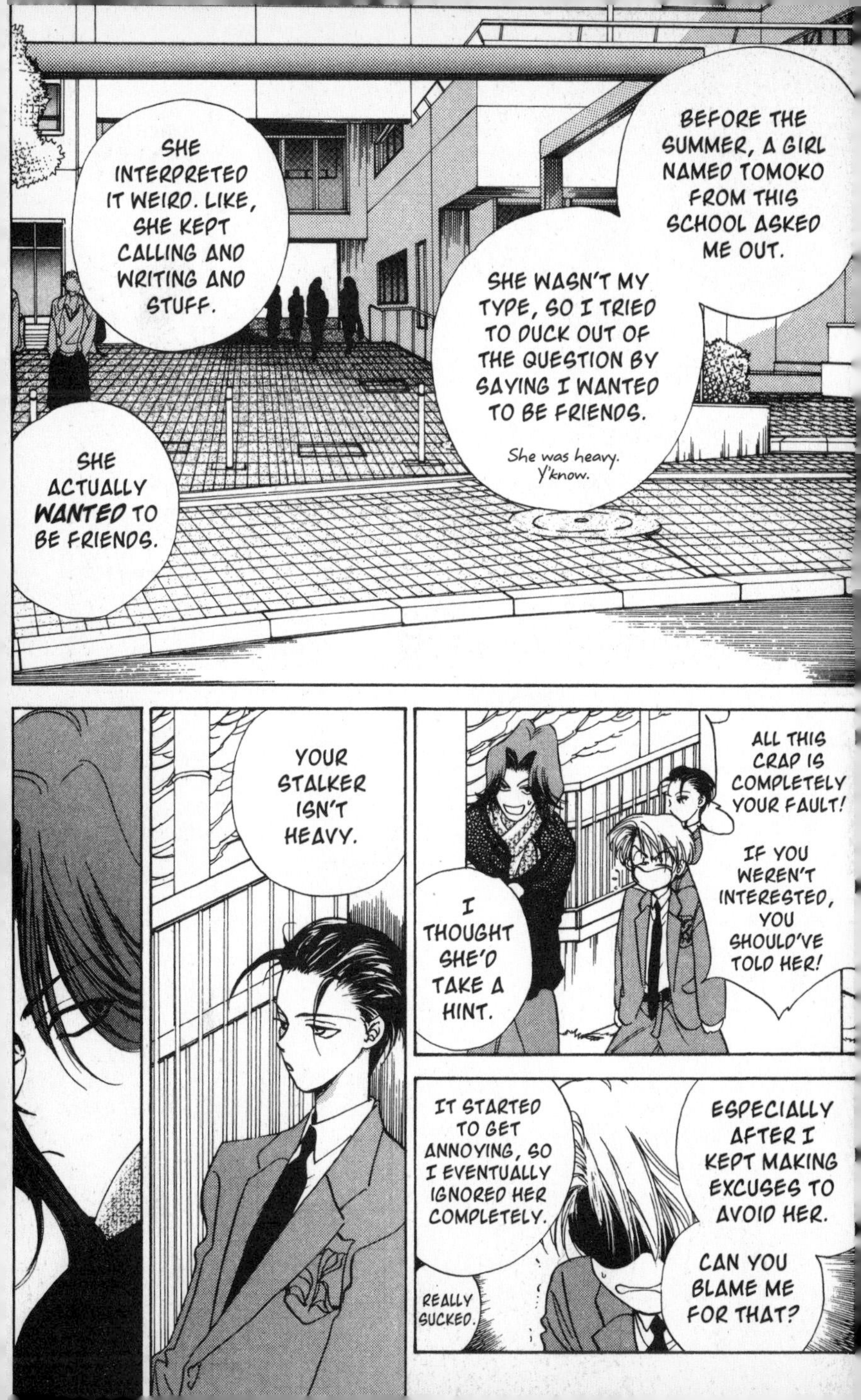
BEFORE THE SUMMER, A GIRL NAMED TOMOKO FROM THIS SCHOOL ASKED ME OUT.
SHE WASN'T MY TYPE, SO I TRIED TO DUCK OUT OF THE QUESTION BY SAYING I WANTED TO BE FRIENDS.
She was heavy. Y'know.
SHE INTERPRETED IT WEIRD. LIKE, SHE KEPT CALLING AND WRITING AND STUFF.
SHE ACTUALLY **WANTED** TO BE FRIENDS.
ALL THIS CRAP IS COMPLETELY YOUR FAULT!
IF YOU WEREN'T INTERESTED, YOU SHOULD'VE TOLD HER!
I THOUGHT SHE'D TAKE A HINT.
ESPECIALLY AFTER I KEPT MAKING EXCUSES TO AVOID HER.
CAN YOU BLAME ME FOR THAT?
IT STARTED TO GET ANNOYING, SO I EVENTUALLY IGNORED HER COMPLETELY.
REALLY SUCKED.
YOUR STALKER ISN'T HEAVY.

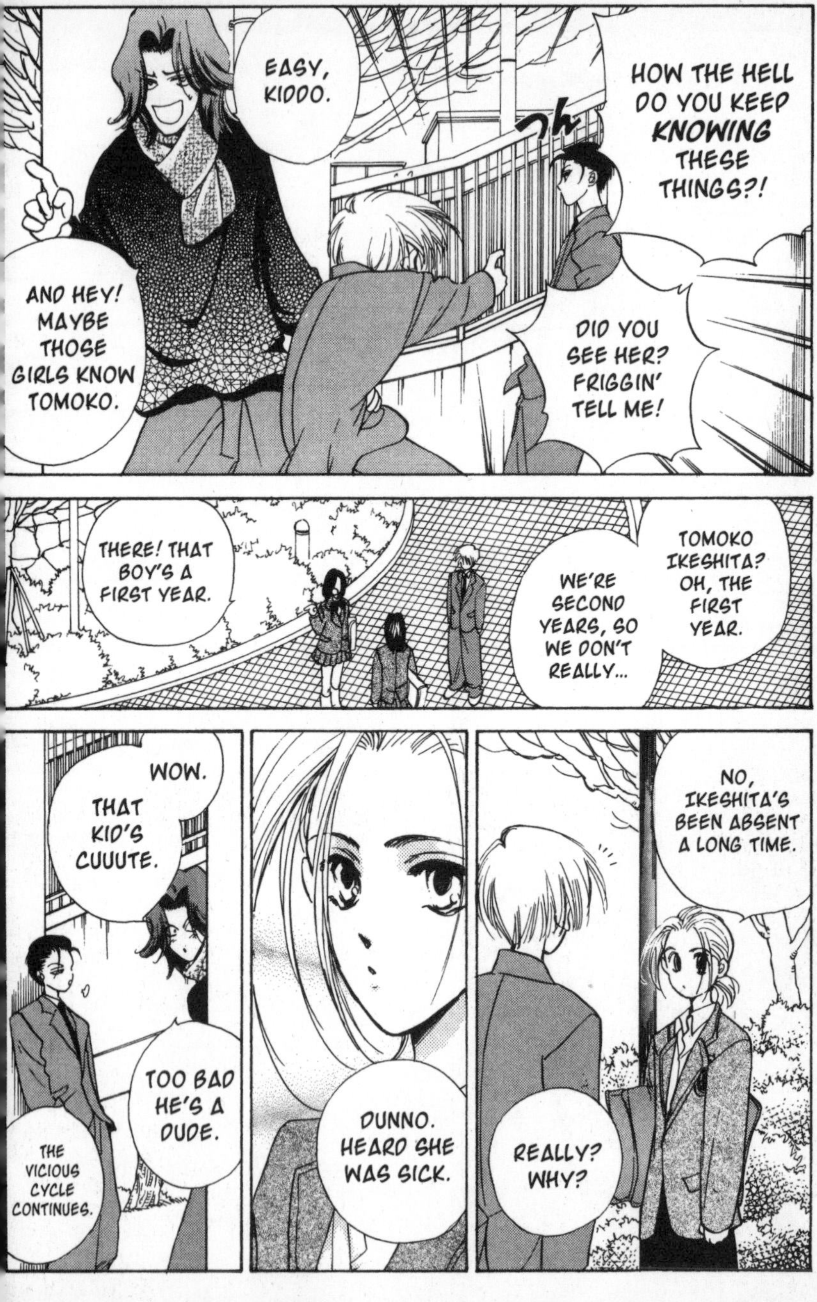
HOW THE HELL DO YOU KEEP KNOWING THESE THINGS?!
つん
EASY, KIDDO.
DID YOU SEE HER? FRIGGIN' TELL ME!
AND HEY! MAYBE THOSE GIRLS KNOW TOMOKO.
TOMOKO IKESHITA? OH, THE FIRST YEAR.
WE'RE SECOND YEARS, SO WE DON'T REALLY...
THERE! THAT BOY'S A FIRST YEAR.
NO, IKESHITA'S BEEN ABSENT A LONG TIME.
REALLY? WHY?
DUNNO. HEARD SHE WAS SICK.
WOW. THAT KID'S CUUUTE.
TOO BAD HE'S A DUDE.
THE VICIOUS CYCLE CONTINUES.

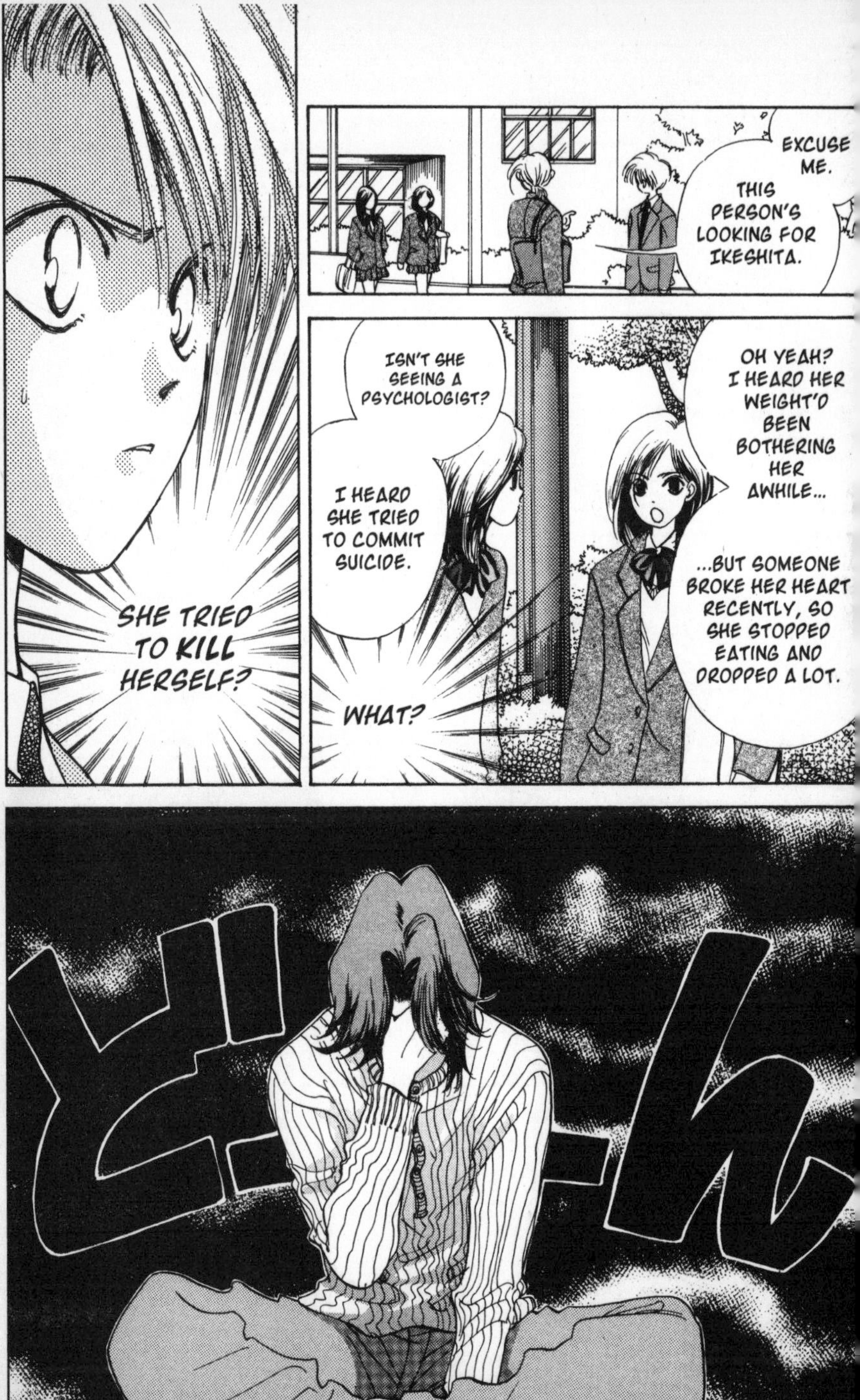
EXCUSE ME.
THIS PERSON'S LOOKING FOR IKESHITA.
OH YEAH? I HEARD HER WEIGHT'D BEEN BOTHERING HER AWHILE...
...BUT SOMEONE BROKE HER HEART RECENTLY, SO SHE STOPPED EATING AND DROPPED A LOT.
ISN'T SHE SEEING A PSYCHOLOGIST?
I HEARD SHE TRIED TO COMMIT SUICIDE.
WHAT?
SHE TRIED TO KILL HERSELF?
どーん

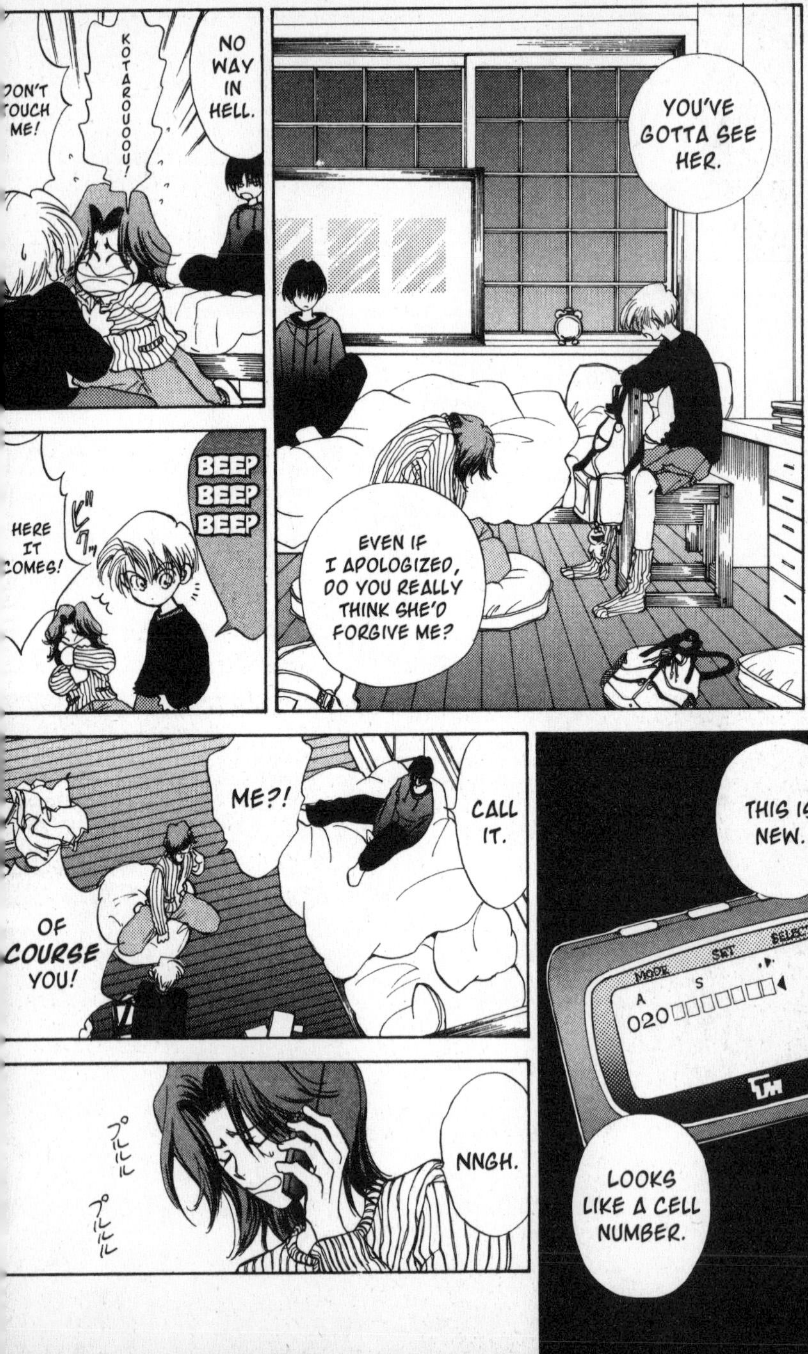
YOU'VE GOTTA SEE HER.
EVEN IF I APOLOGIZED, DO YOU REALLY THINK SHE'D FORGIVE ME?
NO WAY IN HELL.
KOTAROUUUU!
DON'T TOUCH ME!
BEEP BEEP BEEP
HERE IT COMES!
THIS IS NEW.
MODE SET SELECT
A S
020
LOOKS LIKE A CELL NUMBER.
CALL IT.
ME?!
OF COURSE YOU!
NNGH.
プルルル
プルルル

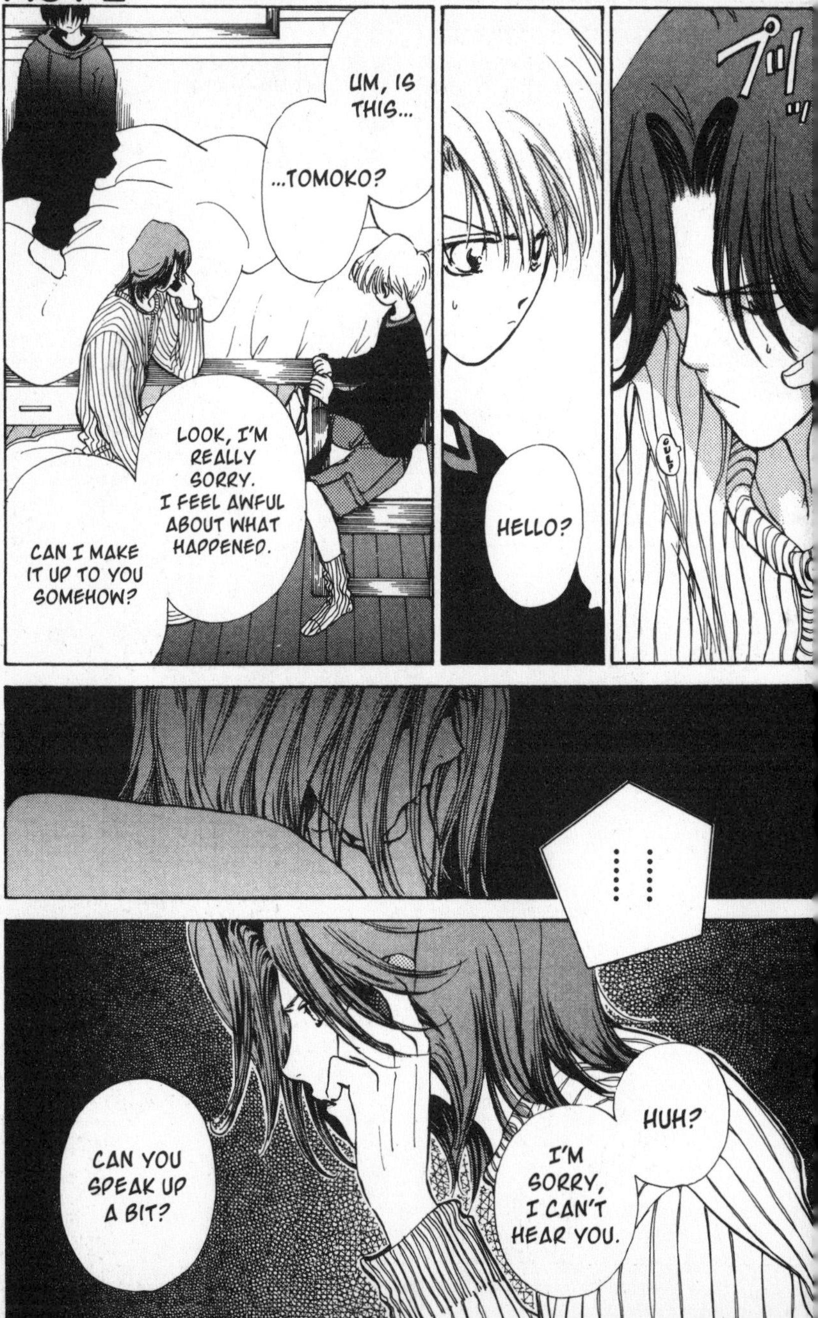
GULP
HELLO?
UM, IS THIS...
...TOMOKO?
LOOK, I'M REALLY SORRY. I FEEL AWFUL ABOUT WHAT HAPPENED.
CAN I MAKE IT UP TO YOU SOMEHOW?
......
HUH?
I'M SORRY, I CAN'T HEAR YOU.
CAN YOU SPEAK UP A BIT?

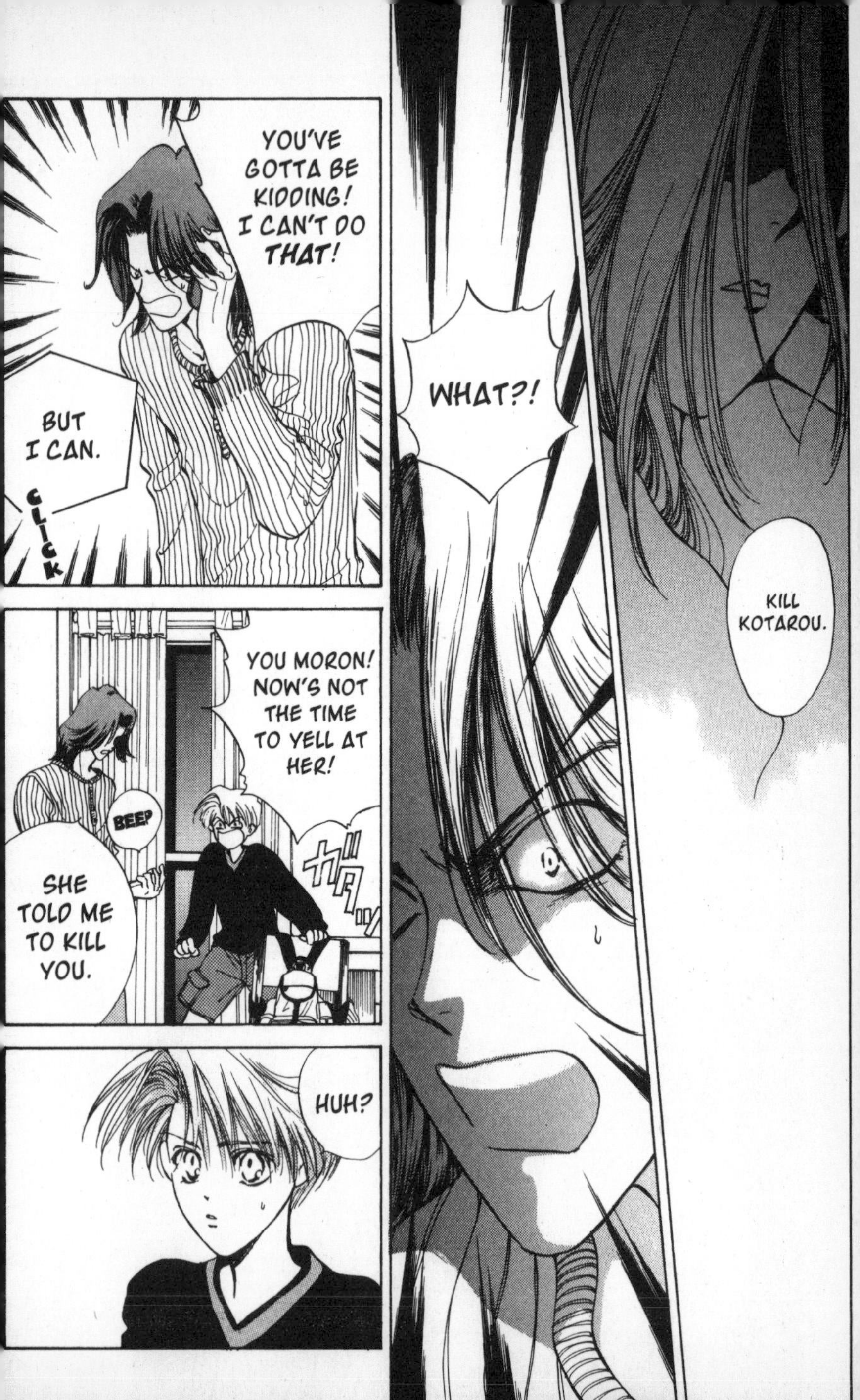
KILL KOTAROU.
WHAT?!
YOU'VE GOTTA BE KIDDING! I CAN'T DO *THAT*!
BUT I CAN.
CLICK
YOU MORON! NOW'S NOT THE TIME TO YELL AT HER!
ガタッ
BEEP
SHE TOLD ME TO KILL YOU.
HUH?

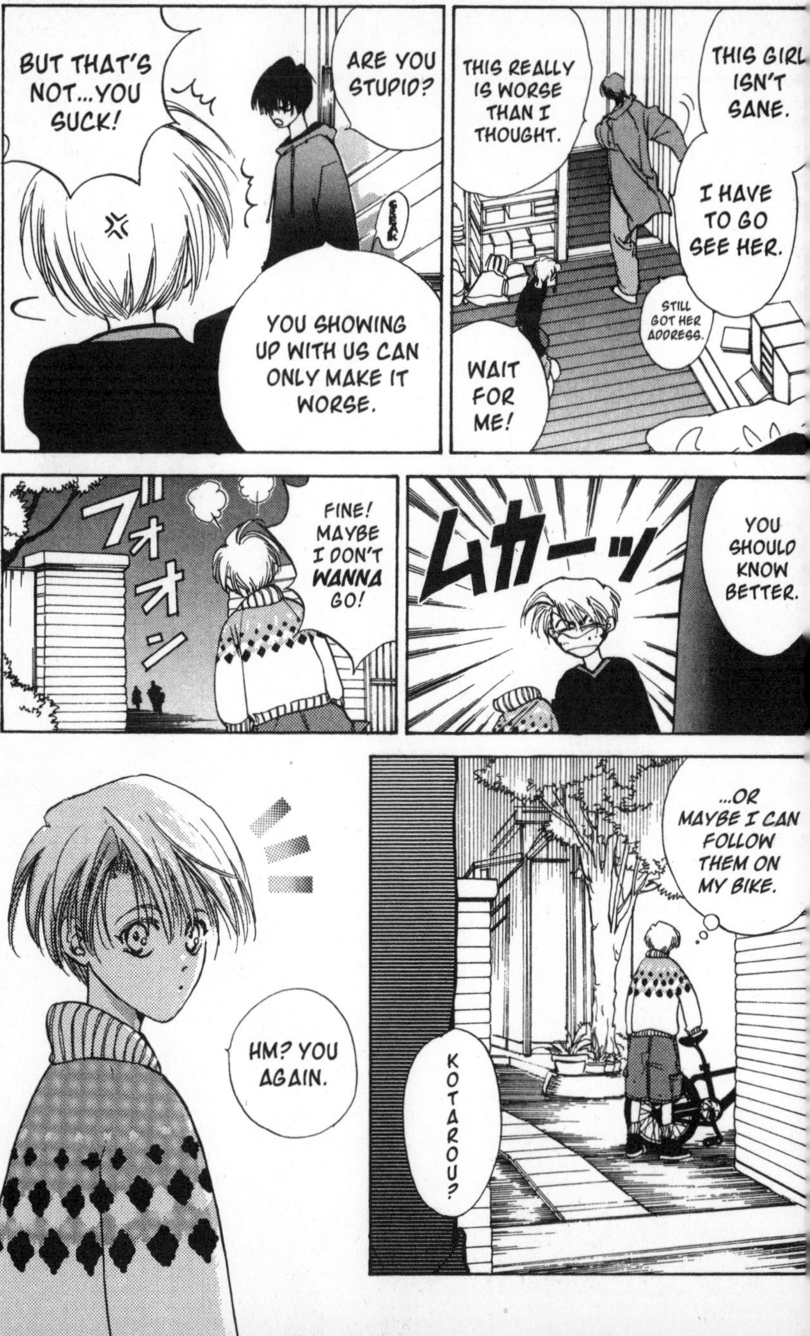
THIS GIRL ISN'T SANE.
THIS REALLY IS WORSE THAN I THOUGHT.
I HAVE TO GO SEE HER.
STILL GOT HER ADDRESS.
WAIT FOR ME!
ARE YOU STUPID?
BUT THAT'S NOT...YOU SUCK!
YOU SHOWING UP WITH US CAN ONLY MAKE IT WORSE.
ムカーッ
YOU SHOULD KNOW BETTER.
ブォオン
FINE! MAYBE I DON'T WANNA GO!
...OR MAYBE I CAN FOLLOW THEM ON MY BIKE.
KOTAROU?
HM? YOU AGAIN.

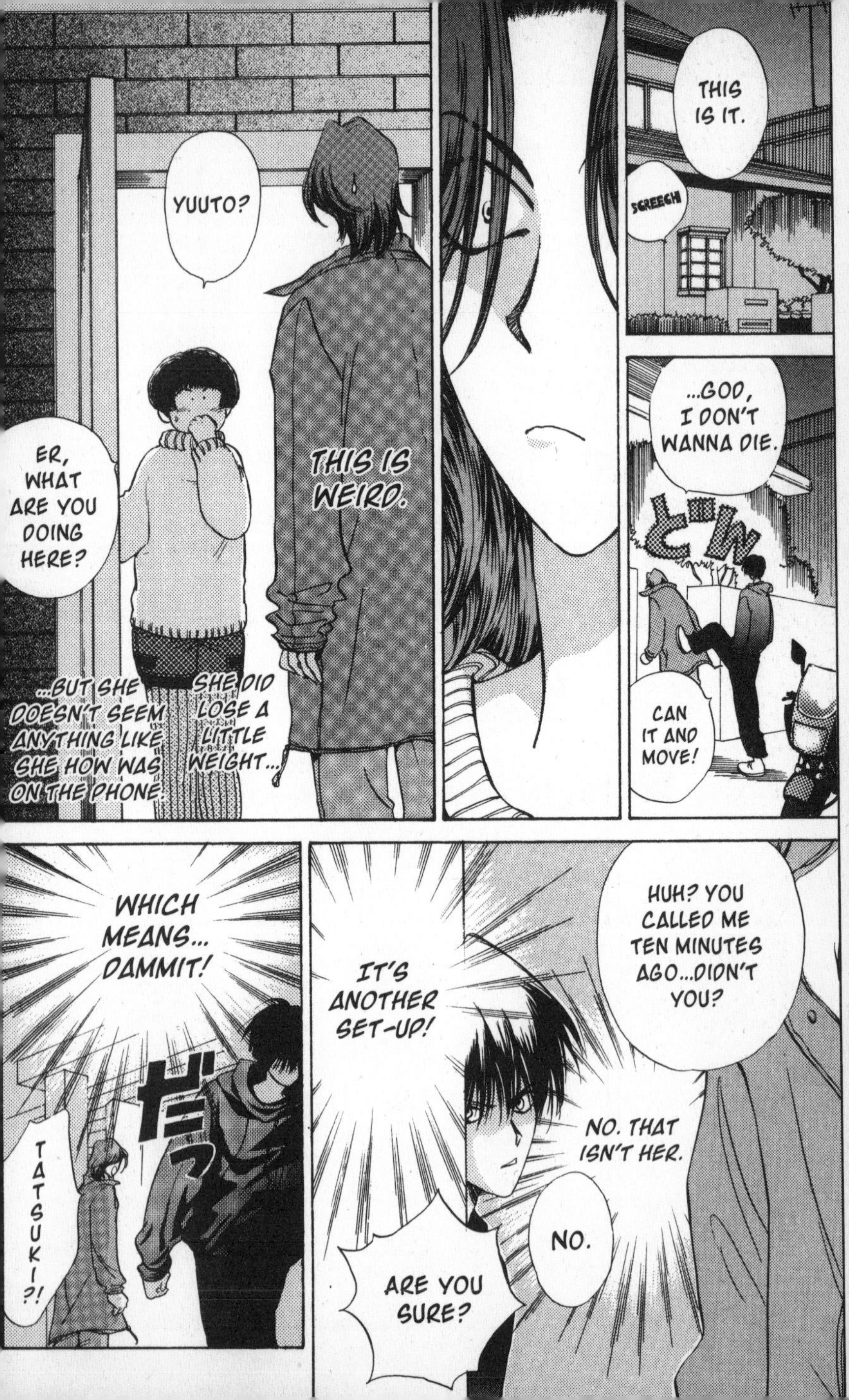
THIS IS IT.
SCREECH
...GOD, I DON'T WANNA DIE.
CAN IT AND MOVE!
YUUTO?
ER, WHAT ARE YOU DOING HERE?
THIS IS WEIRD.
SHE DID LOSE A LITTLE WEIGHT...
...BUT SHE DOESN'T SEEM ANYTHING LIKE SHE HOW WAS ON THE PHONE.
HUH? YOU CALLED ME TEN MINUTES AGO...DIDN'T YOU?
NO. THAT ISN'T HER.
NO.
ARE YOU SURE?
IT'S ANOTHER SET-UP!
WHICH MEANS... DAMMIT!
TATSUKI?!

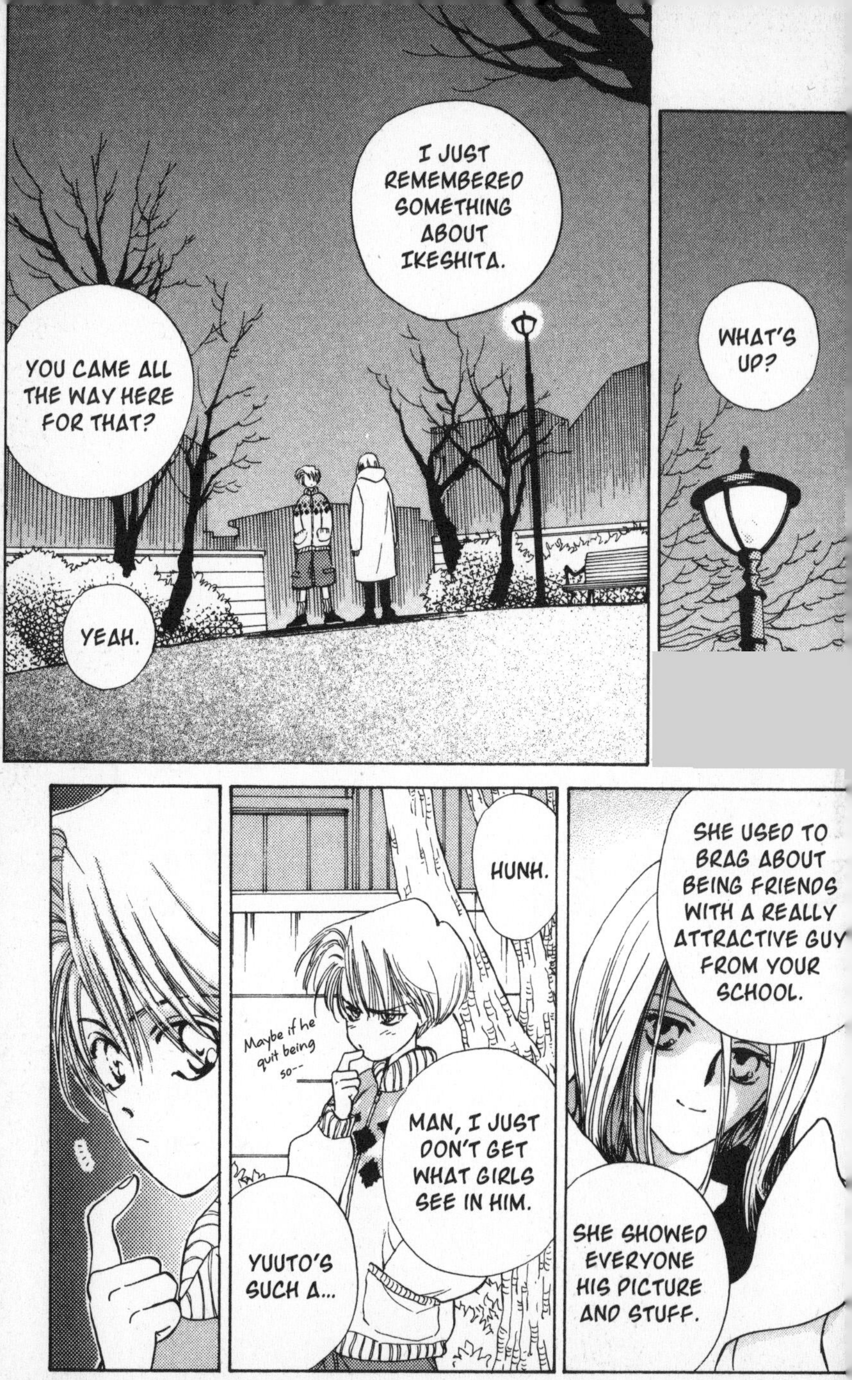
WHAT'S UP?
I JUST REMEMBERED SOMETHING ABOUT IKESHITA.
YOU CAME ALL THE WAY HERE FOR THAT?
YEAH.
SHE USED TO BRAG ABOUT BEING FRIENDS WITH A REALLY ATTRACTIVE GUY FROM YOUR SCHOOL.
SHE SHOWED EVERYONE HIS PICTURE AND STUFF.
HUNH.
MAN, I JUST DON'T GET WHAT GIRLS SEE IN HIM.
Maybe if he quit being so--
YUUTO'S SUCH A...
...

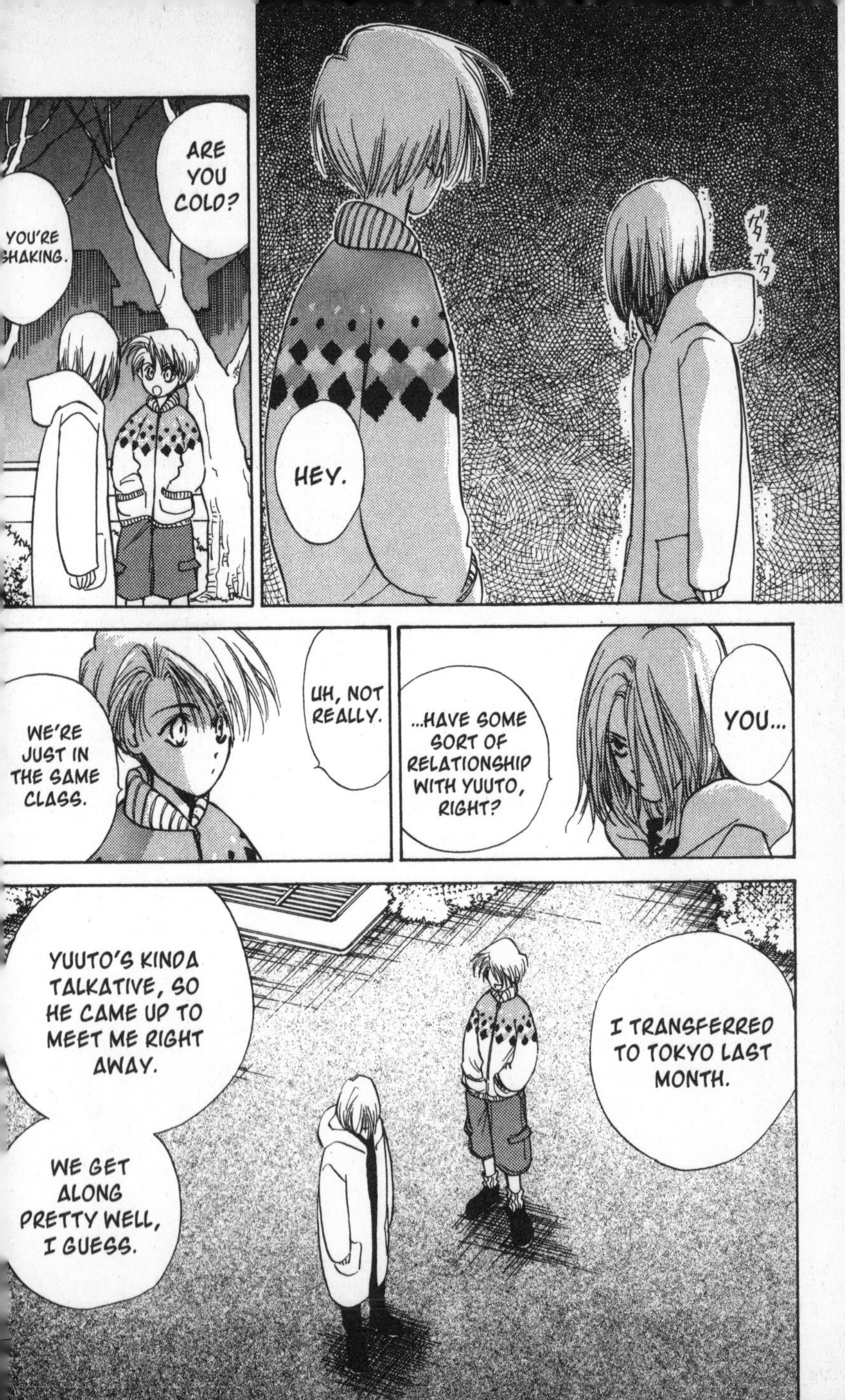
ガタ ガタ
HEY.
ARE YOU COLD?
YOU'RE SHAKING.
YOU...
...HAVE SOME SORT OF RELATIONSHIP WITH YUUTO, RIGHT?
UH, NOT REALLY.
WE'RE JUST IN THE SAME CLASS.
I TRANSFERRED TO TOKYO LAST MONTH.
YUUTO'S KINDA TALKATIVE, SO HE CAME UP TO MEET ME RIGHT AWAY.
WE GET ALONG PRETTY WELL, I GUESS.

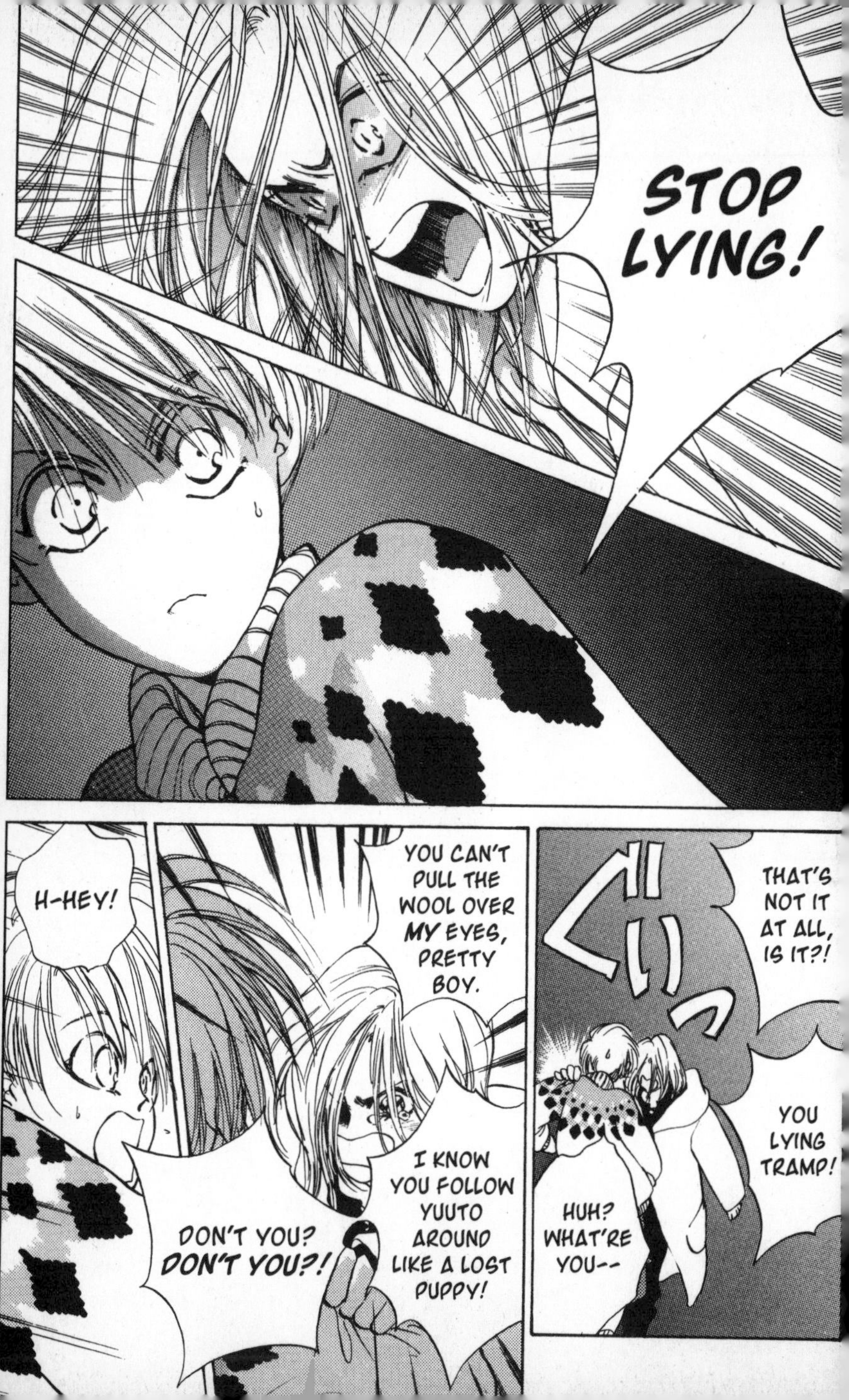
STOP LYING!
ぐいっ
THAT'S NOT IT AT ALL, IS IT?!
YOU LYING TRAMP!
HUH? WHAT'RE YOU--
YOU CAN'T PULL THE WOOL OVER MY EYES, PRETTY BOY.
I KNOW YOU FOLLOW YUUTO AROUND LIKE A LOST PUPPY!
H-HEY!
DON'T YOU? DON'T YOU?!

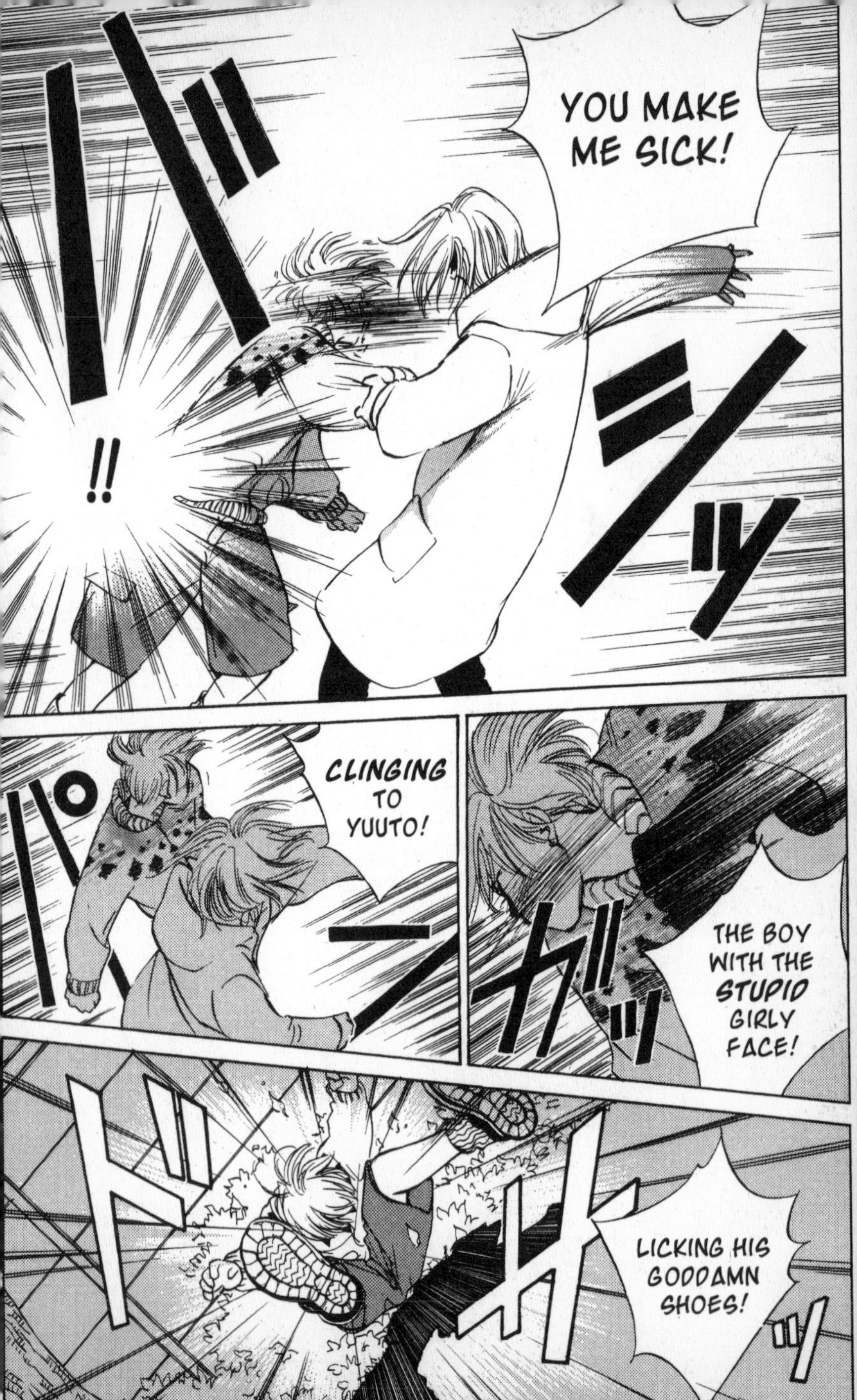
YOU MAKE ME SICK!
!!
THE BOY WITH THE STUPID GIRLY FACE!
CLINGING TO YUUTO!
LICKING HIS GODDAMN SHOES!

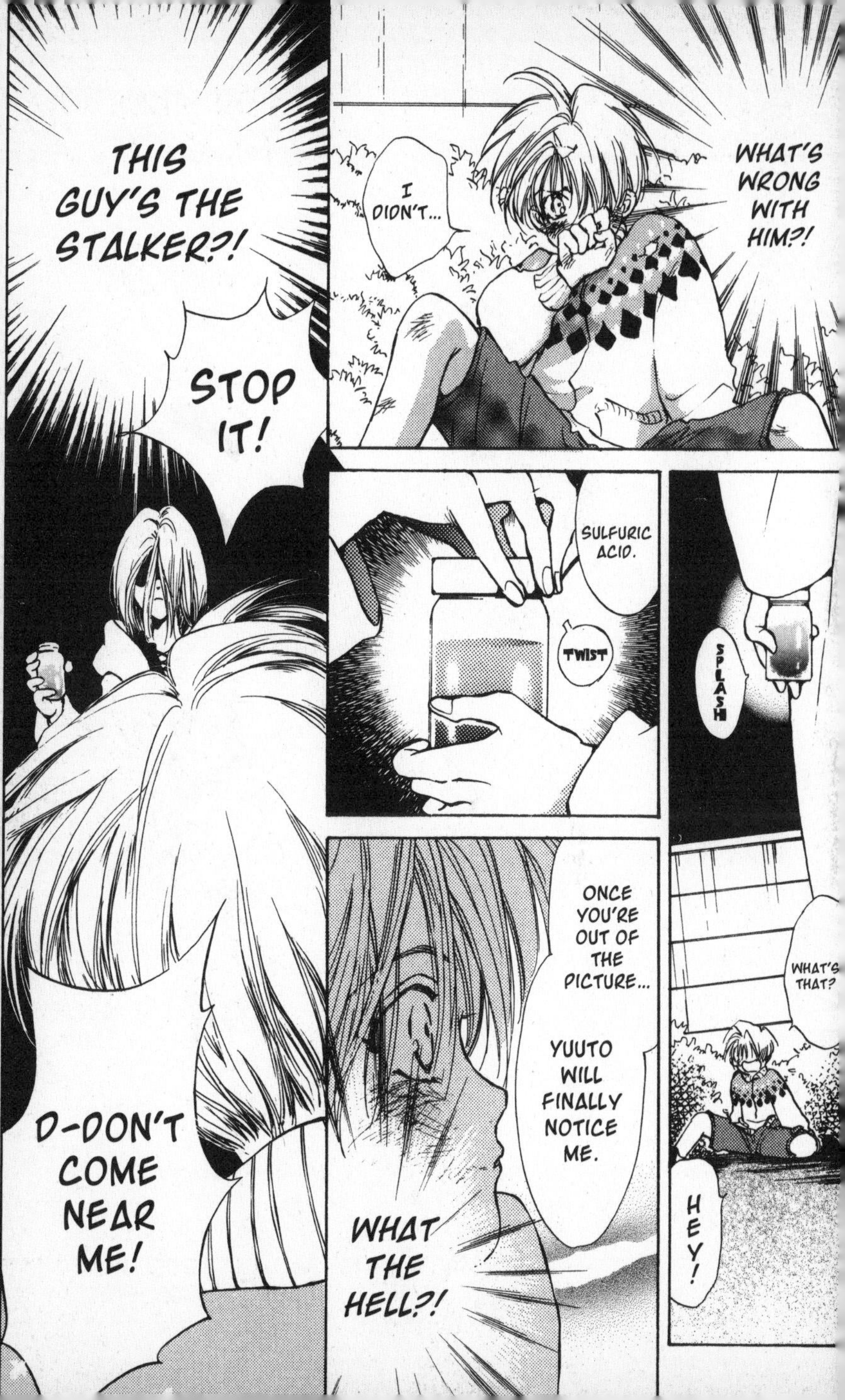
WHAT'S WRONG WITH HIM?!
I DIDN'T...
SPLASH
SULFURIC ACID.
TWIST
WHAT'S THAT?
HEY!
ONCE YOU'RE OUT OF THE PICTURE...
YUUTO WILL FINALLY NOTICE ME.
WHAT THE HELL?!
THIS GUY'S THE STALKER?!
STOP IT!
D-DON'T COME NEAR ME!

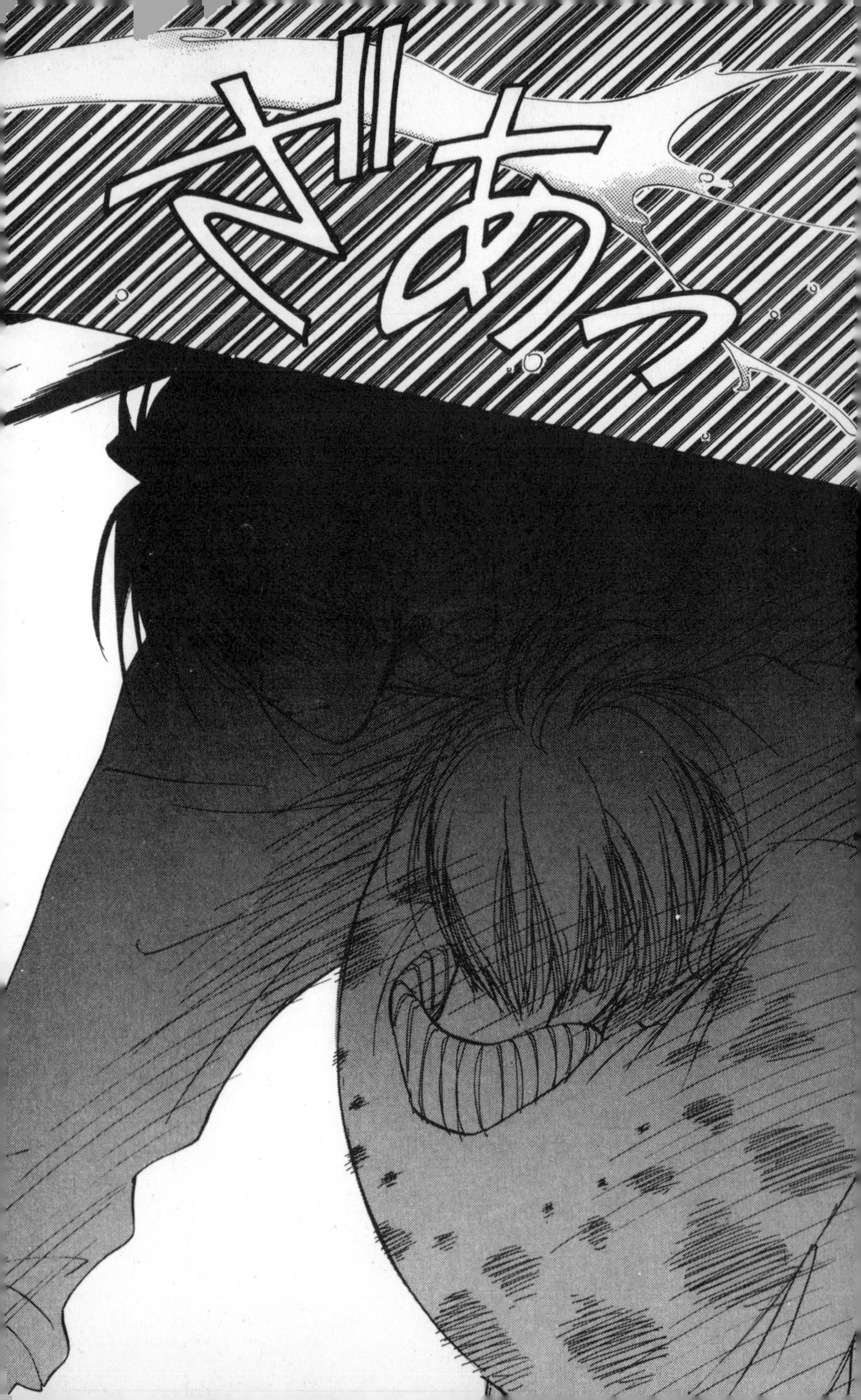
ざあっ

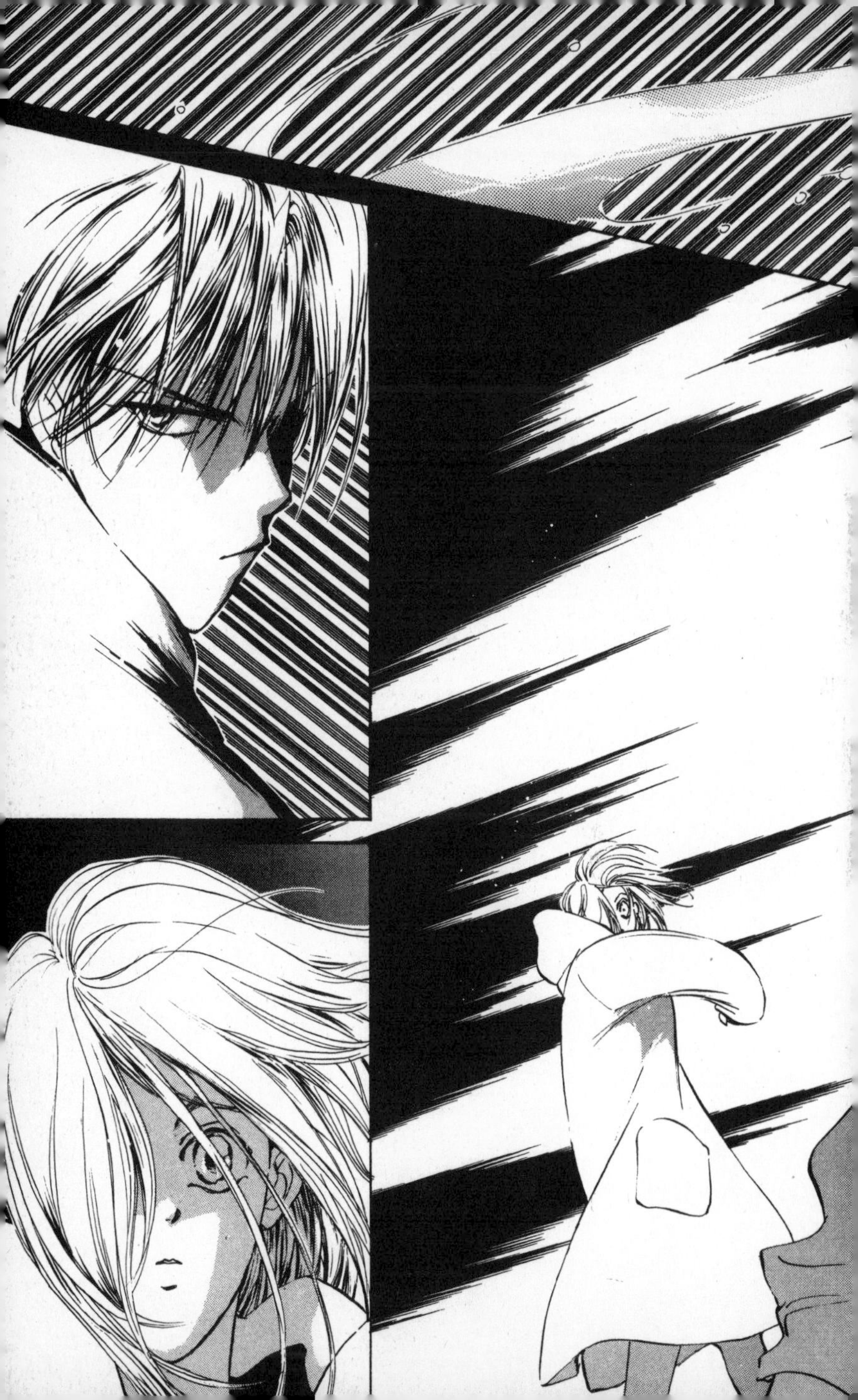

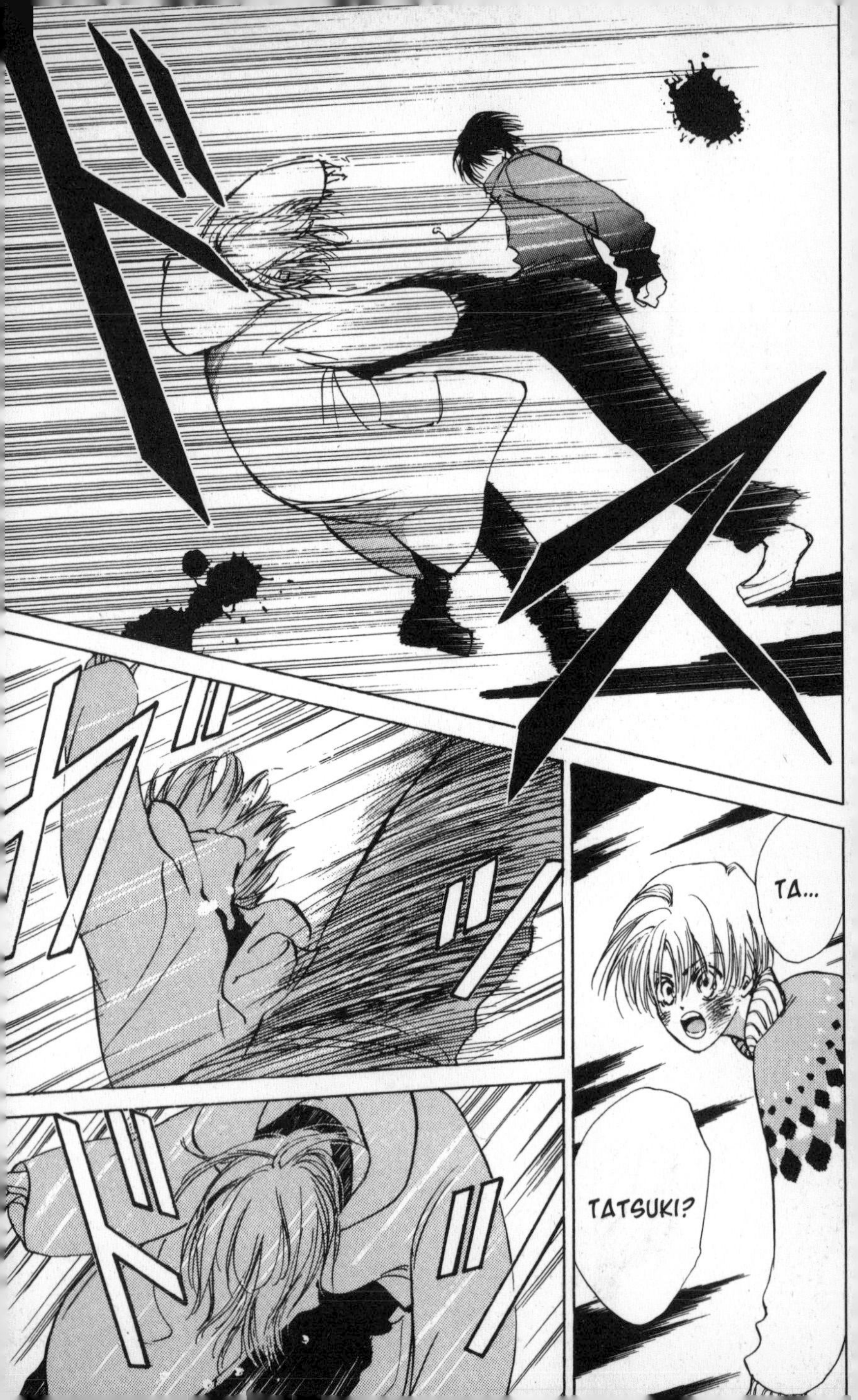
TA...
TATSUKI?

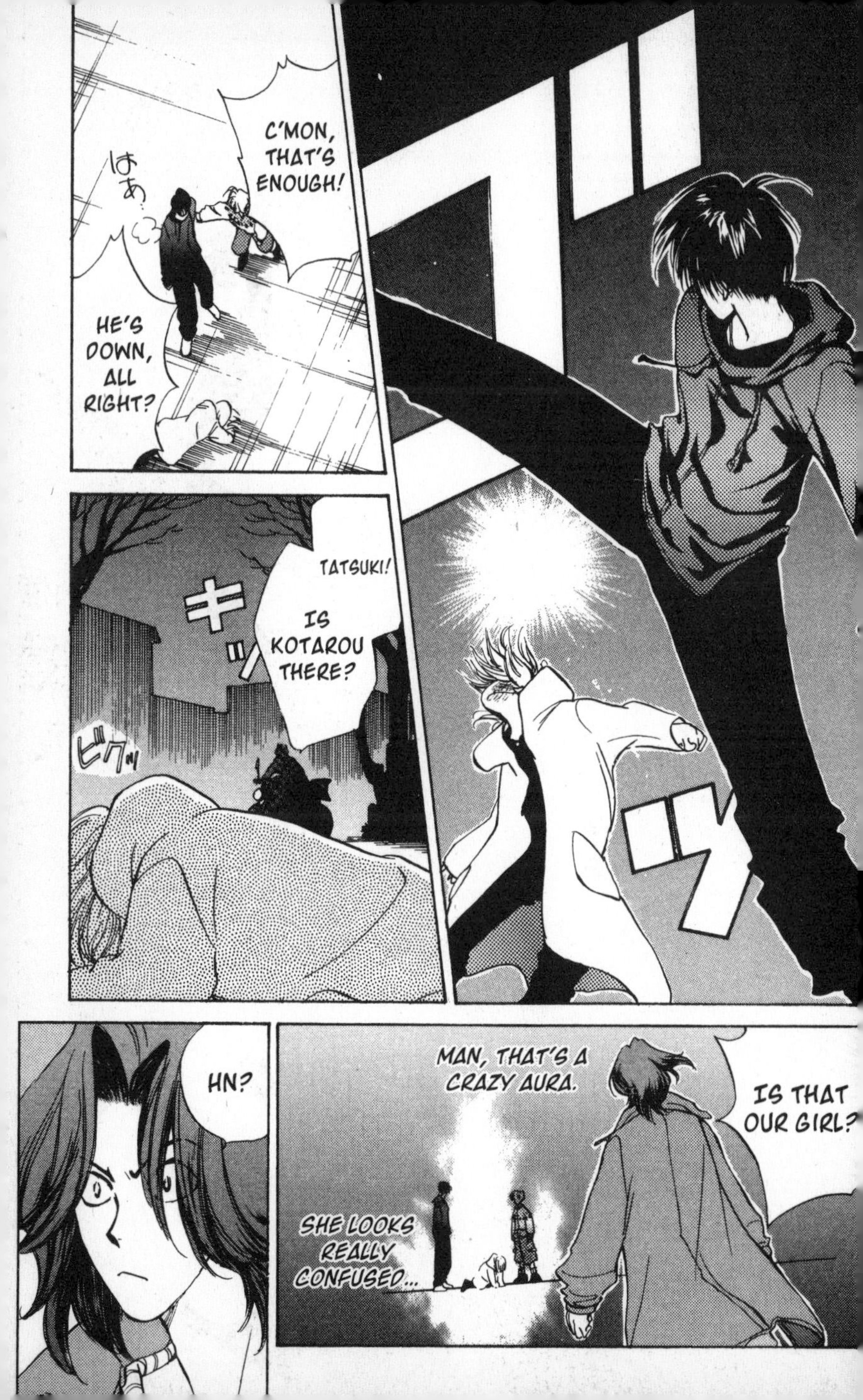
C'MON, THAT'S ENOUGH!
はあ
HE'S DOWN, ALL RIGHT?
TATSUKI!
IS KOTAROU THERE?
IS THAT OUR GIRL?
MAN, THAT'S A CRAZY AURA.
SHE LOOKS REALLY CONFUSED...
HN?

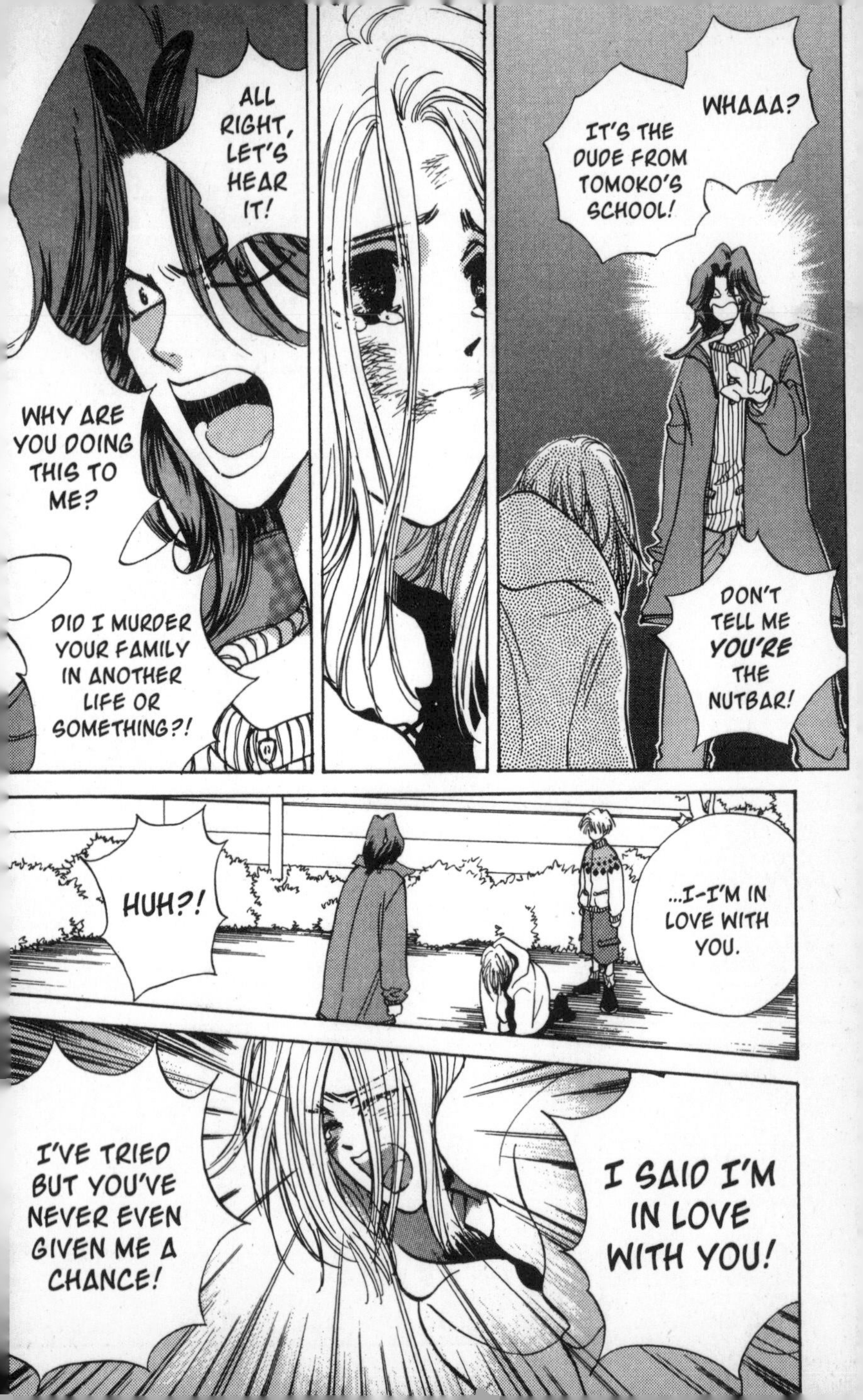
WHAAA?
IT'S THE DUDE FROM TOMOKO'S SCHOOL!
DON'T TELL ME *YOU'RE* THE NUTBAR!
ALL RIGHT, LET'S HEAR IT!
WHY ARE YOU DOING THIS TO ME?
DID I MURDER YOUR FAMILY IN ANOTHER LIFE OR SOMETHING?!
...I-I'M IN LOVE WITH YOU.
HUH?!
I SAID I'M IN LOVE WITH YOU!
I'VE TRIED BUT YOU'VE NEVER EVEN GIVEN ME A CHANCE!

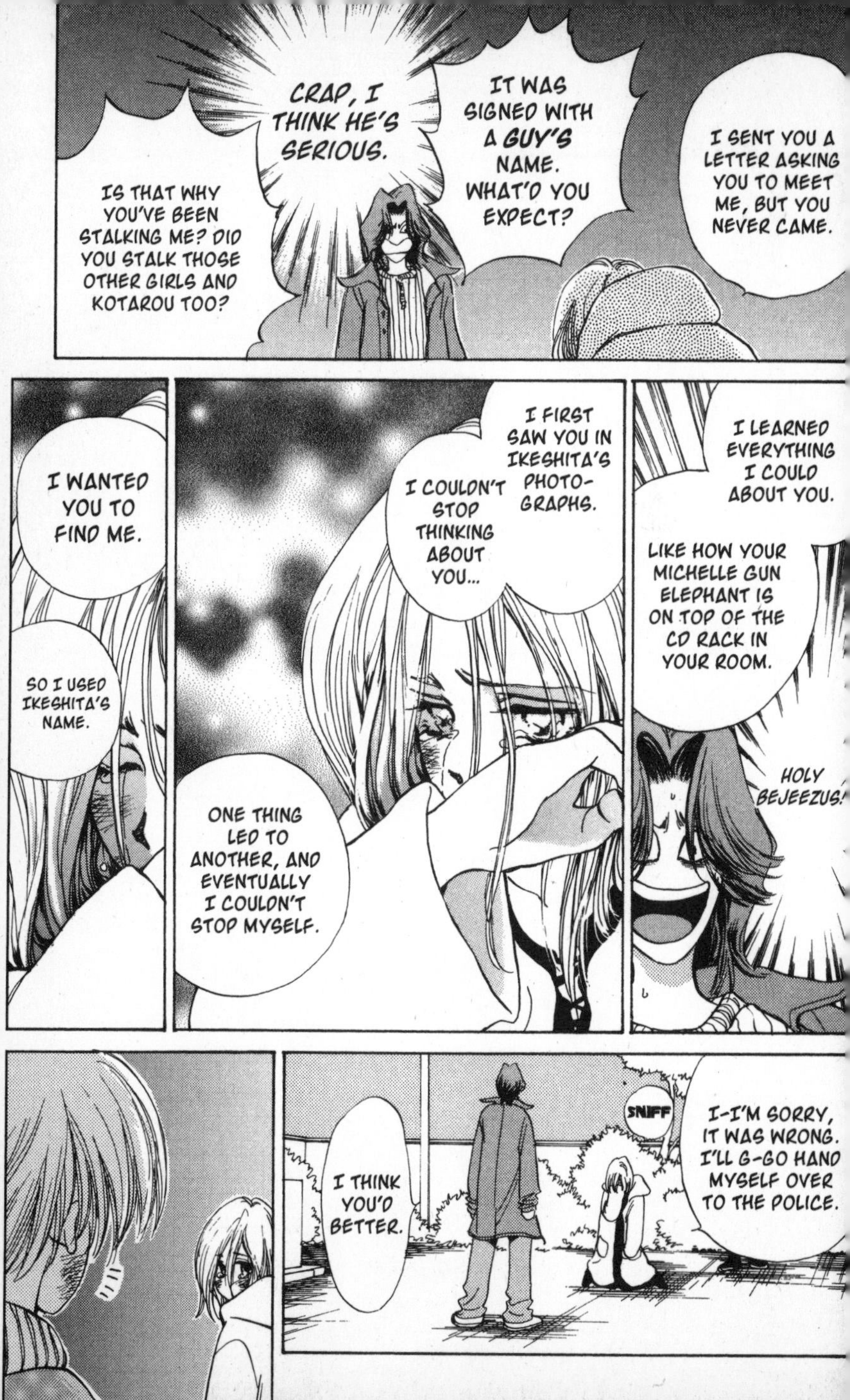
I SENT YOU A LETTER ASKING YOU TO MEET ME, BUT YOU NEVER CAME.
IT WAS SIGNED WITH A GUY'S NAME. WHAT'D YOU EXPECT?
CRAP, I THINK HE'S SERIOUS.
IS THAT WHY YOU'VE BEEN STALKING ME? DID YOU STALK THOSE OTHER GIRLS AND KOTAROU TOO?
I LEARNED EVERYTHING I COULD ABOUT YOU.
LIKE HOW YOUR MICHELLE GUN ELEPHANT IS ON TOP OF THE CD RACK IN YOUR ROOM.
HOLY BEJEEZUS!
I FIRST SAW YOU IN IKESHITA'S PHOTOGRAPHS.
I COULDN'T STOP THINKING ABOUT YOU...
ONE THING LED TO ANOTHER, AND EVENTUALLY I COULDN'T STOP MYSELF.
I WANTED YOU TO FIND ME.
SO I USED IKESHITA'S NAME.
I-I'M SORRY, IT WAS WRONG. I'LL G-GO HAND MYSELF OVER TO THE POLICE.
SNIFF
I THINK YOU'D BETTER.

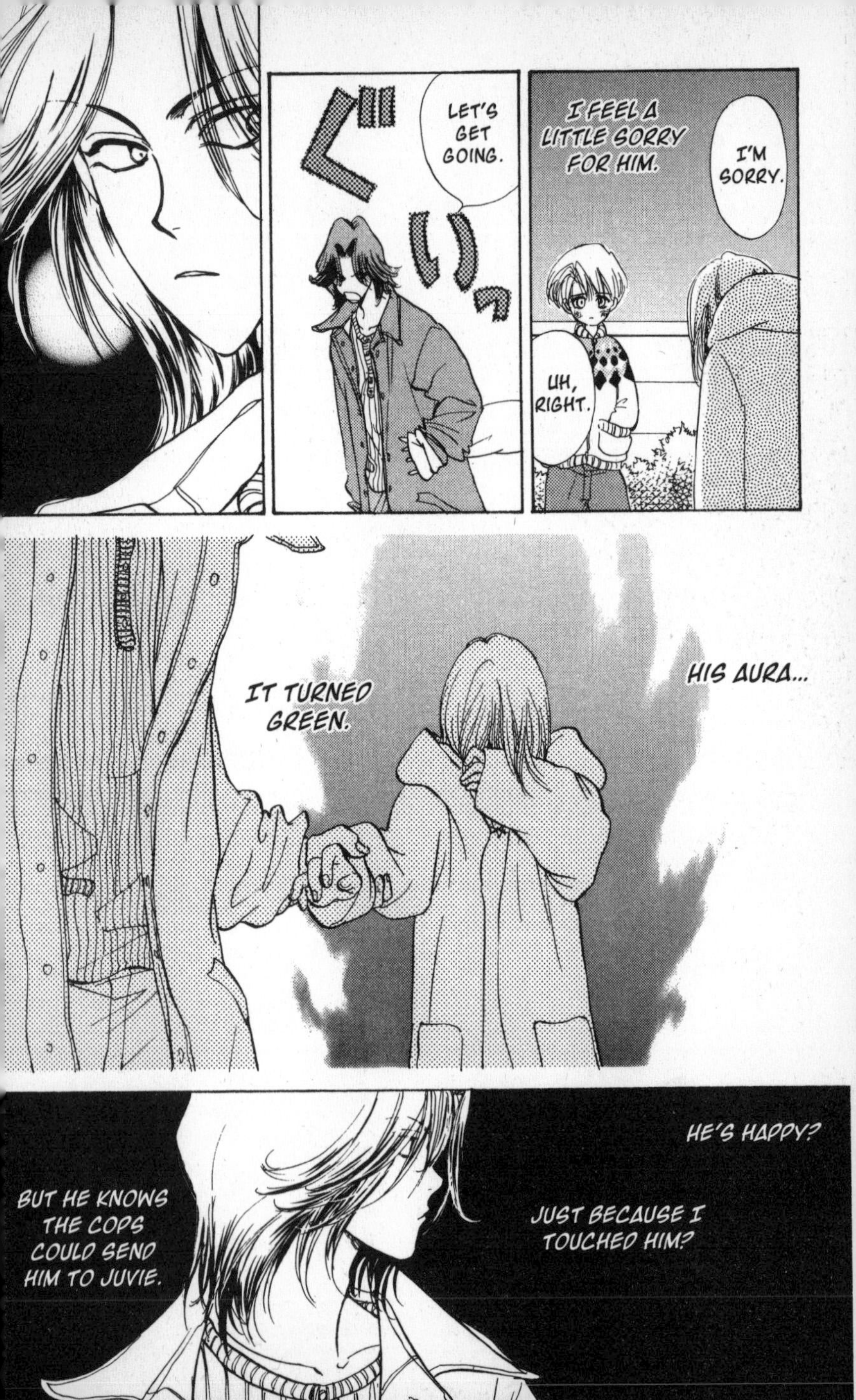
I'M SORRY.
I FEEL A LITTLE SORRY FOR HIM.
UH, RIGHT.
LET'S GET GOING.
ぐいっ
HIS AURA...
IT TURNED GREEN.
HE'S HAPPY?
JUST BECAUSE I TOUCHED HIM?
BUT HE KNOWS THE COPS COULD SEND HIM TO JUVIE.

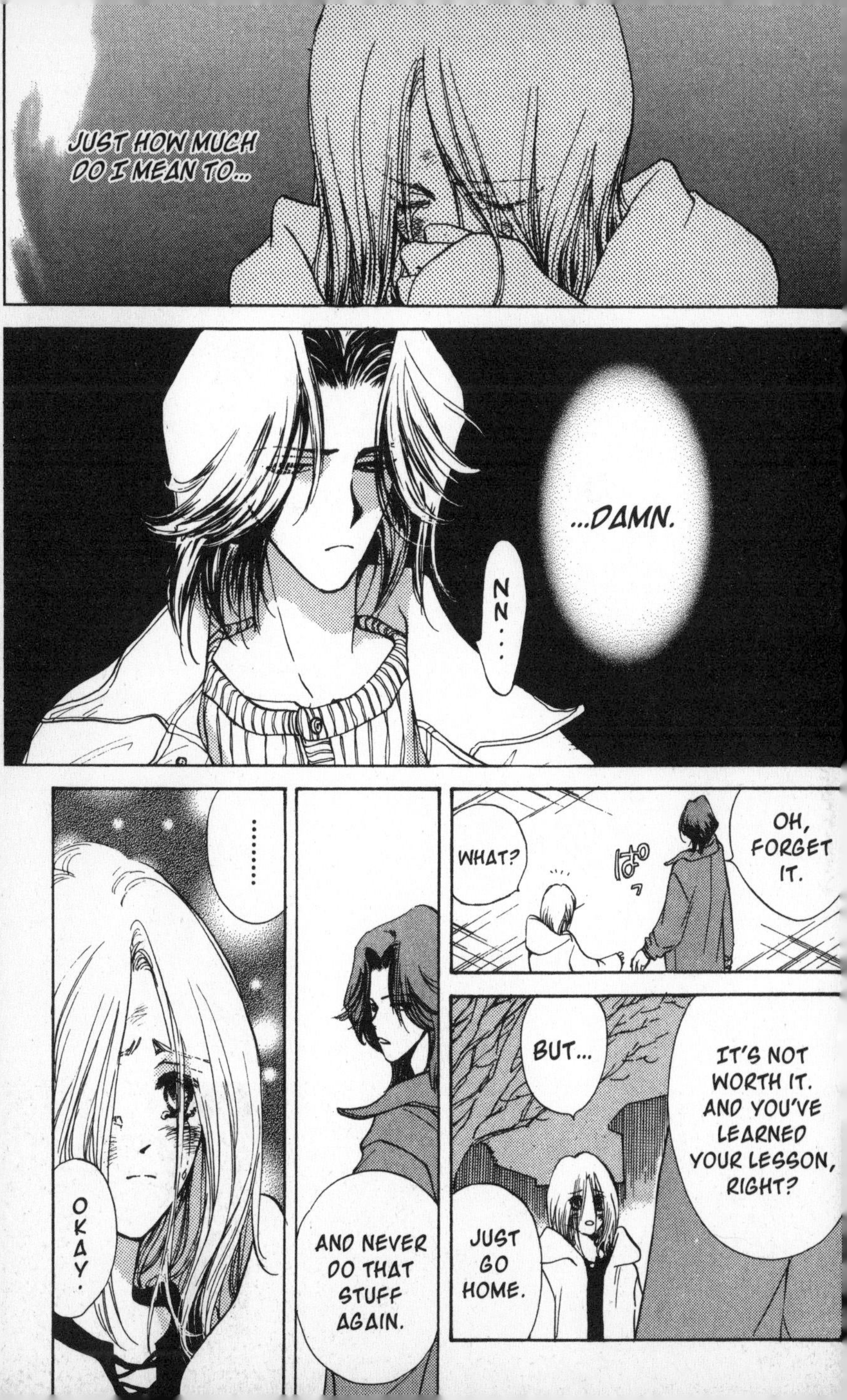

JUST HOW MUCH DO I MEAN TO...
...DAMN.
NN...
OH, FORGET IT.
WHAT?
IT'S NOT WORTH IT. AND YOU'VE LEARNED YOUR LESSON, RIGHT?
BUT...
JUST GO HOME.
AND NEVER DO THAT STUFF AGAIN.
......
OKAY.

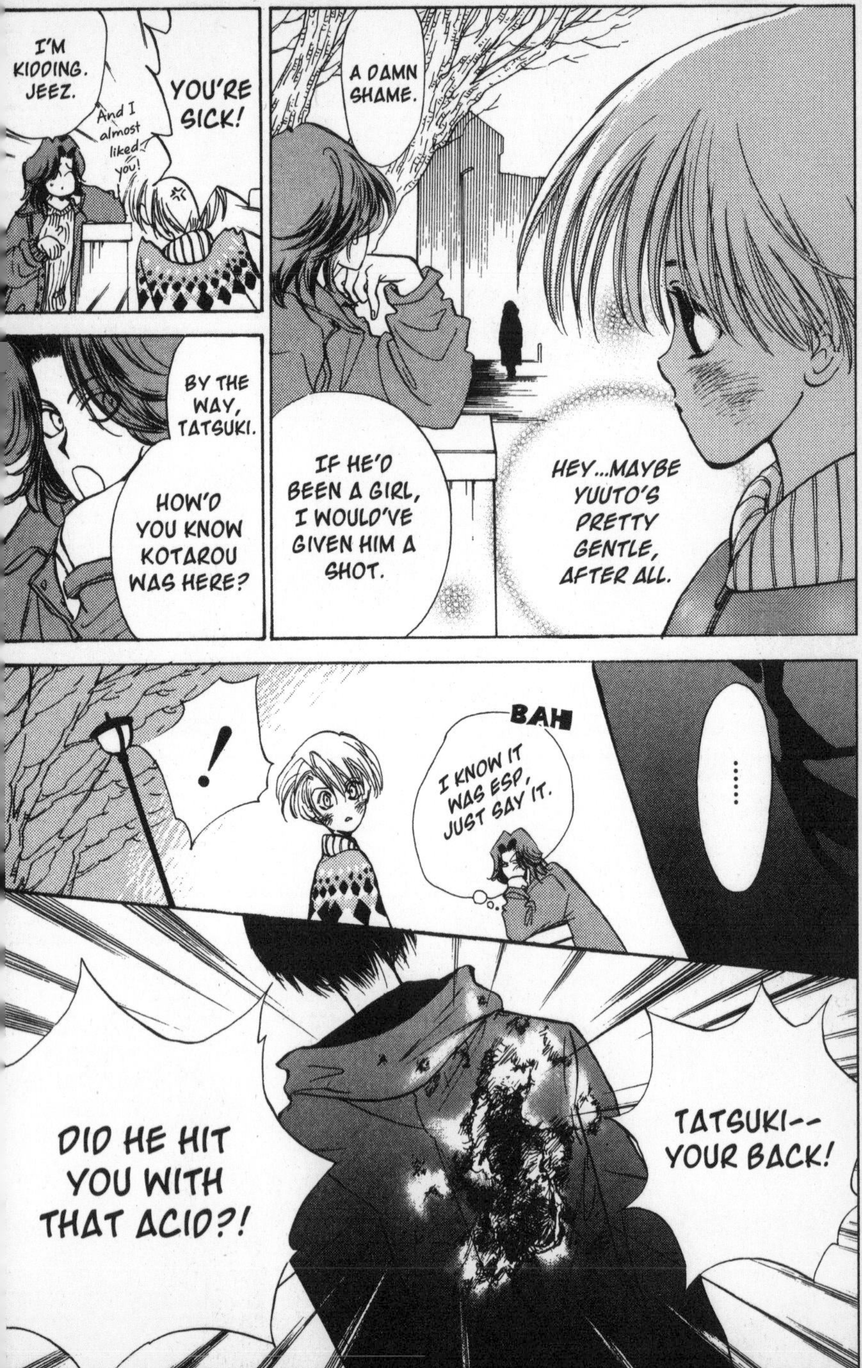

HEY...MAYBE YUUTO'S PRETTY GENTLE, AFTER ALL.
A DAMN SHAME.
IF HE'D BEEN A GIRL, I WOULD'VE GIVEN HIM A SHOT.
YOU'RE SICK!
And I almost liked you!
I'M KIDDING. JEEZ.
BY THE WAY, TATSUKI.
HOW'D YOU KNOW KOTAROU WAS HERE?
......
BAH
I KNOW IT WAS ESP, JUST SAY IT.
!
TATSUKI-- YOUR BACK!
DID HE HIT YOU WITH THAT ACID?!

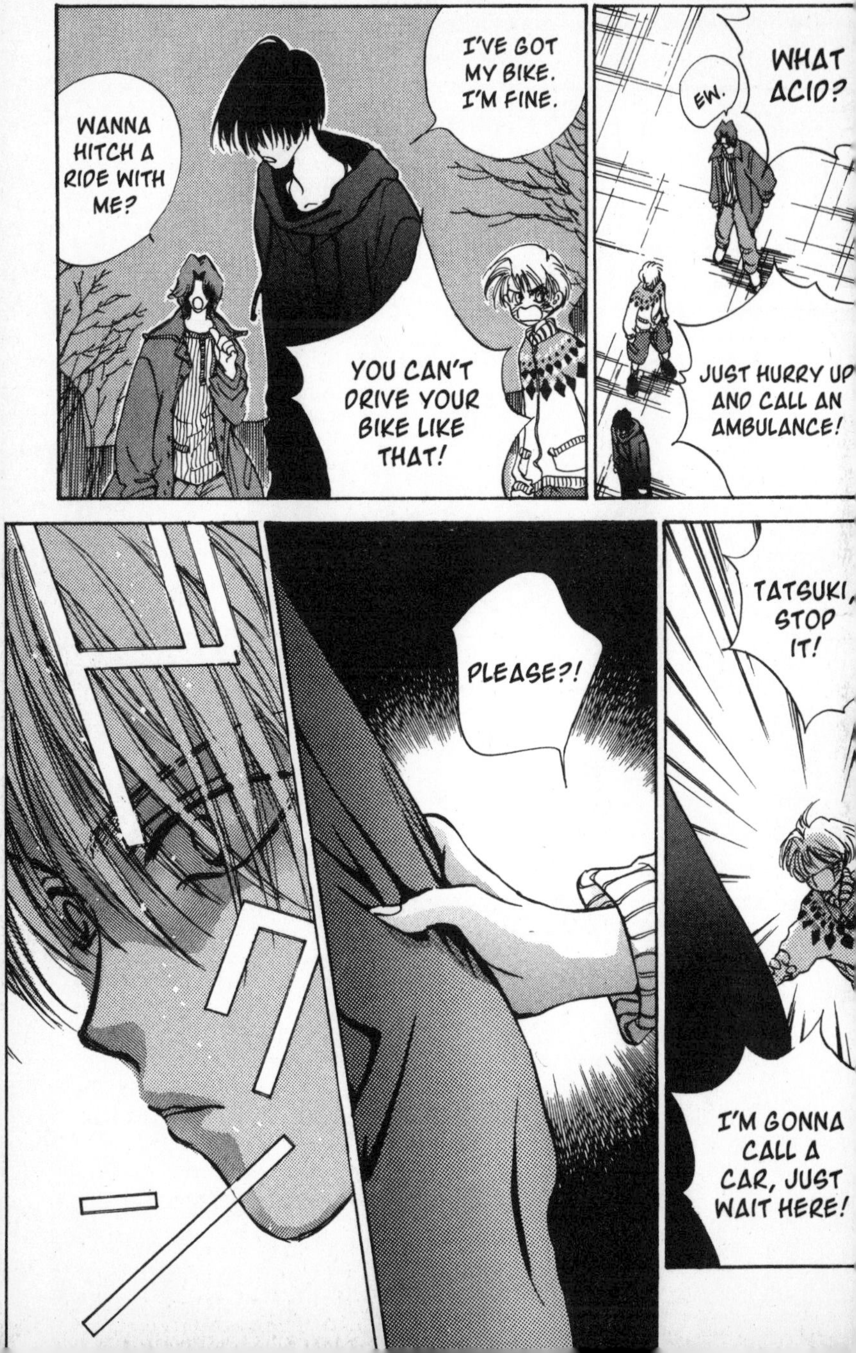
WHAT ACID?
EW.
JUST HURRY UP AND CALL AN AMBULANCE!
WANNA HITCH A RIDE WITH ME?
I'VE GOT MY BIKE. I'M FINE.
YOU CAN'T DRIVE YOUR BIKE LIKE THAT!
TATSUKI, STOP IT!
I'M GONNA CALL A CAR, JUST WAIT HERE!
PLEASE?!

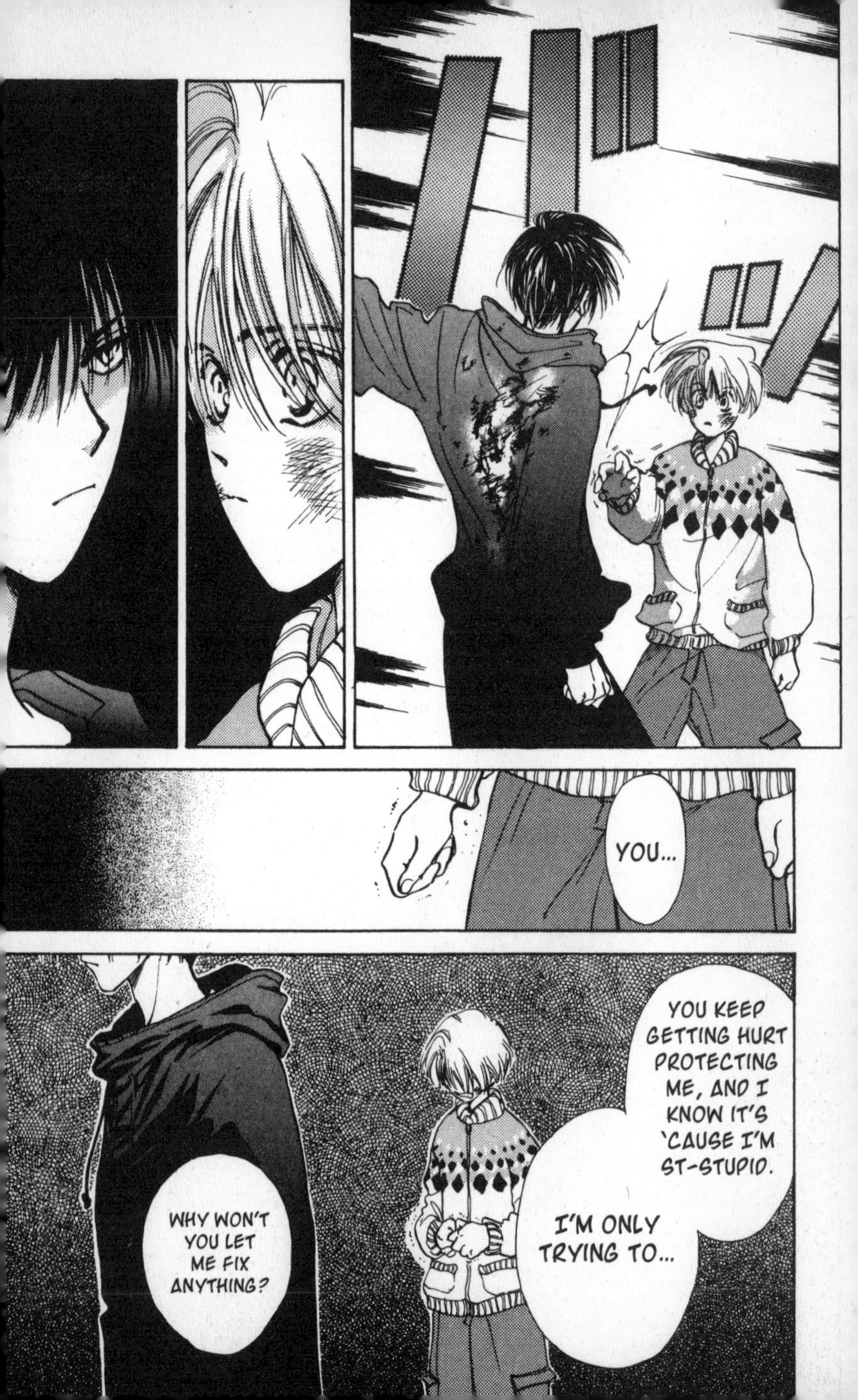
YOU...
YOU KEEP GETTING HURT PROTECTING ME, AND I KNOW IT'S 'CAUSE I'M ST-STUPID.
I'M ONLY TRYING TO...
WHY WON'T YOU LET ME FIX ANYTHING?

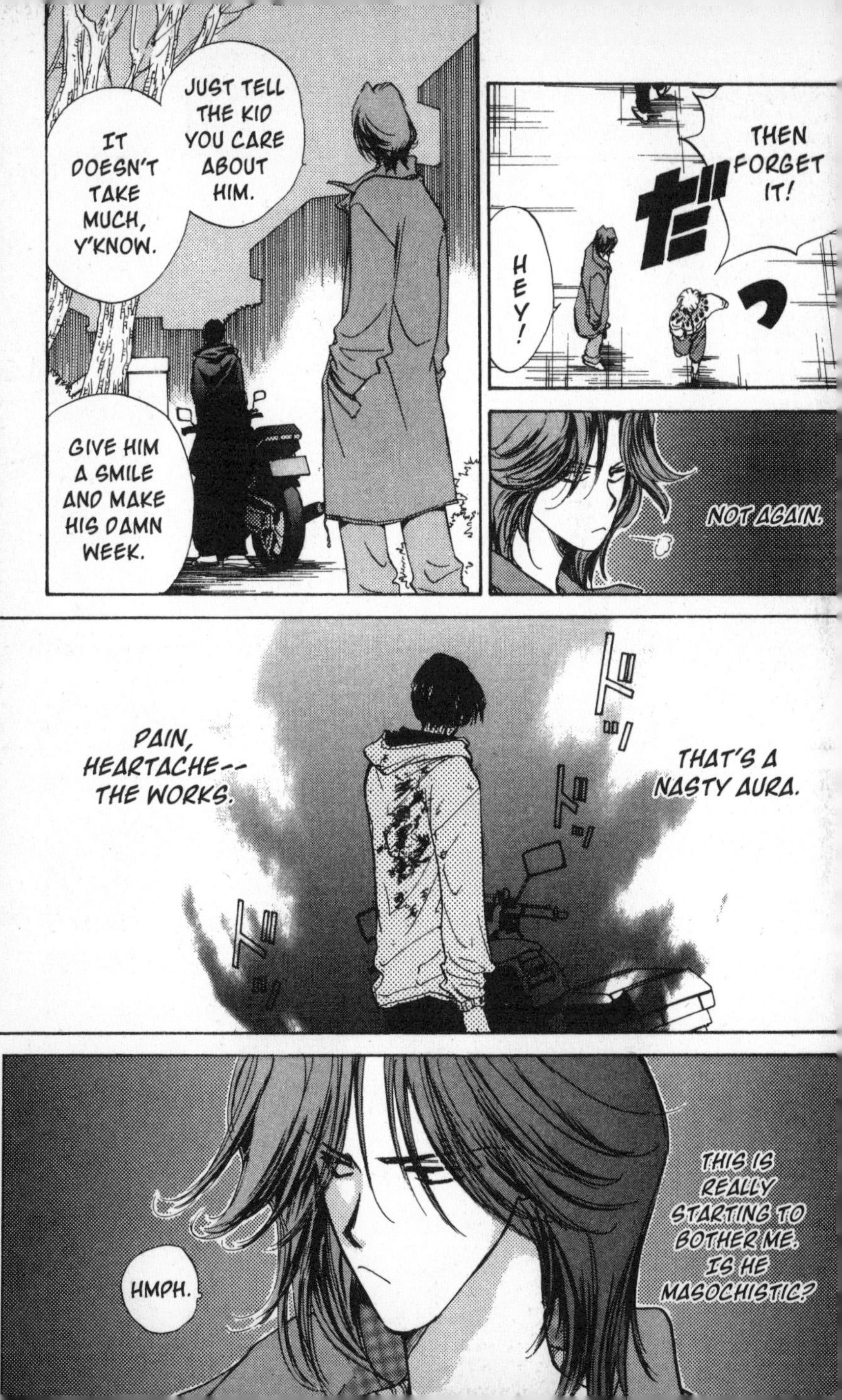
THEN FORGET IT!
だっ
HEY!
NOT AGAIN.
JUST TELL THE KID YOU CARE ABOUT HIM.
IT DOESN'T TAKE MUCH, Y'KNOW.
GIVE HIM A SMILE AND MAKE HIS DAMN WEEK.
THAT'S A NASTY AURA.
PAIN, HEARTACHE-- THE WORKS.
THIS IS REALLY STARTING TO BOTHER ME. IS HE MASOCHISTIC?
HMPH.

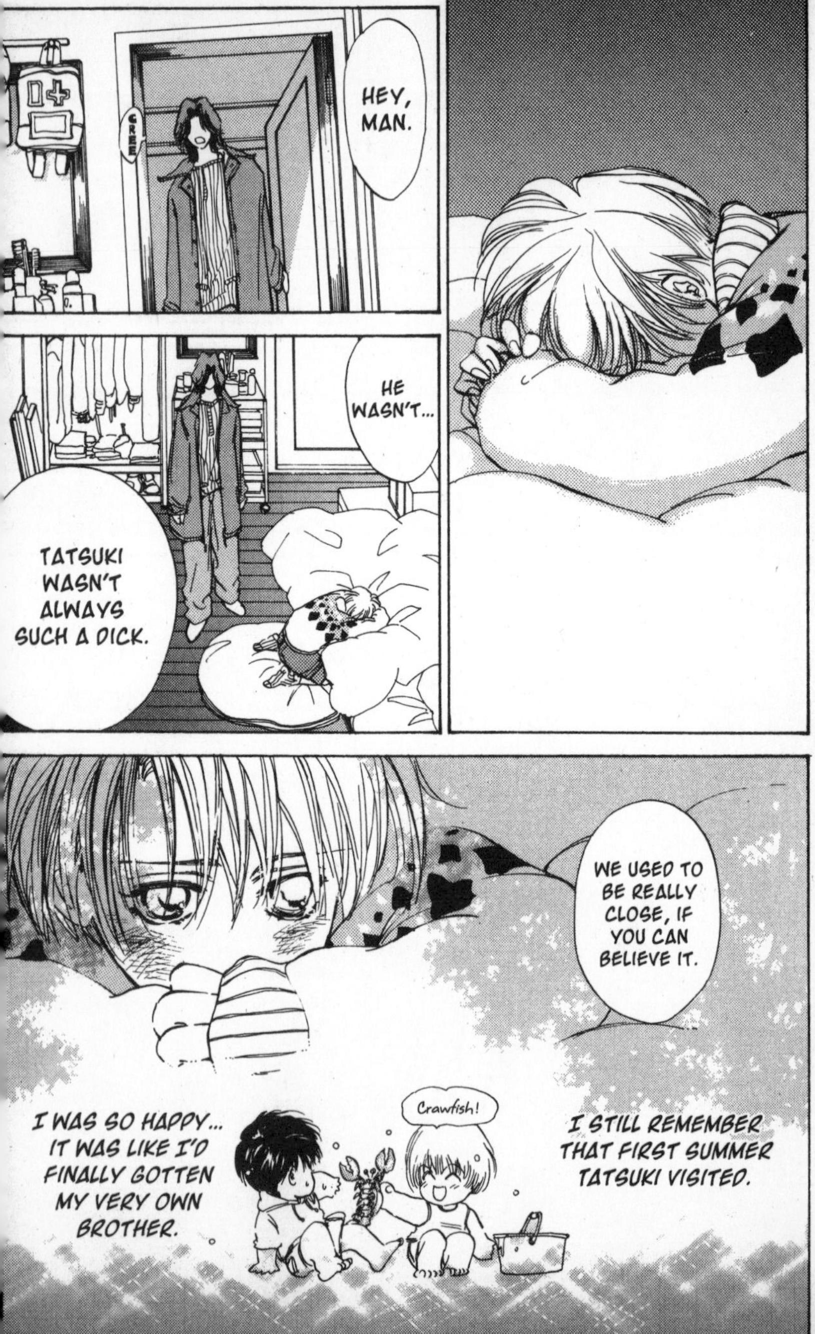
HEY, MAN.
GREE
HE WASN'T...
TATSUKI WASN'T ALWAYS SUCH A DICK.
WE USED TO BE REALLY CLOSE, IF YOU CAN BELIEVE IT.
I STILL REMEMBER THAT FIRST SUMMER TATSUKI VISITED.
Crawfish!
I WAS SO HAPPY... IT WAS LIKE I'D FINALLY GOTTEN MY VERY OWN BROTHER.

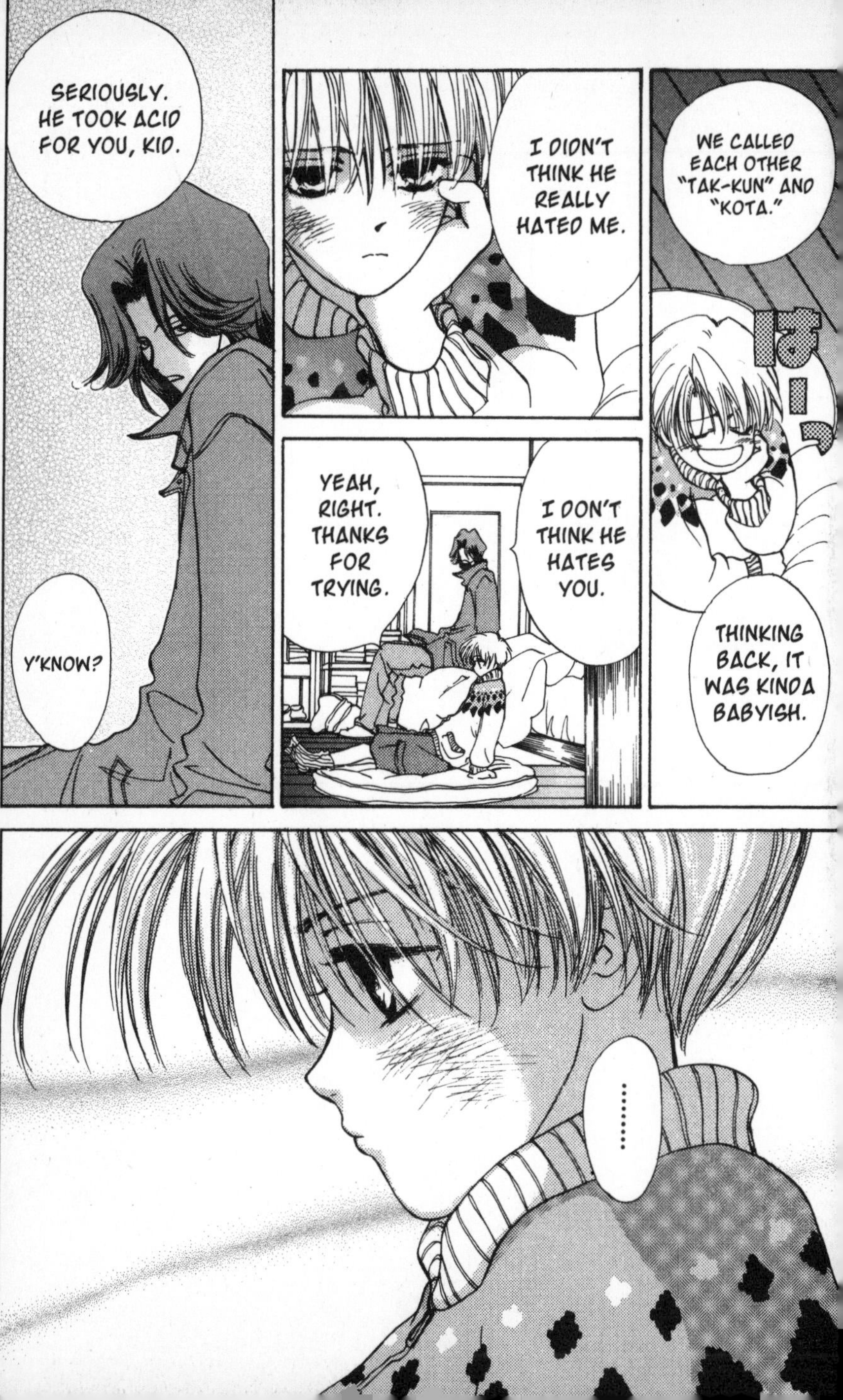

WE CALLED EACH OTHER "TAK-KUN" AND "KOTA."
はーッ
THINKING BACK, IT WAS KINDA BABYISH.
I DIDN'T THINK HE REALLY HATED ME.
I DON'T THINK HE HATES YOU.
YEAH, RIGHT. THANKS FOR TRYING.
SERIOUSLY. HE TOOK ACID FOR YOU, KID.
Y'KNOW?
....

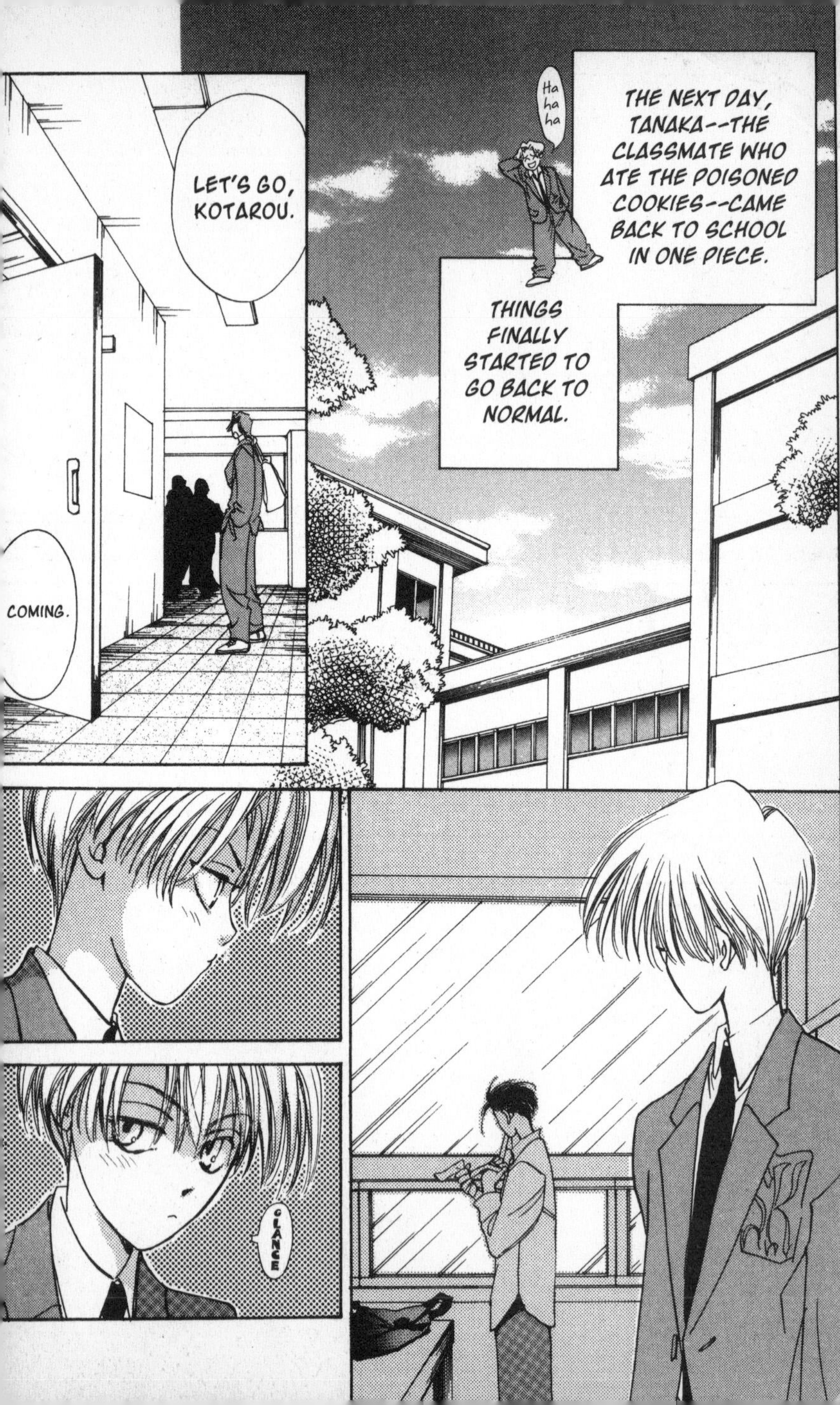
THE NEXT DAY, TANAKA--THE CLASSMATE WHO ATE THE POISONED COOKIES--CAME BACK TO SCHOOL IN ONE PIECE.
Ha ha ha
THINGS FINALLY STARTED TO GO BACK TO NORMAL.
LET'S GO, KOTAROU.
COMING.
GLANCE

ACT 2

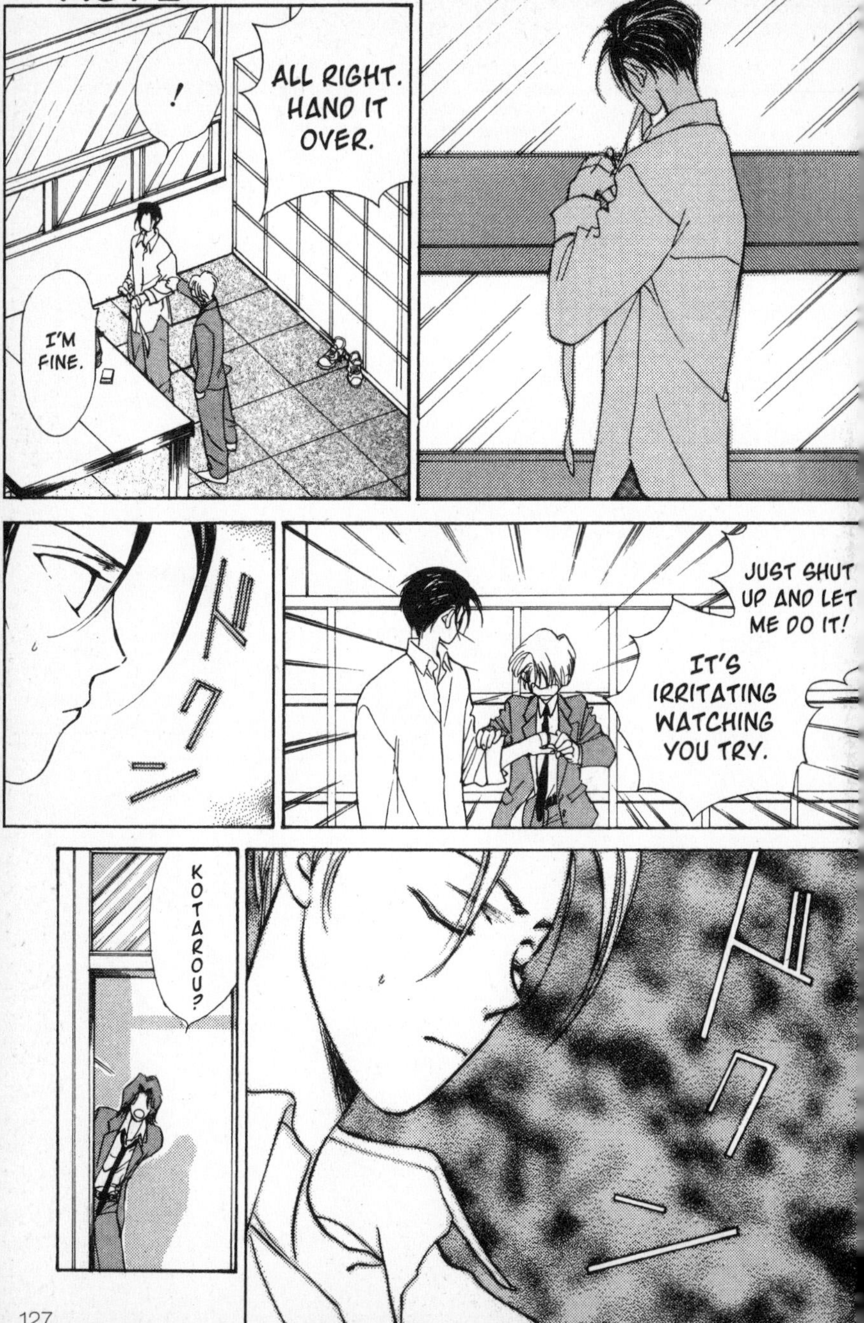
ALL RIGHT. HAND IT OVER.
!
I'M FINE.
JUST SHUT UP AND LET ME DO IT!
IT'S IRRITATING WATCHING YOU TRY.
KOTAROU?

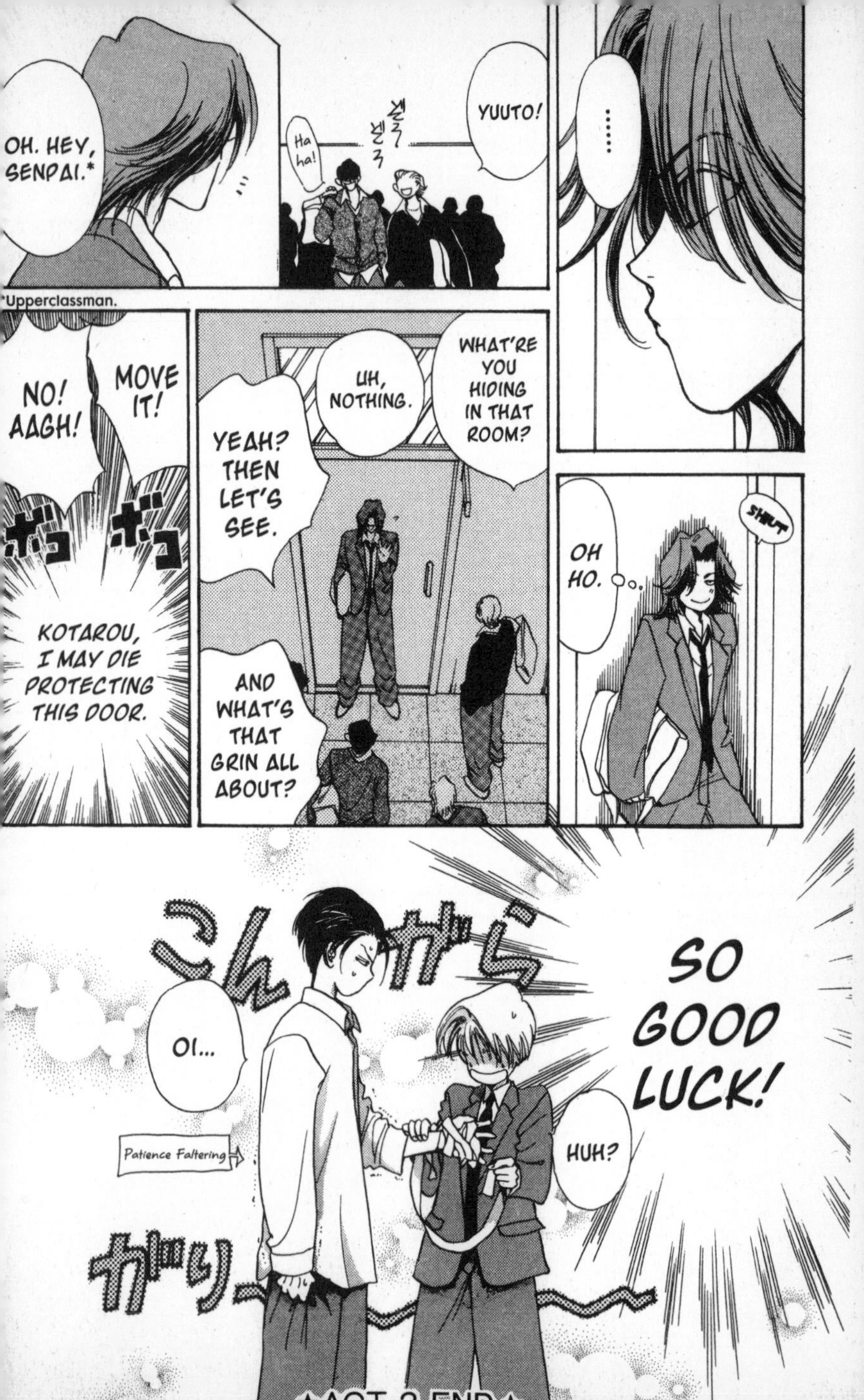
......
YUUTO!
Ha ha!
OH. HEY, SENPAI.*
*Upperclassman.
OH HO.
SHUT
WHAT'RE YOU HIDING IN THAT ROOM?
UH, NOTHING.
YEAH? THEN LET'S SEE.
AND WHAT'S THAT GRIN ALL ABOUT?
MOVE IT!
NO! AAGH!
KOTAROU, I MAY DIE PROTECTING THIS DOOR.
SO GOOD LUCK!
HUH?
こんがら
OI...
Patience Faltering

★ACT 2 END★

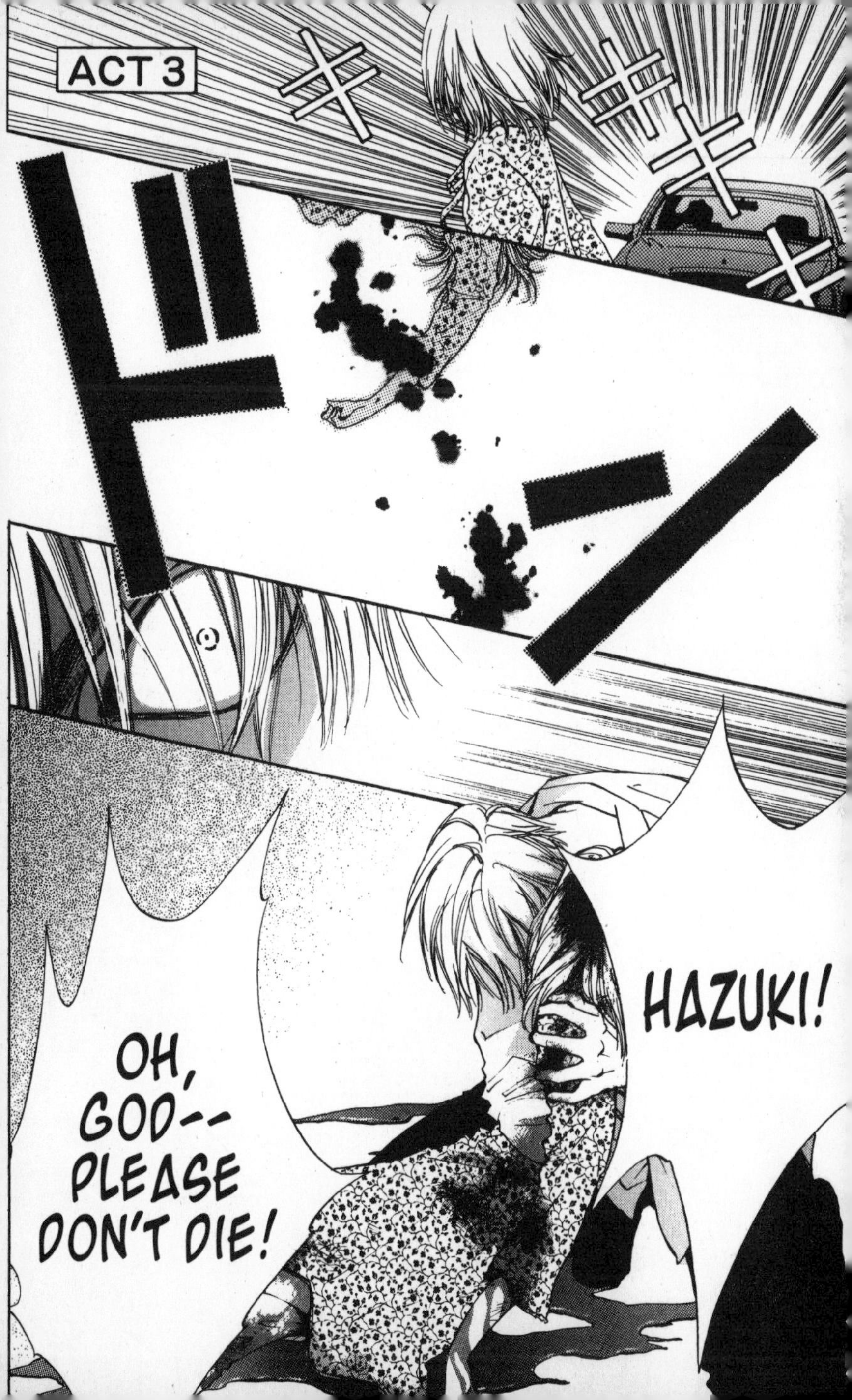
ACT 3
ドーン
HAZUKI!
OH, GOD-- PLEASE DON'T DIE!

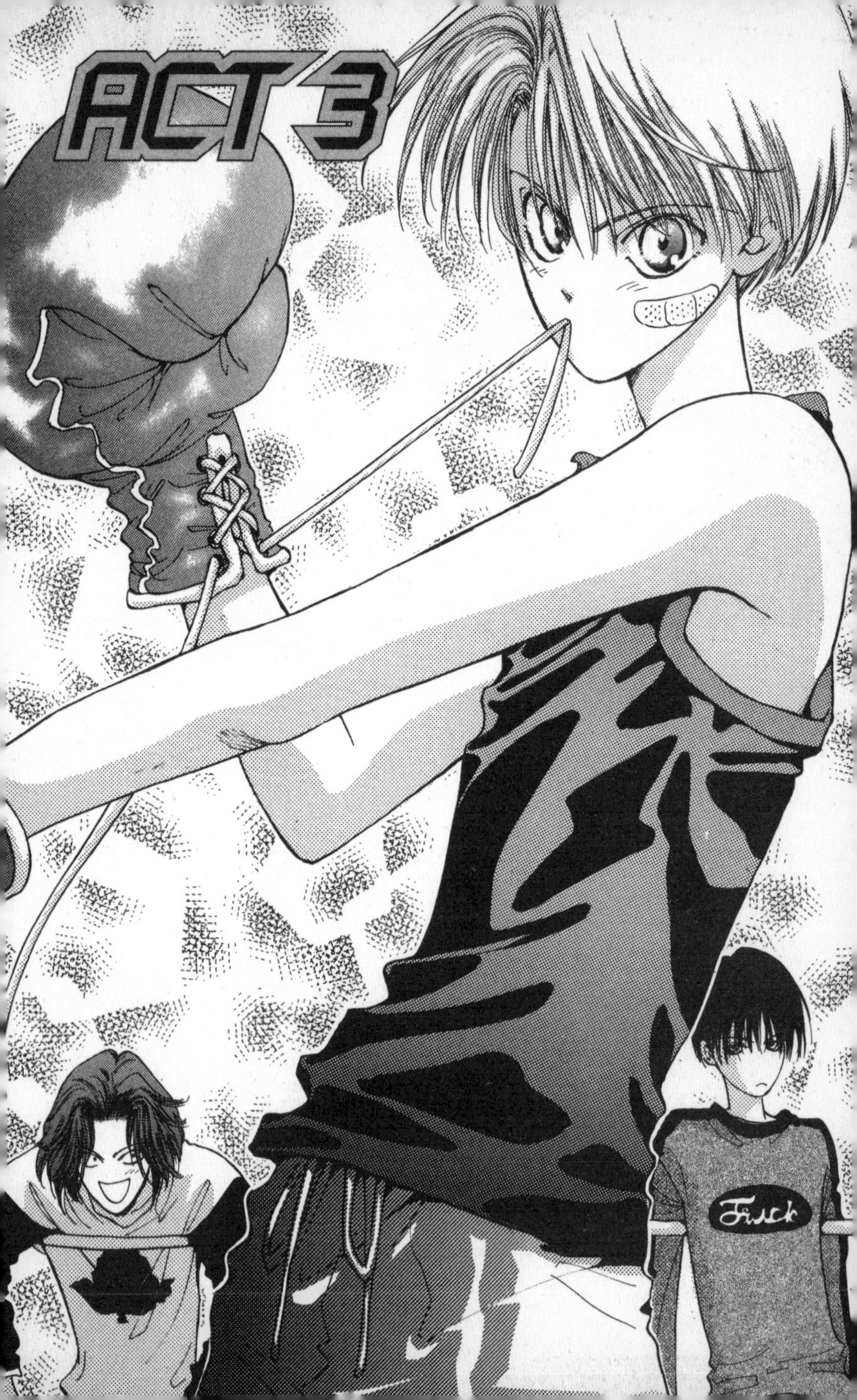
ACT 3

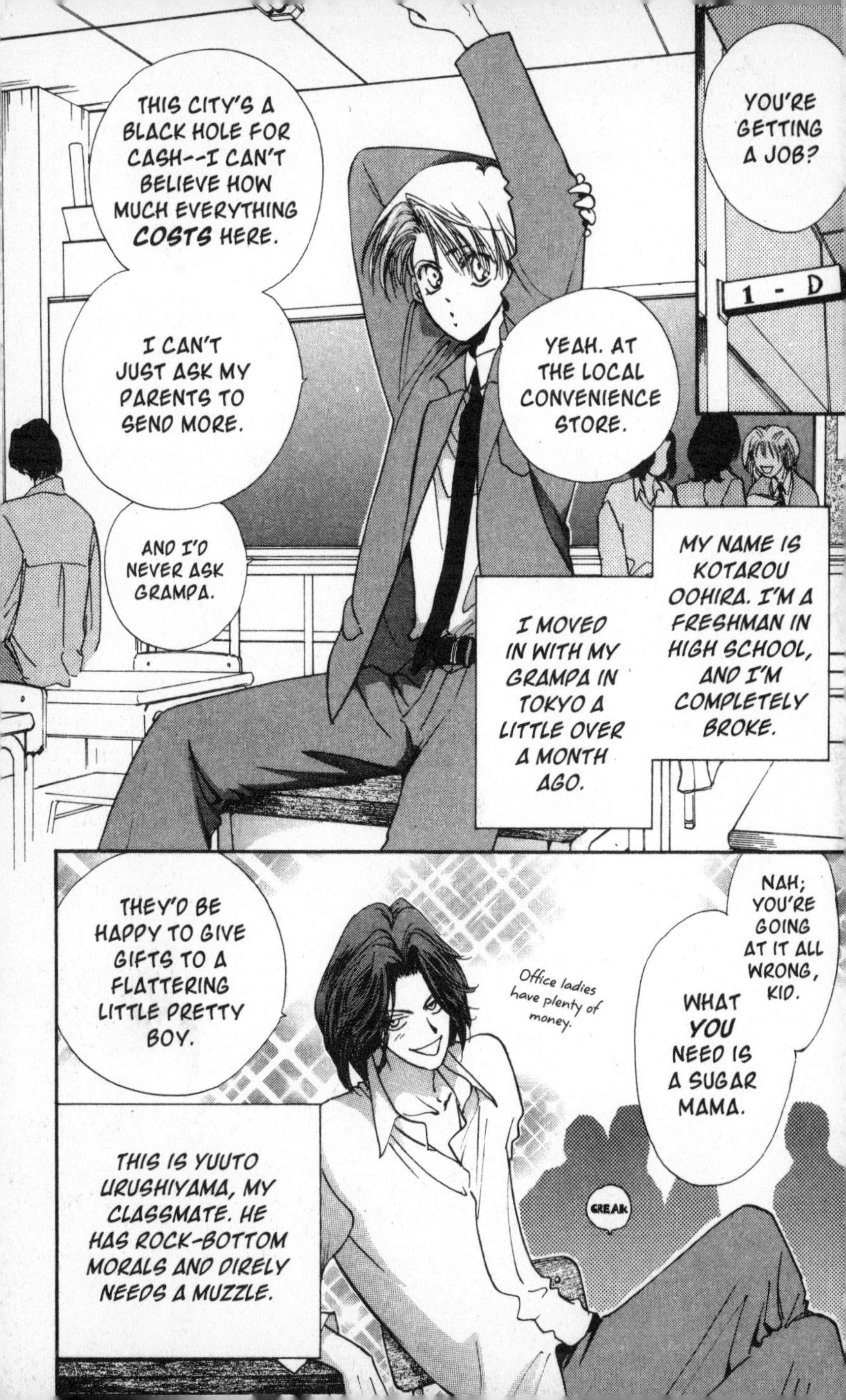
YOU'RE GETTING A JOB?
1 - D
YEAH. AT THE LOCAL CONVENIENCE STORE.
THIS CITY'S A BLACK HOLE FOR CASH--I CAN'T BELIEVE HOW MUCH EVERYTHING **COSTS** HERE.
I CAN'T JUST ASK MY PARENTS TO SEND MORE.
AND I'D NEVER ASK GRAMPA.
MY NAME IS KOTAROU OOHIRA. I'M A FRESHMAN IN HIGH SCHOOL, AND I'M COMPLETELY BROKE.
I MOVED IN WITH MY GRAMPA IN TOKYO A LITTLE OVER A MONTH AGO.
NAH; YOU'RE GOING AT IT ALL WRONG, KID.
WHAT **YOU** NEED IS A SUGAR MAMA.
Office ladies have plenty of money.
THEY'D BE HAPPY TO GIVE GIFTS TO A FLATTERING LITTLE PRETTY BOY.
CREAK
THIS IS YUUTO URUSHIYAMA, MY CLASSMATE. HE HAS ROCK-BOTTOM MORALS AND DIRELY NEEDS A MUZZLE.

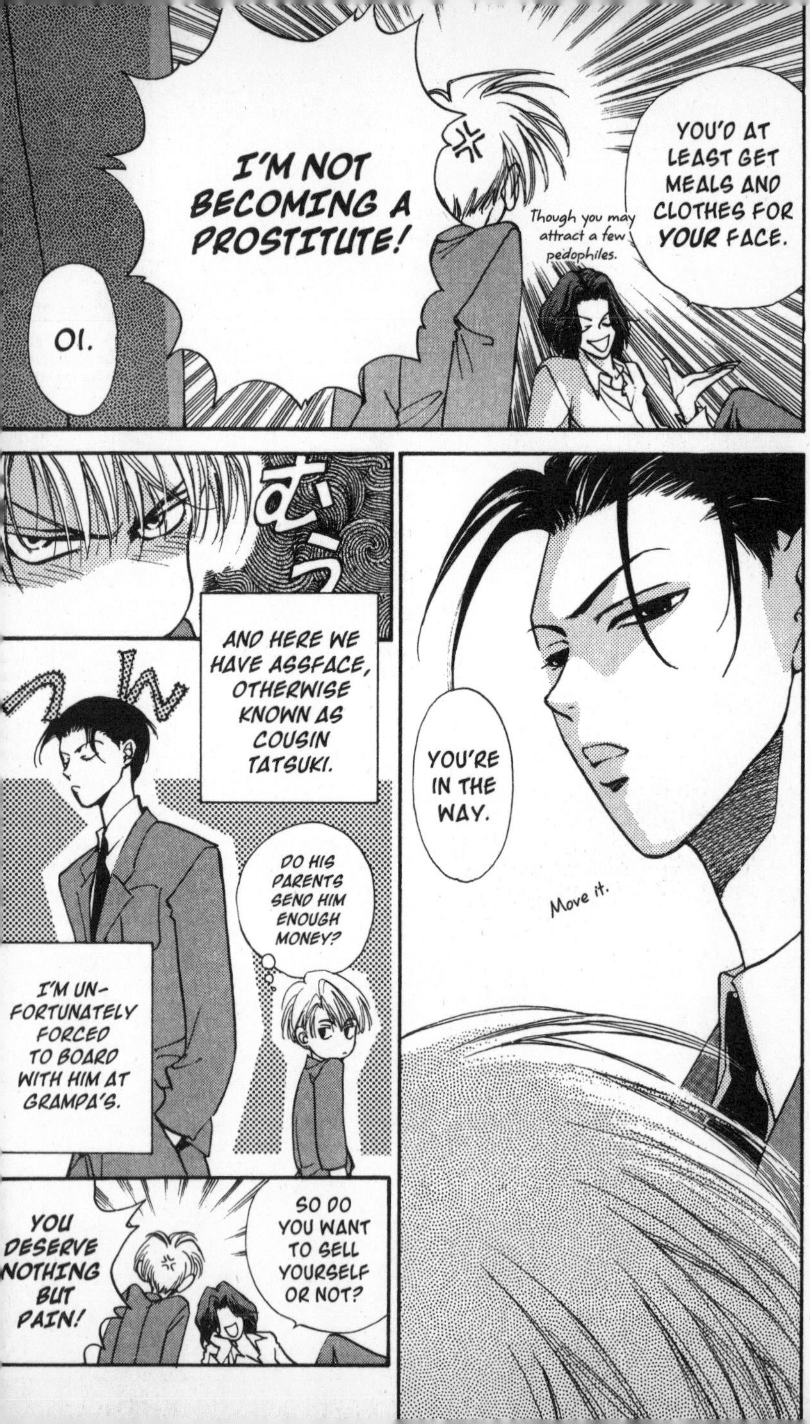
YOU'D AT LEAST GET MEALS AND CLOTHES FOR YOUR FACE.
Though you may attract a few pedophiles.
I'M NOT BECOMING A PROSTITUTE!
OI.
YOU'RE IN THE WAY.
Move it.
むっ
AND HERE WE HAVE ASSFACE, OTHERWISE KNOWN AS COUSIN TATSUKI.
つん
DO HIS PARENTS SEND HIM ENOUGH MONEY?
I'M UN-FORTUNATELY FORCED TO BOARD WITH HIM AT GRAMPA'S.
SO DO YOU WANT TO SELL YOURSELF OR NOT?
YOU DESERVE NOTHING BUT PAIN!

ACT 3

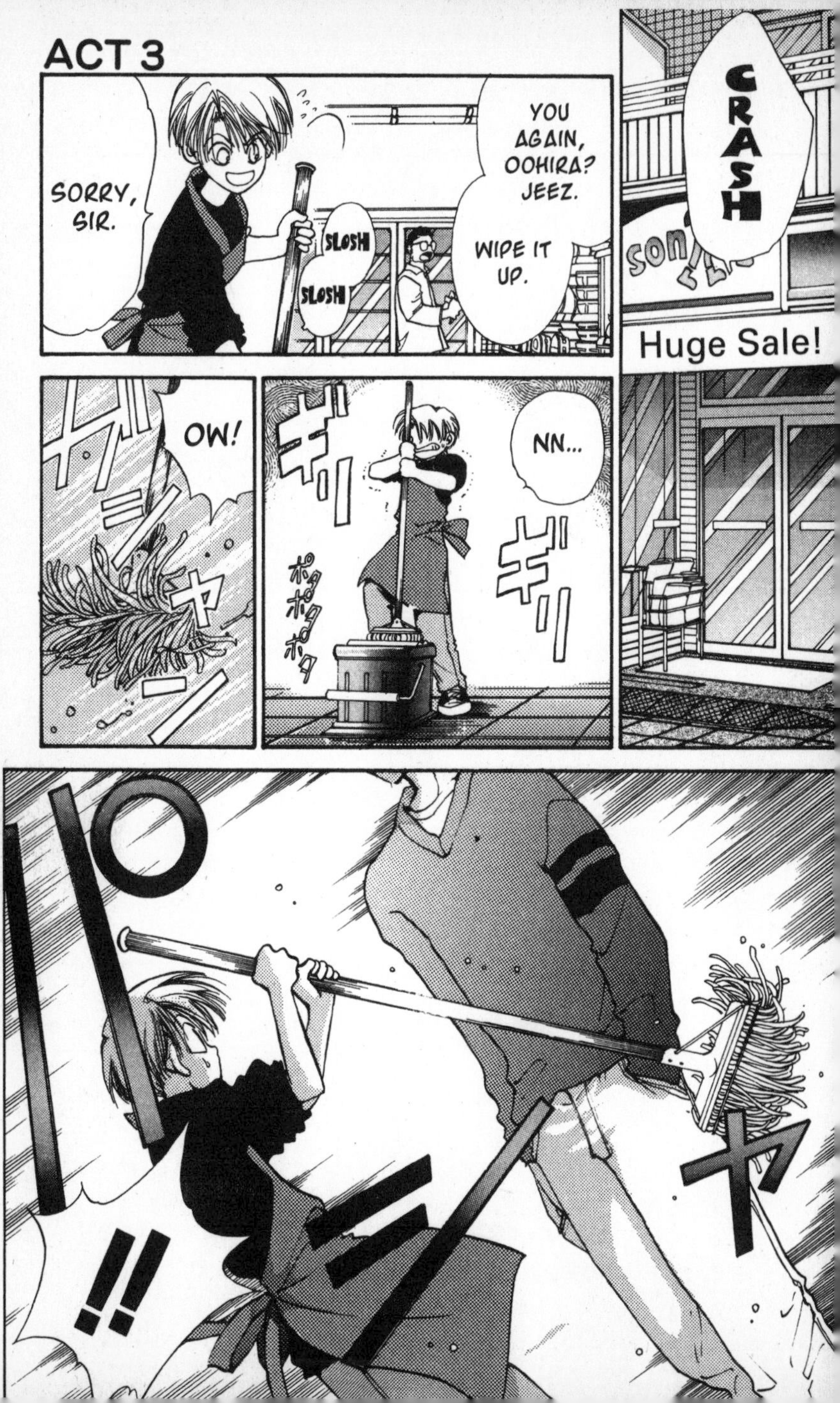
CRASH
Huge Sale!
YOU AGAIN, OOHIRA? JEEZ.
WIPE IT UP.
SLOSH
SLOSH
SORRY, SIR.
NN...
OW!
!!

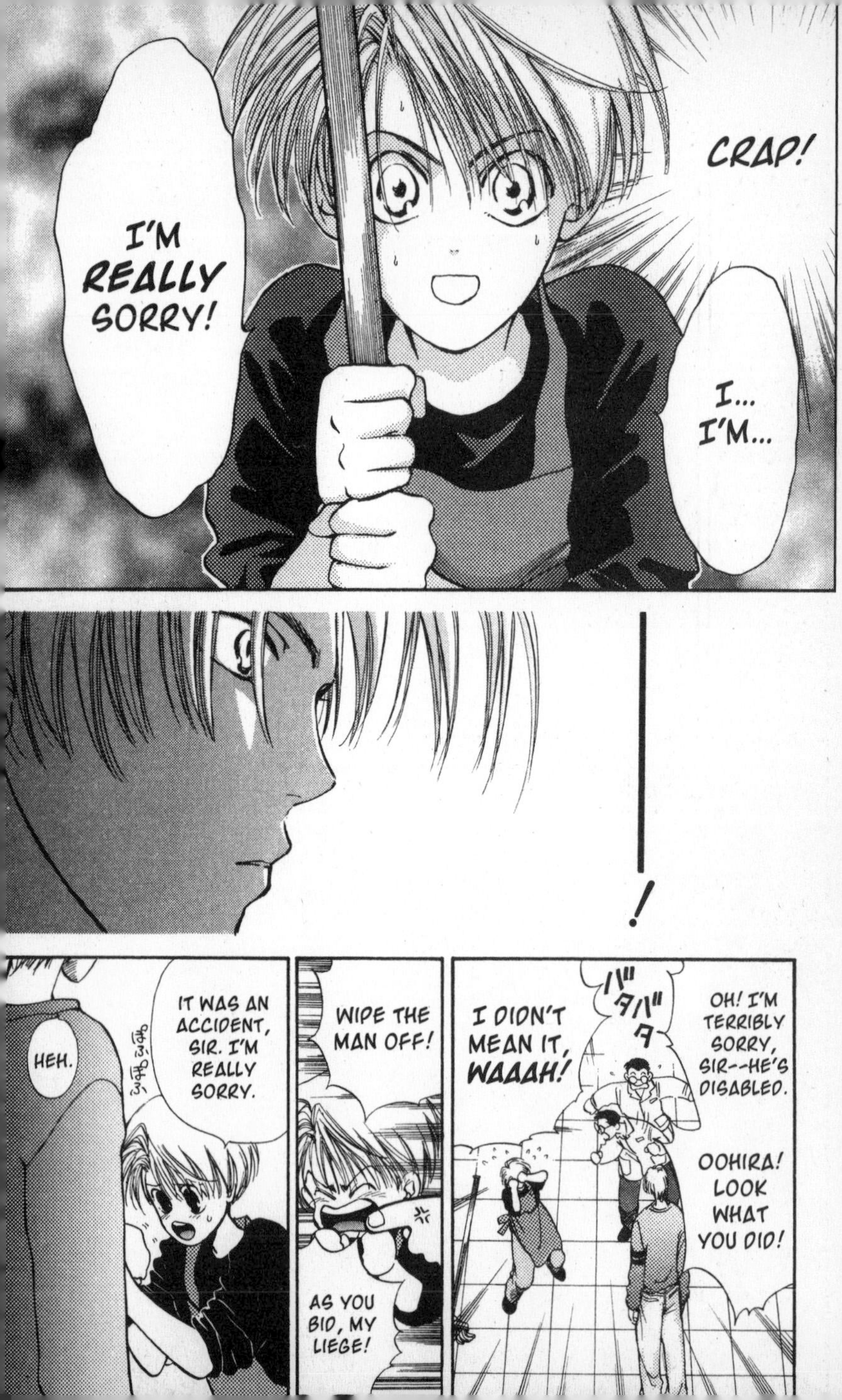
CRAP!
I... I'M...
I'M REALLY SORRY!
—!
OH! I'M TERRIBLY SORRY, SIR--HE'S DISABLED.
バタバタ
I DIDN'T MEAN IT, WAAAH!
OOHIRA! LOOK WHAT YOU DID!
WIPE THE MAN OFF!
AS YOU BID, MY LIEGE!
IT WAS AN ACCIDENT, SIR. I'M REALLY SORRY.
HEH.

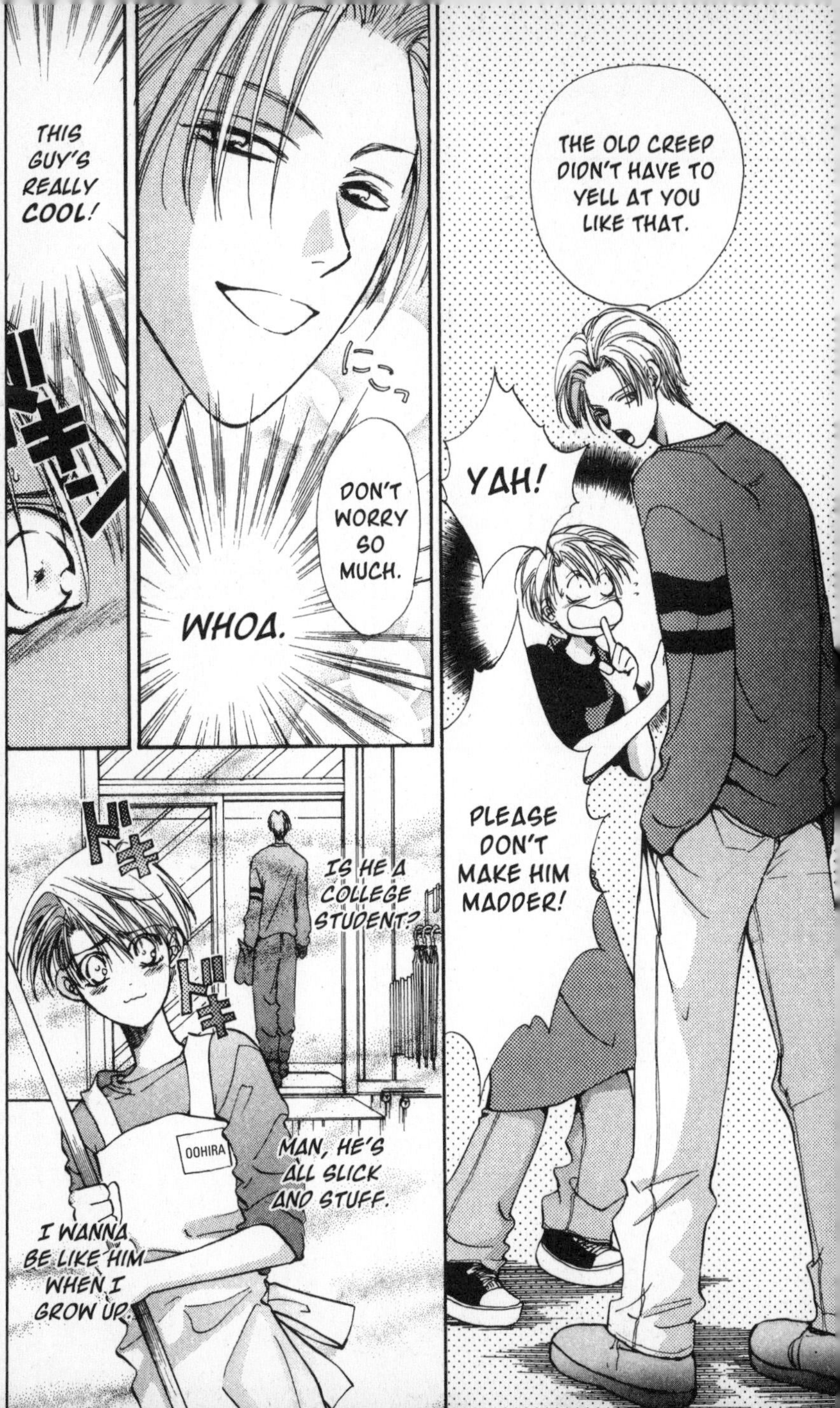
THE OLD CREEP DIDN'T HAVE TO YELL AT YOU LIKE THAT.
YAH!
PLEASE DON'T MAKE HIM MADDER!
にこっ
DON'T WORRY SO MUCH.
WHOA.
THIS GUY'S REALLY COOL!
ドキ
ドキ
IS HE A COLLEGE STUDENT?
MAN, HE'S ALL SLICK AND STUFF.
OOHIRA
I WANNA BE LIKE HIM WHEN I GROW UP...

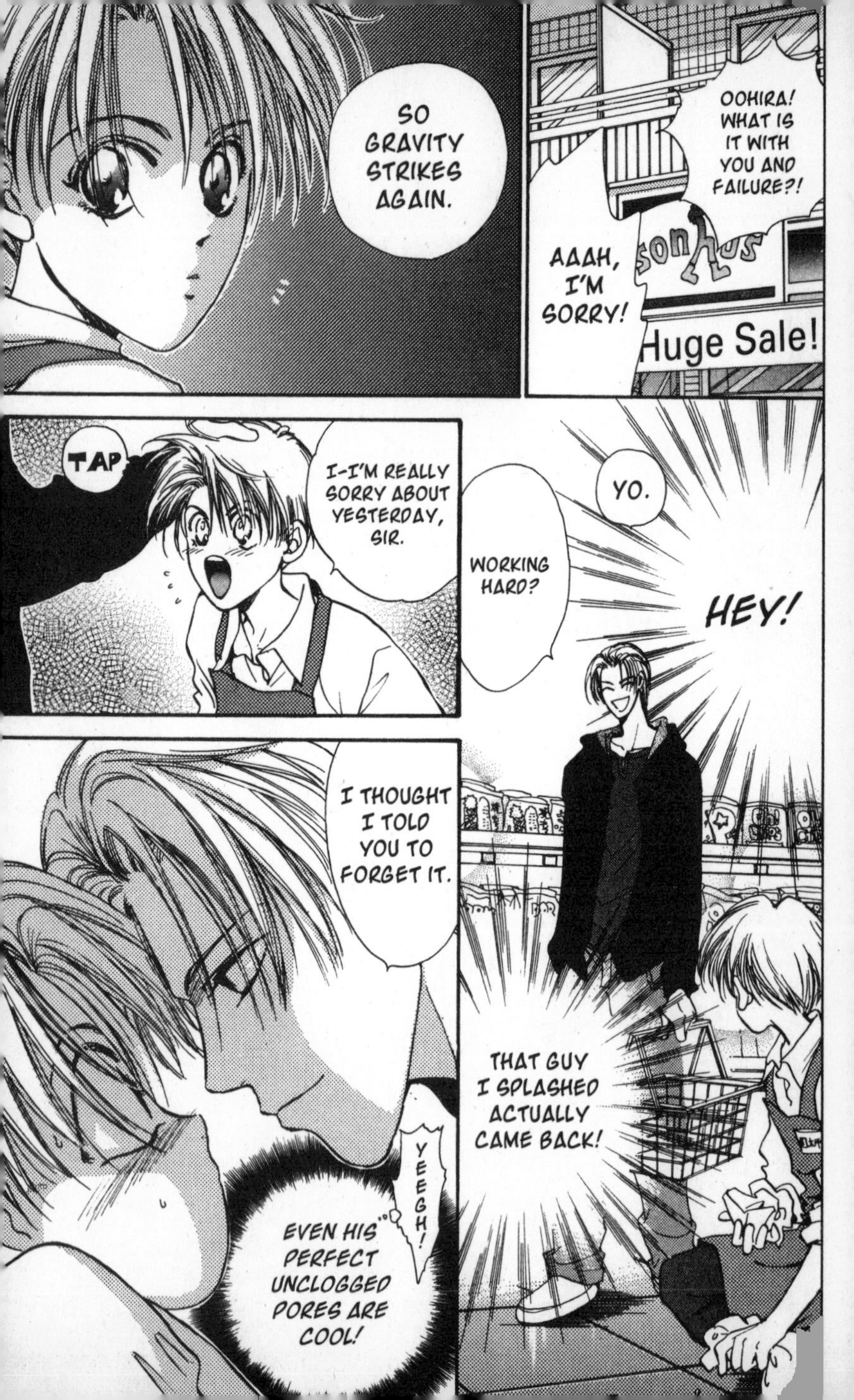
OOHIRA! WHAT IS IT WITH YOU AND FAILURE?!
AAAH, I'M SORRY!
Huge Sale!
SO GRAVITY STRIKES AGAIN.
HEY!
YO.
WORKING HARD?
THAT GUY I SPLASHED ACTUALLY CAME BACK!
TAP
I-I'M REALLY SORRY ABOUT YESTERDAY, SIR.
I THOUGHT I TOLD YOU TO FORGET IT.
YEEGH!
EVEN HIS PERFECT UNCLOGGED PORES ARE COOL!

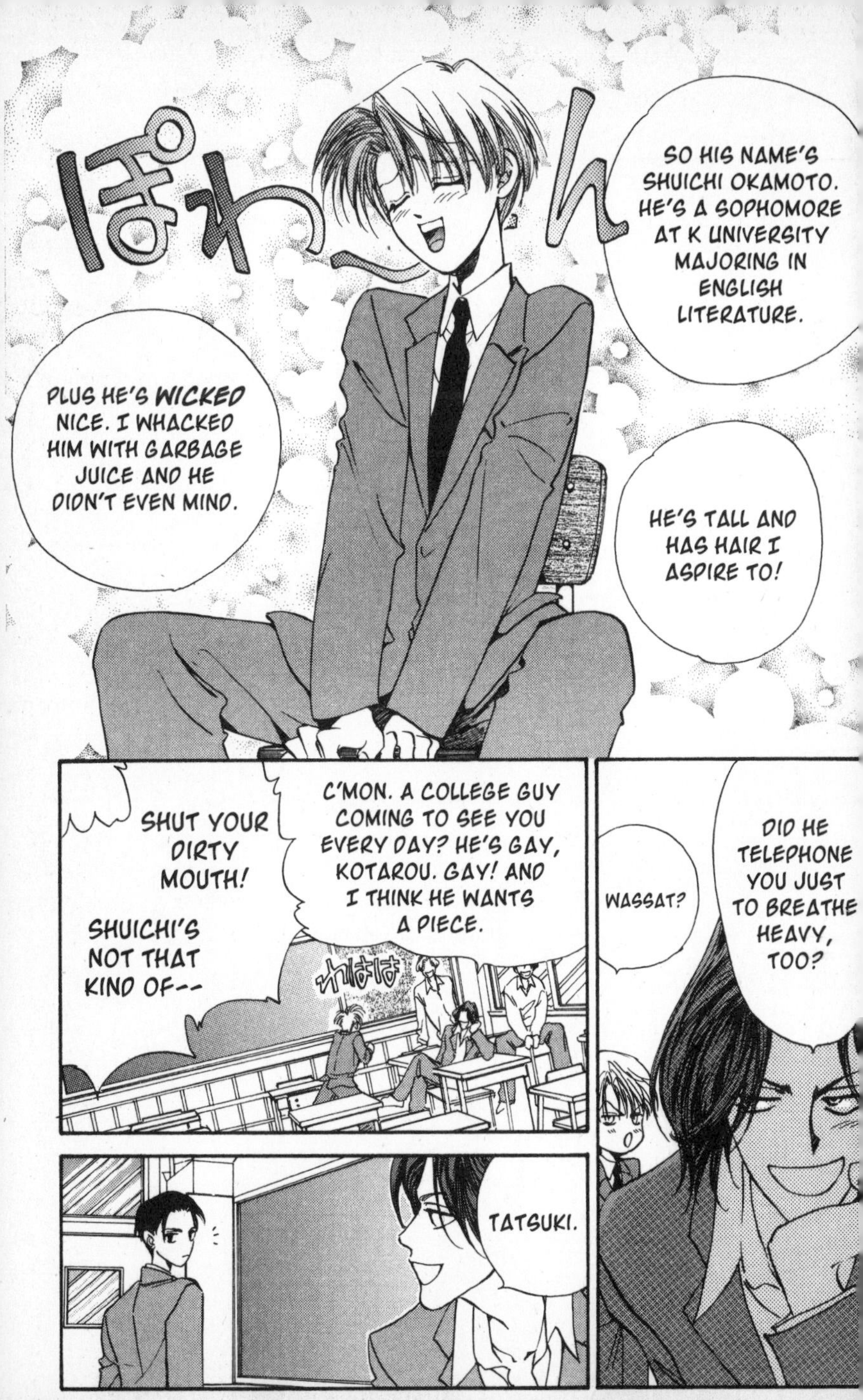
ぽわ〜ん
SO HIS NAME'S SHUICHI OKAMOTO. HE'S A SOPHOMORE AT K UNIVERSITY MAJORING IN ENGLISH LITERATURE.
PLUS HE'S **WICKED** NICE. I WHACKED HIM WITH GARBAGE JUICE AND HE DIDN'T EVEN MIND.
HE'S TALL AND HAS HAIR I ASPIRE TO!
DID HE TELEPHONE YOU JUST TO BREATHE HEAVY, TOO?
WASSAT?
C'MON. A COLLEGE GUY COMING TO SEE YOU EVERY DAY? HE'S GAY, KOTAROU. GAY! AND I THINK HE WANTS A PIECE.
わはは
SHUT YOUR DIRTY MOUTH!
SHUICHI'S NOT THAT KIND OF--
TATSUKI.

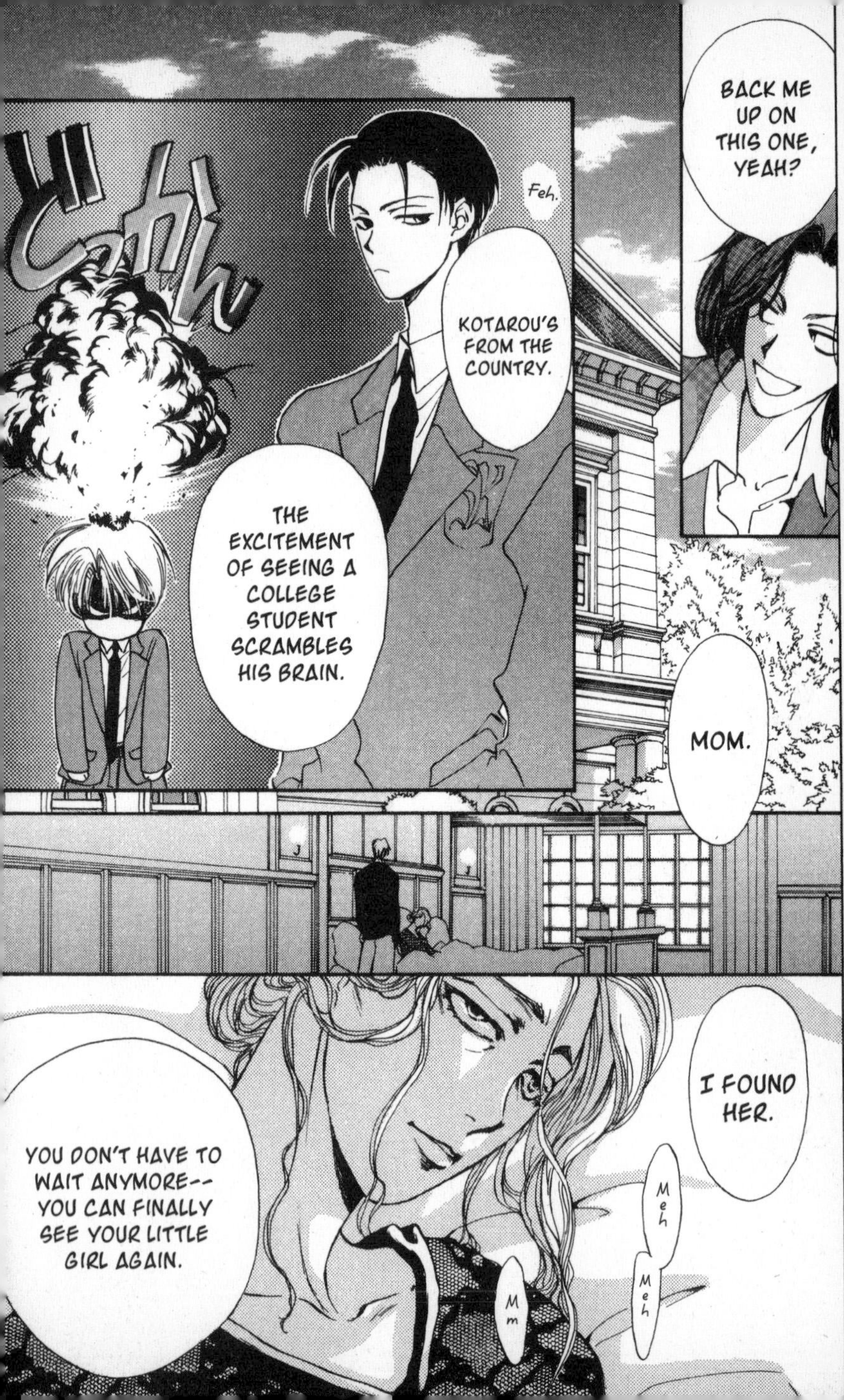
BACK ME UP ON THIS ONE, YEAH?
Feh.
KOTAROU'S FROM THE COUNTRY.
THE EXCITEMENT OF SEEING A COLLEGE STUDENT SCRAMBLES HIS BRAIN.
MOM.
I FOUND HER.
Meh
Meh
Mm
YOU DON'T HAVE TO WAIT ANYMORE-- YOU CAN FINALLY SEE YOUR LITTLE GIRL AGAIN.

ACT 3

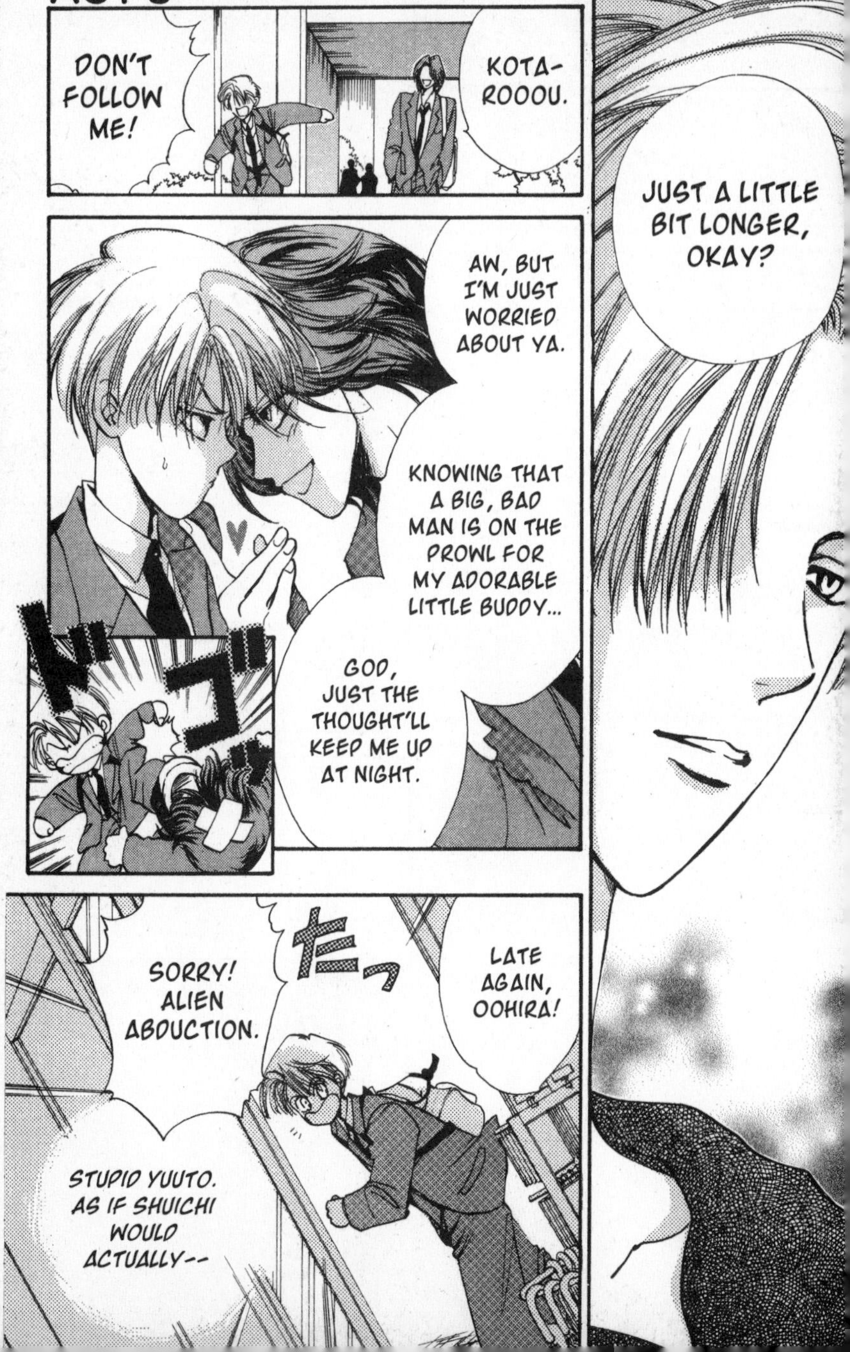
JUST A LITTLE BIT LONGER, OKAY?
KOTA-ROOOU.
DON'T FOLLOW ME!
AW, BUT I'M JUST WORRIED ABOUT YA.
KNOWING THAT A BIG, BAD MAN IS ON THE PROWL FOR MY ADORABLE LITTLE BUDDY...
GOD, JUST THE THOUGHT'LL KEEP ME UP AT NIGHT.
ドゴ
LATE AGAIN, OOHIRA!
たっ
SORRY! ALIEN ABDUCTION.
STUPID YUUTO. AS IF SHUICHI WOULD ACTUALLY--

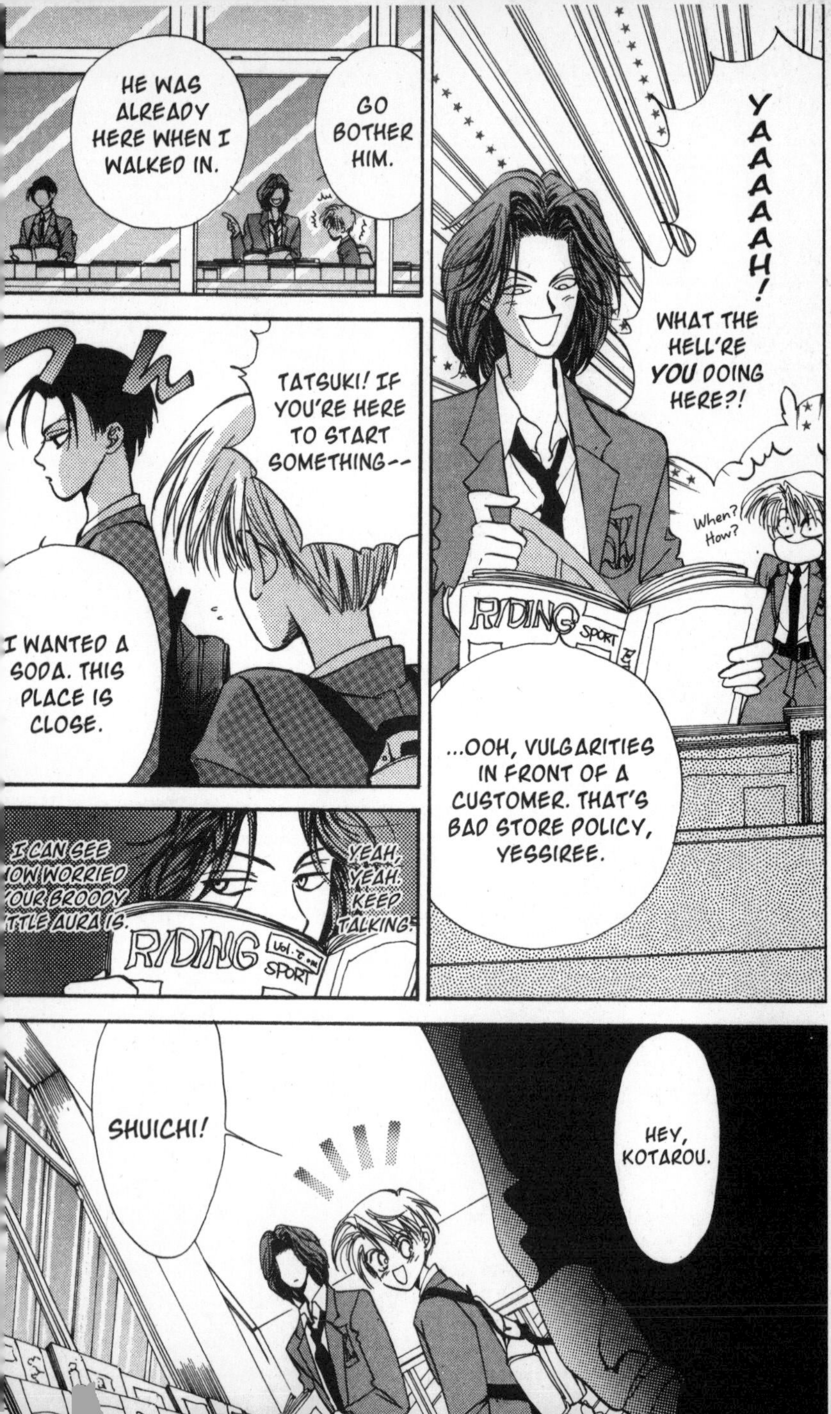
YAAAAAH!
WHAT THE HELL'RE YOU DOING HERE?!
When? How?
RIDING SPORT
...OOH, VULGARITIES IN FRONT OF A CUSTOMER. THAT'S BAD STORE POLICY, YESSIREE.
GO BOTHER HIM.
HE WAS ALREADY HERE WHEN I WALKED IN.
TATSUKI! IF YOU'RE HERE TO START SOMETHING--
I WANTED A SODA. THIS PLACE IS CLOSE.
YEAH, YEAH. KEEP TALKING.
I CAN SEE OW WORRIED OUR BROODY TTLE AURA IS.
RIDING SPORT
HEY, KOTAROU.
SHUICHI!

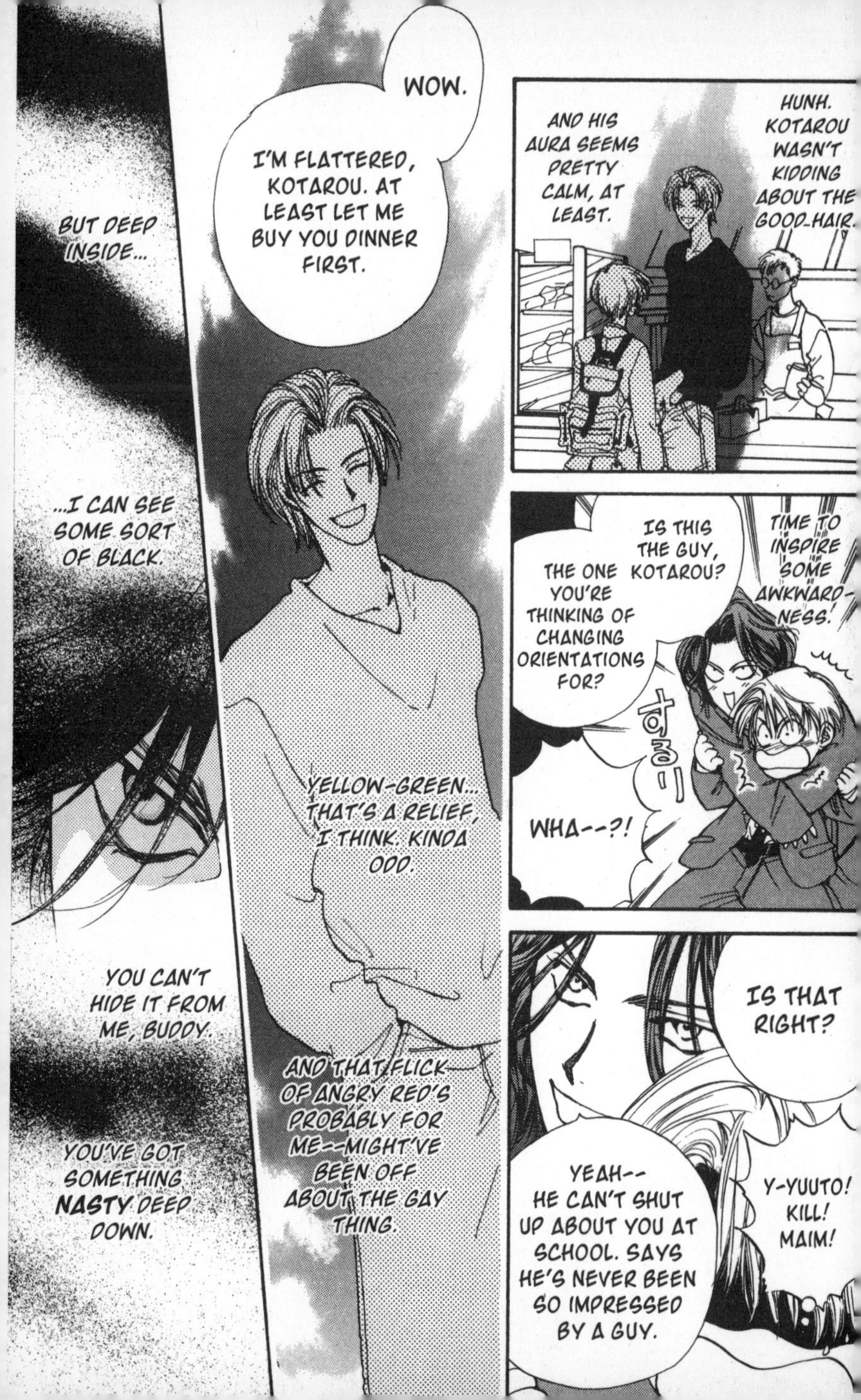
HUNH. KOTAROU WASN'T KIDDING ABOUT THE GOOD-HAIR.
AND HIS AURA SEEMS PRETTY CALM, AT LEAST.
TIME TO INSPIRE SOME AWKWARDNESS!
IS THIS THE GUY, KOTAROU?
THE ONE YOU'RE THINKING OF CHANGING ORIENTATIONS FOR?
するり
WHA--?!
IS THAT RIGHT?
Y-YUUTO! KILL! MAIM!
YEAH-- HE CAN'T SHUT UP ABOUT YOU AT SCHOOL. SAYS HE'S NEVER BEEN SO IMPRESSED BY A GUY.
WOW.
I'M FLATTERED, KOTAROU. AT LEAST LET ME BUY YOU DINNER FIRST.
YELLOW-GREEN... THAT'S A RELIEF, I THINK. KINDA ODD.
AND THAT FLICK OF ANGRY RED'S PROBABLY FOR ME--MIGHT'VE BEEN OFF ABOUT THE GAY THING.
BUT DEEP INSIDE...
...I CAN SEE SOME SORT OF BLACK.
YOU CAN'T HIDE IT FROM ME, BUDDY.
YOU'VE GOT SOMETHING NASTY DEEP DOWN.

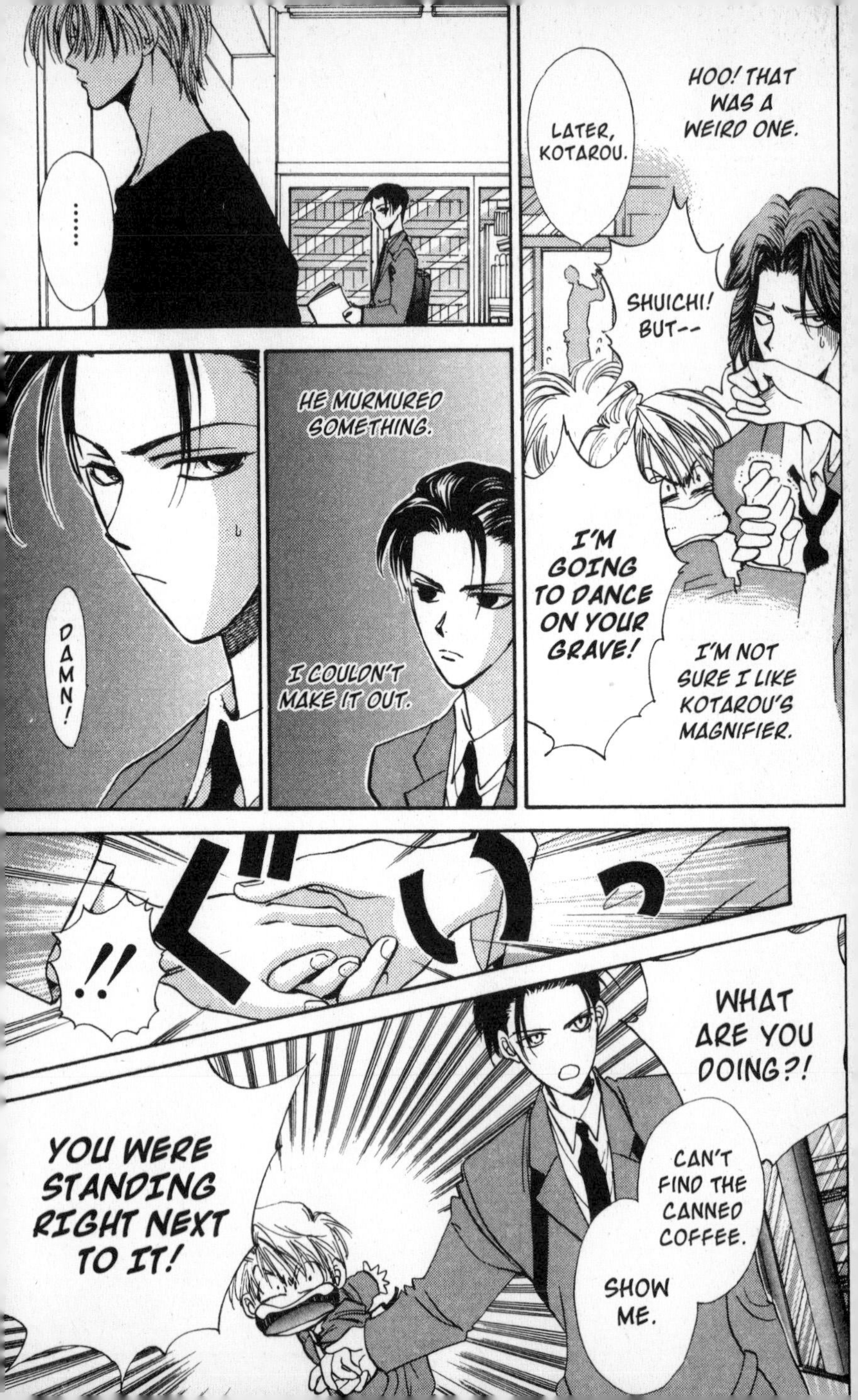
HOO! THAT WAS A WEIRD ONE.
LATER, KOTAROU.
SHUICHI! BUT--
I'M GOING TO DANCE ON YOUR GRAVE!
I'M NOT SURE I LIKE KOTAROU'S MAGNIFIER.
......
HE MURMURED SOMETHING.
I COULDN'T MAKE IT OUT.
DAMN!
ぐいっ
!!
WHAT ARE YOU DOING?!
CAN'T FIND THE CANNED COFFEE.
SHOW ME.
YOU WERE STANDING RIGHT NEXT TO IT!

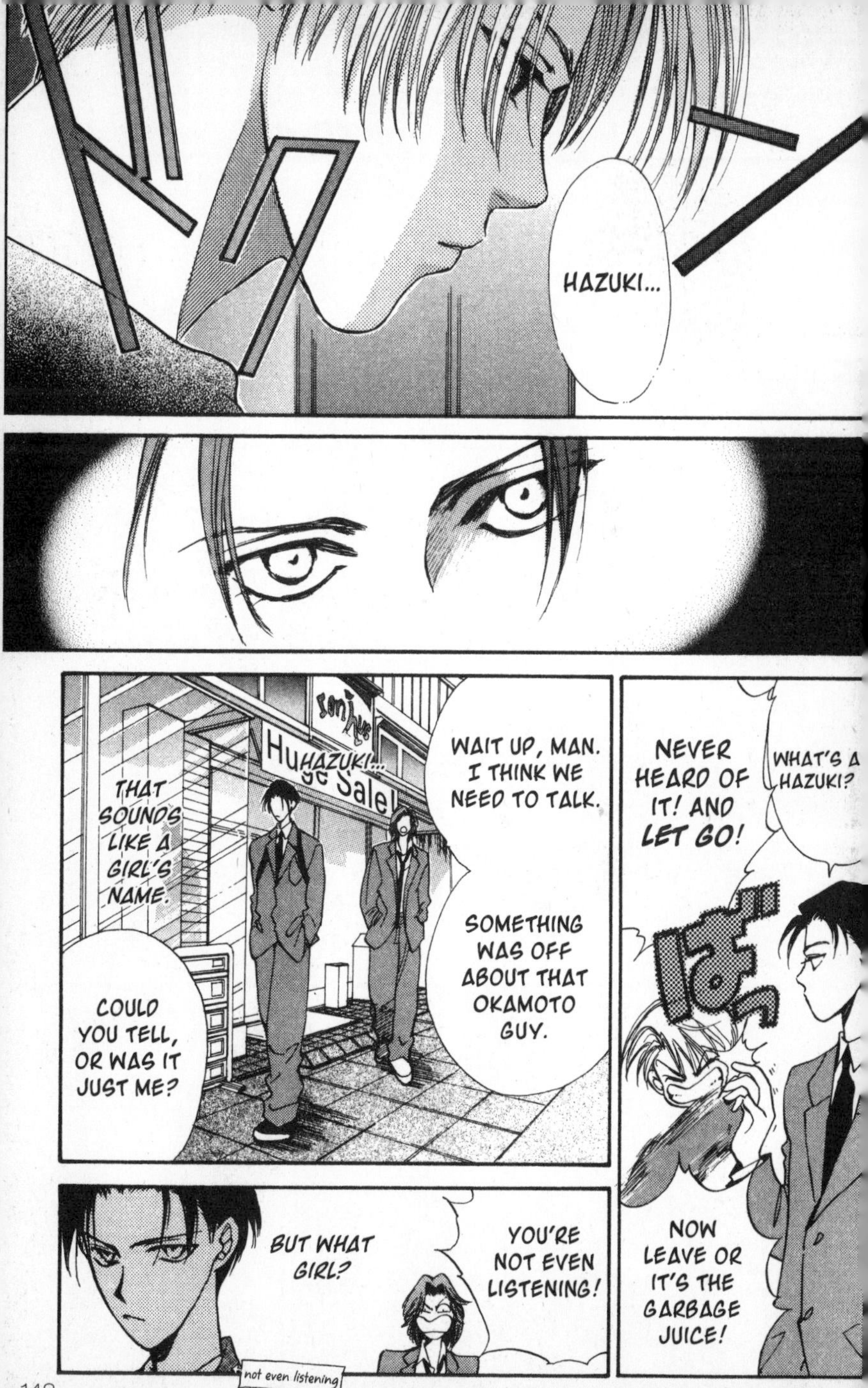
HAZUKI...
WHAT'S A HAZUKI?
NEVER HEARD OF IT! AND LET GO!
NOW LEAVE OR IT'S THE GARBAGE JUICE!
WAIT UP, MAN. I THINK WE NEED TO TALK.
HAZUKI...
THAT SOUNDS LIKE A GIRL'S NAME.
SOMETHING WAS OFF ABOUT THAT OKAMOTO GUY.
COULD YOU TELL, OR WAS IT JUST ME?
YOU'RE NOT EVEN LISTENING!
BUT WHAT GIRL?
not even listening

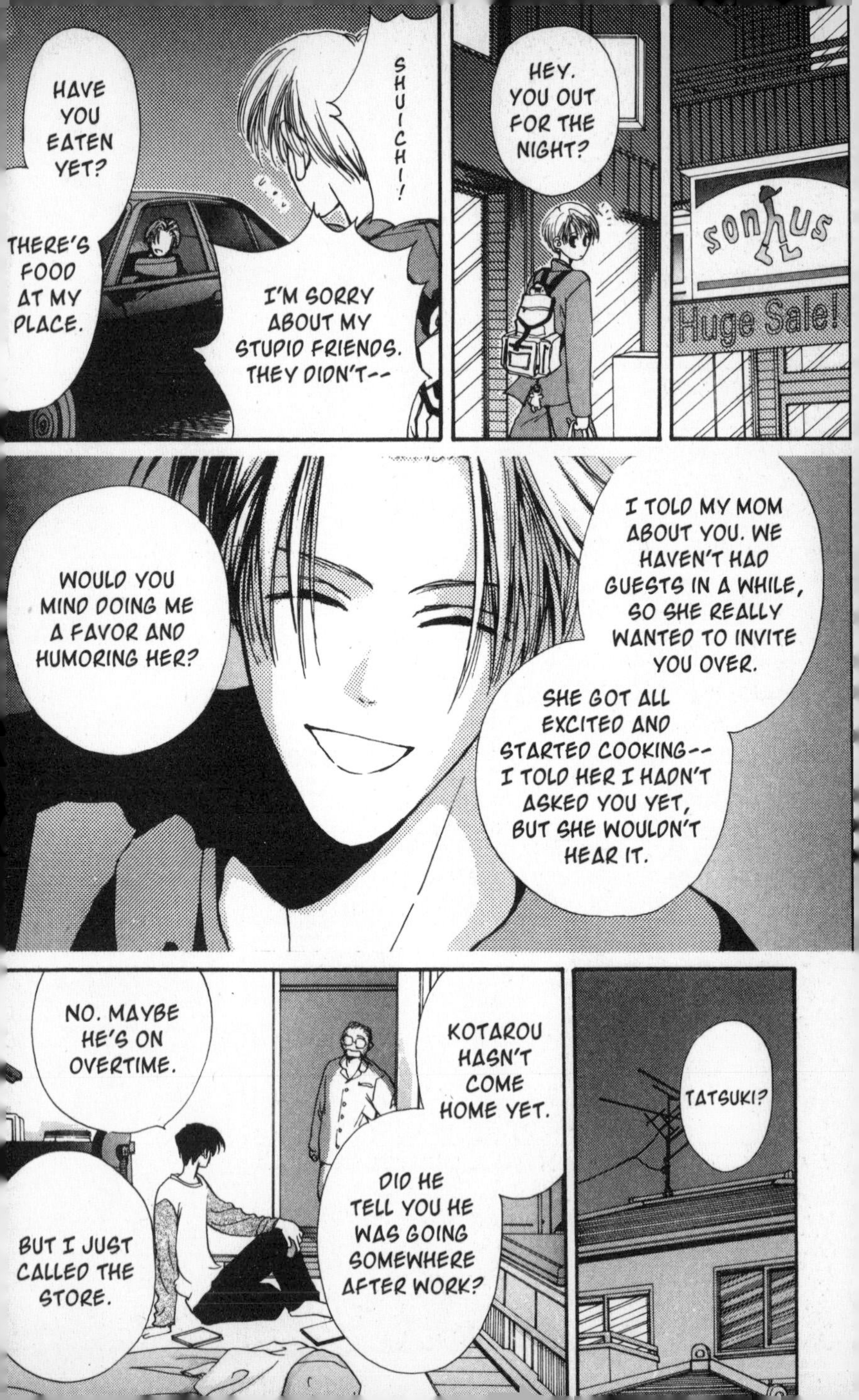
sonhus
Huge Sale!
HEY. YOU OUT FOR THE NIGHT?
SHUICHI!
I'M SORRY ABOUT MY STUPID FRIENDS. THEY DIDN'T--
HAVE YOU EATEN YET?
THERE'S FOOD AT MY PLACE.
I TOLD MY MOM ABOUT YOU. WE HAVEN'T HAD GUESTS IN A WHILE, SO SHE REALLY WANTED TO INVITE YOU OVER.
SHE GOT ALL EXCITED AND STARTED COOKING-- I TOLD HER I HADN'T ASKED YOU YET, BUT SHE WOULDN'T HEAR IT.
WOULD YOU MIND DOING ME A FAVOR AND HUMORING HER?
TATSUKI?
KOTAROU HASN'T COME HOME YET.
NO. MAYBE HE'S ON OVERTIME.
DID HE TELL YOU HE WAS GOING SOMEWHERE AFTER WORK?
BUT I JUST CALLED THE STORE.

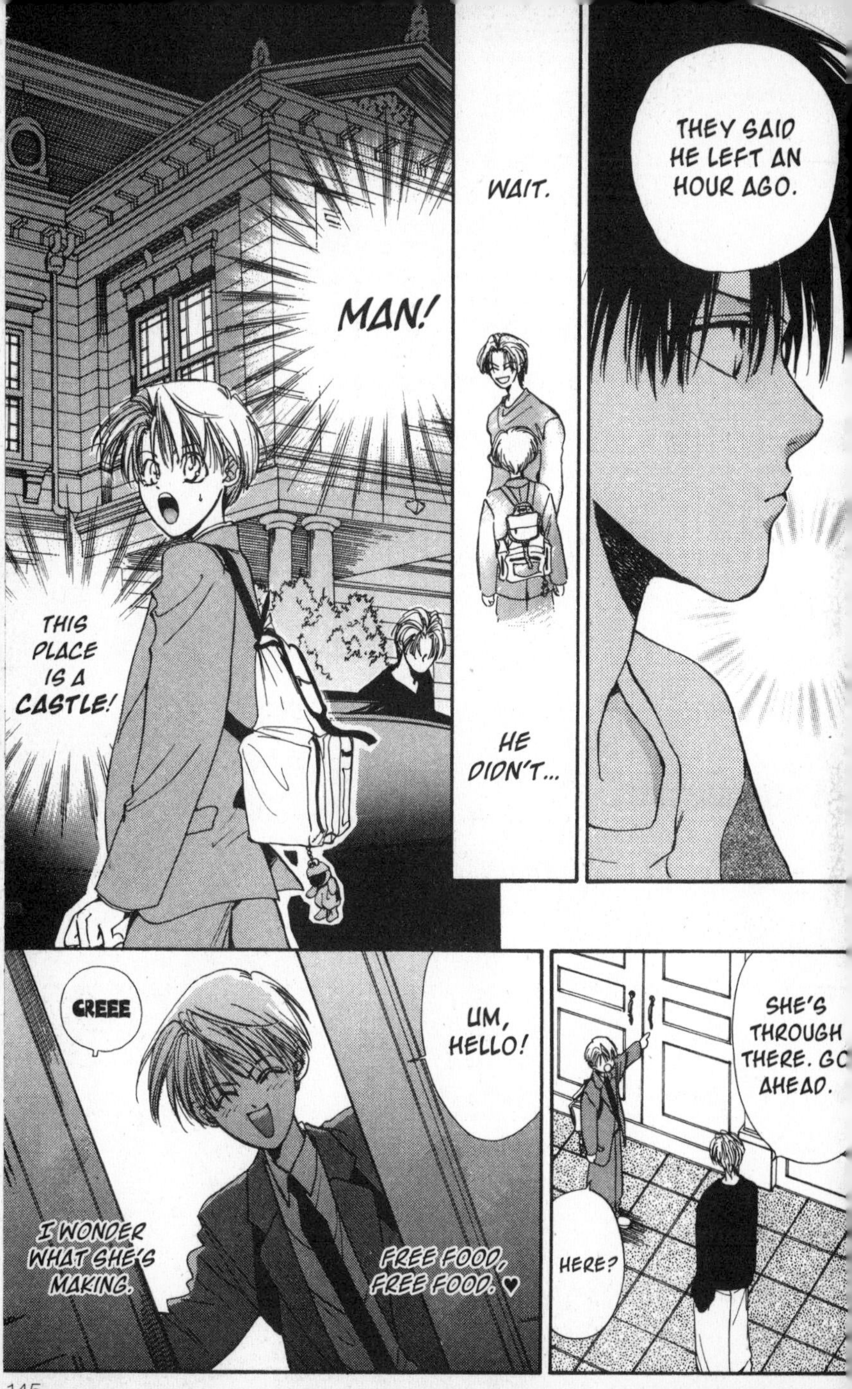
THEY SAID HE LEFT AN HOUR AGO.
WAIT.
HE DIDN'T...
MAN!
THIS PLACE IS A CASTLE!
SHE'S THROUGH THERE. GO AHEAD.
HERE?
UM, HELLO!
GREEE
FREE FOOD, FREE FOOD. ♥
I WONDER WHAT SHE'S MAKING.

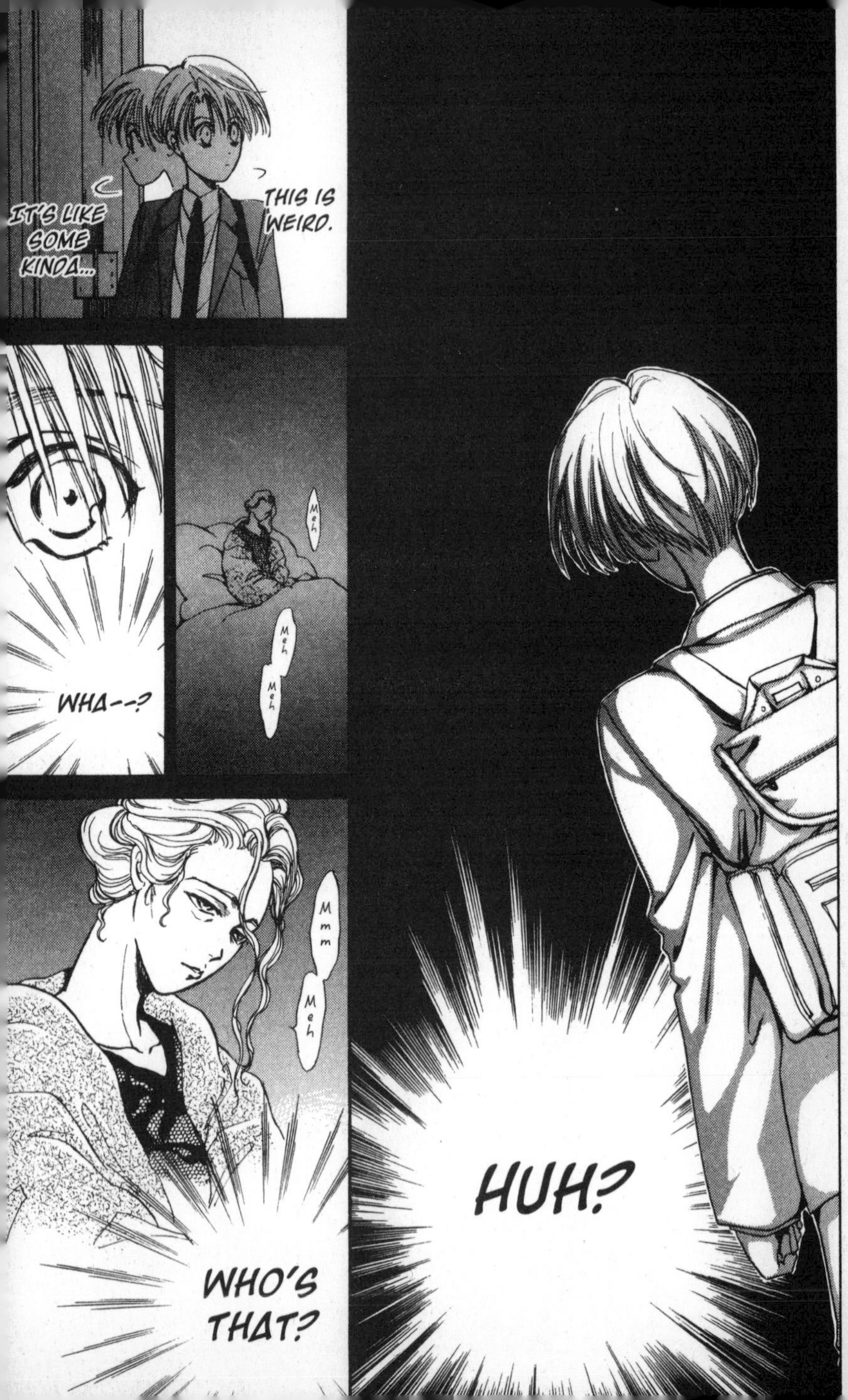
HUH?
THIS IS WEIRD.
IT'S LIKE SOME KINDA...
Meh
Meh
Meh
WHA--?
Mmm
Meh
WHO'S THAT?

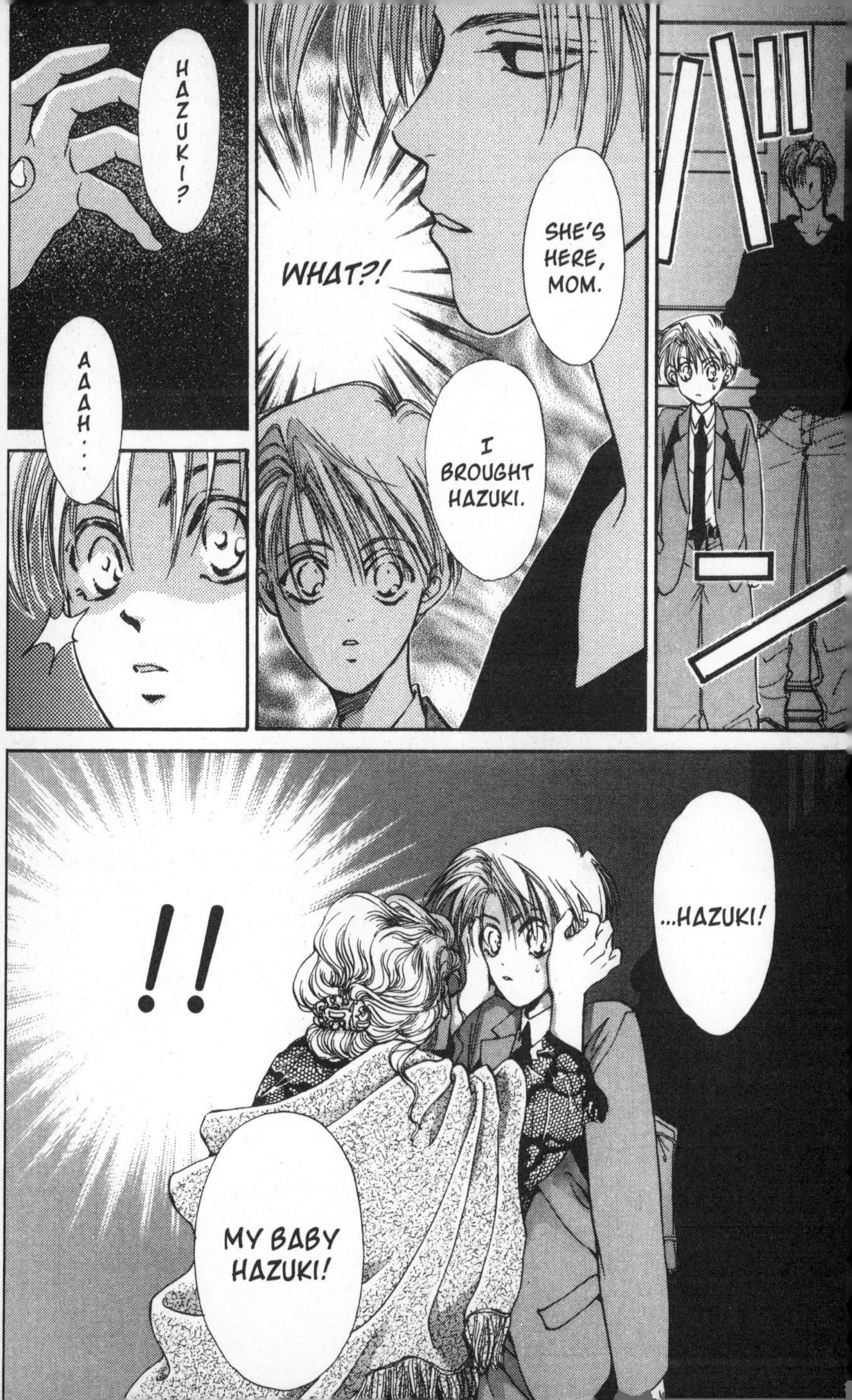
SHE'S HERE, MOM.
WHAT?!
I BROUGHT HAZUKI.
HAZUKI?
AAAH...
...HAZUKI!
!!
MY BABY HAZUKI!

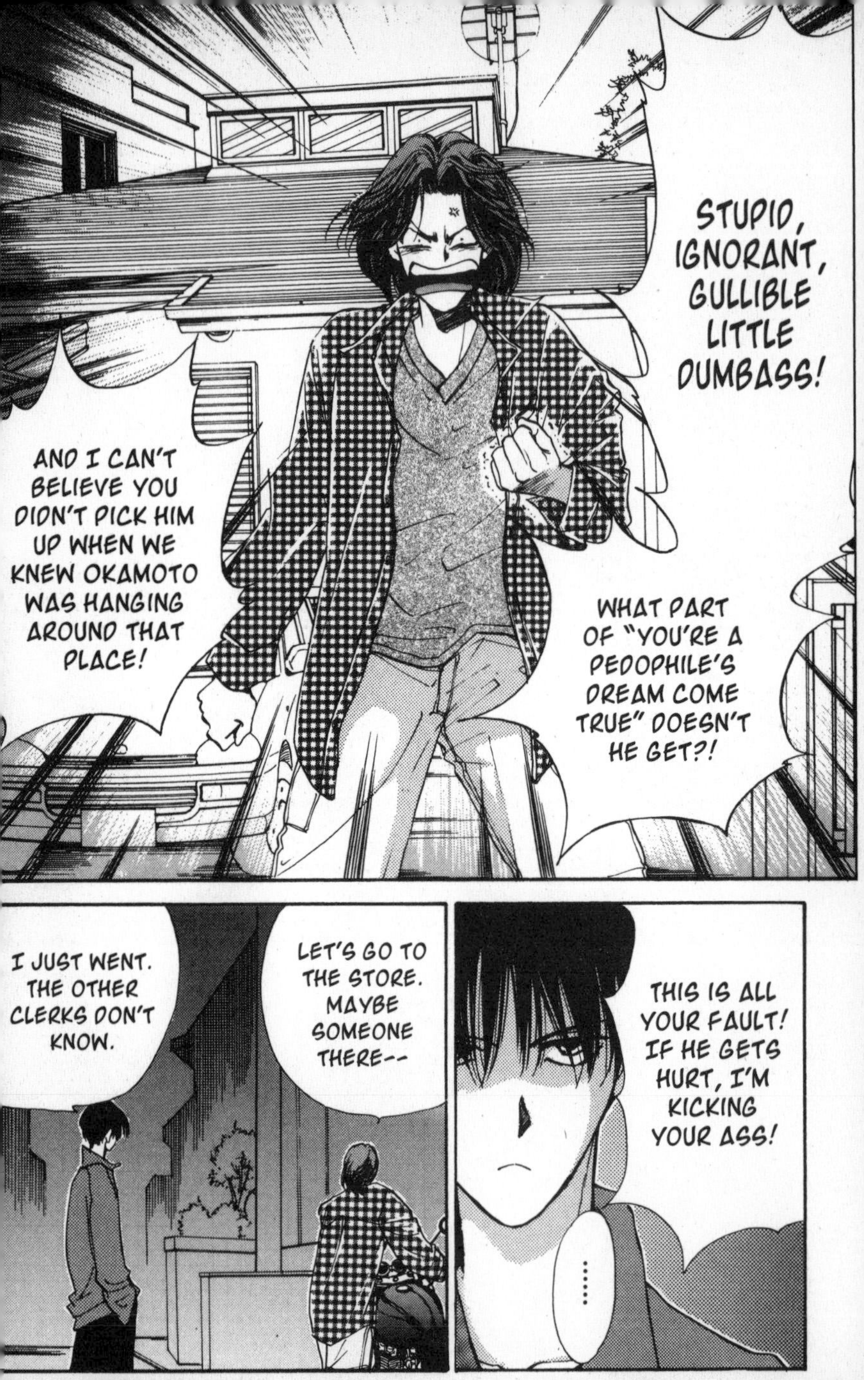
STUPID, IGNORANT, GULLIBLE LITTLE DUMBASS!
WHAT PART OF "YOU'RE A PEDOPHILE'S DREAM COME TRUE" DOESN'T HE GET?!
AND I CAN'T BELIEVE YOU DIDN'T PICK HIM UP WHEN WE KNEW OKAMOTO WAS HANGING AROUND THAT PLACE!
THIS IS ALL YOUR FAULT! IF HE GETS HURT, I'M KICKING YOUR ASS!
......
LET'S GO TO THE STORE. MAYBE SOMEONE THERE--
I JUST WENT. THE OTHER CLERKS DON'T KNOW.

ACT 3

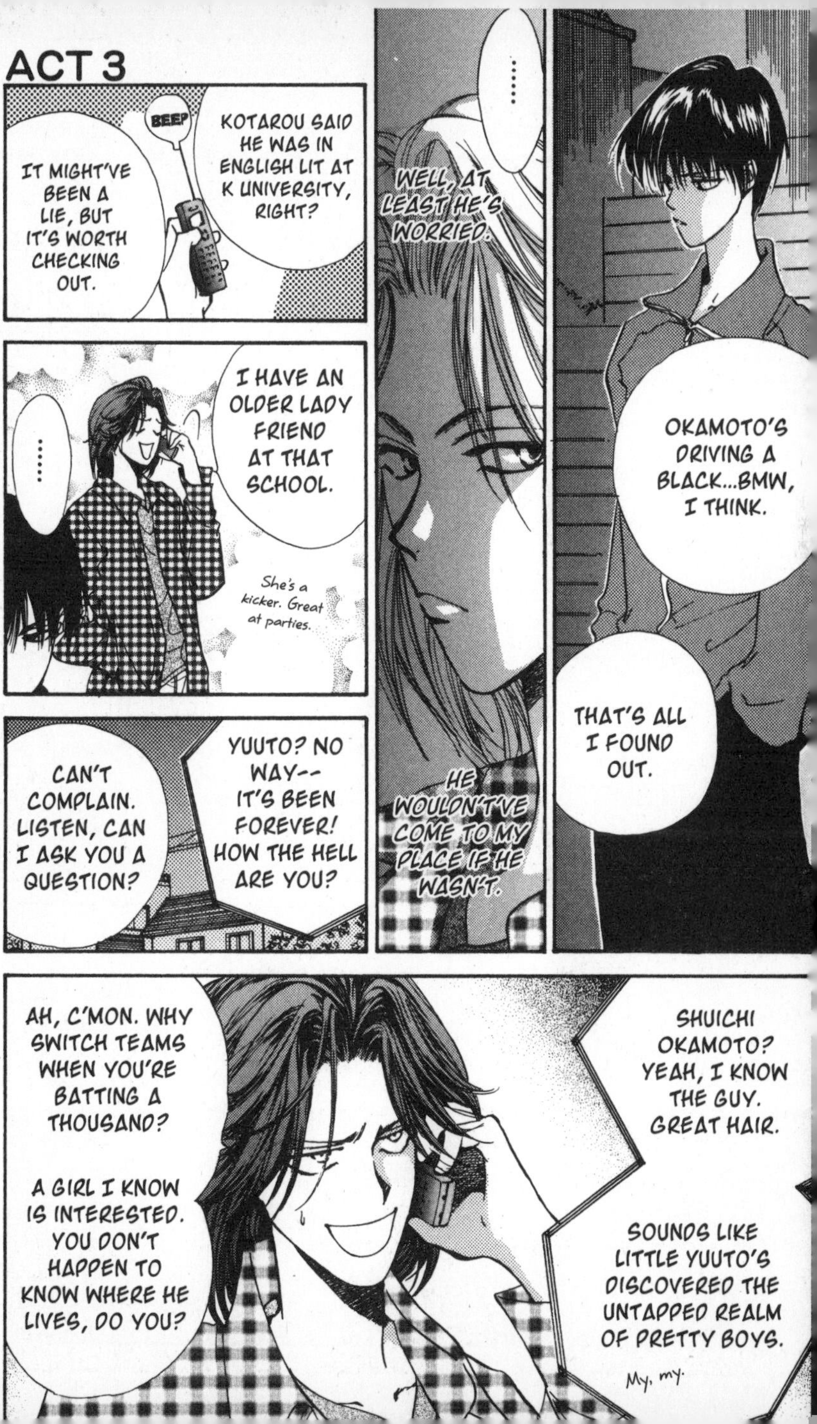

OKAMOTO'S DRIVING A BLACK...BMW, I THINK.
THAT'S ALL I FOUND OUT.
......
WELL, AT LEAST HE'S WORRIED.
HE WOULDN'T'VE COME TO MY PLACE IF HE WASN'T.
BEEP
KOTAROU SAID HE WAS IN ENGLISH LIT AT K UNIVERSITY, RIGHT?
IT MIGHT'VE BEEN A LIE, BUT IT'S WORTH CHECKING OUT.
I HAVE AN OLDER LADY FRIEND AT THAT SCHOOL.
......
She's a kicker. Great at parties.
YUUTO? NO WAY-- IT'S BEEN FOREVER! HOW THE HELL ARE YOU?
CAN'T COMPLAIN. LISTEN, CAN I ASK YOU A QUESTION?
SHUICHI OKAMOTO? YEAH, I KNOW THE GUY. GREAT HAIR.
SOUNDS LIKE LITTLE YUUTO'S DISCOVERED THE UNTAPPED REALM OF PRETTY BOYS.
My, my.
AH, C'MON. WHY SWITCH TEAMS WHEN YOU'RE BATTING A THOUSAND?
A GIRL I KNOW IS INTERESTED. YOU DON'T HAPPEN TO KNOW WHERE HE LIVES, DO YOU?

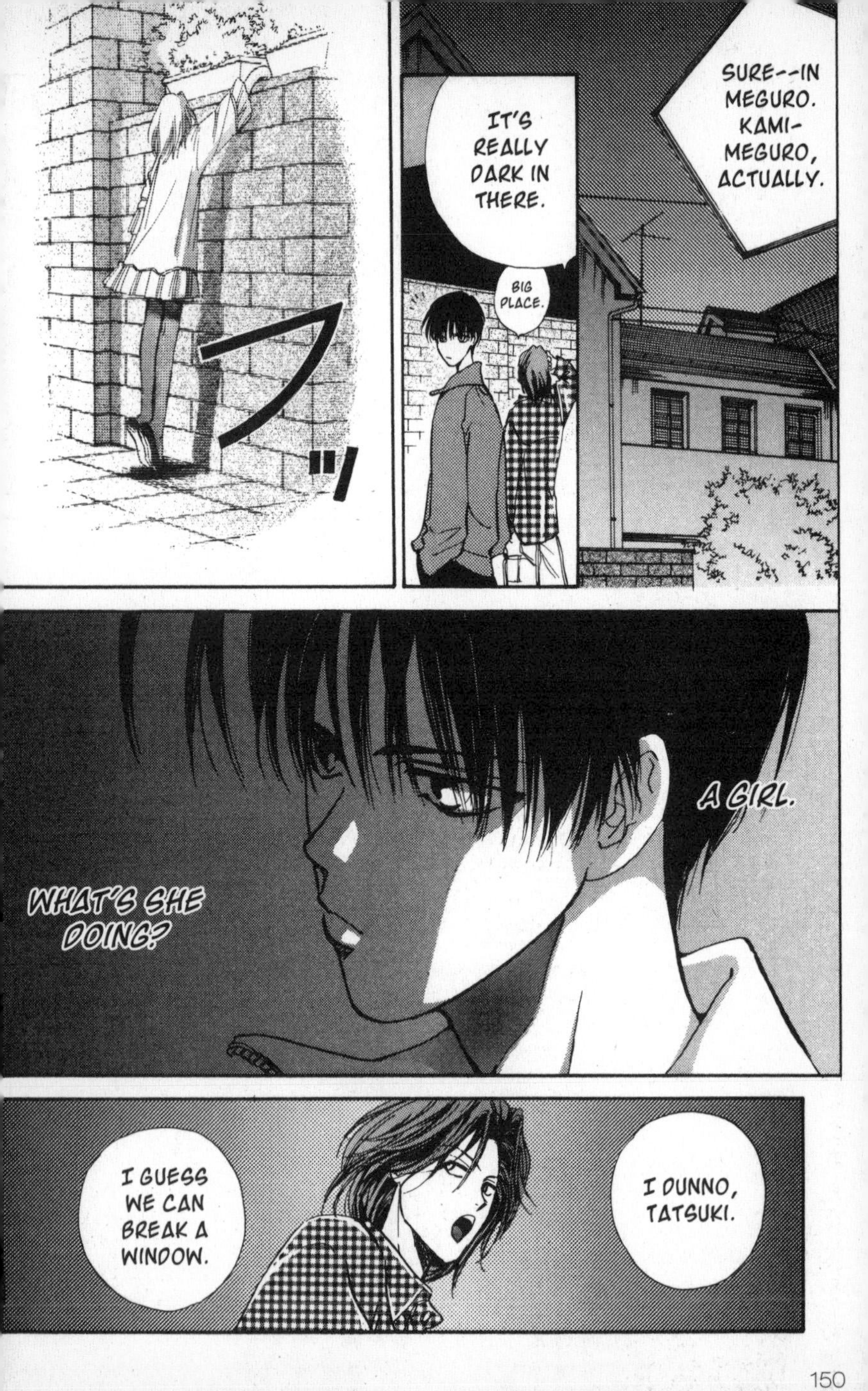
SURE--IN MEGURO. KAMI-MEGURO, ACTUALLY.
IT'S REALLY DARK IN THERE.
BIG PLACE.
A GIRL.
WHAT'S SHE DOING?
I DUNNO, TATSUKI.
I GUESS WE CAN BREAK A WINDOW.

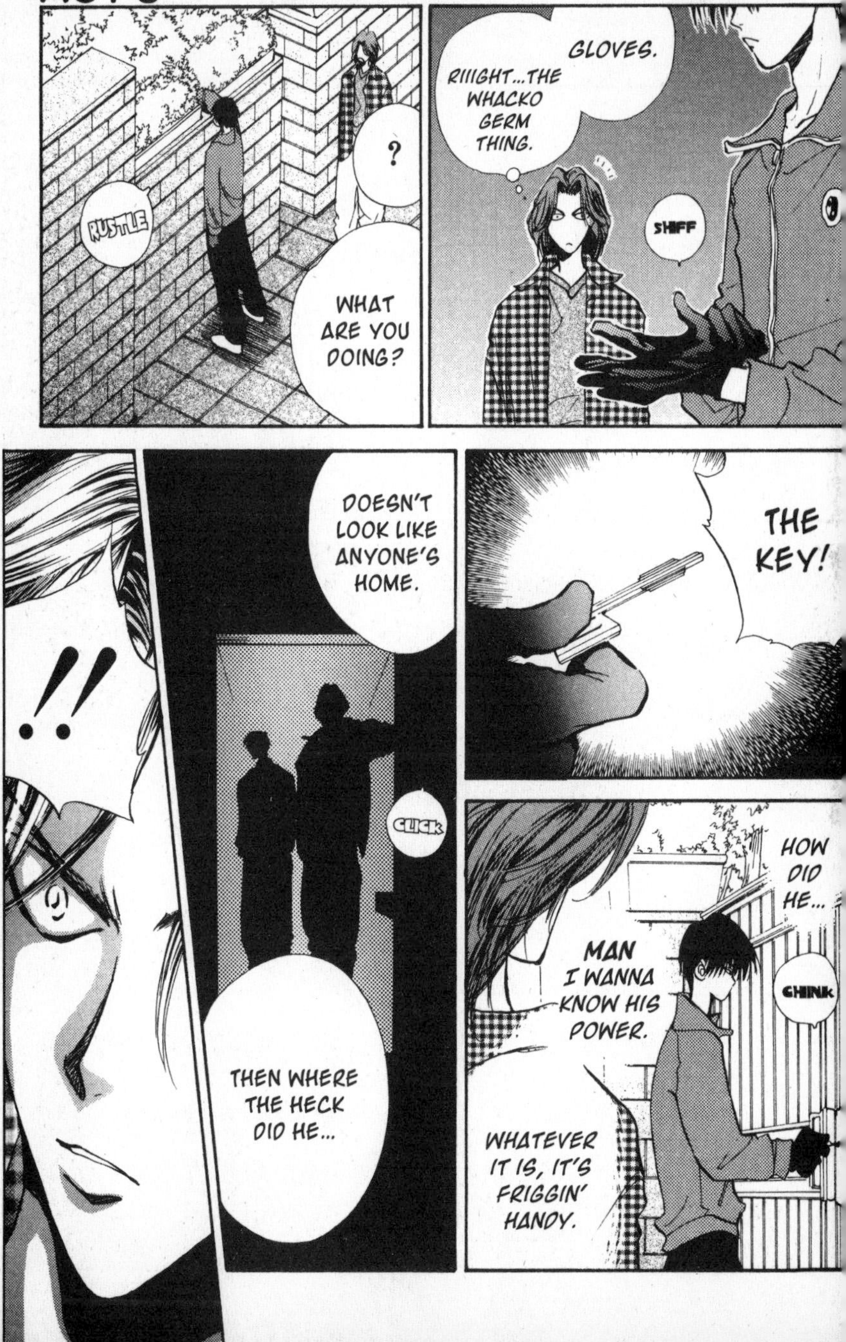
GLOVES.
RIIIGHT...THE WHACKO GERM THING.
SHIFF
?
WHAT ARE YOU DOING?
RUSTLE
THE KEY!
HOW DID HE...
CHINK
MAN I WANNA KNOW HIS POWER.
WHATEVER IT IS, IT'S FRIGGIN' HANDY.
DOESN'T LOOK LIKE ANYONE'S HOME.
CLICK
THEN WHERE THE HECK DID HE...
!!

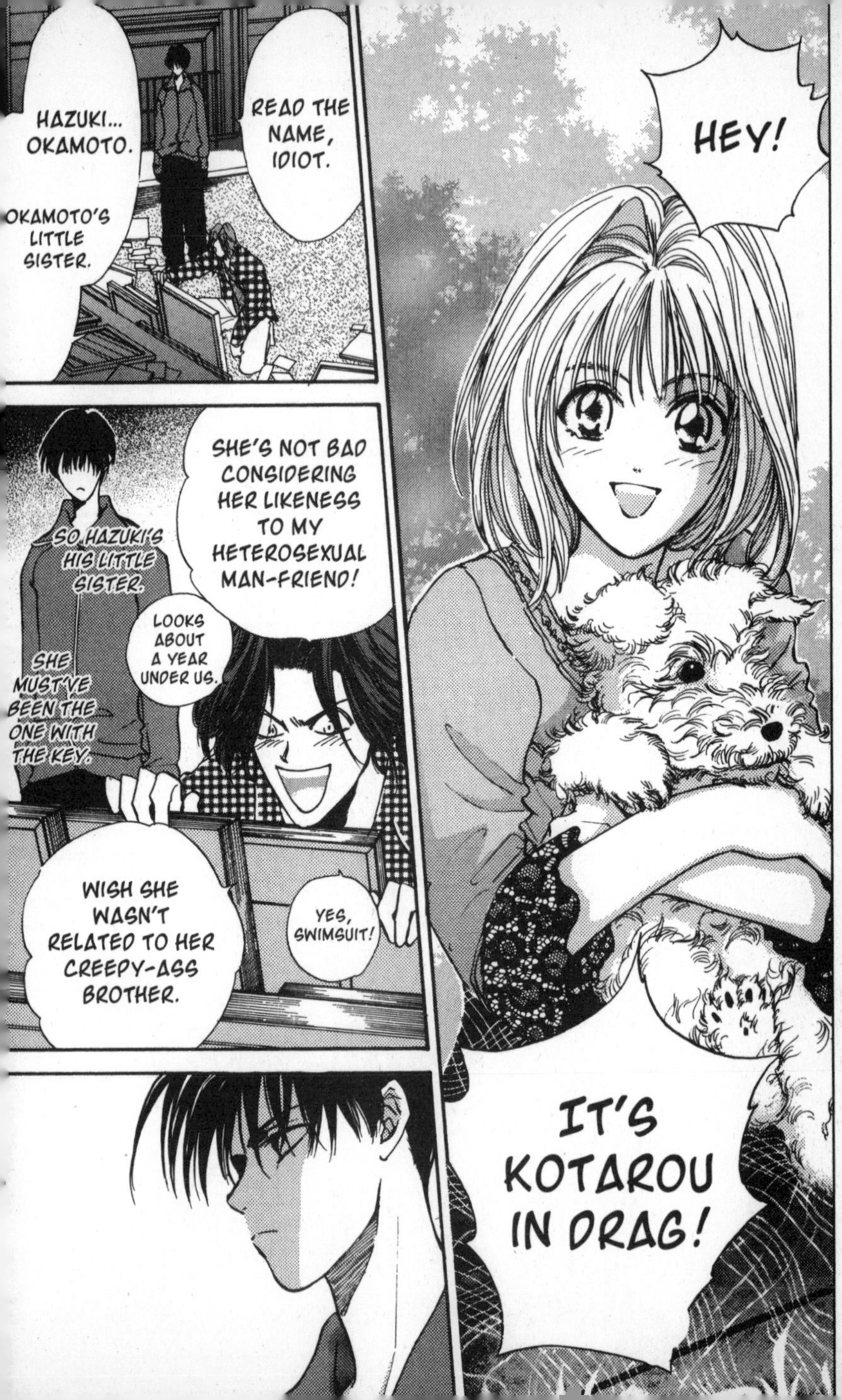
HEY!
IT'S KOTAROU IN DRAG!
READ THE NAME, IDIOT.
HAZUKI... OKAMOTO.
OKAMOTO'S LITTLE SISTER.
SHE'S NOT BAD CONSIDERING HER LIKENESS TO MY HETEROSEXUAL MAN-FRIEND!
SO HAZUKI'S HIS LITTLE SISTER.
LOOKS ABOUT A YEAR UNDER US.
SHE MUST'VE BEEN THE ONE WITH THE KEY.
YES, SWIMSUIT!
WISH SHE WASN'T RELATED TO HER CREEPY-ASS BROTHER.

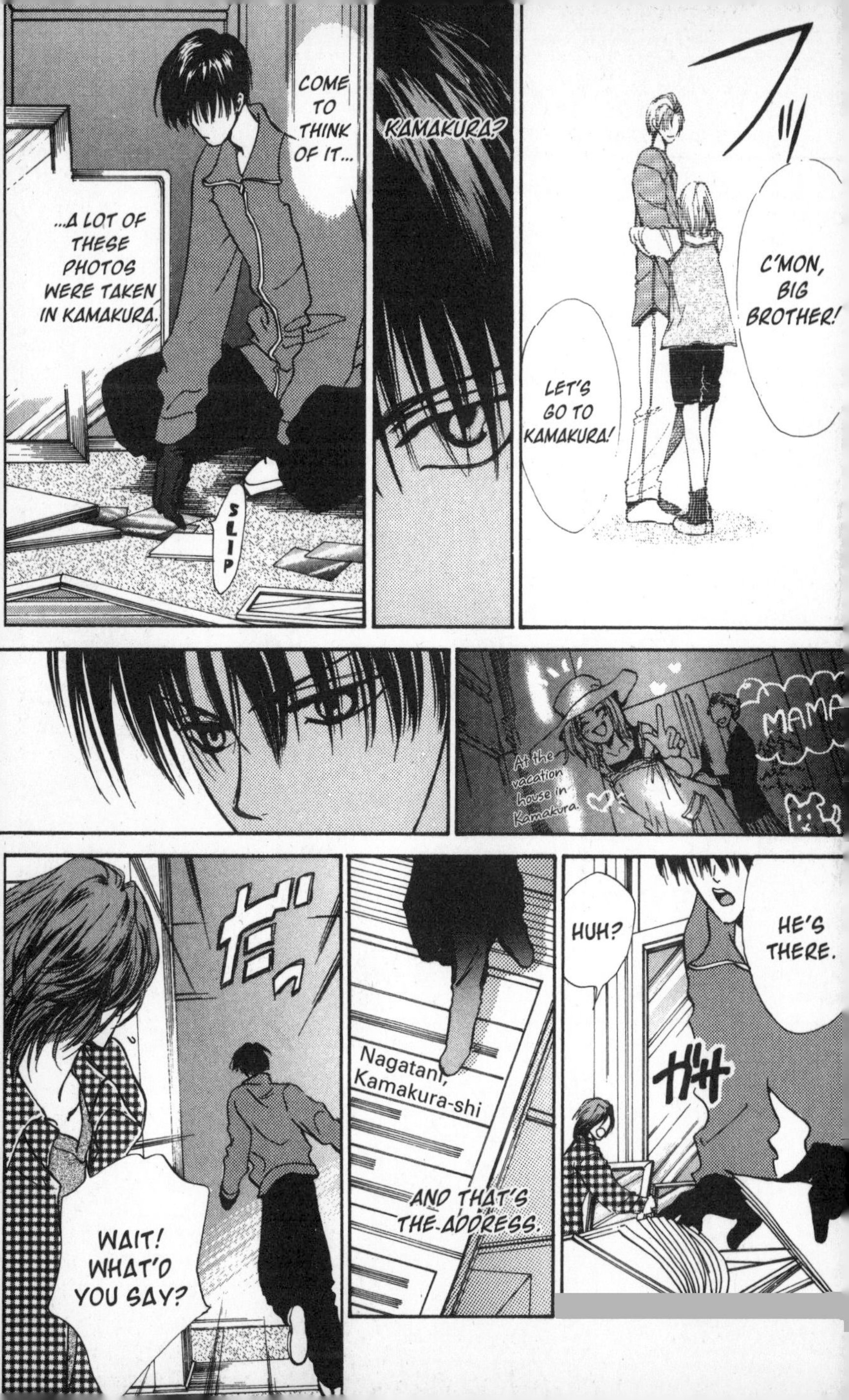
C'MON, BIG BROTHER!
LET'S GO TO KAMAKURA!
KAMAKURA?
COME TO THINK OF IT...
...A LOT OF THESE PHOTOS WERE TAKEN IN KAMAKURA.
SLIP
MAMA
At the vacation house in Kamakura.
HE'S THERE.
HUH?
ガサ
Nagatani, Kamakura-shi
AND THAT'S THE ADDRESS.
だっ
WAIT! WHAT'D YOU SAY?

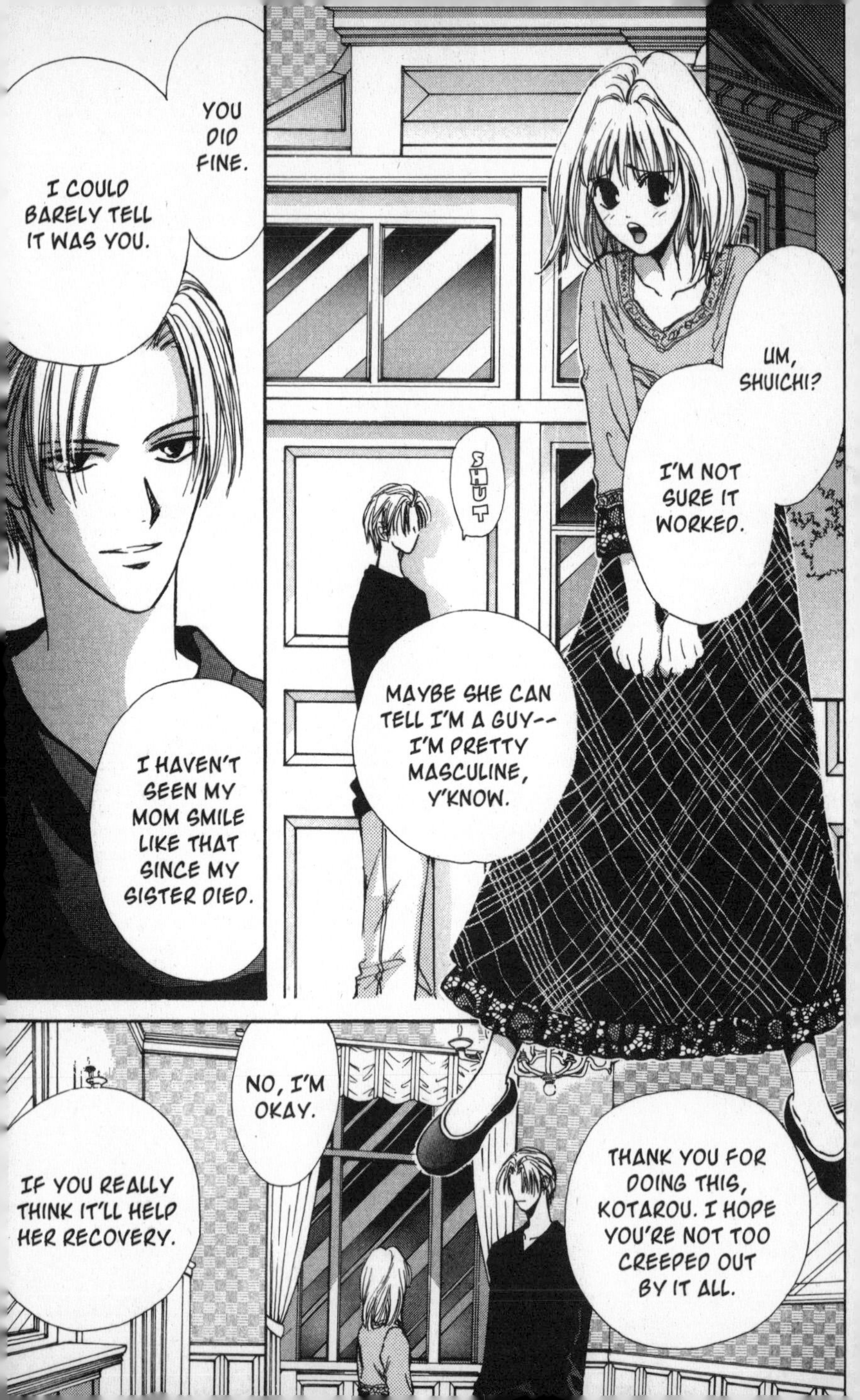
UM, SHUICHI?
I'M NOT SURE IT WORKED.
SHUT
MAYBE SHE CAN TELL I'M A GUY-- I'M PRETTY MASCULINE, Y'KNOW.
YOU DID FINE.
I COULD BARELY TELL IT WAS YOU.
I HAVEN'T SEEN MY MOM SMILE LIKE THAT SINCE MY SISTER DIED.
THANK YOU FOR DOING THIS, KOTAROU. I HOPE YOU'RE NOT TOO CREEPED OUT BY IT ALL.
NO, I'M OKAY.
IF YOU REALLY THINK IT'LL HELP HER RECOVERY.

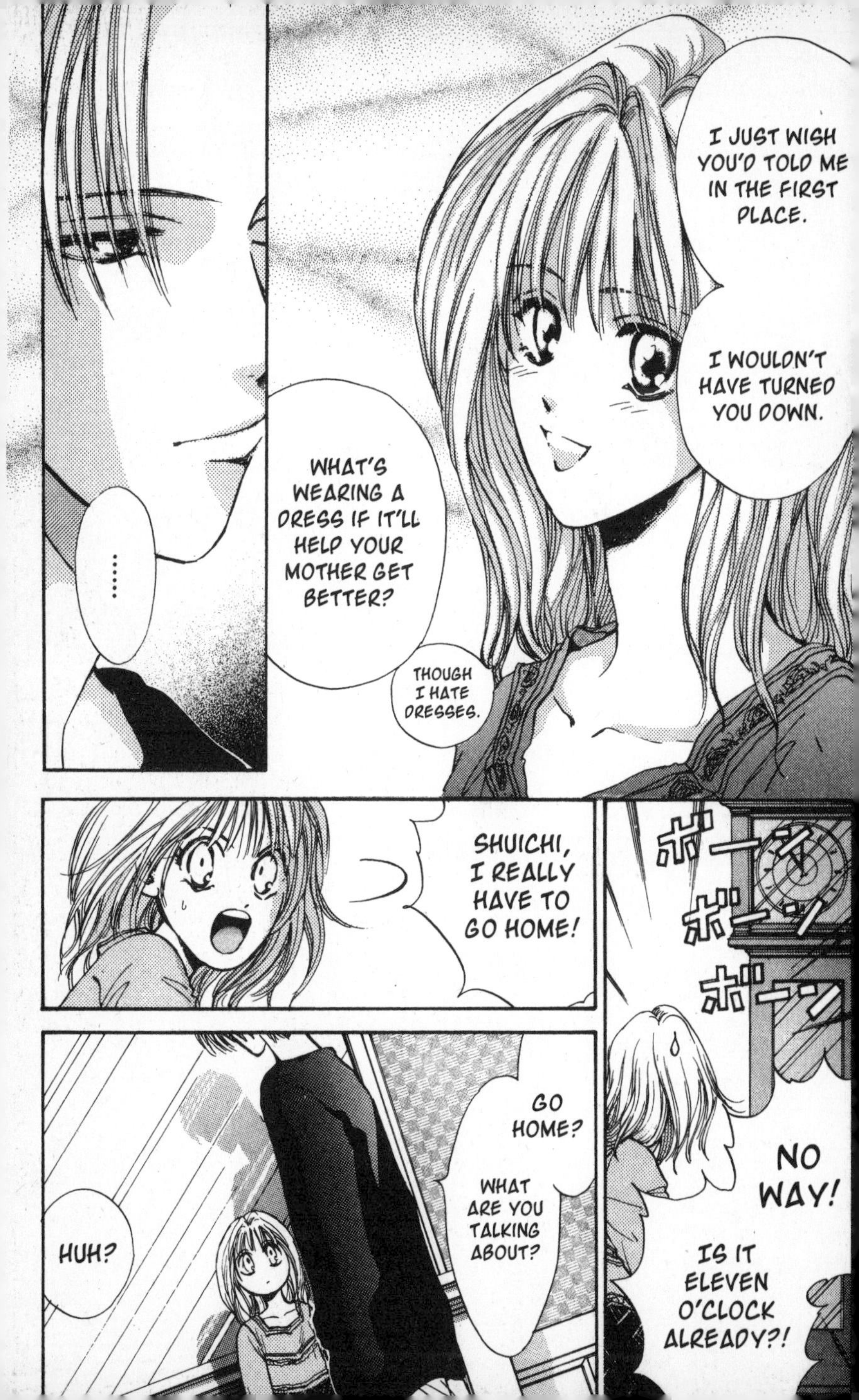
I JUST WISH YOU'D TOLD ME IN THE FIRST PLACE.
I WOULDN'T HAVE TURNED YOU DOWN.
WHAT'S WEARING A DRESS IF IT'LL HELP YOUR MOTHER GET BETTER?
THOUGH I HATE DRESSES.
......
ボーン
ボーン
ボーン
NO WAY!
IS IT ELEVEN O'CLOCK ALREADY?!
SHUICHI, I REALLY HAVE TO GO HOME!
GO HOME?
WHAT ARE YOU TALKING ABOUT?
HUH?

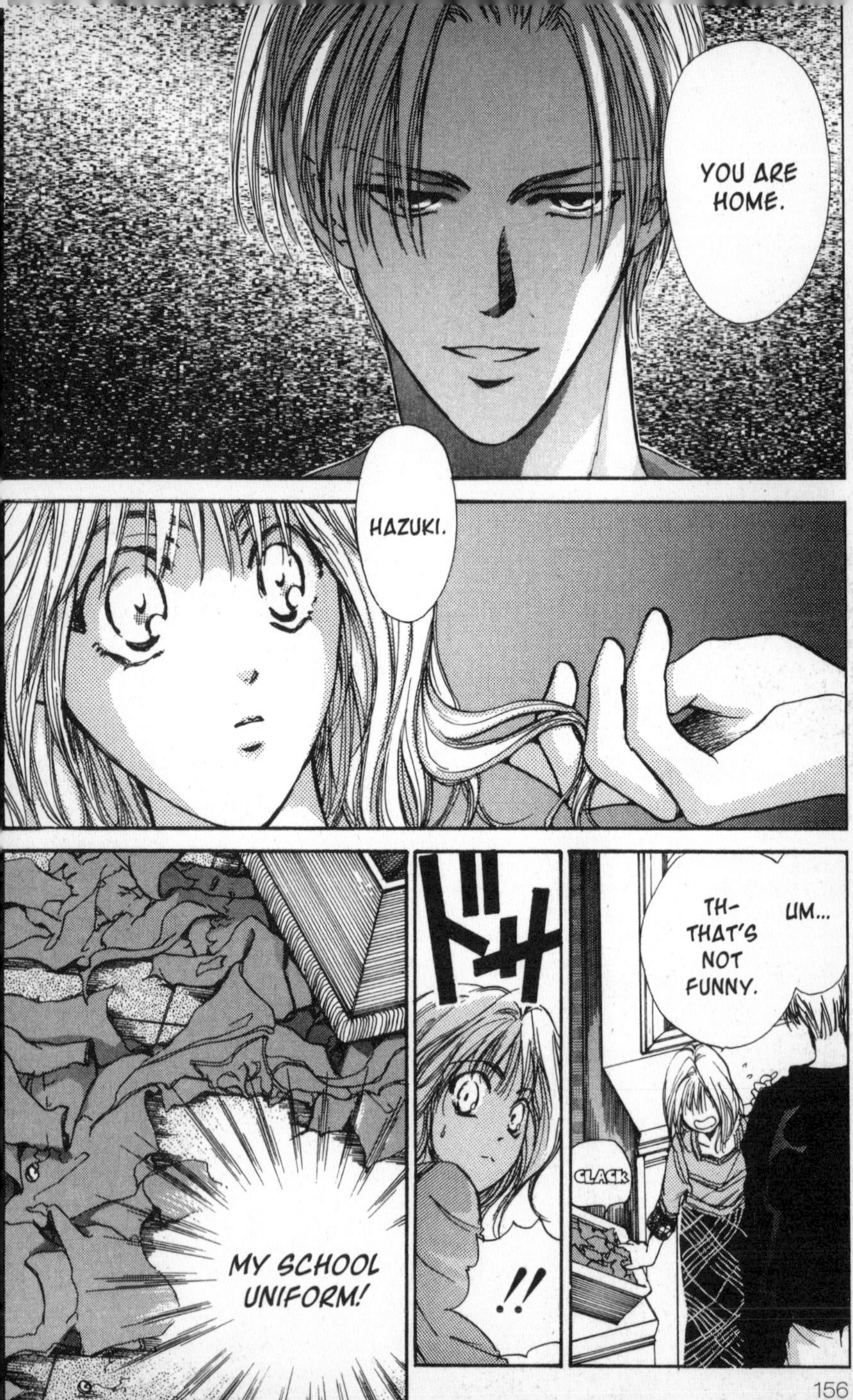
YOU ARE HOME.
HAZUKI.
UM...
TH- THAT'S NOT FUNNY.
CLACK
ドサ
!!
MY SCHOOL UNIFORM!

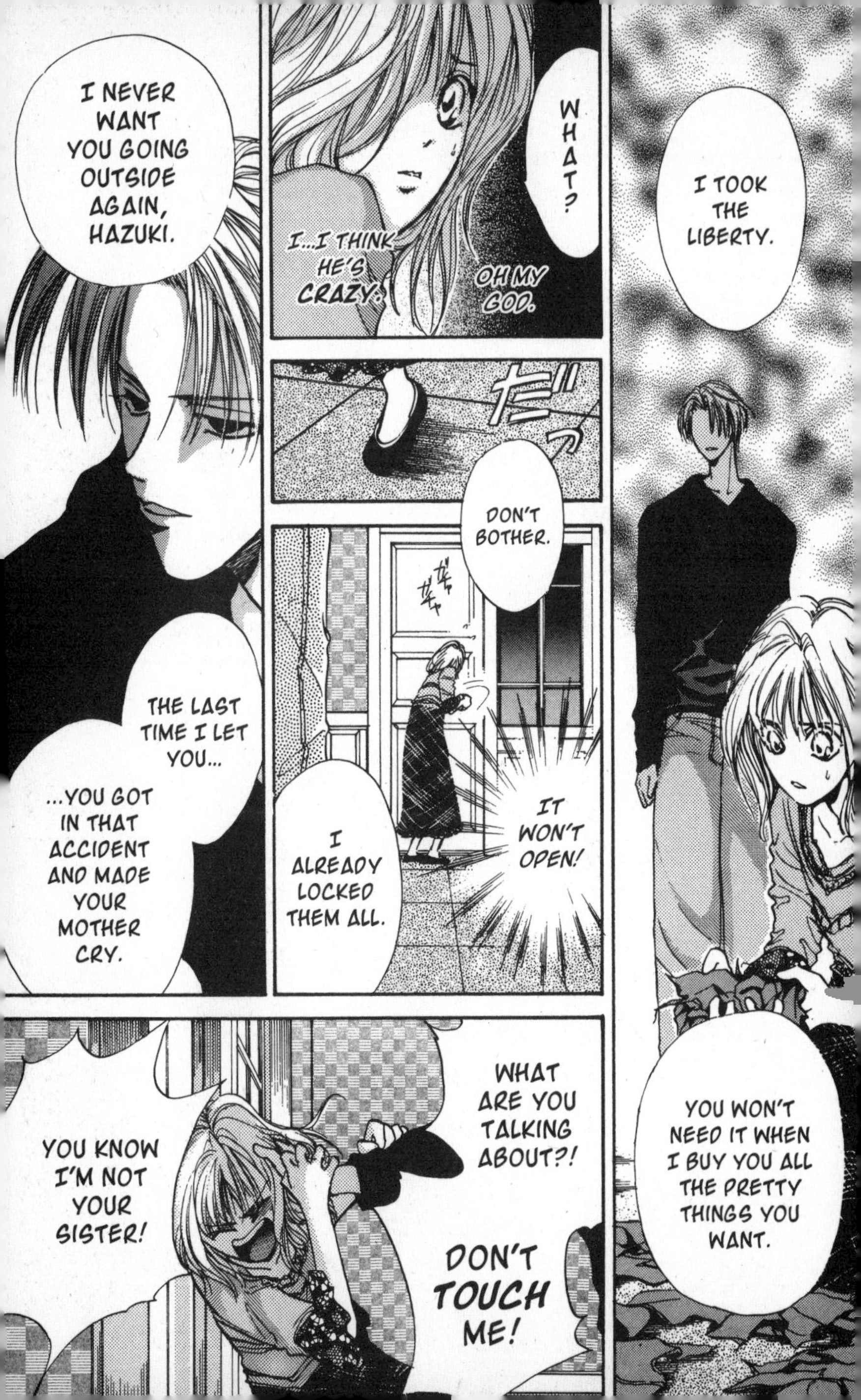
I TOOK THE LIBERTY.
YOU WON'T NEED IT WHEN I BUY YOU ALL THE PRETTY THINGS YOU WANT.
WHAT?
OH MY GOD.
I...I THINK HE'S CRAZY.
だッ
DON'T BOTHER.
IT WON'T OPEN!
I ALREADY LOCKED THEM ALL.
I NEVER WANT YOU GOING OUTSIDE AGAIN, HAZUKI.
THE LAST TIME I LET YOU...
...YOU GOT IN THAT ACCIDENT AND MADE YOUR MOTHER CRY.
WHAT ARE YOU TALKING ABOUT?!
DON'T TOUCH ME!
YOU KNOW I'M NOT YOUR SISTER!

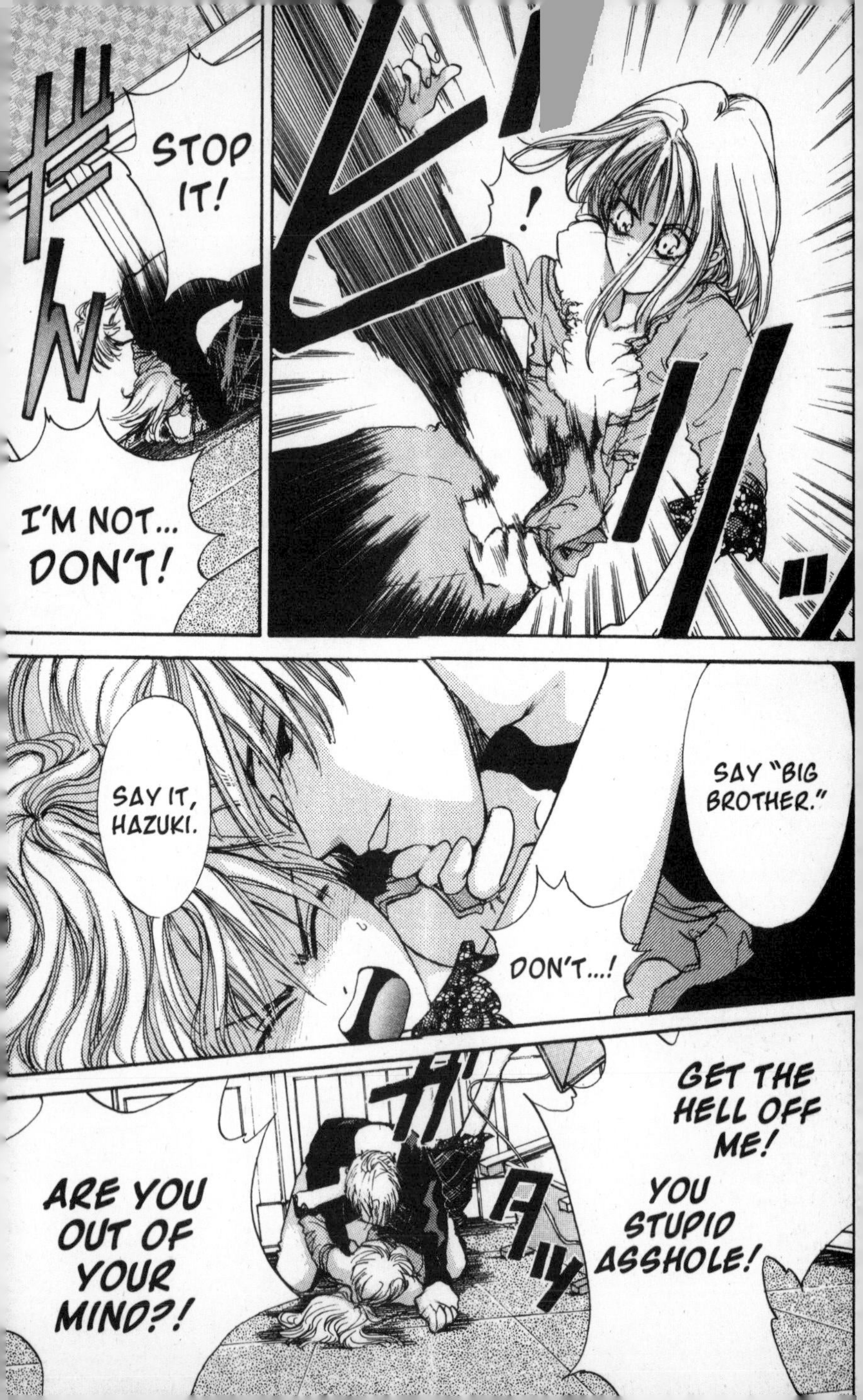
!
STOP IT!
I'M NOT... DON'T!
SAY "BIG BROTHER."
SAY IT, HAZUKI.
DON'T...!
GET THE HELL OFF ME!
YOU STUPID ASSHOLE!
ARE YOU OUT OF YOUR MIND?!

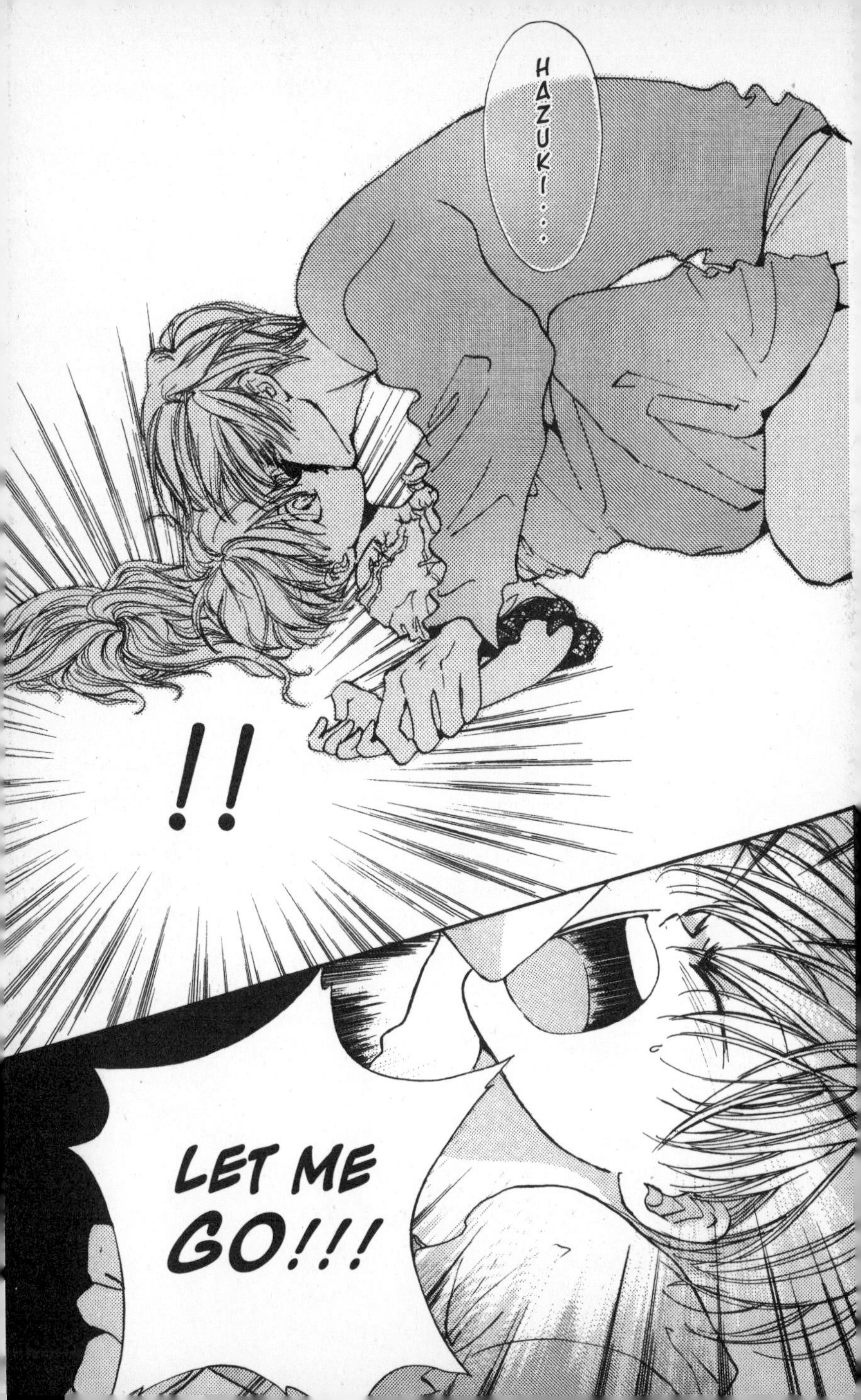
HAZUKI...
!!
LET ME GO!!!

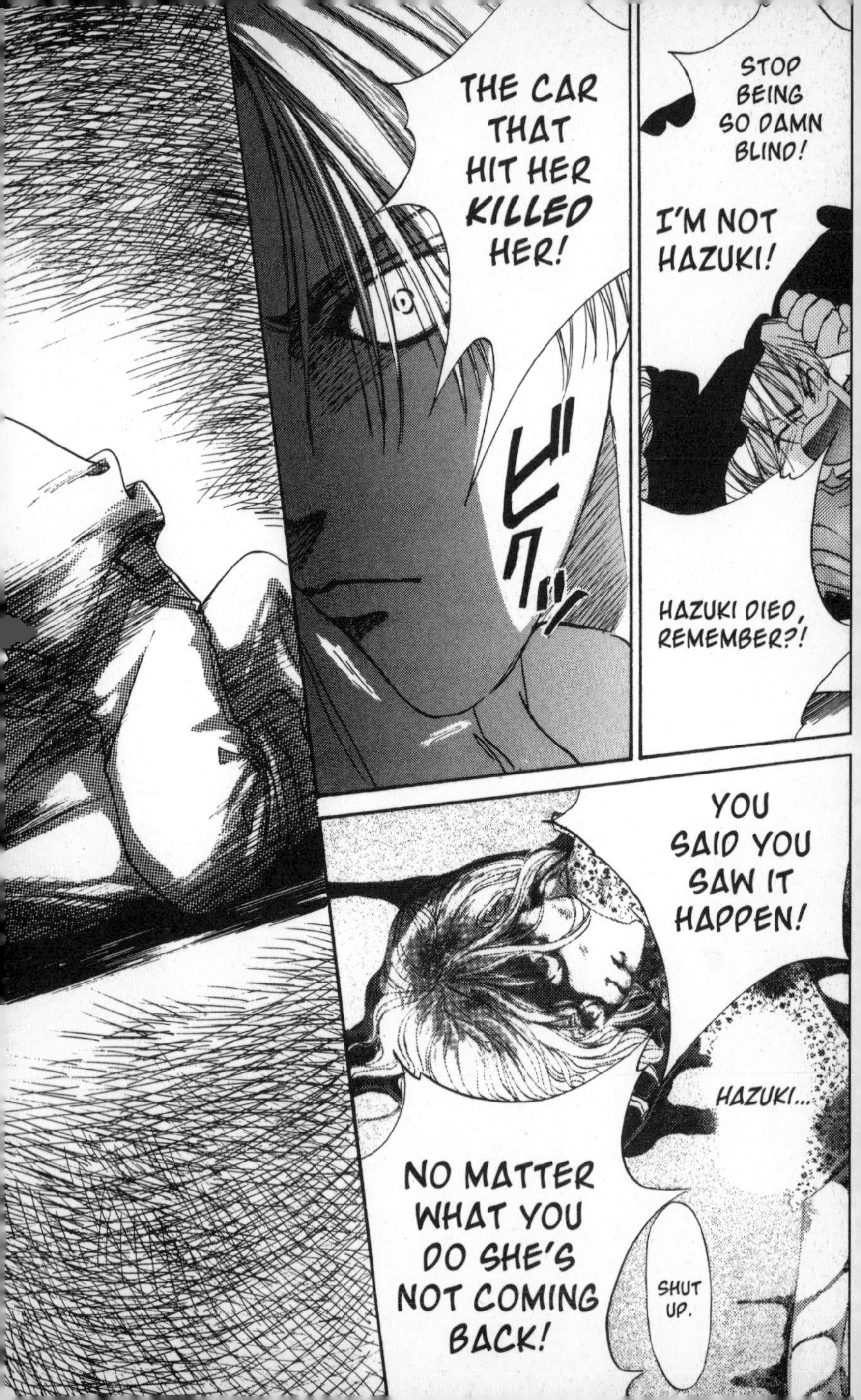
STOP BEING SO DAMN BLIND!
I'M NOT HAZUKI!
HAZUKI DIED, REMEMBER?!
THE CAR THAT HIT HER *KILLED* HER!
ビクッ
YOU SAID YOU SAW IT HAPPEN!
HAZUKI...
NO MATTER WHAT YOU DO SHE'S NOT COMING BACK!
SHUT UP.

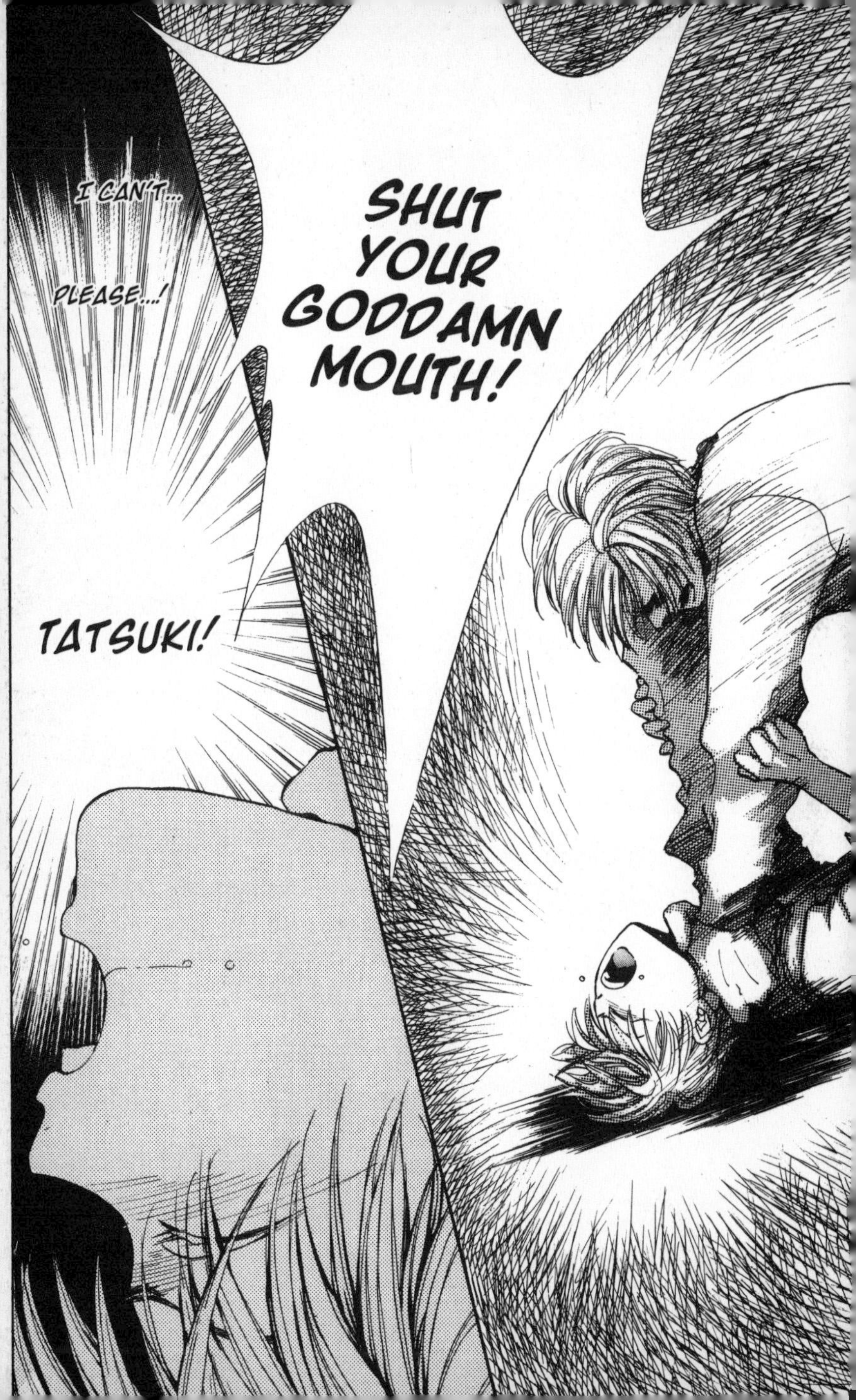
SHUT YOUR GODDAMN MOUTH!
I CAN'T...
PLEASE...!
TATSUKI!

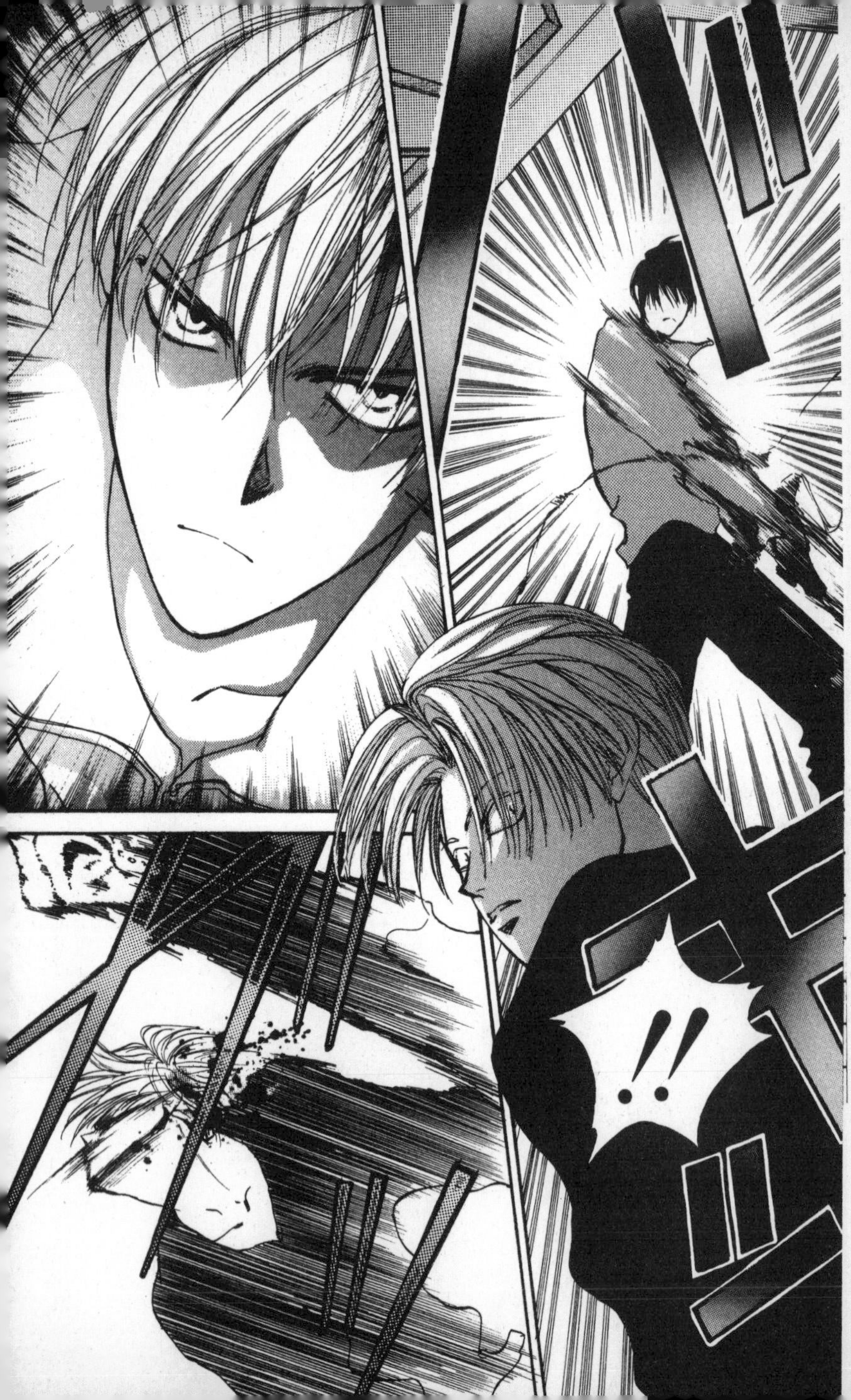
!!

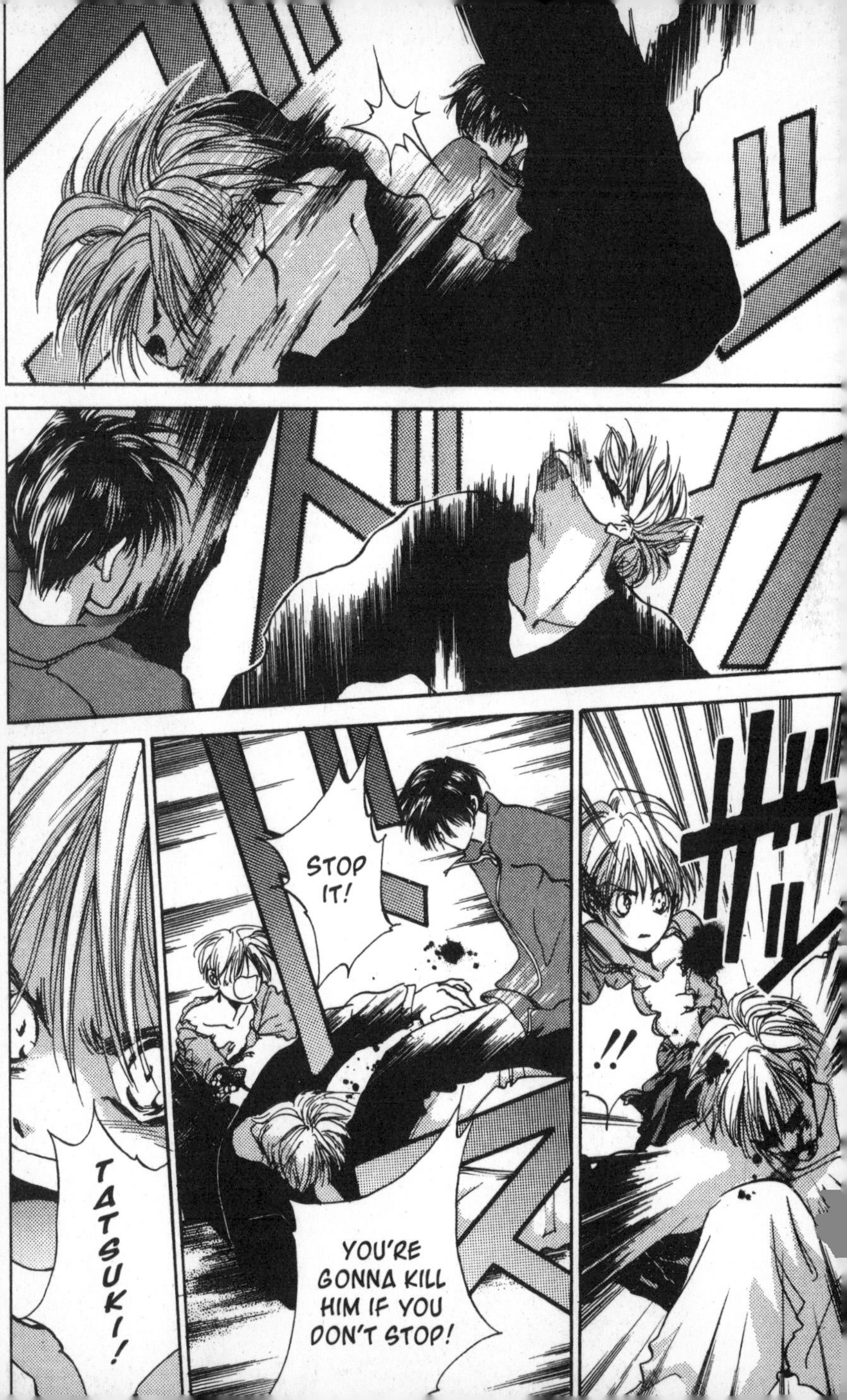
ザッ
!!
STOP IT!
YOU'RE GONNA KILL HIM IF YOU DON'T STOP!
TATSUKI!

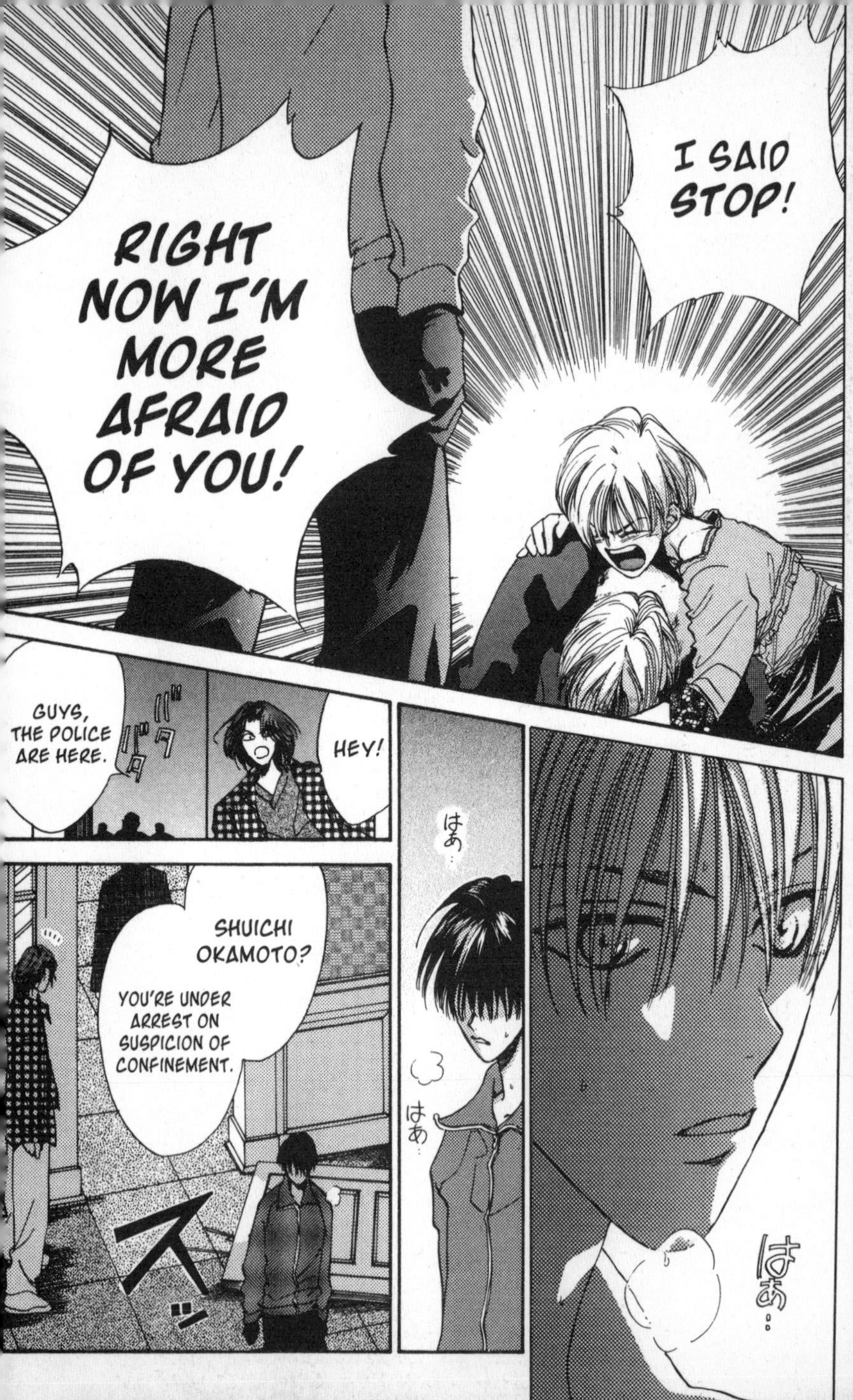
I SAID STOP!
RIGHT NOW I'M MORE AFRAID OF YOU!
はあ…
はあ…
はあ…
HEY!
GUYS, THE POLICE ARE HERE.
バタ
バタ
SHUICHI OKAMOTO?
YOU'RE UNDER ARREST ON SUSPICION OF CONFINEMENT.
ス

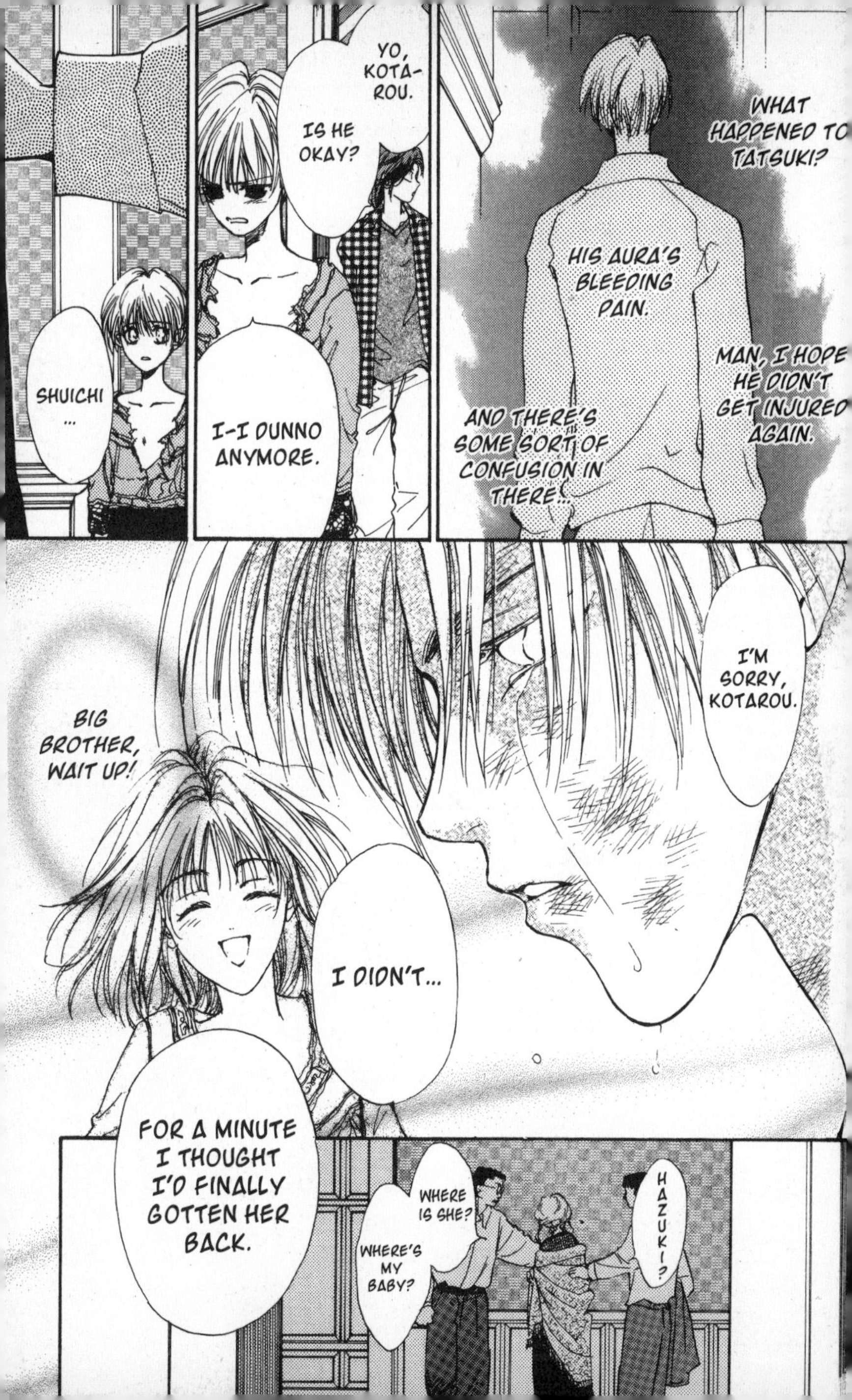
WHAT HAPPENED TO TATSUKI?
HIS AURA'S BLEEDING PAIN.
MAN, I HOPE HE DIDN'T GET INJURED AGAIN.
AND THERE'S SOME SORT OF CONFUSION IN THERE...
YO, KOTA-ROU.
IS HE OKAY?
I-I DUNNO ANYMORE.
SHUICHI ...
I'M SORRY, KOTAROU.
I DIDN'T...
BIG BROTHER, WAIT UP!
FOR A MINUTE I THOUGHT I'D FINALLY GOTTEN HER BACK.
HAZUKI?
WHERE IS SHE?
WHERE'S MY BABY?

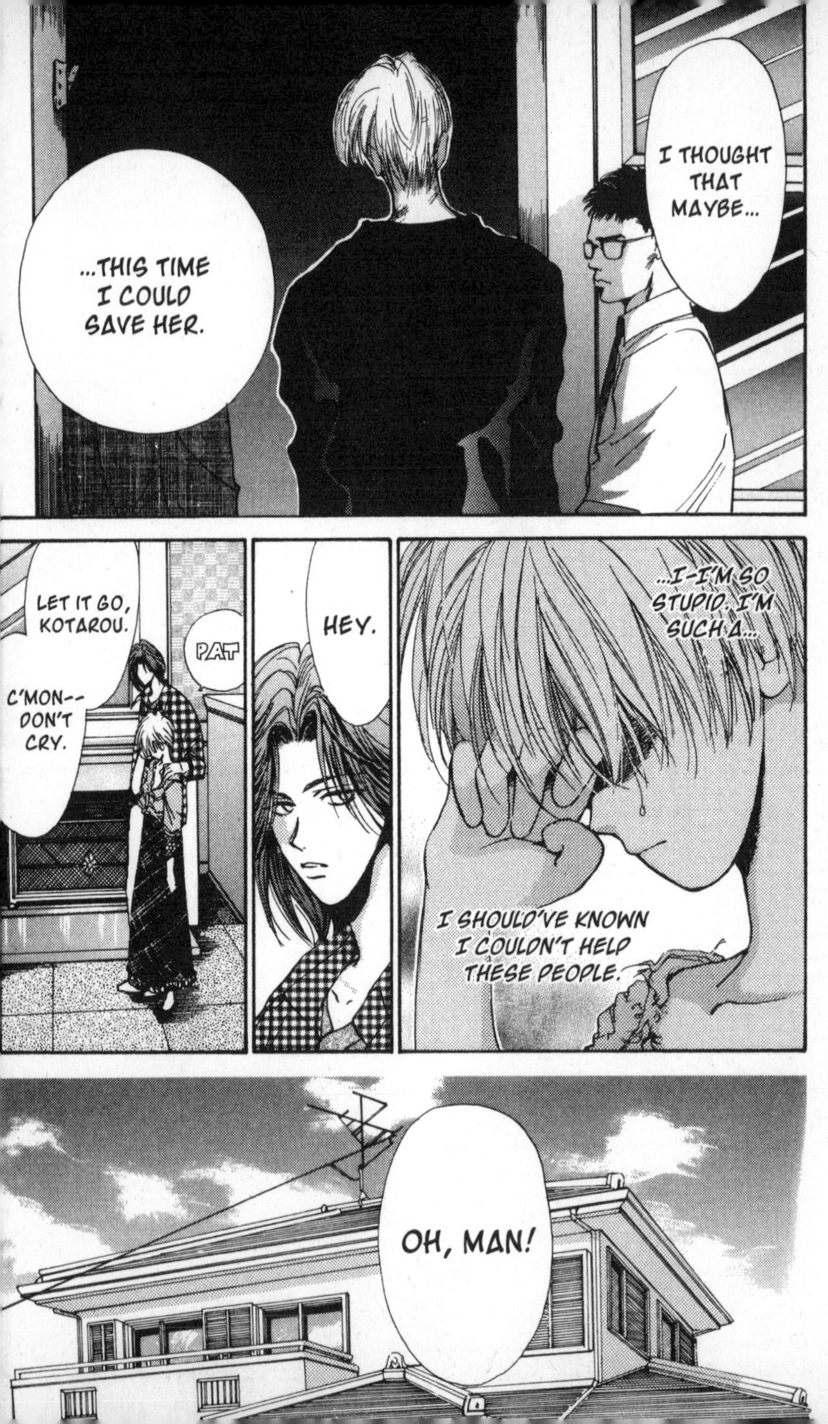
I THOUGHT THAT MAYBE...
...THIS TIME I COULD SAVE HER.
...I-I'M SO STUPID. I'M SUCH A...
I SHOULD'VE KNOWN I COULDN'T HELP THESE PEOPLE.
HEY.
PAT
LET IT GO, KOTAROU.
C'MON--DON'T CRY.
OH, MAN!

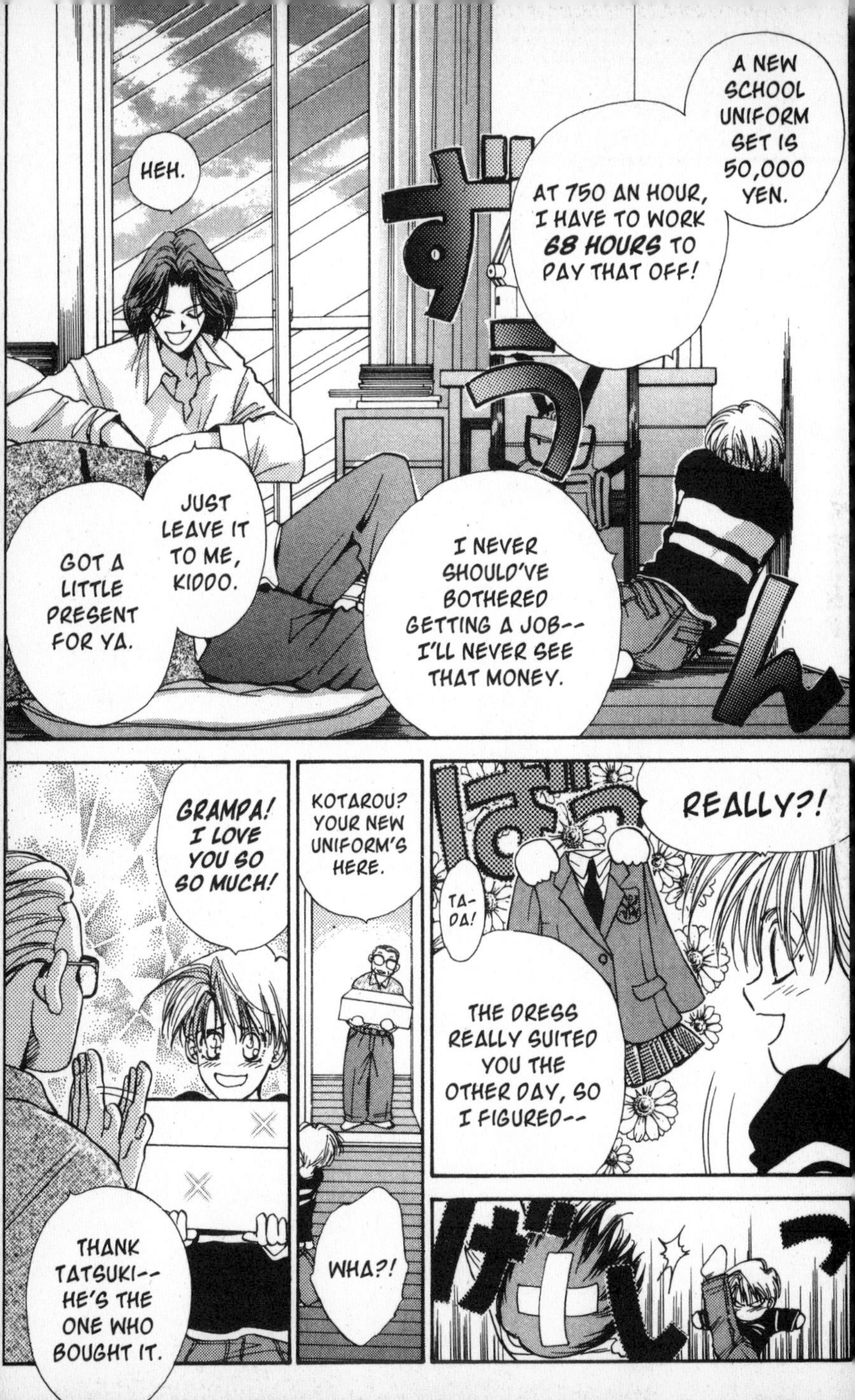
A NEW SCHOOL UNIFORM SET IS 50,000 YEN.
AT 750 AN HOUR, I HAVE TO WORK 68 HOURS TO PAY THAT OFF!
HEH.
I NEVER SHOULD'VE BOTHERED GETTING A JOB-- I'LL NEVER SEE THAT MONEY.
JUST LEAVE IT TO ME, KIDDO.
GOT A LITTLE PRESENT FOR YA.
REALLY?!
TA-DA!
THE DRESS REALLY SUITED YOU THE OTHER DAY, SO I FIGURED--
KOTAROU? YOUR NEW UNIFORM'S HERE.
WHA?!
GRAMPA! I LOVE YOU SO SO MUCH!
THANK TATSUKI-- HE'S THE ONE WHO BOUGHT IT.

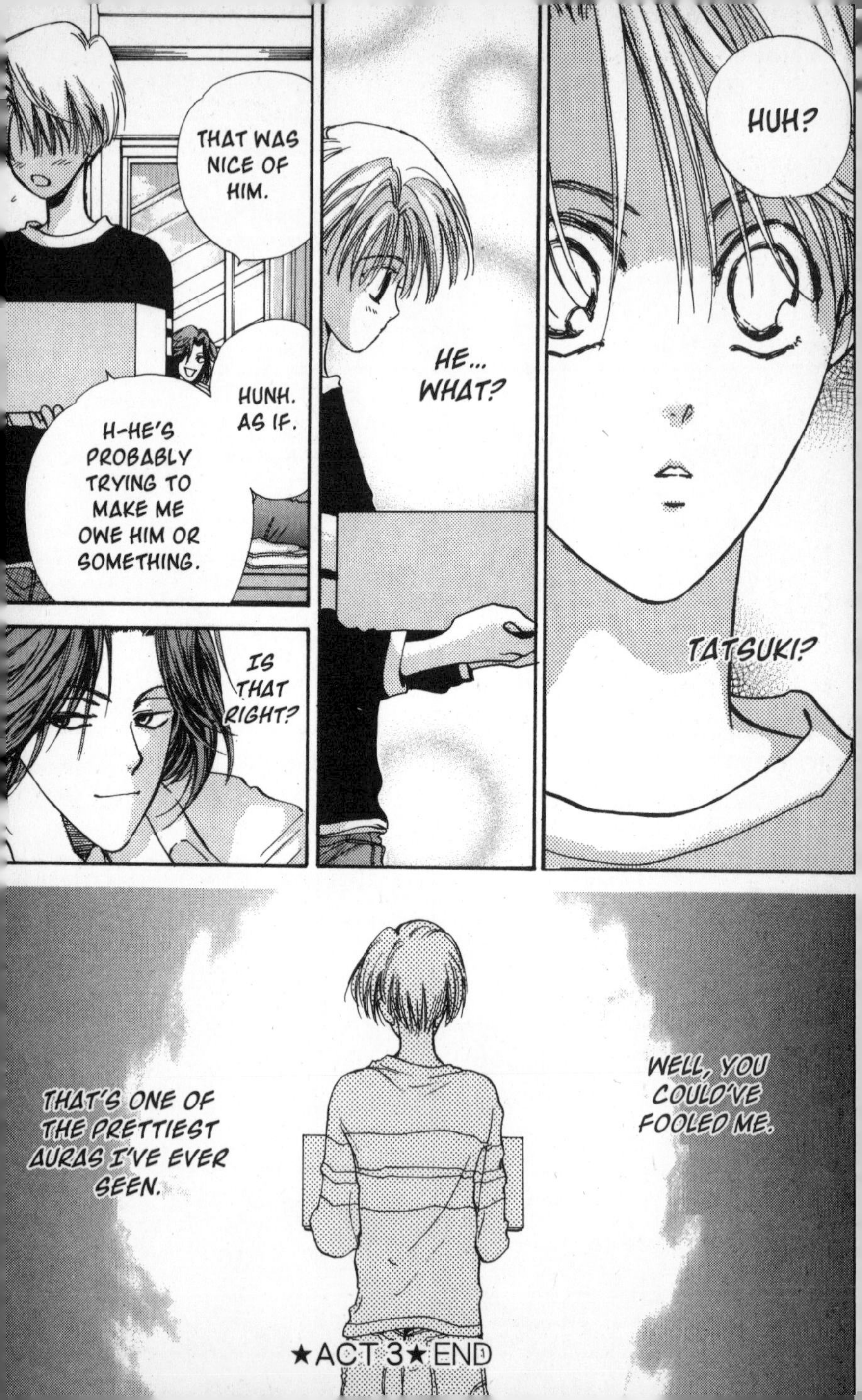
HUH?
TATSUKI?
HE... WHAT?
THAT WAS NICE OF HIM.
HUNH. AS IF.
H-HE'S PROBABLY TRYING TO MAKE ME OWE HIM OR SOMETHING.
IS THAT RIGHT?
WELL, YOU COULD'VE FOOLED ME.
THAT'S ONE OF THE PRETTIEST AURAS I'VE EVER SEEN.
★ACT 3★ END

HANDS OFF, PLEASE

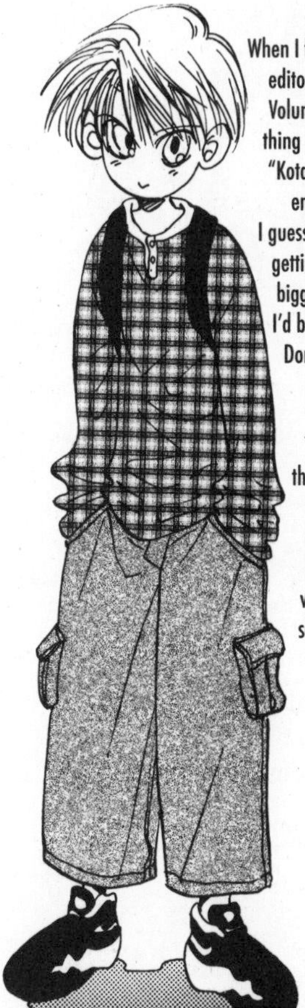

When I first showed my editor the cover for Volume 1*, the first thing mentioned was "Kotarou's eyes are enormous." I guess his eyes are getting bigger and bigger over time... I'd better watch that Don't want anyone getting hurt.

*This refers to the original cover for Volume 1, as opposed to TOKYOPOP'S version, but the same shock still applies.

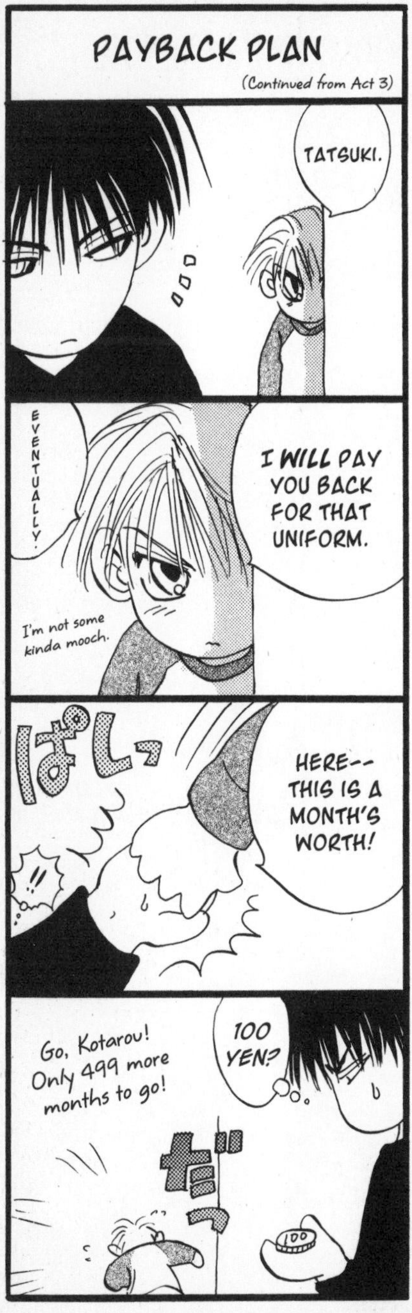

PAYBACK PLAN
(Continued from Act 3)
TATSUKI.
I WILL PAY YOU BACK FOR THAT UNIFORM.
EVENTUALLY.
I'm not some kinda mooch.
HERE-- THIS IS A MONTH'S WORTH!
ぱしっ
!!
100 YEN?
Go, Kotarou! Only 499 more months to go!
だっ
100

Rest In Peace, Friend

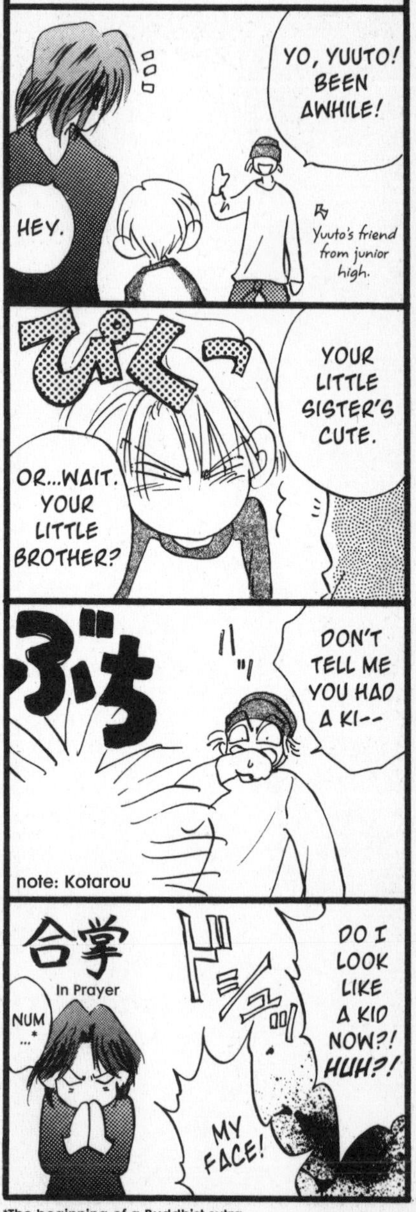
YO, YUUTO! BEEN AWHILE!
HEY.
Yuuto's friend from junior high.
YOUR LITTLE SISTER'S CUTE.
ぴくっ
OR...WAIT. YOUR LITTLE BROTHER?
DON'T TELL ME YOU HAD A KI--
ぶち
note: Kotarou
DO I LOOK LIKE A KID NOW?! HUH?!
合掌
In Prayer
NUM...*
MY FACE!

*The beginning of a Buddhist sutra.

He Is Cool

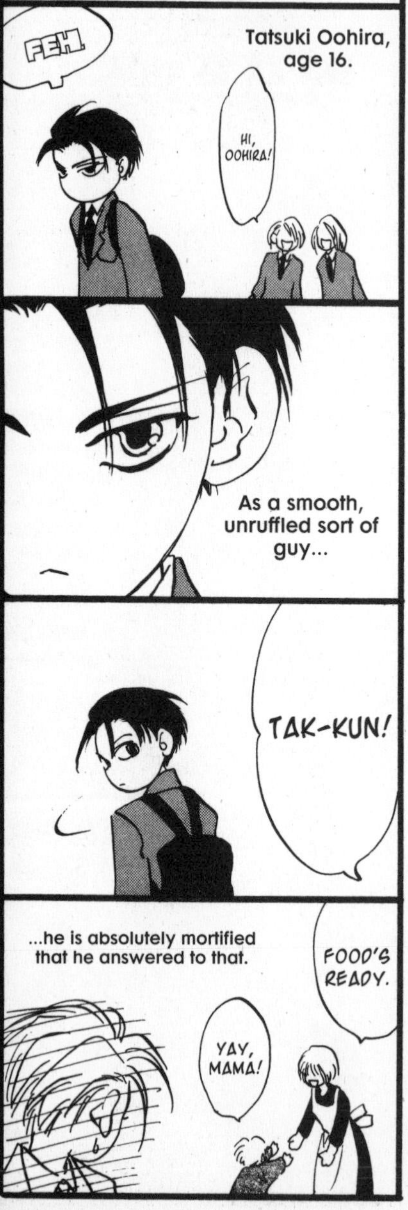
Tatsuki Oohira, age 16.
FEH.
HI, OOHIRA!
As a smooth, unruffled sort of guy...
TAK-KUN!
...he is absolutely mortified that he answered to that.
FOOD'S READY.
YAY, MAMA!

Soap Opera Part 1

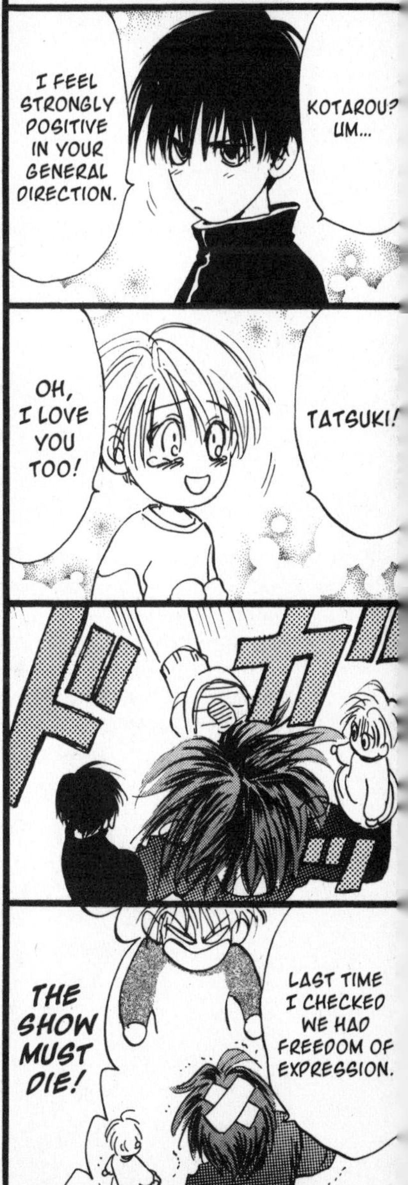
KOTAROU? UM...
I FEEL STRONGLY POSITIVE IN YOUR GENERAL DIRECTION.
TATSUKI!
OH, I LOVE YOU TOO!
ドカッ
LAST TIME I CHECKED WE HAD FREEDOM OF EXPRESSION.
THE SHOW MUST DIE!

Soap Opera Part 2

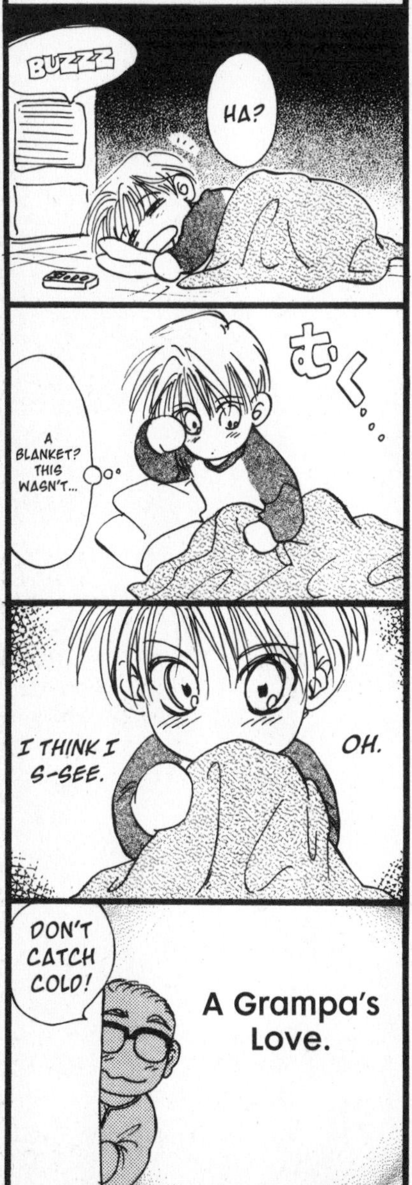
BUZZZ
HA?
むく。。。
A BLANKET? THIS WASN'T...
OH.
I THINK I S-SEE.
DON'T CATCH COLD!
A Grampa's Love.

KOTARO

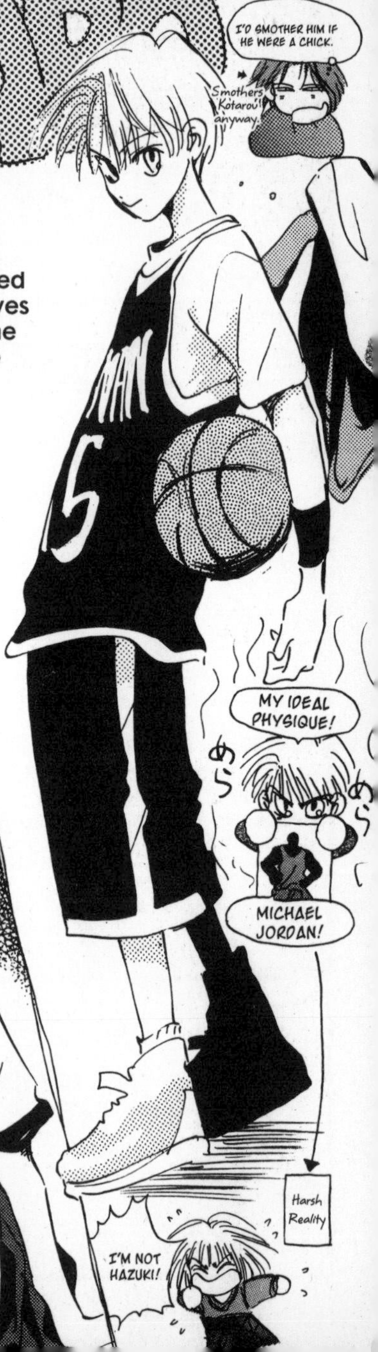
I'D SMOTHER HIM IF HE WERE A CHICK.
Smothers Kotarou anyway.
MY IDEAL PHYSIQUE!
MICHAEL JORDAN!
Harsh Reality
I'M NOT HAZUKI!

Although it hasn't been mentioned in the series just yet, Kotarou loves basketball. He's been playing the kiddie version in a boys' league since elementary school.

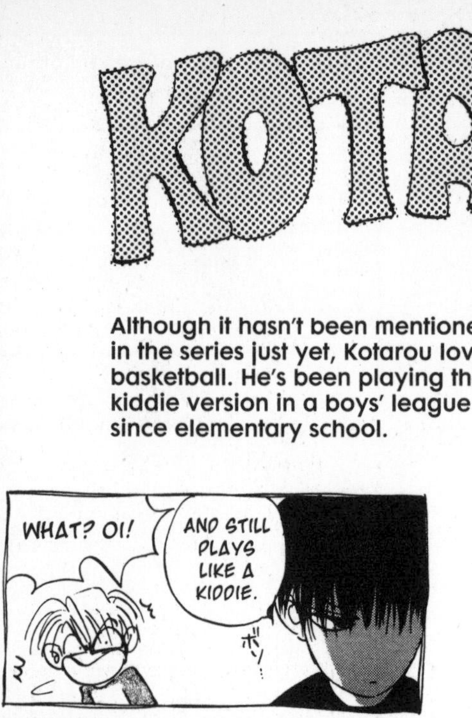
AND STILL PLAYS LIKE A KIDDIE.
WHAT? OI!

Even though it may take awhile for the story to move in that direction, you'll start learning about Tatsuki's special power and his relationship with Kotarou soon enough.

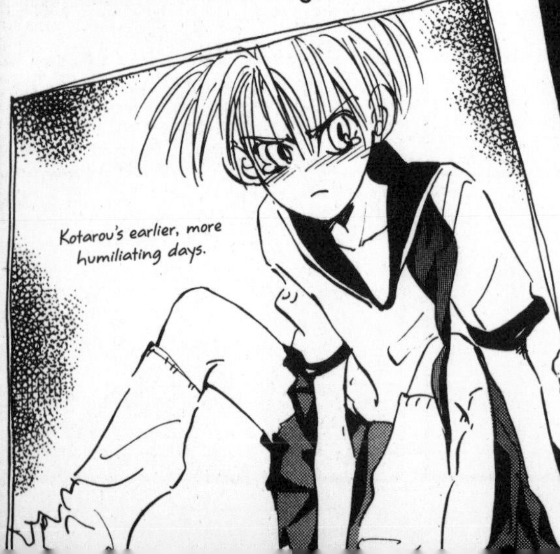
Kotarou's earlier, more humiliating days.

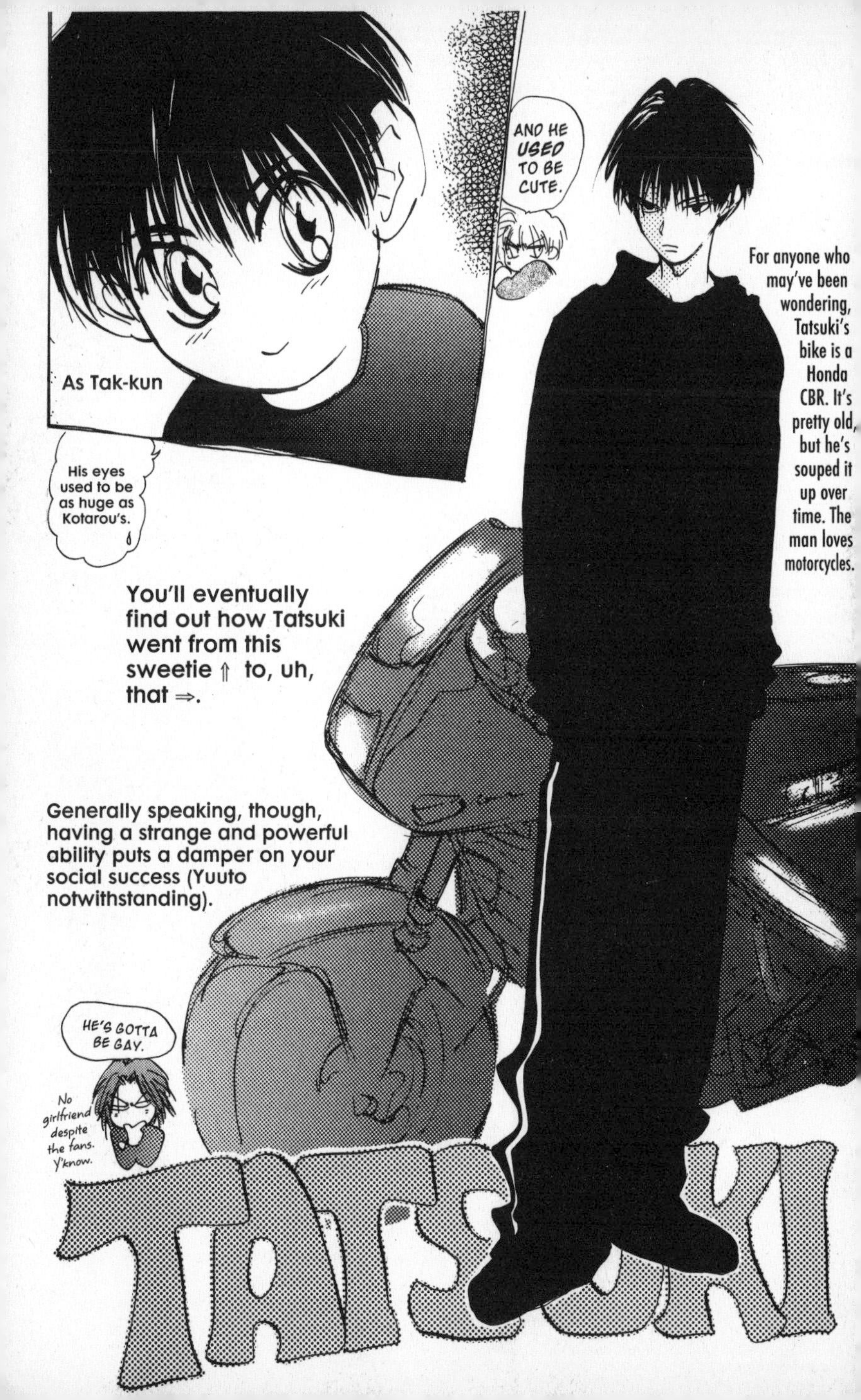

AND HE USED TO BE CUTE.
For anyone who may've been wondering, Tatsuki's bike is a Honda CBR. It's pretty old, but he's souped it up over time. The man loves motorcycles.
As Tak-kun
His eyes used to be as huge as Kotarou's.
You'll eventually find out how Tatsuki went from this sweetie ⇑ to, uh, that ⇒.
Generally speaking, though, having a strange and powerful ability puts a damper on your social success (Yuuto notwithstanding).
HE'S GOTTA BE GAY.
No girlfriend despite the fans. Y'know.
TATSUKI

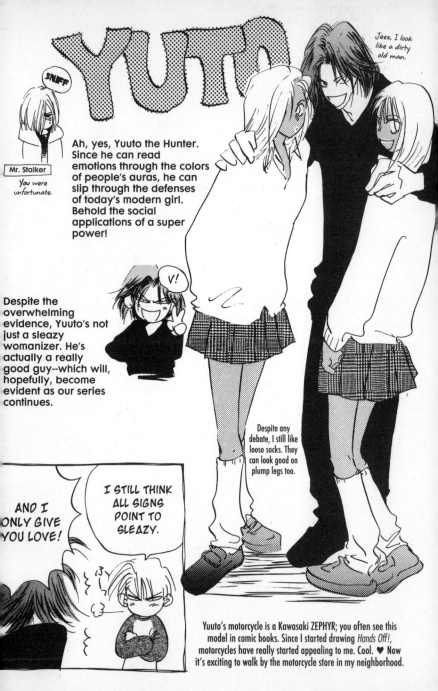

YUTO

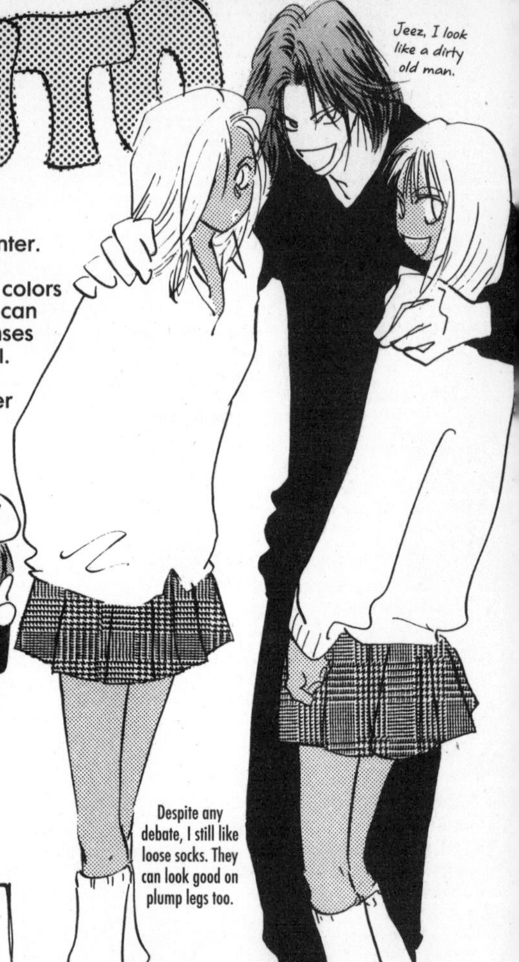
Jeez, I look like a dirty old man.
Despite any debate, I still like loose socks. They can look good on plump legs too.

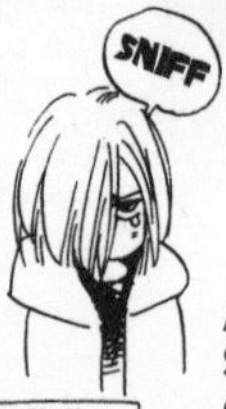
SNIFF

Mr. Stalker

You were unfortunate.

Ah, yes, Yuuto the Hunter. Since he can read emotions through the colors of people's auras, he can slip through the defenses of today's modern girl. Behold the social applications of a super power!

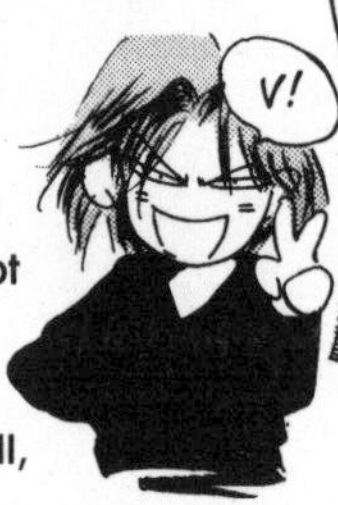
V!

Despite the overwhelming evidence, Yuuto's not just a sleazy womanizer. He's actually a really good guy--which will, hopefully, become evident as our series continues.

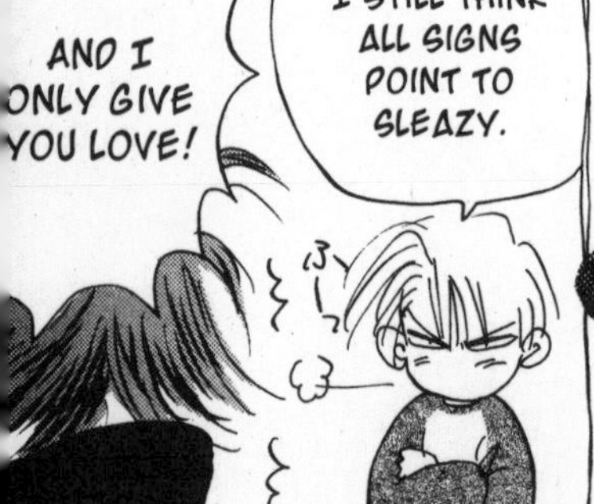
I STILL THINK ALL SIGNS POINT TO SLEAZY.
AND I ONLY GIVE YOU LOVE!

Yuuto's motorcycle is a Kawasaki ZEPHYR; you often see this model in comic books. Since I started drawing *Hands Off!*, motorcycles have really started appealing to me. Cool. ♥ Now it's exciting to walk by the motorcycle store in my neighborhood.

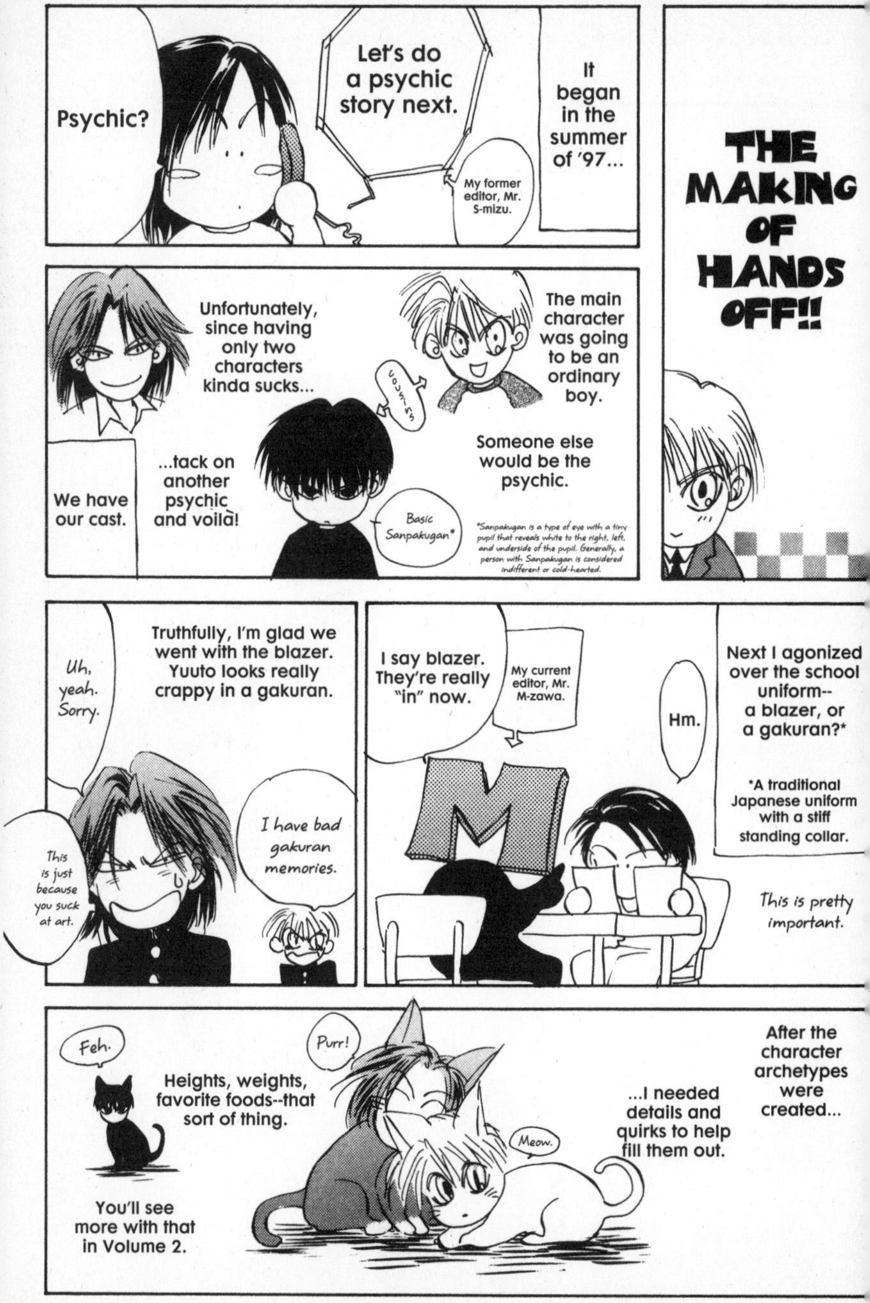
THE MAKING OF HANDS OFF!!
It began in the summer of '97...
My former editor, Mr. S-mizu.
Let's do a psychic story next.
Psychic?
The main character was going to be an ordinary boy.
Cousins
Unfortunately, since having only two characters kinda sucks...
Someone else would be the psychic.
*Sanpakugan is a type of eye with a tiny pupil that reveals white to the right, left, and underside of the pupil. Generally, a person with Sanpakugan is considered indifferent or cold-hearted.
Basic Sanpakugan*
...tack on another psychic and voila!
We have our cast.
Next I agonized over the school uniform-- a blazer, or a gakuran?*
*A traditional Japanese uniform with a stiff standing collar.
This is pretty important.
Hm.
My current editor, Mr. M-zawa.
I say blazer. They're really "in" now.
Truthfully, I'm glad we went with the blazer. Yuuto looks really crappy in a gakuran.
Uh, yeah. Sorry.
I have bad gakuran memories.
This is just because you suck at art.
After the character archetypes were created...
...I needed details and quirks to help fill them out.
Meow.
Purr!
Heights, weights, favorite foods--that sort of thing.
Feh.
You'll see more with that in Volume 2.

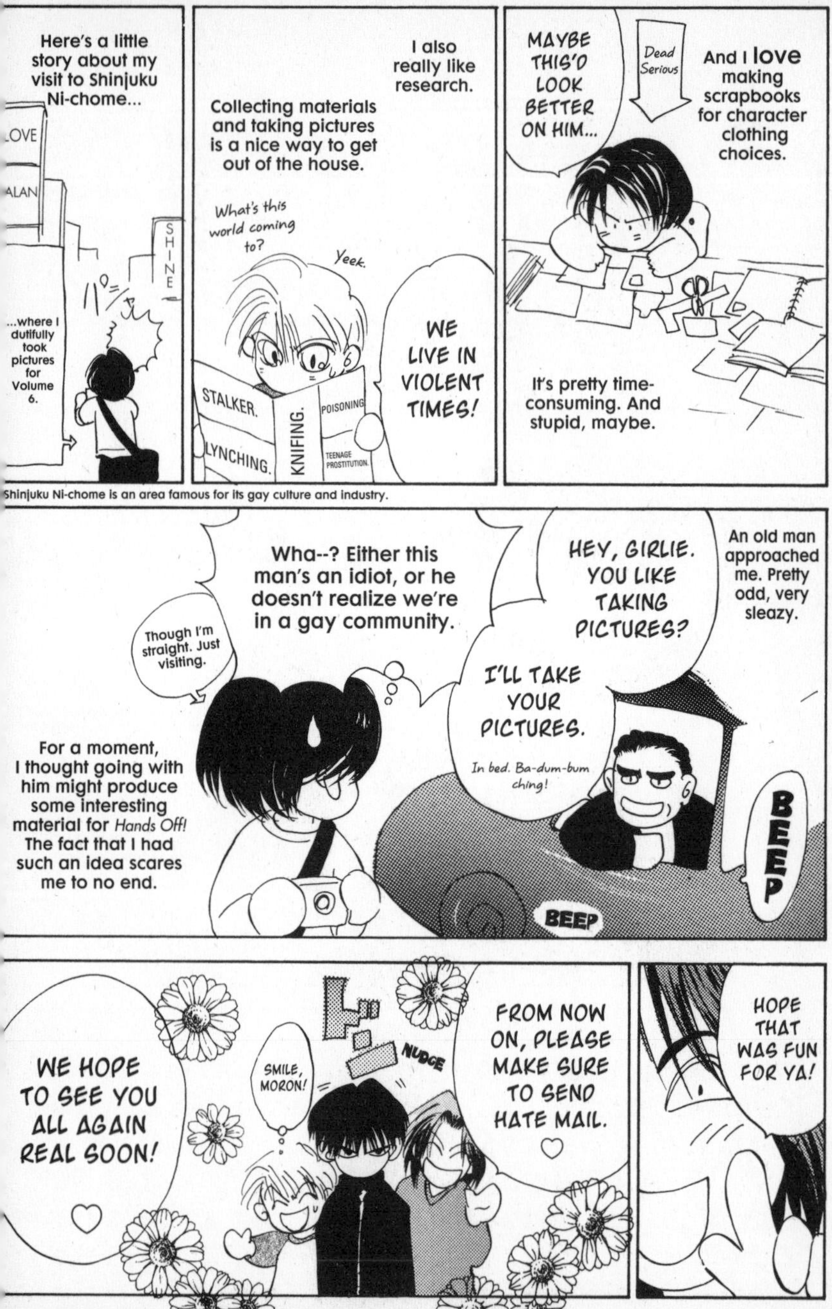

And I love making scrapbooks for character clothing choices.
Dead Serious
MAYBE THIS'D LOOK BETTER ON HIM...
It's pretty time-consuming. And stupid, maybe.
I also really like research.
Collecting materials and taking pictures is a nice way to get out of the house.
What's this world coming to?
Yeek.
WE LIVE IN VIOLENT TIMES!
STALKER.
POISONING
KNIFING.
LYNCHING.
TEENAGE PROSTITUTION.
Here's a little story about my visit to Shinjuku Ni-chome...
LOVE
ALAN
SHINE
...where I dutifully took pictures for Volume 6.
Shinjuku Ni-chome is an area famous for its gay culture and industry.
An old man approached me. Pretty odd, very sleazy.
HEY, GIRLIE. YOU LIKE TAKING PICTURES?
Wha--? Either this man's an idiot, or he doesn't realize we're in a gay community.
Though I'm straight. Just visiting.
I'LL TAKE YOUR PICTURES.
In bed. Ba-dum-bum ching!
BEEP
BEEP
For a moment, I thought going with him might produce some interesting material for Hands Off! The fact that I had such an idea scares me to no end.
HOPE THAT WAS FUN FOR YA!
FROM NOW ON, PLEASE MAKE SURE TO SEND HATE MAIL.
NUDGE
SMILE, MORON!
WE HOPE TO SEE YOU ALL AGAIN REAL SOON!

★ AFTERWORD END ★

Coming Soon!

HANDS OFF!

Volume 2

Kotarou is totally stoked that basketball season has started and he can now fulfill his hoop dreams. Things look even brighter for Kotarou when he meets Mio, a beautiful older woman who's got the hots for Kotarou. Unfortunately, he also meets Chiba, Mio's devious protector. With trouble afoot, Tatsuki and Yuuto must use their ESP to make sure there is no foul play!

ALSO AVAILABLE FROM  TOKYOPOP®

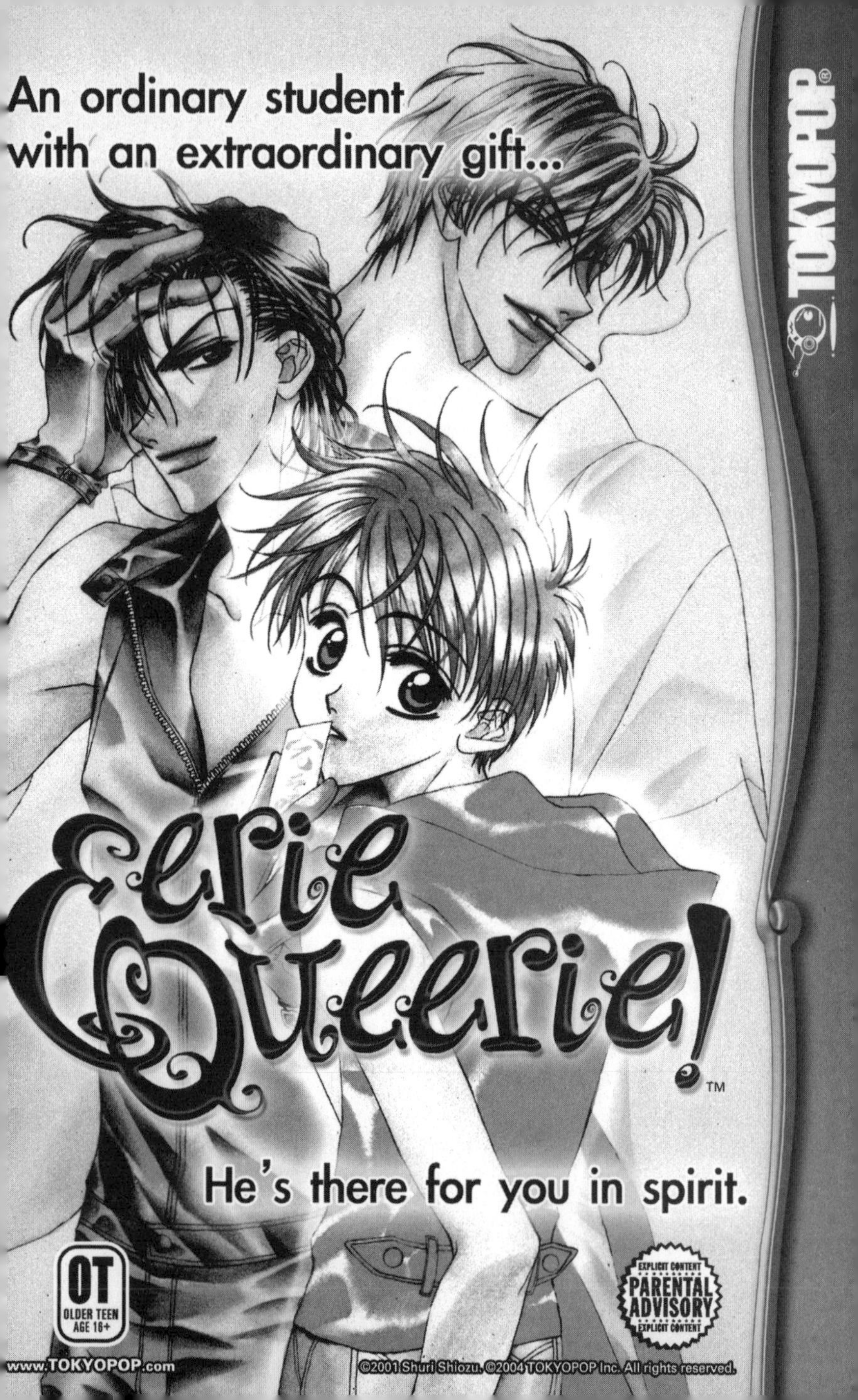
An ordinary student
with an extraordinary gift...
TOKYOPOP
Eerie Queerie!™
He's there for you in spirit.
OT
OLDER TEEN
AGE 16+
EXPLICIT CONTENT
PARENTAL ADVISORY
EXPLICIT CONTENT
www.TOKYOPOP.com
©2001 Shuri Shiozu. ©2004 TOKYOPOP Inc. All rights reserved.

GETBACKERS

They get back what shouldn't be gone...

most of the time.

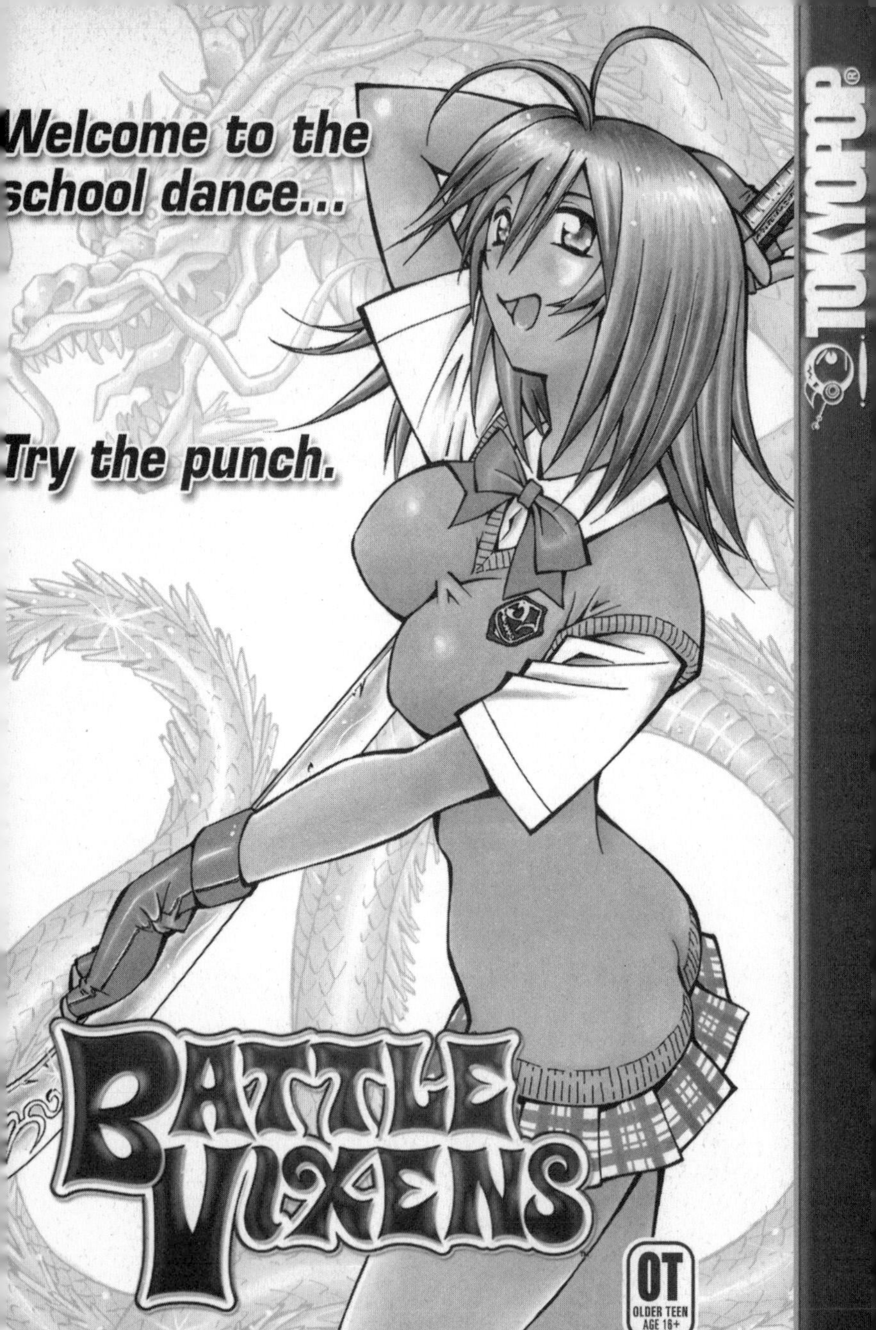
Welcome to the
school dance...
Try the punch.
TOKYOPOP
BATTLE VIXENS
OT
OLDER TEEN
AGE 16+

STOP!

This is the back of the book.
You wouldn't want to spoil a great ending!

This book is printed "manga-style," in the authentic Japanese right-to-left format. Since none of the artwork has been flipped or altered, readers get to experience the story just as the creator intended. You've been asking for it, so TOKYOPOP® delivered: authentic, hot-off-the-press, and far more fun!

DIRECTIONS

If this is your first time reading manga-style, here's a quick guide to help you understand how it works.

It's easy... just start in the top right panel and follow the numbers. Have fun, and look for more 100% authentic manga from TOKYOPOP®!